Zen Time

Zen Time

Dōgen's *Uji* in Context

RAJI C. STEINECK

SUNY PRESS

Cover credit: *Time in the Zen Monastery*, created for the TIMEJ project by Martin Rümmele in collaboration with Fritz Schumann and the author.

Published by State University of New York Press, Albany

© 2025 State University of New York

All rights reserved

Printed in the United States of America

An open access version of this book is available.

No part of this book may be used or reproduced in any manner whatsoever without written permission. No part of this book may be stored in a retrieval system or transmitted in any form or by any means including electronic, electrostatic, magnetic tape, mechanical, photocopying, recording, or otherwise without the prior permission in writing of the publisher.

Links to third-party websites are provided as a convenience and for informational purposes only. They do not constitute an endorsement or an approval of any of the products, services, or opinions of the organization, companies, or individuals. SUNY Press bears no responsibility for the accuracy, legality, or content of a URL, the external website, or for that of subsequent websites.

EU GPSR Authorised Representative:
Logos Europe, 9 rue Nicolas Poussin, 17000, La Rochelle, France
contact@logoseurope.eu

For information, contact State University of New York Press, Albany, NY
www.sunypress.edu

Research for this publication was funded by the ERC Advanced Grant ERC-ADG 741166.

Library of Congress Cataloging-in-Publication Data

Name: Steineck, Raji C., author.
Title: Zen time : Dōgen's *Uji* in context / Raji C. Steineck.
Description: Albany : State University of New York Press, [2025] | Includes bibliographical references and index.
Identifiers: LCCN 2024060106 | ISBN 9798855803600 (hardcover : alk. paper) | ISBN 9798855803624 (ebook) | ISBN 9798855803617 (pbk. : alk. paper)
Subjects: LCSH: Dōgen, 1200–1253. | Spiritual life—Zen Buddhism. | Zen Buddhism.
Classification: LCC BQ9449.D657 S74 2025 | DDC 294.3927—dc23/eng/20250304
LC record available at https://lccn.loc.gov/2024060106

For
Tomoe

Contents

Acknowledgments — xi

Conventions and Abbreviations — xiii

Introduction — 1

Part I
Grounding the Conceptual Analysis

Chapter 1
From *uji* to Philosophy and Back: Thoughts on Methodology — 11
   Philosophical Transpositions — 11
   Restating *uji*: A New Translation — 17
   Time and Symbolic Form — 19
   The Question of Cultural Appropriation — 22
   Zen with Distinctions — 24

Chapter 2
Placing Dōgen in Time: Cultural Constellation, Chronology, Agenda — 27
   Social and Cultural Conditions — 29
   Religious Writing in Early Medieval Japan — 30
   The Religious Field — 33
   Dōgen's Life and Works — 35
   Dōgen in Time — 46

Chapter 3
Time Expressed: Chronography in Dōgen's Works — 49
  A Matrix for Chronographical Analysis — 50
  Chronothesis — 54
  Chronometrics and Chronotypology — 56
  Numerical Chronometry and Its Uses — 61
  Conclusion — 69

Chapter 4
Chronopolitics: Time Regimes and the Social Language of Time — 73
  The Diurnal Rhythm in Monastic Life — 75
  The Monthly Cycle — 91
  The Annual Cycle — 94
  The Social Meaning of Time — 103
  Control and Commitment — 109
  Conclusion — 112

Part II
Chrononoetics: Understanding Time

Chapter 5
Building Blocks and Early Approaches — 119
  Conceptual Heritage: Dōgen and the Tradition of Buddhist Thought on Time — 119
  Setting the Stage: Trans-Temporal Unity in a Transient World — 123

Chapter 6
Time in "What Is:Time" — 137
  "What Is:Time": Structure and Argument — 138
  Central Concepts and Propositions — 145
  Conclusion — 158

Chapter 7
Karma and the "Consummate Now" — 161
  Synchrony and Sequence — 161
  Karma and the "Final Dharma Age" — 168
  Conclusion — 178

Part III
Conclusions and After-Thoughts

CHAPTER 8
Dōgen's Concept of Time in Context 181
   What is:Time: A Brief Reconstruction and Conceptual
      Analysis 181
   Integrating Distinctions 188
   Dōgen and Time in Medieval Japan 191
   Dōgen and the History of Time 196

CHAPTER 9
After-Thoughts: Dimensions of Contemporary Significance 203
   Theoretical: Dōgen and the Concept of Time 203
   Time's Measure and Attributes 207
   Practical: Time- and Task-Orientation Combined ... 211
   Spiritual: Trans-Temporal Synchrony, Holistic Connectedness ... 214

APPENDIX 1
Translation of *Uji* ("What Is:Time") 221

APPENDIX 2
Titles of Dōgen's Writings and Other Original Sources 229

NOTES 235

BIBLIOGRAPHY 293

INDEX OF NAMES 313

INDEX OF TERMS 317

Acknowledgments

Every book, single-authored or not, is the result of collective efforts. This one was written as part of my project "Time in Medieval Japan (TIMEJ)." I owe gratitude to the European Research Council for supporting this project with an ERC Advanced Grant and to the members of our TIMEJ group, Vroni Ammann, Georg Blind, Alexandra Ciorciaro, Kataoka Kōhei, Stefania Lottanti, Simone Müller, Jannick Scherrer, Etienne Stähelin, and Daniela Tan, for many stimulating discussions and helpful comments. I also want to thank our secretaries, Alexandra Harr and Dagmar Löher, for very efficiently dealing with the ERC's administrative requirements. Their unceasing efforts saved us a lot of time and energy.

I began engaging with Dōgen more than thirty years ago in Kyōto, where my host at Kyoto University, Arifuku Kōgaku, took time for weekly one-on-one discussions on Dōgen's writings. The late Matsunami Taiun of Daitokuji's Ryōsen-an offered me and like-minded others a space for regular *zazen* practice, often followed by free-spirited discussions over tea. I am deeply grateful to both for their openness and for liberally sharing their wisdom without ever imposing a predefined way of thought. These encounters continued over many years whenever I had a chance to spend time in Kyōto. Over the past years, the Daishin Zen community has greatly supported my continued practice.

Heartfelt thanks further go to Yorizumi Mitsuko, who agreed to cooperate with our TIMEJ project and came to Zurich for several days of stimulating exchange on Dōgen and his reception in the medieval and early modern periods. The members of two *Shōbōgenzō* reading groups, organized by Ishii Kiyozumi and Ralf Müller, respectively, helped me to calibrate my understanding of Dōgen. Raquel Bouso gently pointed out the merits of some approaches that I initially found counterintuitive. Paulus Kaufmann has been a valued counterpart in discussions on Buddhist philosophy over the years. Three anonymous reviewers and Steven Heine read drafts of the book and gave helpful advice on its organization. James Peltz, Julia Cosacchi and everyone at SUNY Press guided me smoothly through the process toward publication. Special thanks go to reviewer Steffen Doell, who provided numerous further useful hints and kindly agreed to discuss various aspects of the book in person.

As always, my greatest gratitude goes to my wife, Dr. Tomoe Steineck, intellectual companion and sparring partner in debates late into the night. Our daughter, Sora Aruna, patiently sat through many such conversations at the dinner table. Both have supported me in many ways, opening my heart and mind to things within and beyond the scope of this book that have been important in shaping its content.

Conventions and Abbreviations

Conventions

- Dōgen's works are quoted according to his collected works, edited in two volumes by Ōkubo Dōshū (*Dōgen zenji zenshū* 道元禪師禅宗, Kyōto 1969)
- Japanese names are presented in East Asian style, with family names first and personal names second. Except for direct quotes, persons from medieval Japan, who generally had many names, are represented with the name by which they are best known in the Anglophone world.
- The characters for Japanese names, work titles, and so forth are given according to the sources cited. This means that, in many instances, the old forms of Chinese characters are used instead of the simplified versions customary in present-day Japan.
- The transcription of Japanese text follows the Hepburn style. Medieval Japanese is rendered in transcriptions according to the old *kana* style used in the edited sources.
- To improve readability, in the main text I refer to Dōgen's works using English titles. A two-way list of the titles is provided in appendix 2.
- For the same reason, I univocally refer to the tradition that Dōgen belongs to as "Zen," even in relation to sources and

persons from China, where the school is pronounced "Chan." However, personal names are transliterated according to their original language.

- Quotes from Japanese sources in English are my translation if no other reference is given. I provide the Japanese original and, if possible, references to other translations where my translation involves a high degree of interpretation and alternative interpretations are possible. For reasons of space, transcriptions are provided for specific phrases only, but not for longer quotations. For quotations from the composite vernacular (*kana*) *Shōbōgenzō*, I provide references to the translation by Nearman, which is published in open access, and to the widely used translation edited by Tanahashi.

Abbreviations

CBETA	*Chinese Buddhist Electronic Texts Association*
Ch.	Chinese
DZZ	*Dōgen zenji zenshū*, edited by Ōkubo Dōshū
GA	Heidegger, Martin. *Gesamtausgabe.*
GG DZZ	*Genbun taishō gendaigo yaku Dōgen zenji zenshū*, edited by Kagamishima Genryū et. al.
MYS	*Manyōshū*
Jp.	Japanese
T	*Taishū shinshū daizōkyō*, edited by Takakusu Junjirō et al.
X	*Xuzangjing*, edited by CBETA

Introduction

> A full circle sheet approaches spring, and arrives
> Opening and closing according to the times, it resembles a picture
> Stoking with char, watching the ashes, adding a snowflake on top
> Patch-robed monks call out, declaring it a furnace.[1]

Zen master Dōgen 道元 (1200–1253 CE), the founding abbot of Eiheiji in Western Japan, offered this poem to his congregation in early spring of 1252. It marked the closing of the fireplace which during winter had heated the hall where monks meditated, ate, and slept. Confronting the limited measure and changing course of human life had always been an essential part of Dōgen's religious views. The poem by the simile of the "full circle" expresses how he found perfection in these temporal conditions; by living through each occasion and "adding a snowflake on top"—neither detaching himself from trivial necessities nor merely giving himself up to the moment.

One of his most cited statements expresses this attitude in more abstract terms: "time is altogether what there is, and what there is, each and all of it, is time." He offers this formula to explain the word *uji* 有時, the central term and title of a fascicle in his magnum opus, "Treasury of the True Dharma Eye."[2] Originally a standard Sinitic expression meaning "at a certain time" or "sometimes," Dōgen famously converted it into a term indicating enlightened understanding of time, by playing on the semantic potential of its components 有 "to be, to have, to exist" and 時 "time, hour, moment, season, occasion." For him, the term ultimately indicated the omnipresence of Buddhist enlightenment; an omnipresence that played out within and through the distinctive characteristics of each specific time.

In the modern context, the term *uji* and its above-quoted explanation have prompted associations with Heidegger's *Sein und Zeit* (*Being and Time*). In English, *uji* therefore has often been translated as "being[-]time" and discussed as an ontological and existential rather than a soteriological concept. In line with the explanatory sentence quoted above, I propose "what is:time" as an alternative translation because I believe it is now time to question this existential-ontological interpretation and the association with Heidegger.

Timing played a certain part in how that association came about. Heidegger's book appeared just one year after the renowned cultural philosopher Watsuji Tetsurō (1889–1960) had published a book that placed Dōgen on the intellectual agenda of early Shōwa Japan.³ Watsuji and other prominent Japanese philosophers quickly made Heidegger's ideas known in Japan. Akiyama Hanji's (1893–1980) study of Dōgen's "theories," published in 1935, initially highlighted the connection with *Being and Time*.⁴ A number of Japanese and Western scholars adopted his approach in the following decades.⁵ The first monographs on Dōgen's idea of time in English—namely, Steven Heine's *Existential and Ontological Dimensions of Time in Heidegger and Dōgen* and Joan Stambaugh's *Impermanence Is Buddha Nature*—reinforced the link for Western audiences.⁶ Comparisons with a host of other modern Western philosophers followed suit.⁷

There was a certain "cunning of reason"⁸ at work in this integration of Dōgen's thought on time into modern philosophical discourse. Without that reception, his ideas on the subject hardly would have gained the recognition they have today. Dōgen did not return to the expression *uji* in his subsequent writings, and later commentaries therefore saw no reason to highlight this particular term.⁹ Nonetheless, the recognition that the text and Dōgen's thought on time have gained since the twentieth century is well deserved. In the chapter in question, he presented an intricate concept of time, conceived as the intrinsic and omnipresent medium of liberation from suffering. One of the objectives of this book is to explain how time, for him, gained this salvific status. However, the modern philosophical reception has also involved a certain degree of diversion, whereby the focus has shifted away from Dōgen's concern with the salvific engagement with time and its practical implementation in the various aspects of monastic life.

As signaled by the title of Heine's volume, analyzing Dōgen in parallel with Heidegger has led to the former being considered primarily as a philosopher who formulated an original "existential" and "ontological" analysis of time. Accordingly, the reception of Dōgen's engagement with time in the past century has focused on those texts and aspects that speak to the fundamental philosophical interest in knowledge and understanding.

Elements in Dōgen's work that were dedicated to the presentation of specific doctrinal beliefs, expressions of devotion to sacred figures, or elucidation of the details of religious and monastic practice were relegated to the background. This has helped contemporary concerns about the oppressive "rationalization" of time to become connected with Dōgen's texts. The result can be seen in readings that place his concept of time squarely in opposition to "chronology and the calculation of time."[10]

Putting Dōgen's various doctrinal expositions, poetic expressions, and monastic regulations back into the picture provides us with a more nuanced and detailed image of Dōgen's own agenda and his pertinent ideas. "What Is:Time" comes to life as an argument in favor of realizing (conceptually and practically) a distinct, salvific form of cross-temporal synchrony with enlightened beings. According to Dōgen, this synchrony can be lived in every moment of monastic life. Its realization involves a certain mode of attending to the distinctions of the experiential world, including chronology and the quantitative measure of time. The extensive treatment of the details of monastic life that we find in Dōgen's texts spells out this possibility. A paradigm for connecting time's measure with topics of existential significance can be derived from it, and this may be transferred beyond the confines of the "Buddha Way"[11] that he expounded.

On a conceptual level, this paradigm offers an opportunity to overcome two kinds of dualism: First, that between rational distinctions (temporal and otherwise) and enlightened insight, which dominates much of the literature on Zen; and second, the dualism between "subjective, authentic, lived" time and "objective, rationalized, measured" time that dominates the modern philosophical debate, especially on the "continental" side. As I demonstrate in this book, Dōgen allows for the validity of the mystical perspective. It is, however, incomplete and must be complemented by others. The distinct and specific attributes of each given situation or occasion are indispensable features in deepening insight and widening its meaning. In his more theoretical ideas, as well as in their implementation in the realm of religious practice, Dōgen thus integrates the "objective" and the "subjective" features of time; its quantitative aspects with its qualitative ones. Similarly, Dōgen does not simply deny duration in favor of simply "living the moment": He denies that there is a *causa materialis* for duration, as an inert and unchanging substance. Duration occurs because certain "objects" retain features that are relevant to certain types of observers over a certain period of time. Duration in this sense is "real," not imaginary or a matter of mere convention; and it is, again, an essential feature of religious practice. In the ontological terms of the "Heart Sutra," the reading of Dōgen that I offer here corresponds to fully appreciating its formula of "form is emptiness, emptiness is form"[12]—in other words, we must understand "form," without any need for further "reduction" or "negation," as the mode in which "emptiness" exists, and vice versa.[13] Insight into "emptiness," then, does not require a leap beyond distinctions, but instead a close attention to the way reality with its distinctions actually unfolds. This reading allows us to integrate prominent and well-known aspects of Dōgen's teaching—including his concept of a mystical, all-encompassing present where sentient beings are united with the enlightened ones—with others that have been denied or marginalized, such as the affirmation of causal sequence, duration, and time's measure.

The book is structured in three parts. Part I, "Grounding the Conceptual Analysis," first details my approach and the questions that guide the investigation. It then examines the biographical circumstances of Dōgen's writings, the linguistic forms he used to represent time, and the time regimes he installed in his monasteries to embed the analysis of his concept of time in its proper referential, expressive, and conative dimensions. Part II, "What Is:Time," discusses his ideas on time as they unfolded in his work. Finally, part III offers conclusions and afterthoughts. It presents a conceptual reconstruction of Dōgen's view of time, locates it in its historical context, and offers some reflections concerning its relevance for the present world.

In part I, the first chapter explains the book's agenda and methodology with an eye to Dōgen's reception in modern and contemporary scholarly discussions. I show how this reception is largely informed by philosophical interpretations of Dōgen that have isolated his discourse on the concept of time from his overall endeavor to transmit the Buddha's teaching. This has helped his views to become aligned with specific modern concerns: most importantly, the opposition between the quantitative measurement of time and an intuitive approach to lived time. To address this problematic, I propose a new translation for the term *uji* and a systematic investigation of Dōgen's time-related writings as a point for reciprocal comparison and reflection.

My investigation starts from Dōgen's stated aim to "spread the Buddha's teaching and save sentient beings"[14] and relates his conceptual explanations to the ways in which he expressed and regulated time. Through analysis of his multiple ways of expressing time, I expose determinants of time that go beyond quantitative measurement. The examination of Dōgen's instructions on time use and their doctrinal foundations presents practical methods of integrating time's metric with its typological, content-rich attributes. Analyzing his thematic expositions on time in relation to the dimensions of expression and practice leads to an interpretation that is conceptually rich and intellectually compelling—even if some of Dōgen's ideas turn out to be based on metaphysical premises that many modern readers will not readily share.

To place Dōgen's ideas in their proper context, some information on his life and his cultural and social environment is necessary. In chapter 2, I briefly sketch the cultural constellation that shaped the field of religion in early medieval Japan. I then present an outline of Dōgen's life, discussing the timeline and periodization of his works. I follow Steven Heine in arguing in favor of the fundamental continuity and conceptual coherence in his writings; however, I also emphasize more strongly the connections that link Dōgen to concepts and practices outside of the Zen tradition. Recognizing these relations is important for two reasons: First, they help to explain Dōgen's central idea of the unity of practice and attainment, which has strong esoteric undertones. Second, recognizing these links also fosters awareness of the commonalities between different denominations and across medieval Japanese society, such as in terms of shared ritual calendars and schedules. As I demonstrate in more detail in chapter 4, Dōgen strove to secure the autonomy of his monastic communities as worlds apart from secular ambitions and strife. But he also maintained a certain degree of synchronization with other religious institutions, and even with the courtly ritual calendar. Such synchronization helped to convey the fact that these monasteries, in their conscious seclusion from worldly affairs, were nonetheless intended to create benefits for society and the country as a whole.

Chapter 3 begins the exploration of time in Dōgen's texts with an investigation of *chronography*: the ways in which time and temporal relations are expressed in his works. I use a matrix of temporal determinations, derived from Kant's table of categories, to systematically register what aspects of time Dōgen addresses, in which fashion, and to what ends. Admittedly, this methodology builds on a classic modern and "Western" theory. Nonetheless, it ensures that a spectrum of temporal determinations is recorded that includes, but also goes beyond, quantitative expressions.

Besides, far from imposing a preconceived notion of time on Dōgen's texts, this analysis ultimately goes against the grain of Kant's own idea of time: Instead of asserting time as a unitary, a priori "form of intuition," it evokes a variety of ways in which time may be determined. I demonstrate that typological expressions of time are more prevalent in Dōgen's texts than metrical ones, and that Dōgen favors words for time that indicate specific occasions, while avoiding terms that function as general hyperonyms. He also prefers to express temporal location and sequence by "material," metonymical denominators. Sequence is determined by stating which event follows which, instead of localizing each in a chronological framework. Nevertheless, elements of the latter, such as numerical dates, have an important function to play. They are used to indicate the authenticity of Dōgen's writings and emphasize the factual character of extraordinary and portentous events—like the meeting of the first Chinese ancestor of Zen, Bodhidharma, with the Liao emperor Wu. Numerical chronography is also very often linked to material, typological expressions. This indicates that, at least on the level of expression, they are not mutually exclusive.

Chapter 4 moves from modes of expression to the field of action and addresses the time regimes Dōgen installed in his monasteries and the religious and social meaning he attached to them; or, in short, his *chronopolitics*. I first analyze the daily schedule that Dōgen prescribed for his monastic congregation and compare it with similar documents from the Zen school and other denominations. I show that Dōgen's regime conformed to a general framework of four daily practice periods, which Dōgen dedicated exclusively to seated meditation. An intricate system of visual and aural signals informed monastics of the beginning and end of events; they were thus able to concentrate on their present actions. Planning was important in coordinating monastic life, but this was left to experienced temple officers.

I further examine the structure and content of monthly and annual events. For instance, there was a telling shift in the allocation and frequency of memorial days. Dōgen's collected sayings show that he observed memorial days for his teachers, independent of their denomination. With Keizan, the "second ancestor" of the Sōtō school, this practice changed, and only teachers from this lineage were ritually remembered. But identifying dates of particular significance was not only a tool in strengthening the Sōtō school's identity; it also synchronized life in the monastic community with that in other Buddhist institutions and society at large. Numerical chronography was furthermore relevant in regulating the hierarchy of the monastic community. Using iterations of the summer retreat as a criterion, Dōgen ensured that proven commitment to practice decided about monastic rank. Here again, the measurement of time became a significant element of the soteriological agenda.

Based on these findings, part II turns to Dōgen's understanding of time, or his *chrononoetics*, and follows the development of his thought. Chapter 5 demonstrates how his early texts equate time with impermanence, imbuing its notion with a strong sense of urgency. In this context, I also discuss the momentarist aspect of Dōgen's concept of time, but argue against reducing his view to that perspective. I show how the example of the seasons provides him with a paradigm that allows for limited duration without assuming an underlying, permanent substance. Early on in his writings, Dōgen also expresses the idea that within religious practice, a cross-temporal unity occurs between practitioners and all enlightened ones. Chapter 6 is dedicated to Dōgen's most famous text on time, which offers a perspective that unites transiency and time-transcendence. I propose "what is:time" as a new translation for its central term and title (*uji* 有時 in Japanese) instead of renderings such as "being-time" or "existence-time." With this term, Dōgen posits that whatever exists (he mentions the self, but also pine trees, bamboo, or mountains) is also temporal. This holds not only for sentient beings or insentient matter, but also for the enlightened ones and "Buddha nature" (the quality that defines them). I show how "being temporal," in his view, implies that everything at every moment comprises a "lining-up" of the whole world, including the past, present, and future. As a consequence, there is no clear line of separation between present practitioners and their future state as enlightened beings, or between them and the Buddhas, past, present, and future. This alone implies that every given occasion involves all times, as indicated by Dōgen's strong use of the term *nikon* 而今 in the sense of a "consummate now." But Dōgen further contends that religious practice creates a synchrony between practitioners and all enlightened beings. This appears to clash with the directionality of time and a linear understanding of causality. Chapter 7 therefore explores how Dōgen expands on these ideas in his writings after "What Is:Time."

I propose an interpretation where the validity of temporal distinctions is maintained. I show that this explanation fits better with the textual evidence than views that relegate distinctions to the secondary level of "provisional" truth. Dōgen affirms temporal distinctions in general, and temporal sequence in particular, in the very texts that appear to question their validity. His position, however, requires trust in the authoritative insights of the enlightened ones, which were transmitted by the canonical texts. The belief in the moral retributive causality of karma is of primary importance in this regard. Karma, according to Dōgen, can be modified at any moment by the salvific power of insight and proper religious practice.

Part III, "Conclusion and After-Thoughts," starts with a brief reconstruction and conceptual analysis that summarizes the findings of the previous parts and compares them with earlier interpretations. I elucidate how the mystical aspect of cross-temporal unity works jointly with that of quantitative and typological temporal distinctions. Moreover, Dōgen's position is rationally consistent, but it requires acceptance of certain premises that cannot be proven by ordinary human means of insight. The conceptual analysis is followed by reflections on the position of Dōgen's ideas in medieval Japan and, more generally, the history of human time consciousness. Dōgen's more sophisticated ideas were not widely known, let alone shared, by medieval society. However, the themes he addressed and the time-regimes he installed in his monasteries were well within the realm of generally shared concerns and practices. Concerning the global history of time, his position provides an argument against modernist assumptions that want to reserve fully operational ideas of time for modernity, as it integrates abstract and quantitative aspects of time.

Chapter 9, "After-Thoughts," turns the spotlight from medieval Japan to our time and asks what Dōgen's thoughts have to offer people today, beyond the confines of Zen Buddhist communities, in theoretical, spiritual, and practical terms. On the theoretical plane, I argue that his modes of temporal expression and his concept of time challenge the reduction of time to number, and I posit that the typological determination of time is a necessary condition for its quantitative measurement. I further demonstrate that the metaphors Dōgen employed to present intuitive images of time belong to different temporal morphologies. That is often precisely their point: By introducing unexpected imagery, Dōgen subverts simplified notions of time, such as "time is like a river." The alternatives he offers are still worth contemplating today. I argue that his integration of time's measure with spiritual attributes and the time regimes he installed in his monasteries hold significant lessons for building healthy and sustainable social organizations. Spiritually, I highlight his notion of cross-temporal synchrony as a remedy for the existential anxiety caused by the isolation of the individual that is a hallmark of contemporary societies.

Part I
Grounding the Conceptual Analysis

1

From *uji* to Philosophy and Back

Thoughts on Methodology

Philosophical Transpositions

The philosophical interpretation of Dōgen's work has been essential for putting the significance of his thoughts on time into relief. However, as I demonstrate below, reading Dōgen as a philosopher has also entailed a shift in the frame of reference, from the domain of religion to that of cognition. As a consequence, Dōgen's doctrinal expositions on time have been cut off from essential elements of their reasoning. This has resulted in a kind of transposition or modulation that has made his ideas more amenable to modern and philosophically minded readers. But it has also removed a great deal of detail, shape, and color, which are necessary to illustrate the basis of his ideas as well as their practical implications. In the ensuing discussion, I place some emphasis on examples by Japanese philosophers to avoid the impression that what happens in such philosophical readings is a matter of "Western" philosophical rationality appropriating "Japanese" thought. In fact, it is more a question of transposing Dōgen's ideas from the realm of religion into that of modern philosophy, Japanese or otherwise.

One of the earliest English-language presentations of Dōgen's ideas on time was published as the Japanese contribution to a high-profile UNICEF volume on *Time and the Philosophies*.[1] Its author was Seizo Ohe [Ōe Seizō 大江精三], then president of the Japan Philosophy of Science Society and a specialist in philosophy of science. He started his piece by presenting the following excerpt from the "opening part" of *Uji*.

Time is existence and all existence is time. [...] Because time's transit leaves traces, man does not doubt it. Though he does not doubt, he does not understand. Because the ordinary man does vaguely doubt everything he does not understand, his future doubts may not agree with his present doubts. Even doubt is nothing but a part of time. There is no world without this doubting self, for this self is the world itself. We must regard everything in this world as time. [...] Thus we see that the self is time itself. [...] And each grass and each appearance are time.[2]

This excerpt is typical of the philosophical presentation of Dōgen in two regards. First, Ohe uses a decidedly modern philosophical vocabulary in his rendition of Dōgen's ideas. Second, he omits elements from the original text that would demand explanation and might alienate contemporary readers. The result, however, robs the passage of its immediate frame of reference.

A closer look at Dōgen's text reveals that the statement rendered here as "existence is time" and above as "whatever there is, is [also] time" is further explained by way of reference to the traditional description of the Buddha's body and its measure: "The golden body of one *jō* six [ca. 5.9yd/4.85m] is time. Because it is time, there is the sublime light of time." Dōgen goes on to connect this statement to Buddhist teaching and practice: "Study and practice this in the current twelve [zodiacal] hours. The three-headed, eight-armed is time. Because it is time, it is one and the same as the current twelve hours." "Three-headed, eight armed" either refers to an *asura* (a bellicose demon inhabiting one of the six lower realms of Buddhist cosmology) or to a "wisdom king": a manifestation of the Buddha's enlightened insight, usually depicted with a stern or angry expression and holding military implements that symbolize the intent to ward off and subdue evil forces. In other words, the sentences left out by Ohe place Dōgen's statement firmly in the Buddhist cosmos, with its sacred and demoniacal figures, its demand for devoted religious practice, and its promise of support through the beneficial and superhuman powers of the enlightened ones.

In fact, Dōgen's explanatory words directly relate to the initial lines of *Uji*, which Ohe completely omits. Dōgen presents them as a quote from an "old Buddha."[3] They form four couplets in Chinese, with seven characters per line in the first couplet and six in the following three. Each line begins with the two characters *uji*, and each describes a certain action, state of being, or insight—apparently one that the person speaking experienced at some point. The first two lines suggest *uji* indicates that "at a given time" (*aru toki / uji* 有時) the speaker was "standing on the top of a high, high mountain" (line 1), and at another "walking the bottom of the deep, deep sea" (l. 2). These two lines, however, are not merely presenting grandiose vistas. They allude to phrases from a discourse by the Chinese master Yaoshan on the challenges of keeping up monastic life.[4] As such, they point to what one is required to do to fulfill the promise to work toward saving all suffering beings, which is part of the monastic vows. The next line continues the reference to the path of enlightened beings by stating that at one time the speaker was or will be a being with three heads and eight arms (l. 3), and at one time the Buddha himself, standing "one *jō* six [*shaku*]" tall (l.4). As Arifuku Kōgaku has explained, this is an allusion to the Lotus Sutra's chapter on Kannon, the Bodhisattva of universal compassion, who promises to appear in whatever form is necessary to convert and save sentient beings.[5]

Dōgen's famous statement accordingly is primarily about phases of the Buddhist path. It posits that all these phases are not events "in time," separated by time's passing; rather, they are themselves time. By way of being time, they are not isolated instances, but interconnected. They participate in the "sublime light of time" emitted by the golden Buddha body. Ultimately, everything that exists does so. I review the details of this conceptual move in chapter 6. For now, it is important to note how this passage has embedded itself in Buddhist soteriology, including a rich catalog of mysterious beings and a salvific agenda that promises liberation from the cycle of suffering.

One can read Ohe's elimination of references to golden Buddhas and beings with multiple arms and heads charitably, as an attempt to relieve Dōgen's soteriological discourse of elements that might alienate modern minds. Others have gone further and completely stripped Dōgen's concept of all religious connotations. An extreme example is the analytical philosopher Ōmori Shōzō. To Ōmori, the "golden body of one *jō* six" simply represents a Buddha statue in Dōgen's monastery. He treats it as an example of an object present in everyday life, analogous to a kitchen pot.[6] In contrast, Ohe distills from Dōgen's text a soteriological essence that, to his mind, stands the test of time and holds up to philosophical scrutiny. He further admits the central role of seated meditation and religious practice. Nevertheless, Ohe describes meditation in rather abstract terms, ridding it of any references to monastic context and pious ritual:

> Dōgen knew very well the epistemological primacy of time, just like Kant, because he knew that our cognitive consciousness does rise and fall with our time-experience. [. . .] He went deeper (as did Heidegger or Husserl), into the very basis of our experienced time, where the essence of human existence may reveal itself at any moment. Even then he did not stop. Dōgen proposes to all truth-seekers to sit cross-legged quietly and try to think the unthinkable, i.e., to keep the mind as empty as possible of all the illusions and delusions of everyday life [. . .]. Only by this practice of *Zazen*, he thinks, can man attain true enlightenment in a timeless void of the "eternal now," overcoming the temporality of human existence.[7]

Ohe's twofold abstraction from religious cosmology and the monastic context is typical of much of the philosophical reception of Dōgen. Two prominent examples suffice to illustrate this; the first is Akiyama Hanji (1893–1980), a Sōtō priest and student of Nishida Kitarō. His study of Dōgen,[8] published in 1935, was the first scholarly monograph dedicated to latter's ideas. Akiyama resorted to Husserl's idea of "withholding" and "inhibiting" all judgment on the existence of the "Objective world"[9] to explain the enlightened view of time. He equated Husserl's "natural" belief in the existence of the world (and time) with the common, secular view of time. "Phenomenological epoché," which "parenthesizes" that assumption[10] to focus on how our experience of that world comes about, in Akiyama comes to stand for the enlightened view. In the common view, time is linear; the cause precedes the effect; and past, present, and future are distinct temporal spheres that follow each other in sequence. When their objectivity is "parenthesized," however, and they are reduced to experience, they all coexist as distinct parts of the present moment of consciousness, which always already comprises the totality of past, present, and future.[11] Akiyama applies Husserl's distinction between the "noematic" analysis of a given mental object and the "noetic" analysis of the mental acts responsible for producing that object[12] to the experience of time and causation: "Not obscuring cause and effect in the higher sense actually refers to the noematic knowledge of continuous causation that spans the eternal past, present, and future, which is contained in the noetic, discontinuous present moment."[13] In the enlightened view, each moment arises spontaneously and without connection to the previous or following one. At the same time, each moment is the "now of eternity," comprising the totality of past, present, and future.¹⁴ In contrast, the natural view is immersed in the moment. From this standpoint, it sees past, present, and future as a continuum. Consequently, the illusion of duration arises. Things apparently exist beyond the moment, but that is a figment of the imagination. Clock-time, based on the measurement of duration, belongs to this imaginary level. The "now of eternity" (and therefore *uji*) knows of no duration; it is beyond any measure. Like Ohe, Akiyama does not deny the necessity of meditative practice in Dōgen. But practice here assumes the meaning of exercising a certain cognitive standpoint, which is essentially characterized by the phenomenological and ontological insight characterized above.

Second, Joan Stambaugh took this one step further in her monograph on Dōgen's ideas on time. Expressly softening the link to monastic practice, she posits:

> [T]he term "monastery" refers less to a place than to a state of being, or perhaps better, a way of being. [. . .] Ceaseless practice, perhaps in the trackless world monastery, liberates us from words, especially from the ordinary, unthinking, automatic use of words, and renders us truly the opposite of deaf and dumb: listening and soundlessly "speaking," giving expression (*dōtoku*), i.e., articulating suchness. Other examples of sustained exertion might be found in an actor performing in a play, a musician playing in a concert or an athlete engaging in a competition.

The result is once more a presentation of Dōgen's practice as the experiential realization of a particular ontological insight:

> Since everything is impermanent, there is no substance whatsoever in any sense of that word. Thus no thing or being obstructs any other being, and every moment is a total manifestation of the entire world. To see phenomena in this way is to see them in their suchness. Blake expressed something very close to this when he wrote:
>
> To see a world in a Grain of Sand
> And a Heaven in a Wild Flower
> Hold Infinity in the palm of your hand
> And Eternity in an hour.¹⁵

The analogy Stambaugh has drawn to Christian mysticism and, later on, to the holistic view of philosophers like Leibniz, is not entirely misplaced. In Part II of this book, I examine the mystical and holistic element entailed in Dōgen's concept of time, which may translate into experiences of the kind indicated by Ohe and Stambaugh. As will become clear in this discussion, however, presenting this element as the essence of his thought robs the concept of *uji* of its intrinsic relation with temporal distinctions (the manifold aspects of the "twelve hours" mentioned above), the salvific power of enlightened beings, and karmic causation. In fact, reference to "experience" is all but absent from Dōgen's discourse. Nevertheless, it becomes a necessary element in these philosophical readings, where it takes the place of the more specifically Buddhist ideas mobilized in Dōgen's texts. The result is a somewhat generic mysticism and one that, in contrast to Dōgen, accepts distinctions only as secondary, provisional attributes of reality. Writes Stambaugh: "It is a matter of utter indifference whether things are good (Buddha) or bad (demon), grandiose or commonplace; without *uji*, nothing at all is, or can be."[16]

Not all philosophical readers of Dōgen would concur with this somewhat extreme statement. But the tendency to loosen the ties between his ideas on time and specific ritual, doctrinal, and soteriological elements of the Buddha Way, and to replace them with a certain epistemological stance, identified with the cognitive stance and mode of experience in Zen meditation, can also be observed in other influential authors, such as Tanabe Hajime, Abe Masao, and the early Steven Heine or Rein Raud.[17] This mode of reading opens up analogies that can be helpful in understanding certain aspects of Dōgen's position, and it has greatly facilitated the integration of his thought into philosophical discourse. These two advantages, however, have come at a price. In pitting Dōgen's concept of *uji* against the ordinary experience of time (and especially all measuring of time), such readings have obscured the way Dōgen actually worked to integrate ordinary modes of time experience and measurement into his comprehensive notion of time. Furthermore, they have cut off his concepts from essential elements of their justification, which also serve to explain Dōgen's insistence on standards of monastic propriety and ethical behavior. Putting the full gamut of Dōgen's expressive, prescriptive, and doctrinal references to time back into the picture gives us a more nuanced understanding of his notion of time and its justification. As outlined above, the result is a highly complex and inclusive concept of time. This concept holds important lessons both theoretically and practically, even if it rests on fundamental assumptions that defy proof by ordinary means of knowledge.

Restating *uji:* A New Translation

Given the problems that have arisen from associating Dōgen's *Uji* with various strands of modern philosophy, and Heidegger's *Being and Time* in particular, I propose retranslating Dōgen's term in a fashion more in line with the meaning of its components and its usage in his texts, which helps to avoid a facile alignment with modern philosophical concerns.

As a reminder, the term *uji* is originally an inconspicuous expression that would be read *aru toki* in Japanese, and may be rendered in English with the conjunction "when" or the expression "at a certain time." Dōgen introduces it in the eight-line stanza at the beginning of the chapter bearing that title. This stanza depicts, on first sight, various situations or modes of existence recalled by an "old Buddha." The compound *uji*, which stands at the beginning of each line, therefore seems simply to indicate, in line with its usual reading, an indefinite temporal location. The stanza starts out with rather grandiose perspectives ("standing on top of the high, high mountain / walking at the bottom of the deep, deep sea"), but moves on to mention more inconspicuous things like a fly whisk, a staff, or a stone lantern, only to return to the larger perspective ("the great earth, the empty sky") at the end. Notably, the first two lines are taken from a discourse by the Chinese master Yaoshan on how difficult it is to keep up the monastic life,[18] and the more mundane elements mentioned in the ensuing lines are either ritual implements of the Zen master, or they are connected to enlightened insight by episodes from Zen lore, collected by Dōgen in his "Three Hundred Cases of the Treasury of the True Dharma Eye."[19] Each scene depicted in the stanza therefore has some connection to the question of insight and the ultimate liberation from the cycle of suffering that Dōgen identifies with monastic life.

Dōgen then gives a surprising twist to the word *uji* with his first explanatory sentence. Suddenly the compound is read as a fixed term signifying the inherent temporality of everything that exists: "*Uji* here means that time is altogether what there is, and what there is, each and all of it, is time." The original Japanese sentence is more succinct and uses the term's two components *u* ("to be present; to exist; to have") and *ji* ("time, hour, moment, season, occasion") as stand-alone nouns.[20] Transposed into

English, this may be rendered as "Concerning *uji*: *ji* is altogether *u*, and all *u* are *ji*" (or "every *u* is *ji*"). The quantifier "all/every" (*mina*) in the second part of the sentence shows that *u* stands for a quantifiable particular. This supports Rolf Elberfeld's etymological note that *u* 有 originally "indicates a given, concrete something."[21] The ensuing sentences, which present "the golden body of one *jō* six" and "three heads, eight arms" from the stanza as examples, corroborate that observation. In conclusion, *u* here does not stand for an abstract noun like "being" or "existence"; it represents something particular that is given in a certain situation. This is why I propose "time is altogether what there is [in the sense of 'every given something'], and what there is, each and all of it, is time" as the full translation of the sentence in question. A translation of *uji* may be derived from this. The forced consolidation of *uji* into a compound that defies dissolution into the standard Japanese reading *aru toki* ("at a certain time") justifies the use of an equally forced English term. I propose to contract "time is what there is" and "whatever there is, is time" into "what is:time," with the colon indicating the inseparability of the term's two parts.

Two qualifications are in place regarding this choice of terminology. First, the "what" in "what is:time" is an indefinite pronoun, and not the interrogative. In a different context, Dōgen uses the interrogative to stand for "Buddha nature." It is tempting to read "what is:time" in the same vein. The chapter on time, however, does not use this rhetorical device. It therefore would be a creative intervention to do so. Second, just like the word *uji*, "what is:time" does not in and of itself express the salvific content of the term. Since Dōgen's first explanatory statement uses a universal quantifier, it does read like a general ontological proposition. That proposition is, however, at the same time conjoined with the assurance that once one has committed to practice, one is already living the life of enlightened beings. As I explain in chapters 5 to 8, time for Dōgen provides precisely the link that makes that connection possible. "What is:time" suggests that everything is at once a given individual time and the whole of time. This seemingly paradoxical unity of each time with the totality of time becomes apparent when one queries precisely "what" there is. Dōgen, through this query, leads practitioners to understand how they, in their current efforts, are one with all enlightened beings. Practice creates a trans-temporal unity with sacred reality—or, vice versa, it realizes the trans-temporal sacred in the present. The term "what is:time" in this manner serves to elucidate how time in itself is salvific.

Time and Symbolic Form

The theoretical and methodological approach I take in this book is strongly inspired by Ernst Cassirer's *Philosophy of Symbolic Forms* (1923–1929). Cassirer's work has received renewed attention over recent decades, especially with an eye to the potential his ideas hold for the theory and ethics of interculturality.[22] The key insight at the basis of his philosophy is that reality can only be comprehended through the prism of the "forms of human culture."[23] Each of these forms, such as science, religion, art, technology, or law, structures perception in a specific way and construes a particular kind of "objectivity." Symbols play an essential part in this process, and each form has its constitutive class of signs and modes of signification; this is why Cassirer coined the term "symbolic forms." Because symbols comprise material expression, they exist as part of a spatiotemporal nexus. Symbolic forms therefore are intrinsically historical; they are instantiated in different ways according to place and time, and they evolve in a path-dependent fashion. This provides the philosophical key to understanding and accepting different expressions of universal norms and values such as "truth," "justice," or "beauty." Although Cassirer's writings display the influence of the Eurocentric, colonialist ideologies of his environment and the traditions he received, his ideas nonetheless can serve to question these traditions and move beyond their Eurocentric and imperialist values.

Regarding the problematic examined in this book, the theory of symbolic form offers valuable insights on two levels, the theoretical and the methodological. Theoretically, the concept of symbolic forms asks us to consider cultural artifacts, such as Dōgen's writings on time, within the context of the symbolic form they belong to and its particular mode of objectifying reality, which also specifies the meaning of "time." Methodologically, the theory suggests assessing Dōgen's ideas on time, first, based on a systematic exploration of the mode in which time is expressed and symbolized in his writings, and, second, in their connection with the way of life they imply.

To start from the level of theory, in Kantian terms, symbolic forms are "conditions of possibility" for any kind of objectivity. For Cassirer, the notion of reality depends on symbolic mediation: Symbols create the reflective distance necessary to question what is given in perception. For the same reason, experiential reality is altogether configured according to the terms of a specific symbolic form. Each of these forms has a particular function in the totality of human relations with the world, and each has its own mode and range of validity. What is "beautiful" in an artistic sense might not be theoretically or scientifically "true"; what is "sacred" or "salvific" may conflict with what is legally "just" or technically "efficient," and so forth. At the same time, the "beautiful" and the "salvific" involve a higher degree of individual subjectivity than "truth" and "justice," and therefore command a lower level of validity. Propositions made by Dōgen, or by anyone else within the realm of religion for that matter, cannot be simply accepted into the realm of theory, even if they come with claims for universal validity.[24]

As Cassirer was quick to point out, each symbolic form, by creating a totality of its own, is prone to take its limited world for the whole.[25] Furthermore, historical instantiations of a certain symbolic form often see themselves as its one true representative—just as classical modern Protestants typically saw their form of Christianity as the only fully evolved and true form of religion. Dōgen, incidentally, held a similar view. Not only was he convinced that the Buddha Way (*butsudō* 仏道) was the supreme path for human existence; he also posited that his was the one and only correct understanding of the Buddha's teaching, in perfect accord with that of all previous enlightened ones.[26] The theory of symbolic forms asks us to consider such claims as phenomena related to a particular mode of thinking and to critically explore how they are being validated.

Finally, while Cassirer held fast to an idealist philosophical position, the fundamental role he assigned to symbolic mediation opens up the theory of symbolic forms to a perspective that includes historical materialism's insights into the social conditions that enable (or constrict) the articulation and transmission of a given view.[27] In our context, this means to appreciate not only, in the Kantian vein, the ideal or conceptual "conditions of possibility" related to a specific modality of engendering time, but also the social and material conditions that support its relevance, if not necessity, in a given cultural setting. This moves the argument back from the purely philosophical to the historical plane, and to questions of cultural semiotics.

The methodological upshot of these theoretical considerations is that we need to explore the particular mode of "objectivity" of time within the religious context that is established through Dōgen's express intention to transmit the "Buddha Way" for the benefit of those earnestly seeking liberation from the cycle of suffering. Such an exploration must include time's quantitative aspects together with other kinds of attributes, and the particular function and relative importance of each mode of determination.[28]

In other words, we need to look closely and comprehensively at the ways that time is expressed and used in Dōgen's works in order to understand which aspects of time were salient to him and his followers, how they impacted life on a practical level, and how they related to their way of understanding the world. Such an investigation best starts from the rhetorical situation in which Dōgen was speaking and writing; this means describing how the fundamental factors of communication at play in his works related to the interventions he attempted with them. I base this part of my analysis on Roman Jakobson's model of communication, which identifies six such elementary factors: addresser, addressee(s), message, code, channel, and environment.[29] Texts that seek to influence the attitude and behavior of their recipients regularly design their representation of these factors in a manner conducive to their aims.[30] To achieve a plausible interpretation of Dōgen's writings, we thus need to consider the basic facts concerning the changing environments in which he wrote, the composition of his audiences, the channels of communication available, and the linguistic and cognitive repertoire that mediated their understanding and intellectual exchange.

On an operational level, the theory of symbolic forms further demands close attention to the way time is expressed. Therefore, the main part of the argument starts with a section on *chronography*, and the conceptual analysis of Dōgen's thematic disquisitions on time systematically reviews the metaphors and images he uses to make his notion of time intuitive and palpable. I work from an understanding of chronography that incorporates chronometry, but is not restricted to it. My analysis therefore includes all ways of predicating time, and their functions in the text, to better grasp the specific *modality* in which time appears in Dōgen's writings.[31] On the conceptual level, I take inspiration from Lakoff and Johnson's recognition of metaphorical mapping as an essential and irreducible part of ideational meaning. Furthermore, based on their observation that "[most] of our understanding of time is a metaphorical version of our understanding of motion in space,"[32] I closely attend to the patterns of motion and change that Dōgen refers to, and draw on the dynamic morphology of time proposed by Maki Yūsuke in his "Comparative Sociology of Time."[33] From a practical perspective, I gauge which aspects of time assume importance in guiding or shaping human action, and, conversely, which attitudes toward time are expressed in the conduct of ritual and daily affairs. Because direct observation of the past is impossible, and independent reports of the actual events are scant, the main sources concerning this plane are prescriptive in character. I have chosen to speak of *chronopolitics* in this regard, not least because Dōgen and his followers used temporal duration and sequence to establish and express monastic hierarchy, as well as temporal location and iteration to implement a politics of memory,[34] which was important in the formation of Sōtō school identity.

Exploring the expressive and pragmatic aspects of time in Dōgen provides a firm foundation for conceptual analysis of his thematic discussions of the subject. The analysis follows the development of his ideas over the course of his teaching and writing career; this allows me to address changes in emphasis and topic—although the interpretations rest on the assumption of a fundamental coherence in Dōgen's agenda. Only after this diachronic survey do I attempt a brief systematic reconstruction, which unites all the elements in question.

The Question of Cultural Appropriation

A research project such as this, which is based on modern scholarly methods and terminology, is liable to be accused of imposing an epistemology that is alien to its subject. The application of such alien terms, it is assumed, must lead to a distortion of content and structure. If the methods and terminology are derived from authors who are identified as "Western," these concerns invite the additional accusation of a wrongful mode of cultural appropriation. Such concerns are often warranted. For example, the initial reception of Japanese Pure Land Buddhism by researchers such as Hans Haas[35] or Alfred Bloom[36] was strongly informed by Christian religious notions, as was visible in the very title of Bloom's book *Shinran's Gospel of Pure Grace*. Christian soteriological terminology was, in these instances, applied as a matter of course and was not scrutinized for its potential to cause distortions. Similarly, one of the earliest comparative studies of Zen meditation[37] emerged in the context of Rudolf Otto's endeavor to present Christianity as the highest form and complete realization of religiosity.[38]

The rationale of the theoretical framework chosen for the present volume, however, is to acknowledge the distance between the present world and that of Dōgen in general, and between the scholarly goals of this investigation and his own aim of transmitting the "Buddha Way" in particular. A scholarly work cannot aim to "reproduce" the subject of its investigation; that would be a meaningless endeavor. We cannot return to Dōgen's world; thus, as scholars, our aim must be to understand it, not to "relive" it. Understanding implies familiarity, but also difference and distance. In this context, the methods used to build my interpretation were chosen to ensure that his texts can function as points of resistance against projections and misappropriations. This is yet another reason why my analysis starts from the modes in which time is expressed in his works and considers thematic articulations of time only later.

In the context of this fundamental orientation and methodological strategy, identifying Dōgen's aim as belonging to the symbolic form of religion does not entail, as in the case of Rudolf Otto, a rich normative notion of religion. On the contrary, the notion of "symbolic form" as I employ it accepts that this form can never appear "as such." There is, in other words, no "pure" or "perfect" expression of religion (or any other symbolic form). There are only specific historical formations, binding together multiple individual articulations. We may survey these to deepen our understanding with regard to the multiple and often starkly contrasting ways in which "religion" can be realized. What is crucial in this regard is the readiness to be corrected in one's assumptions about "religion" (or "art," or "science," or "law" for that matter) by the sources in question. That said, identifying Dōgen's own project as one belonging to the symbolic form of religion, and within that form to the class of "religions of salvation," is justified by his own, expressly stated agenda. Dōgen in his first doctrinal exposition describes it with the words "to spread the [Buddha] Dharma and to save sentient beings."[39] *Not* acknowledging Dōgen's own statements about his aims, and refraining from any conscious attempt at relating them to more general categories, would mean neglecting the normative context he himself attributes to his work. It would also be self-defeating in terms of scholarship. Categorization cannot be avoided; one may strive to steer clear of "loaded" terms like "religion" or "salvation," and find oneself using less conspicuously burdened, but equally rich, terms such as "belief" or "rescue" instead.[40]

Furthermore, projection and appropriation are by no means the prerogative of Western readers. Influential Japanese readers of Dōgen, such as Watsuji Tetsurō, Akiyama Hanji, or Tanabe Hajime, showed no compunction in projecting their own agendas and theoretical inclinations on his works.[41] Western readers came mostly a generation later, and by and large followed in their footsteps. In light of this evidence, it appears colonialist to assume that modernist appropriation must originate with Western agents, however one defines the "West." Moreover, not all appropriation or projection is illegitimate in and of itself. Traditions live by reinventing themselves, and Dōgen would hardly have gained such a broad readership today without the creative interventions of the above-named and many other authors. Yet, as I hope to show in this volume, it is worthwhile now to take a step back from the modes of interpretation they established and to see what may be gained from reading Dōgen not as a precursor to Hegelian dialectics, Heideggerian existential phenomenology, or Derridean postmodernism, but as an advocate of the Buddhist, monastic path to liberation from suffering—as strange as that may seem in our world. The point here is not to exoticize Dōgen, but to take his texts as reference objects for reciprocal comparison, which allows for similarities with, as well as differences from, contemporary views and issues.

Zen with Distinctions

To reiterate some of the points that make this a worthwhile endeavor, I intend to demonstrate the following:

(1) In opposition to views that contrast "rationalist" modern views of time, which emphasize chronometry, with "intuitive" views from earlier periods in history, I show that Dōgen employs a complex notion of time that integrates metric and typological distinctions. The specific difference from the homogeneous, quantified time (which dominates modern, capitalist relations of production) is twofold: First, Dōgen employs time's measure to identify and characterize specific occasions and to explore their particular meaning in relation to the Buddha Way. Second, Dōgen installs time regimes that largely free his congregation from the pressure of "running against the clock" and allow them to focus on the action at hand. Planning, and struggling with time pressures, is left to senior monastic officers.

(2) In contrast to views that work with a simple opposition between a "conventional" view of time that includes linearity, duration, and causal connections, and a "higher truth" where none of the aforementioned obtain, I demonstrate that Dōgen (with his signature term of *uji*) seeks to deepen rather than negate the understanding of temporal connectivity, duration, and karmic retribution by showing how they serve to realize a fundamental mystical unity of practitioners with enlightened ones. Such

unity is, however, realized not beyond but through the distinctions between the various situations and attributes of different times. This version of the Buddhist "non-dual" view of "forms" and "emptiness" is "rational" in the sense that it is free from contradictions and does not have recourse to elements or views that lack rational connection and coherence. However, Dōgen's concept is based on assumptions that cannot be proven by ordinary human means of knowledge. It therefore cannot be simply transferred into a philosophy that claims to have no epistemological basis external to the ordinary human mind.

(3) That said, Dōgen's writings on time offer a process-based relational ontology that is of interest beyond the confines of his religious endeavor. Earlier interpretations, such as Rein Raud's work on momentarism, or Yorizumi Mitsuko's and Steven Heine's exploration of emptiness and time, have helpfully highlighted essential aspects of this view, but need to be put in perspective. As I show in the concluding chapter, Dōgen's integration of the quantitative and qualitative aspects of time, and his combination of a holistic view with attention to temporal distinctions, hold promise on both the theoretical and practical levels. His concept of time and the time regime he derived from it skillfully blend clock-time coordination with a personalized focus to create a model that is relevant to contemporary society.

2

Placing Dōgen in Time
Cultural Constellation, Chronology, Agenda

This chapter serves a double purpose within the overall agenda of mobilizing Dōgen's thought on time for reciprocal comparison. First, it places his pertinent writings in their biographical and cultural context; and second, it argues for a basic consistency in his doctrinal agenda in general, and his ideas on time in particular.

Dōgen and his writings became thoroughly modernized in the twentieth century. Selected works, primarily those written in with the use of Japanese grammar and vocabulary, were integrated into the canons of national intellectual history and literature. They were further presented in popular editions and explained as philosophical analyses of the human condition or spiritual guides to a better life. These modes of presentation and interpretation involved substantial alterations in all semiotic dimensions: Pragmatically, "esoteric" instructions for an inner circle of trusted disciples became public knowledge. Syntactically, they were dissociated from the more public statements and performances recorded in Literary Sinitic. Semantically, their message was disconnected from monastic, renunciant life—and thereby, as we shall see in Part II, from the axis of Dōgen's instructions. It therefore seems important to remind even knowledgeable readers of the circumstances of his life, the agendas he pursued, and the state of the religious "field" in which he intervened.

Second, the argument in this book is based on the premise that Dōgen's thought on time remained fundamentally consistent throughout his life as a religious teacher and writer. Not that all its elements were in place right from the start, but there was no break or turning point after which he embraced an entirely new or different position. Furthermore, although his ideas were not widely shared during his lifetime, they were firmly rooted in the Buddhist traditions he had studied in his youth, including, but not limited to, the Zen tradition. This view builds on biographical research by Japanese and Western scholars such as Kawamura Kōdō, Nakaseko Shōdō, Steven Heine, Tsunoda Tairyū, and William Bodiford, but stands in contrast to two earlier views that dominated the discussion for many decades and are still present in the debate.

Many modern authors in the mid-twentieth century embraced the image of Dōgen as representative of a "new Buddhism" that cared for and catered to the masses, which is believed to have emerged in Japan in the early medieval period (1192–1333 CE, styled the Kamakura era after the seat of the military government). More importantly for the topic of this book, he was even regarded as a philosopher with a universal message. Defendants of these views needed to account for Dōgen's numerous expressions of more parochial interests: for example, his investment in intra- and intersectarian struggles[1] and the definition of proper ritual and procedure. They have done so by establishing what Steven Heine has labeled the "decline theory" of Dōgen. They posited that the said interventions occurred only later in his life, when he founded his second monastery in the remote province of Echizen.[2] In this view, the "real" Dōgen, whose ideas are worth discussing and promoting, is the author of a select number of writings in the composite vernacular style that display a distinct philosophical flavor and a universalist message with a strong mystical tendency. In terms of time, this links to an emphasis on the "absolute now" beyond all distinctions. This interpretation is sometimes connected to more sectarian Sōtō school agendas, such as immersion in a state free of all conceptual thought, or "just sitting" (*shikan taza* 只管打坐). For proponents of this view, which aligned smoothly with the modern agenda of building a national cultural consciousness, Dōgen's Literary Sinitic writings, as well as his later expositions on doctrine, were the products of a changed outlook of inferior intellectual quality. They have no bearing on the interpretation of the earlier, "philosophical" works.[3]

Others, most prominently the representatives of the "Critical Buddhism" movement in the 1980s and 1990s,[4] have argued quite the opposite. To their mind, Dōgen later in life became increasingly aware of the shortcomings of the mystical view that placed the highest value on a realm beyond distinctions. Heine has called this the "renewal theory." According to this view, Dōgen chose to completely rewrite the *Treasury* in order to base it firmly on elementary Buddhist doctrines, especially the doctrine of karmic retribution. The "real Dōgen" in this view is to be found in his latest writings, especially in the twelve fascicles of the *Treasury* drafted in his final years.[5] Anything at odds with the views expressed therein is to be regarded as the product of an earlier, immature stage of his thought. It should be discarded, just as Dōgen allegedly renounced his earlier writings when he chose to start his most important doctrinal project anew. In this hypothesis, the turning point is linked to a prolonged visit Dōgen reportedly made to Kamakura at the behest of his most important patron, a senior retainer of the Shōgunate, between the fall of 1247 and spring of 1248.[6]

Representatives of "Critical Buddhism," such as Matsumoto Shirō and Hakamaya Noriaki, unleashed a powerful polemic against doctrines that underwrote the unquestioning affirmation of a social order that dehumanized certain social groups.[7] Conceptually, the most important object of their critique was the idea of a realm of truth beyond distinctions. Where insight was defined by access to that realm, they argued, this would result in an unquestioned affirmation of the world as it presented itself. Such thinking lent itself to the legitimation of repressive social orders. When ultimate truth is posited to lie in a realm beyond distinctions, this works against any attempt to critically assess a given situation, because such assessment itself would be seen as exemplifying "discriminative thought."[8]

Since the 1980s, historical and philological studies by Kawamura Kōdō, Steven Heine, Tsunoda Tairyū, William Bodiford, and others evidenced that both the decline and the renewal theory encounter problems of chronology when the complete scope of Dōgen's writings and their sequence are taken into account.[9] In what follows, I build on their findings to argue in favor of the basic consistency in Dōgen's position over time and to demonstrate its links with Buddhist doctrinal tradition beyond the confines of the Sōtō school. I further use evidence from biographical studies on Dōgen; most importantly, those of Nakaseko Shōdō,[10] which provide information on his social background, networks, intellectual exchanges, and religious commitments. These are all important aspects for understanding the interventions he attempted to make and their practical implications at the time.

Social and Cultural Conditions

The early medieval period in Japan is broadly understood as a time of turmoil. An uneasy power balance existed between the military government in Kamakura and the imperial court. The erosion of the centralized system of law and land administration, which had begun in the late eighth century, had by this time led to constant political intrigue and attempts at land-grabbing and bickering between the "gates of power" (*kenmon* 権門)—that is, the powerful houses of the court, the leading families of the warrior aristocracy, and the major fanes.[11] The less powerful were often caught in the middle of such disputes. They were also vulnerable to hunger and disease, which were both notoriously endemic in all periods before the modern era. In the eyes of those writing at the time, especially when they were members of the court aristocracy, this period was one of disorder and decay. Its calamities fit all too well with the Buddhist historical scheme of the "Final Dharma Age" (*mappō* 末法)—the last and degenerate age, in which the Buddha's teaching would be present in the world—which was calculated to have begun in 1052 CE. This pessimistic outlook dominates the more elaborate sources of the period, a prime example being Kamo no Chōmei's "Ten Foot Square Hut" (*Hojōki* 方丈記, 1212).[12]

The dark tone of this literature, however, contrasts with the somewhat brighter picture emerging from a purview of general living conditions and population statistics: A steady growth in population bears witness to heightened productivity, which was based on and further supported increased specialization and the proliferation of crafts and trades. New groups of wealthy commoners emerged, including agricultural managers, traders, and workshop masters.[13] This development broadened the basis for the production and reception of symbolic artifacts; it also created new demands. The growing segments of the common population who had time and resources to devote to issues beyond survival aspired to see their hopes and needs reflected in the symbolic realm. Moreover, increasing trade with the continent fostered an influx of monies, goods, and ideas. Matsuo Kenji has demonstrated how the creation of new religious congregations and doctrines was linked to the growth of urban populations, where many people were no longer embedded in transgenerational spiritual communities, and consequently looked for prospects of individual salvation.[14] Furthermore, Satō Hiroo showed how, in response to the concomitant trend for commoners to visit temples to offer their prayers, temple architecture changed to accommodate larger numbers of the faithful.[15]

Religious Writing in Early Medieval Japan

In step with these developments, a new style of writing emerged beside the logographic Literary Sinitic (*kanbun* 漢文) and the purely phonographic indigenous (*wabun* 和文) styles.¹⁶ This "composite Japano-Sinitic style" (*wakan konkō bun*, short: "composite vernacular") brought together the rich lexicon of Chinese terms (*kango* 漢語) and the highly differentiated options offered by indigenous grammar to qualify semantic and pragmatic relations. It proved an apt and adaptable medium to express and disseminate a broad variety of ideas. Dōgen's aforementioned *Treasury of the True Dharma Eye* is among the early masterpieces of this style, as are Kamo no Chōmei's musings, along with the various redactions of the "Tale of the Heike" (*Heike monogatari* 平家物語, first half of the thirteenth century), which describes the conflicts that led to the establishment of the Shogunate in Kamakura. That said, Literary Sinitic remained an important and highly prestigious mode of expression. Nor did this "conservative" style stand in the way of new ideas: The period's famed religious innovators, from Hōnen 法然 (1133–1212) and his disciple Shinran 親鸞 (1173–1263) of the Pure Land School to Eisai/Yōsai 栄西 (1141–1215) of the Zen and Nichiren 日蓮 (1222–1282) of the so-called Lotus School, all explained and defended their teachings in works written in Literary Sinitic.¹⁷

Dōgen was no exception to this rule; indeed, substantial parts of his oeuvre are written in Literary Sinitic. These comprise his initial *Manual for the Universal Promotion of Seated Meditation* (*Fukan zazen gi* 普勧坐禪儀, 1227; short: *Manual*), the 1234 *Collection of Essentials in the Study of the Way* (*Gakudō yōjin shū* 學道用心集; short: *Essentials*), his *kōan* collection "300 Cases of the Treasury of the True Dharma Eye" (*Shōbōgenzō sanbyaku soku* 正法眼蔵三百則; short: *300 Cases Treasury*), the various expositions on monastic rules posthumously collected in the *Pure Rules of Eternal Peace* (*Eihei shingi* 永平清規, 1237–1248), and, last but not least, the official record of his sayings, *Extensive Record of Eternal Peace* (*Eihei kōroku* 永平廣錄; short: *Extensive Record*). Together, these straddle all phases of his life as a religious teacher and guide and cover the realms of the doctrinal-theoretical as well as the practical. The modern predilection for his works in the composite vernacular style is related to the project of defining and promulgating a "national literature," in which works written in the "foreign" idiom had to take second place—although excluding them proved impossible.¹⁸

Whether in the composite vernacular or the Literary Sinitic style, such writings were both drafted and reproduced as manuscripts. This was not due to the absence of printing technology: Already in the Nara period, canonical Buddhist texts had been printed in large numbers, mostly for ritual purposes.¹⁹ But during Dōgen's lifetime, this mode of reproduction was largely reserved for established and widely accepted texts that were thought to contain meritorious power (*kudoku* 功徳).²⁰ In Dōgen's second monastery Eiheiji, it appears that a text used for the daily "transfer of merit" (*ekō* 回向・廻向) ritual was printed to spare the labor of copying; this demonstrates the availability of the technology and exemplifies its preferred use at the time.²¹ On the other hand, a decade after Dōgen's death, one of his disciples planned to print an anthology of his formal instructions and took a manuscript to China for editing. He received help and even secured the endorsement of pre- and postscripts by three established masters.²² Although the plan did not materialize in the end, it attests to an increase in printing activities, especially in the Zen school, where anthologies of "recorded sayings" (*goroku* 語録, marked by highly formalized, Literary Sinitic style) started to be printed to preserve and promulgate the insight and style of established masters.²³ Incidentally, the first work of Dōgen to appear in print was his *Essentials*²⁴—again, a presentation of elementary, and largely uncontroversial, injunctions in the Literary Sinitic style, rather than a discussion of doctrinal intricacies.

Explications on the details of new and still-debated doctrines or interpretations were often accessible only to the select few of trusted followers and were not meant to be "published" or circulated widely. This connected to a culture of lineage, where firsthand knowledge—and even more so, possession—of these texts came with the prestige of being an acknowledged "successor" to the teaching. This does not mean that there was no debate between lineages and schools.²⁵ On the contrary, it was expected that new doctrines would be exposed to scrutiny and debate, as is evident from contemporary complaints by the Enryakuji, the powerful head monastery of the Tendai School on Mount Hiei to the northeast of Kyoto, against the Zen and Pure Land schools.²⁶ Documents answering to such requests often took the form of "disquisitions" (*ron* 論) or "collections" (*shū* 集) of passages from canonical scriptures. They needed to prove that the teaching in question was in line with established tradition.²⁷ In keeping with their official character—many of them were submitted to either the imperial court or the Shogunate—they were written in the Literary Sinitic style, and they were more widely circulated. This is visible, for example, in Nichiren's or Myōe's refutations of Hōnen's teachings. Dōgen's vernacular "Treasury of the True Dharma Eye" (which contains the instruction "What Is:Time"), however, was not of that type. It belonged to the group of expositions directed at the inner circle of trusted disciples. Accordingly, it was kept secret for centuries and was only publicly circulated from the eighteenth century, when the culture of reading and writing, as well as conditions in the religious field, had changed considerably. Until then, access and possession were limited and conferred prestige on those to whom they were granted. Concomitantly, as many colophones show, reading and copying was guided by an attitude of reverence rather than critical examination. This reverential mode continued and extended also to printed text, as shown in the following injunction in a later commentary on the *Essentials*: "These ten chapters exhibit the deepest, unsurpassed great benevolence and compassion. [We] remote descendants should recite it day after day, to polish ourselves and recompense the ancestors."[28] Performative reproduction of the text was clearly more important than critical examination.

The Religious Field

As indicated above, writing and reading practices reflected certain premises pertaining to the religious field. Upon its establishment in the seventh century, the imperial court had reserved the right for its government to oversee and regulate the institutions dealing with divine powers, enlisting them to work in its favor. Shrines that engaged in rituals central to the state, as well as officially recognized Buddhist monasteries, received their funds out of tax coffers. On the other hand, the legal codes restricted the numbers of Buddhist clerics, who were exempt from tax and corvée labor. This system eroded over time, requiring monasteries to seek new sources of income—either through securing their own estates or through private patronage, endowments, and donations. This implied an increased investment in secular matters, which was often perceived as a sign of degeneration in line with expectations concerning the "Final Dharma Age." On the other hand, the very same development provided incentives to cater more to individual religious needs and fostered the generation of new rituals and doctrines. The power of the court to control the religious field was greatly diminished in this process. However, as the complaints cited above show, in the early medieval period the court was still regarded as the authority that could call for and sanction the establishment of "new teachings"—that is, teachings promoted apart from the network of established institutions, which were still dominated by the great temples in Nara (especially Tōdaiji and Kōfukuji) and the leading monasteries of the Tendai and Shingon schools. Most of the figures in the Kamakura era who were later revered as founders of new schools remained affiliated with one of these institutions during their lifetime.

The main doctrinal pièce de résistance was the promotion of a specific, narrowly defined religious practice as the exclusive path to salvation. This idea, forcefully endorsed by Hōnen and Nichiren for the invocation of the name of Amida and the title of the Lotus Sutra respectively, went against the grain of the fundamental pluralism that governed the religious field in general and the coexistence of Buddhist schools in particular. This pluralism was based on the idea of "skillful means" (*hōben* 方便) and viewed the plethora of teachings and practices as so many adaptations to the varying cognitive and moral capacities of those in need of salvation. Within this paradigm, there was space for competing claims to superiority of insight and efficacy, as long as alternatives remained an accepted part of the system in question. However, as was famously argued by Kuroda Toshio, the general inclusive framework combining esoteric and exoteric doctrines and practices still held sway. For much of the medieval period, the field was dominated by the old schools and major monasteries in Kyoto and Nara.[29]

In this environment, teachings that defined a single, exclusive path to salvation were regarded as disruptive. Their proponents could be exiled, as happened to Hōnen, Shinran, and Nichiren, and their congregations were threatened by the "teeth and claws of the Buddha,"[30] that is, soldier monks from the major fanes. There was no official suppression of pertinent books, but a threat of violent intervention loomed over congregations that promulgated censored writings. Thus, in the "Dharma-disturbance of the Karoku era" of 1227, militant monks of Enryakuji not only destroyed Hōnen's grave, but also burned the printing blocks of his *Collection of Passages on the Nenbutsu Chosen in the Original Vow*.[31] Similarly, the first Zen community in Japan, the Nihon Daruma shū centered around Dainichibō Nōnin 大日房能忍 (fl. around 1190), was accused of antinomianism and suppressed—a fact that would greatly influence Dōgen's career.[32] As Satō Hiroo has pointed out, the old institutions wielded overwhelming power, and they were willing to use it against those who threatened their ideological basis. This is why the majority of the new communities that formed in the Kamakura era—even the Pure Land and Nichiren/Lotus Schools, which have been regarded as prototypical for "Kamakura New Buddhism"—eventually reneged on the tenet of "exclusive practice" and sought their place in the established, pluralistic paradigm.[33]

To sum up, the religious sphere in the early Kamakura era was a dynamic field of power in which no single institution could exert complete control. It was more an oligopoly, dominated by established major fanes that were competing with each other, but willing to cooperate to maintain the fundamental structure of the field. These institutions had successfully rebuilt their income base, acquired major landholdings, and secured patronage and political protection by cultivating ties with the imperial court and the major houses of the aristocracy. On the ideological plane, a pluralistic paradigm held sway in which, arguably, esoteric teachings and practices commanded the highest esteem. This paradigm, in combination with the growing numbers of the urban population and rural petty elites, provided space and demand for new and more individualistic teachings and religious practices. The established institutions themselves had incentives to respond to this demand. They were therefore open to innovation and intellectual exchange, as long as these did not question their legitimacy and basis of power.

Successful operation in this field, and especially the establishment of a new congregation, then, required fulfilling three demands: the dexterous cultivation of patronage, a theoretical and practical appeal to the religious needs of a significant group of individuals, and the ability to efficiently mobilize intellectual and cultural resources in favor of the doctrine or practice proposed. In the following sections, we shall review the biographical research on Dōgen to sketch out his position in the field and see how and with what degree of success he negotiated the above-named demands. This will help us to understand the interventions he was attempting to make with his writings.

Dōgen's Life and Works

Later hagiographers[34] have claimed that Dōgen was a late child of Minamoto no Michichika 源通親 (1149–1202) and Ishi 伊子, daughter of Fujiwara no Motofusa 藤原基房 (1144–1230) and previous spouse to the ill-fated Minamoto Yoshinaka 源義仲 (1154–1184), a cousin of the first Shogun Minamoto Yoritomo 源頼朝 (1147–1199). This would place Dōgen in the highest echelons of the court aristocracy and further connect him to the major political conflicts of the day. Minamoto no Michichika was a central figure at court during the tumultuous 1180s and 1190s who attained high offices during his career. Motofusa was his counterpart from the still-influential Fujiwara family. However, as Nakaseko's careful scrutiny of the available sources has shown, Dōgen was in all probability only a grandson of Michichika. His parents were Michichika's second son,

Michitomo 通具 (1171–1227), a famed poet but less prodigious politician, and an unnamed concubine of the third court rank, probably with close family ties to Fujiwara no Motofusa. Since Dōgen therefore was not part of the hereditary line, he did not have much prospect of a glorious political career. However, subsequent to his mother's death in 1207, he was taken in as a foster child by Motofusa, who recognized his talent and educated him in court procedures.[35]

Even if the factual genealogy is less glorious than its popular, embellished version, it still connects Dōgen to the highest ranks of the court aristocracy and the clergy. Among his paternal uncles were, for example, the general administrator of the clergy (daisōjō 大僧正) Shin'en 親縁, who was acting abbot (bettō 別当) of Kōfukuji, and the Tōji abbot Jōshin 定親.[36] Another relation was Michichika's foster child Shōkū 證空 (1177–1244), a prominent disciple of Hōnen and founder of the Seizan-ha 西山派 branch of Pure Land Buddhism, with whom Dōgen maintained friendly ties and an exchange of acolytes in his adult years.[37]

Furthermore, there is no doubt that Dōgen in his youth had the opportunity to study secular as well as Buddhist literature—a privileged position, given the culture of protection surrounding canonical works at the time.[38] A highly intelligent and promising student, he was groomed for a career in the aristocratic bureaucracy. However, he abruptly absconded from secular life just before his coming-of-age ceremony. The early sources mention that he left "during the night" and "in secret."[39] He joined his maternal uncle Ryōken 良顕 on Mount Hiei. Ryōken held the rank of "Dharma-Eye" (hōgen 法眼),[40] the second tier in the official, state-sponsored Buddhist hierarchy, and he was also an affiliate of Kōen 公円, then abbot of the Enryakuji, who oversaw Dōgen's taking of the tonsure in 1213. This marked the formal start of young Dōgen's religious career. Given his intellectual proclivity and his prominent connections, he was well positioned to achieve office within the hierarchy of the most powerful religious institution of the day. But again, he chose a different path early on.

As mentioned above, the ensuing course of his life has been interpreted in various ways. Much of the literature, including the recent study by Steven Heine, follows later hagiography in assuming that in 1215 Dōgen met with Eisai, one of the first promulgators of Rinzai Zen in Japan, and left Mount Hiei only one year after his ordination.[41] However, Nakaseko, in his rigorous study of the available sources, convincingly argues that both assumptions are wrong and that Dōgen only entered

Eisai's Kenninji in 1218.[42] This means that he spent five years studying in the framework of traditional branches of the Tendai school, where a broad range of traditions were brought together. The formative influence of these studies can be seen in several aspects of Dōgen's teachings. First, the Lotus Sutra—the primary canonical source in Tendai doctrine—remains a paramount reference in his writings, even though his commentary at times subverts the surface meaning of its text.[43] Second, as Sueki Fumihiko has pointed out, Dōgen's basic idea that seated meditation leads to a mystic unity with enlightened beings is analogous to the ideas that support esoteric ritual.[44] (In spite of this, Dōgen consistently avoided any reference to the literature and terminology of Esoteric Buddhism.) Finally, Kegon school doctrine also exerted a significant influence on his thought. Frédéric Girard has observed that Dōgen's works give "the strong impression of an omnipresence of the doctrines of the Huayan / Kegon (華厳) in its background," even though "we find scarcely partial quotations and almost no trace of Huayan texts surely read by Dōgen."[45] Again, this is probably due to the fact that he learned about Kegon ideas through the filter of Tendai doctrinal studies.

The reasons why Dōgen transferred to Kenninji after five years are not entirely clear. Traditional hagiography frames them in terms of a doubt concerning the Tendai doctrine of "original enlightenment" (*hongaku* 本覚), which posited that all living beings were originally endowed with the highest insight. If that were true, Dōgen reportedly inquired, why was there a need for teaching and practice?[46] This, however, was an oft-disputed question in the "original enlightenment" literature and could hardly have been left unanswered by his teachers.[47] From the records of his own sayings, it appears that he was unhappy with an environment that encouraged the aspiration for fame and office over earnest religious practice, and that he was pointed to Eisai's monastery as a place better suited to his spiritual zeal.[48]

Situated close to the residence of the Shōgun's governor in Kyōto, Kenninji had been founded by the Tendai monk Eisai/Yōsai 栄西, who was famous for bringing the tradition of Song-period Zen as well as tea drinking to Japan. Along with the exoteric and esoteric Tendai ritual, a certain emphasis in this monastery lay on seated meditation (*zazen* 坐禅) and the study of Zen. Dōgen studied with Myōzen 明全 (1184–1225) for about five years before joining him on a privately financed study trip to Song China in 1223.[49] Having visited several prominent Zen temples, he settled in 1225 at Tiantongshan 天童山, where he was accepted as a personal student by the abbot Rujing (Jp. Nyojō 如浄, 1162–1227), a master of the Caodong/Sōtō line. Two years later, Rujing acknowledged Dōgen's enlightenment and mastery of the tradition, presenting him with a document of Dharma-Inheritance. He returned to Japan and, in late 1227, took up residence again at Kenninji. While in China, he had composed fifty poems in Literary Sinitic[50] and may have made notes from his interviews with Rujing, which were later reported in his *Record from the Baojing Era* (*Hōkyō ki* 寶慶記, DZZ II, 363–88).[51] Upon his return to Japan, he composed his first more extensive religious writings; a memorial regarding the relics of Myōzen (*Shari sōden ki* 舎利相傳記, DZZ II, 395–96), who had died while in China in 1225; and a first, no longer extant, draft of his *Manual of Seated Meditation*.[52]

In other words, from this point onward Dōgen began to act as an authorized teacher. Apparently he attracted some visitors at Kenninji in the ensuing years, among them Jakuen 寂円 (Chin. Jiyuan, 1207–1299), a Chinese fellow student at Tiandongshan, and Kōun Ejō 孤雲懐奘 (1198–1280), who later became his trusted adjunct and successor. He started to build a following, but also encountered problems. In 1230, he relocated to the dilapidated Gokurakuji temple in Fukakusa, at that time a half-day's journey south of Kyōto. The grounds belonged to the Konoe 近衛 branch of the Fujiwara family, with whom he had apparently developed ties after his return to Kenninji.[53] Although the following years are described in some early records as a time of seclusion, he continued to teach those who sought his advice. He wrote a number of religious instructions ("Dharma words," *hōgo* 法語) in Literary Sinitic[54] and in 1231 drafted his first larger doctrinal exposition in the composite vernacular style, *Discourses on Negotiating the Way* (*Bendōwa* 辨道話, DZZ I, 729–46; short: *Discourses*).

It is not clear to whom these *Discourses* were addressed. However, Dōgen clearly stated his aspiration to be recognized as the sole legitimate heir to the teaching of Śākyamuni in Japan, and he promoted seated meditation (*zazen*) as the one practice that immediately realizes superior insight. At the same time, his rhetoric also reflected the ambiguity of his station. On the one hand, he followed Zen mythography and likened himself to the legendary Indian patriarch/"ancestor," Bodhidharma. On the other hand, he apologized for offering a new interpretation without invitation by the court. Similarly, he highlighted his familiarity with the teaching and style ("house wind"; *kafū* 家風) of Linji 臨済 and the traditions of Chinese Chan, while carefully avoiding identification of his teaching with a specific "Zen school." The practice of seated meditation that he extols and equates with enlightenment is therefore framed as the practice of all "Buddha-ancestors" (*busso* 仏祖) rather than that of a specific denomination.

With a first formulation of his central doctrine in place, Dōgen then sought and quickly found support for establishing a monastery under his guidance. In 1233, he opened up his residence on the Gokurakuji grounds for his first congregation, turning it into the "Treasure Grove Temple [where the Bodhisattva] Kannon/Avalokiteśvara Guides, Benefits and Promotes Sages" (Kannon dōri kōshō hōrinji 観音導利興聖宝林寺, variously known as Kannon dōri'in or Kōshōji). The last part of this name indicates Dōgen's ambition, as it is identical with the name of Baolinsi in China, where the legendary sixth ancestor Huineng 慧能 (638–713) resided. He conducted a summer retreat and gradually collected and composed teaching materials. He produced a new copy of his *zazen* manual and in the following year drafted his *Essentials*. Furthermore, he collated (in Literary Sinitic) 300 authoritative cases from Zen lore. The collection's title, "Treasury of the True Dharma Eye" (*Shōbō genzō* 正法眼蔵), is provocative, as it is identical with a work from the line of Dahui Zonggao 大慧宗杲, which provided legitimation for the Nihon Daruma shū.[55]

The chief initial support for building the monastery probably came from Konoe Motomichi 近衛基通 (1160–1233).[56] But when Dōgen undertook major construction two years later, he also wrote a mission statement to elicit donations from a wider circle of patrons. This addressed "all buddhas in the ten directions, [. . .] sages and monks in the heavenly and human worlds, [. . .] the eight types of guardians in the dragon realm, and [. . .] generous men and women," and announced the plan to build a monastics' hall after the Chinese model: "We plan to build a seven *ken* (about seventy feet) square with no interior walls. We will set up long platforms on which we will reside, practicing day and night without fail. A sacred figure [. . .] will be enshrined in the center of the hall, to be surrounded by the practicing monks."[57] Important contributions to the further consolidation of the monastery came from a wealthy nun of unknown background, Shōkaku 性覚, and from Kujō Moroie 九条師家 (1172–1238). The support from Shōkaku, as well as written instructions given to other female recipients, shows that Dōgen's community transcended gender divisions. In his view, clearly and famously stated in the "Paying Obeisance and Attaining the Mark" (*Raihai tokuzui* 禮拜得髄) fascicle of the *Treasury*, renunciation (*shukke* 出家) rendered these and other secular distinctions irrelevant.

By late 1237, the monastery was in place and operational. The congregation had grown, with Ejō—Dōgen's later successor and an erstwhile member of the prohibited Daruma shū—having joined a year earlier. In 1236, Dōgen had given his first formal instruction (*jōdō* 上堂), recorded in Literary Sinitic in the first volume of the *Extensive Record*.⁵⁸ However, his teaching and writing in this period was still leaning toward the informal and vernacular, as befitted a still small community. Ejō recorded more than a hundred informal lectures (*shosan* 小参) over the years and edited them in his *Record of Things Heard*.⁵⁹ The emphasis was, in Heine's words, on "creating a picture of Zen training based on three pillars of training, *zazen*, *shingi* (or precepts in a general sense), and *kōan* study."⁶⁰

Establishing proper monastic discipline and sustained practice was apparently a daunting task. In 1237, Dōgen drafted the first of his several works pertaining to monastic offices and procedures, his *Instructions for the Head Cook* (*Tenzō kyōkun* 典座教訓). Rules for the monastery's study hall followed in 1239. Their detailed prohibitions give evidence that many monastics were routinely engaged in secular activities. They traded, entertained guests, or studied astrology and secular literature (probably to give advice to individual patrons and sponsors). Dōgen apparently struggled to keep at least the communal rooms free from such affairs.

Informal instructions from the same year on "Washing the Face" or "Cleansing" (*Senjō* 洗浄) bring together the interpretations of sayings from the sutras and Zen *kōan* literature with detailed prescriptions for how, for example, to clean one's teeth. In this manner, they imbue everyday monastic activity with spiritual significance while patterning it on the model of an idealized life of "Buddhas and ancestors." From 1240 onward, the composition of these informal instructions increased markedly in number. "What Is:Time" is one among seven fascicles drafted in this year, followed by ten in 1241, sixteen in 1242, and twenty-two in 1243.⁶¹ It is likely that Dōgen formed the idea of collecting them into a composite vernacular version of the "Treasury of the True Dharma Eye" during these years. At the same time, he performed formal instructions in even greater number: thirty-one in 1240, forty-eight in 1241, twenty-six in 1242, and twenty-one in the first half of 1243.⁶² This indicates that he saw formal and informal instructions as complementary and that he was moving toward a regular schedule for both types of activities.

The consolidation, growth, and success of Kōshōji eventually led to a crisis that culminated in the relocation of the core community to Echizen Province, about eighty miles north-west of the capital, in the late summer to early fall of 1243. Here, Dōgen founded his second monastery. There is no evidence that provides a clear explanation for this move, but several factors contributing to the crisis are by now well established.

One of them was the increasing number of Daruma shu followers. A second, larger cohort (after Ejō's group) had joined the congregation in 1241. This had two effects: First, it opened up the congregation to attacks from the clerical establishment, although this aspect may have been exaggerated in the Sōtō tradition.[63] Second, the advent of this group also created tensions between different understandings of proper lineage, practice, and doctrine. Increased references to Rujing, insistence on proper procedures of transmission, and a heightened degree of polemic in Dōgen's writings from the period bear witness to these tensions.[64] The arrival of the recorded sayings of Rujing is thought to have stimulated discussion of his master's teaching. Dōgen apparently felt that the document needed to be complemented in important respects, because his own references to Rujing frequently deviate from the record.[65]

External competition was another factor in relocating his community. In 1241, the monk Enni Ben'en 圓爾辯圓 (1202–1280) had returned from China with impeccable credentials of Linji/Rinzai Zen lineage. He secured recognition by the court and the favor of the head of the Kujō branch of the Fujiwara, Kujō Michiie 九条道家 (1193–1252).[66] In 1243, Michiie made Enni abbot of his newly founded Tōfukuji 東福寺 ("Eastern Bliss Monastery," a name that combined elements from two major temples of the old capital Nara, Tōdaiji 東大寺 and Kōfukuji 興福寺). Like Dōgen's Kōshōji, it was situated south of the capital, but slightly closer to the city. Nakaseko showed that at the same time there was a rapprochement between the Kujō and the Konoe branches of the Fujiwara family; this resulted in unified support for Enni and Tōfukuji (over Dōgen and Kōshōji).[67] Enni further had the support of the Tendai school, an advantage that Dōgen lacked.[68]

On the other hand, and as a third factor, Dōgen was able to deepen his already long-standing ties with Hatano Yoshishige 波多野義重 (–1258), a member of the Shogun's advisory council. Yoshishige and his relatives held land in Echizen Province, where they further acted as stewards for estates of the Konoe family.[69] Dōgen's congregation also had ties to the region through the above-mentioned group of Daruma shū adherents. These in turn were connected with the second large faction of the Tendai school, its Miidera or "Temple" branch. Such links apparently helped to foster local community support, which must have been strong given the expeditious construction of the monastery there. As Moriya Shigeru has suggested, the Tendai connections in the region may also have helped to politically clear the waters.[70] Taken together, the relocation to Echizen may have been a solution to Dōgen's increasingly difficult position in the capital. It helped his present and erstwhile supporters, as well as his opponents, to keep their face, and provided him with a new basis for pursuing his vision.

Last but not least, the factor of intrinsic motivation should also be mentioned. Traditional hagiography may have overstated Dōgen's wish to emulate ancient masters—especially his teacher Rujing—and train in a remote mountain community.[71] Recent authors equally may have projected on him a "love of nature," which is, after all, a modern concern. To speak of his wish to leave "urban commotion"[72] behind seems an anachronistic view in regard to the location of Kōshōji, which was several miles south of the capital and full of the "sounds of valleys and mountain colors."[73] But after the prospects of winning over the court to his brand of Buddhism had turned stale, and with growing disputes within his congregation about questions of lineage, doctrine, and discipline, a more isolated place may have held an appeal. Removed from political intrigue, the traffic of visitors, and, generally, outside influence, Dōgen could hope to realize his vision of a monastic life that would, at each and every step, resonate with spiritual significance and conform to the model of the canonical scriptures.[74]

Even though the relocation to Echizen clearly constituted a rupture, the transition was executed swiftly and smoothly. The congregation (or major parts of it) left Kōshōji after the summer retreat of 1243 had been conducted in the regular fashion; it moved to transitory quarters in Echizen in the fall. Already by late summer 1244, the new monastery Daibutsuji ("Great Buddha Temple")—renamed Eiheiji ("Eternal Peace Temple") in 1246—was complete. Between 1244 and summer 1245, it received not only (major parts of) the Kōshōji congregation, but also "numerous Zen followers," who joined when formal instructions in the Dharma Hall were resumed. In the meantime, between autumn 1243 and spring 1244, Dōgen had composed and delivered about thirty informal instructions,[75] which formed a significant portion of his vernacular *Treasury*. This manner of teaching was well suited to the environment of the provisional quarters, but it also facilitated sustained doctrinal exposition, which was important in forging coherence within a community in transition.

The aforementioned peak in text production was followed by a gap between spring 1244 and spring 1245,[76] although several of the informal instructions from the earlier years were copied during that time and may have been reused.[77]

Summer 1245 not only saw the resumption of formal instructions, but also of the regular summer retreat. Its details, apparently, also needed to be explained to newcomers—prompting another extensive vernacular instruction that later went into the *Treasury*. But the emphasis of textual composition from this time onward was on formal teachings, recorded in Literary Sinitic. While 126 of such texts were produced and performed at Kōshōji between 1236 and 1243 (but mostly between 1240 and 1243), 405 were drafted and delivered at Daibutsuji/Eiheiji between 1245 and 1253. They were complemented by texts concerned with monastic organization and discipline, most notably the *Pure Rules for Temple Officers* (*Chiji shingi* 知事清規). The vernacular teachings, however, were not simply given up or abandoned. Instead, they were reviewed and edited to produce a sustained collection. A first stage led to the 75-fascicle *Treasury*, consisting mostly of instructions first drafted between 1233 and 1245. A second compilation comprising twelve texts (two older and ten newly drafted) was started in the final year(s), apparently with a plan to expand and reorganize the vernacular *Treasury* into a compendium of one hundred fascicles.[78]

Dōgen was to remain at his new monastery until the last months of his life, leaving only once for a prolonged visit to Kamakura, the residential city of the Shogun, from fall 1247 to spring 1248. This visit has caused much debate. According to Dōgen's words recorded in his *Extensive Record*, its purpose was to "explain the Dharma to [my] patrons and lay disciples" (*danna zoku-deshi no tame ni seppō su* 為＿檀那俗弟子＿説法). Traditional hagiographers held that Dōgen had been called by the regent Hōjō Tokiyori 北条時頼 (1227–1263),[79] but there are no primary sources to directly support this. As Nakaseko's careful review of the available material shows, it is most likely that Dōgen stayed with his main patron, Hatano Yoshishige, who was in Kamakura at the time. Yoshishige may have arranged for a meeting with the regent, but mainly Dōgen must have catered to the spiritual needs of Yoshishige and his family.[80] The visit is often contrasted with an earlier statement in Ejō's *Record of Things Heard*, where Dōgen had rejected going to Kamakura to seek political favor. Instead he proposed that those seeking the true dharma should demonstrate the strength of their resolution by "crossing mountains, rivers, bays, and the ocean" (*sanzen kōkai o watarite* 山川江海ヲ渡リテ).[81]

Some authors argue that Dōgen lost his spirit of independence and capitulated to political considerations. They draw a connection to his leaving the monastery in summer 1253 to seek medical help in the capital—for an illness that had begun to show in fall 1252 and would cost him his life soon after the transfer to Kyoto. As mentioned above, the "Critical

Buddhists," on the other hand, have seen the visit to Kamakura and the extended experience of teaching to non-specialists as trigger for a spiritual renewal, one that finally brought Dōgen in line with "true Buddhism." They point to a renewed emphasis on ethics and karmic retribution visible in his instructions from that time onward. In their interpretation, Dōgen came to finally reject the ethical ambiguities inherent in the often enigmatic style of his earlier work. They argue that the twelve vernacular instructions drafted in the last years of his life were meant to introduce a new redaction of the *Treasury* that would clear away such ambiguities—an endeavor that, unfortunately, was interrupted by his premature death.

To sum up, and largely following Steven Heine's identification of five distinct periods in Dōgen's life,[82] the main stages in the development of his career as a religious thinker and spiritual guide may be characterized as follows:

1. 1200–1213. Childhood and courtly education. The first period of Dōgen's life was marked by an education for a career at court. This period comprised extensive study of Chinese classics and literature, as well as training in Literary Sinitic and Japanese poetry, with some study of Buddhist scriptures alongside.

2. 1213–1223: Monastic education in Japan. This second preparatory period can be further divided into:

    2.1. A first phase spent in elementary monastic training and advanced study within the traditional doctrinal and ritual framework of the Tendai school. Dōgen received significant influences during this period, which lasted from 1213 to 1218.

    2.2. A second phase between 1218 and 1223, which was spent at Kenninji under the tutelage of Myōzen. Here, Dōgen received his first training in accordance with the Rinzai Zen tradition and apparently formed a deep bond with his teacher, whom he later memorialized regularly in the monasteries he founded.

3. 1223–1233: The formation of Dōgen as a religious teacher. The time spent in China completes his education and leads to his emergence as a religious teacher in his own right.

This period lasts from 1223 and 1233 and comprises:

- 3.1. Dōgen's travel and sojourn in China, where eventually he was acknowledged by Rujing as his legitimate dharma heir; and

- 3.2. The phase after his return until the opening of his first monastery. Only a few works were produced during this period, among them a first draft of his *Manual for the Universal Promotion of Seated Meditation*, which is no longer extant.

4. 1233–1246: Initial Success, Crisis, and Reorientation. This period, termed "reformational" by Heine, saw in its first phase:

    - 4.1. The establishment of Kōshōji, the composition of the first formal instructions, the compilation of his *kōan* collection, and the earliest texts of the vernacular *Treasury*.

    - 4.2. Its second phase coincides with what I have described above as the period of crisis, starting with the advent of Daruma shū followers in 1241 and leading to the composition of a major part of the 75-fascicle vernacular *Treasury*, just before and during the relocation to Echizen Province in 1243.

    - 4.3. The third phase comprises the initial years after the opening of Dōgen's second monastery until it was renamed Eiheiji in 1246, and sees a transition in text production from the informal instructions collected in the vernacular *Treasury* to formal instructions that became part of the *Extensive Record*.

5. 1246–1253: Securing the monastic domain. The final period in Dōgen's life as a religious teacher was labeled "developmental" by Heine because it was dedicated to the full realization of Dōgen's monastic vision. The project was to create a realm where a dedicated congregation could implement the standards set by "Buddha-ancestors" and be largely free from outside interference.

5.1. In its earlier phase, the focus was on establishing the necessary procedures and organization, visible in various texts concerning monastic regulations. The visit to Kamakura was an important element of securing stable support for the project.

5.2. The last phase (1248–1253) saw the monastery in full operation, with regular formal instructions, summer retreats, and ritual interaction with lay supporters.

Dōgen in Time

By considering the historical context and timeline of Dōgen's writings, we have obtained important information concerning his position and how he perceived it, or wanted it to be perceived. While the rhetorical situation he faced varied over time and according to the occasion, there are several factors that remained fairly stable during the course of his life, as follows.

He clearly placed himself within the religious field. His writings in general addressed an audience that shared the general aim of seeking salvation by following the path explained in the Buddhist teachings. With few exceptions, they were directed at those who sought his instruction and accepted him as an enlightened master. This is especially true for the writings collected in the composite vernacular *Treasury*, which were designed as teachings for those who had joined his congregation and entrusted themselves to his guidance. But even the teachings collected in the more official and public *Extensive Record* were delivered to those in support of his monasteries, and not to a general public. In accordance with this choice of addressees, his works were, during his lifetime, only reproduced as manuscript copies. Furthermore, their circulation was limited to channels secured by relations of mutual trust. This was a conscious choice: Reproduction by printing would have been technically feasible, and Dōgen used the technology in Eiheiji for the replication of ritual texts,[83] but open circulation of the *Treasury* texts would have entailed considerable risks.

Dōgen joined the religious field as a member of the aristocratic elite and would have had access to an illustrious career within the established Tendai institutions; however, he broke away from such a career at an early stage. Having left this path, he found himself in an uneasy position as soon as he emerged as a teacher and religious leader in his own right. He belonged to the higher echelons of the court aristocracy, but his connections did not reach its highest ranks. Thus, they did not match his initial aspiration to establish a new paradigm for the realm. At the same time, he was vulnerable because of his association with members of the outlawed Nihon Daruma school, who had joined his congregation in two waves, in the 1230s and in 1241. This further meant that even within his own community he needed to increasingly address dissenting opinions from 1241 onward. Outside his community, he was eventually outcompeted in the region of the capital by a rival with similar formal credentials but more prestige and powerful support. Hence, a rescaling of his project and a reorientation concerning its proper place in Kamakura society were required. The transition to a rural monastery, where he enjoyed protection of the regional magnates and the local population, turned out to be a successful move. As a result of this relocation, we also find a clearer differentiation between the way Dōgen addressed lay patrons and disciples on the one hand and monastic renunciants on the other. The shift to formal instructions, recorded in Literary Sinitic, and the simultaneous complementation of his composite vernacular instructions with twelve additional fascicles that emphasize the basics of the initial stages on the Buddhist path can be seen as corresponding to this strategic reorientation.

The intellectual and moral compass he followed in his youth when he first left the secular world, and then the clerical environment on Mount Hiei, continued to characterize his life, and later, his work. As a religious teacher and monastic leader, he established himself as an independent voice, although one strongly rooted in the cultural repertoire of his time. He did not shy away from criticizing received practices and views, among them the pessimistic outlook related to the concept of the "Final Dharma age." His ideas failed to gain broad recognition in his time, but resonated with a substantial number of people who became his dedicated companions and supporters. In his own time, he thus was neither a marginal nor a highly prominent figure in the religious field and certainly was not considered important beyond that sphere. References to his person in diaries, chronicles, or other records are scant; his poetry never became part of prominent collections; and he did not figure as a subject of popular lore or theatrical plays. The recognition he has gained today as one of the foremost thinkers and writers of medieval Japan is, as with so many other figures in cultural history, the result of much later developments. By now, his works are therefore wrapped in layers of convictions and expectations that belong to later ages in history. This is why it is so important to build the analysis from the ground up when studying Dōgen's thought on time.

3

Time Expressed

Chronography in Dōgen's Works

While Dōgen stayed in Kamakura in late 1247, away from his reclusive "Monastery of Eternal Peace," the regent Hōjō Tokiyori reportedly asked him to compose a series of twelve "brief poems" (*tanka* 短歌) on key phrases of the Zen tradition. Among them is the following, on the subject of the "Original Face"[1]—an expression often associated with the trans-temporal Buddha nature inherent in all human beings, or even everything that exists.[2] It is also the poem that Kawabata Yasunari quoted in his Nobel prize acceptance speech—albeit without reference to its subject—as embodying the "Japanese spirit" and love of nature:[3]

> Haru wa hana
> Natsu hototogisu
> Aki wa tsuki
> Fuyu yuki saete
> suzushikarikeri[4]
> (In spring, the flowers
> Summer: mountain cuckoo
> In fall, the moon
> Winter: snow glistens
> —cold and clear!)

With the combination of its theme and the body of its text, this poem connects calendrical units (the four seasons) and emblematic natural phenomena to the "original face."⁵ Ostensibly, it posits a strong link between the sphere of enlightenment on the one hand and both calendar time and the annual cycle of natural phenomena on the other. It thus encapsulates the main themes and problems to be addressed in this chapter, which is dedicated to exploring the ways in which time (and timelessness) are expressed in Dōgen's writing. In the overall argument of this book, this investigation serves to demonstrate the relative weight and functions of temporal differentiation in his writings vis-à-vis expressions of timelessness or trans-temporality. Observing which forms of temporal differentiation Dōgen employs, and to achieve what ends, provides textual evidence that will help to build our understanding of his thoughts about time. It will point us to aspects usually overlooked when only his thematic statements about time are taken into account, and it will give us a clearer picture of how the different aspects of time (and timelessness) are actually connected in his writings.

In the first part of the chapter, I emphasize variety: the various ways and modes of expressing time, the different aspects of time so expressed, and the different attitudes to time exhibited. The second part focuses on a subject central to the conceptual problematic explored in this book: the status and functions of temporal differentiation and, specifically, numerical chronometry, or clock-time. Since the received view equates clock-time with the unenlightened, inauthentic view of time, it should follow that it has only a marginal position in Dōgen's writings. We will find that this is true to some extent, but that the situation turns out to be more complex upon closer inspection.

A Matrix for Chronographical Analysis

To fully grasp and describe the modes and aspects of time expressed in Dōgen's writings, it is helpful to have a matrix of ways in which humans engage with and make sense of the world, its structures and objects. In this regard, I turn to philosophy as a guide—more specifically, the philosophical system of Kant. In doing so, I do not wed my argument to his specific theorems, especially not to his idea of time as an a priori form of intuition. Instead, I use him as a guide to (a) fundamental modes of apprehending the world and (b) basic functions in determining what there is.⁶

(a) Kant's three critiques explore the foundations of human reason with respect to three essential orientations or dimensions of human existence: the theoretical, or contemplative, which is directed to understanding what there is; the practical, directed toward making changes through action; and the aesthetic, or the sensitive rapport between the world and the human being engaged with it. Dōgen's above-quoted poem, for example, starts out in the contemplative mode—positing seasonal phenomena as so many articulations of the "original face"—but contains a strong aesthetic element in its final line. Its overall message, however, is arguably a practical one and may be summed up in two lines from his earlier works: "Buddhas are those who gain great clarity in delusion," and "Human beings are on their part fully equipped with this truth, but it does not appear before being practiced, it is only achieved when it is authenticated [in one's own conduct]."[7] Our poem thus exemplifies the fact that the three orientations are by no means mutually exclusive; an expression can address one, two, or all of them with varying degrees of emphasis. In terms of chronography, the English adjective "urgent," for example, contains (a) the theoretical observation that time is short in relation to a given objective, (b) the aesthetic component of being pressed to do something, and (c) the practical injunction to actually do it, and to do it now. When exploring the ways in which time is conveyed in writing, it is evidently important to keep all three of these dimensions in mind.

(b) Independently of Kant's own philosophical agenda, the table of categories presented in the "transcendental analytics" part of his *Critique of Pure Reason* provides a matrix of the ways in which an object may be determined. It is a matter of dispute whether this table is exhaustive—Hegel, for example, famously argued that further categories are necessary to grasp the operations of the self-reflective mind. But since we are here concerned with time as an object of expression and description, Kant's survey seems concise and inclusive enough to serve as a heuristic. In any case, and contrary to his own theory of time, it will lead us to aspects beyond the quantitative determinations of time that have dominated the literature.[8] Furthermore, we shall use it in a non-restrictive manner, as a "logic of investigation" to explore the variety of possible temporal determinations and distinctions.

Kant's categories are arranged in four groups, titled (1) quantity, (2) quality, (3) relation, and (4) modality.

To begin with a term that invites misunderstanding, **quality** in Kant is not directly concerned with attributes or characteristics; it is about the fundamental question of whether a predicate is affirmed, negated, or limited in its applicability. With regard to chronography, this means to affirm or deny that something is connected to a certain time or any time, or to locate something generally outside the dimension of time. We can call such a determination "chronothetic," from the Greek "chronos" = "time" and "thesis" = "position, affirmation." Dōgen's above-quoted poem illustrates the notion of the "original face" by way of the seasons and thus generally affirms its place in the temporal realm. Chronothetic negation, absent in this poem, would state that something does not happen at a specific time or at any time at all. The fascicle "Sustained Practice" from the *Treasury* contains an example of general prescriptive/ethical chronothetic negation, when Dōgen enjoins his disciples to quietly contemplate the twenty years a patriarch spent in assiduous practice in the mountains, and "*let there be no time* when you forget about it."[9]

The function of chronothetic limitation is to deny that something belongs to the realm of time altogether. Dōgen's poem seems to argue against the idea that the "original face" is somehow outside time. The antithesis, assuming that the "original face" is outside time, would constitute a chronothetic limitation. Unsurprisingly in light of Dōgen's position, previously quoted in chapter 1, that "everything real is also time," he does not utter such limitative statements himself.

Quantity is about a first, formal identification of the object, and includes unity, plurality, and totality. Applied to chronography, it can be taken to stand for the broad area of chronometric expressions, which traditionally has been virtually identified with chronography as such.[10] Our poem, with its reference to the four seasons, indicates that it is temporally plural; one might argue that listing the full cycle of the seasons also implies totality. On a different plane, the poem further exemplifies that chronometric expression, often associated with clock-time, is not necessarily numeric: on the contrary, numerals assume temporal meaning by being connected to temporal units, such as hours, months, or, in our case, the seasons. Where such units are mentioned, we can speak with Roland Harweg of "formal" metric chronography. The opposite is the informal measuring of time in relation to an event or action, as in "Venerable, it's been a long time since you started to live in the mountain" from a dialogue between a monk and the Chinese master Dabai, mentioned by Dōgen in the fascicle on "Sustained Practice."[11] Another pertinent distinction is that between absolute and relational chronometry. Our poem uses the absolute mode because it does not connect its temporal units to a specific place or period in time with a measurable distance to the present of the reader. Such absolute chronography is often used when sequences or measures of iterable events or actions are described—be it in a poem, a recipe, or a natural law. The above quote concerning Dabai, in contrast, is at least partly (or internally) relational, since it ties the event in question (Dabai's arriving at the mountain) to the present of his dialogue with the monk. To be fully (internally and externally) relational, however, the readers would need information on how to connect that latter event, the moment when the temporal determination is made, with their own present. We will return to the conditions for such fully relational chronography below.

Like chronothetic information, chronometric information can also be conveyed implicitly, simply by mentioning actions or events that imply a beginning, end, or certain duration. The phrase "A flower opens with five petals,"[12] quoted at the beginning of the "Emptiness Flowers"[13] fascicle, points to a beginning, a new segment of/in time, and thus indicates temporal plurality.

This also brings us to the third group of Kant's categories, **relation**, which again comprises three items: the relation of substance and attribute, that of causation, and that of mutual implication. It is intuitive to also subsume temporal relations, such as the sequence of the seasons expressed in our poem, under this heading. Kant, for systematic reasons,[14] shies away from affording them a separate position in his table, but later interprets sequence as an analogy of causation and synchrony as analogy of mutual implication. We need not decide the issue here.[15] Iteration could likewise be seen in analogy to the substance–attribute relation: We say that something, an event or action, is repeated because it has the same characteristics as an earlier instance. Suffice it that we systematically account for iteration, sequence, and synchrony together with their derivatives, such as temporal limits like a beginning and an end.

Even more importantly, Kant's first relation, that of substance and attribute, leads us to an essential function in the determination of time, and one that is again clearly expressed in Dōgen's poem: the specification of time by way of attributes, as in "Summer: mountain cuckoo." In contrast to the Aristotelian reduction of time to number, the segmentation of time that forms the basis for its countability relies on the possibility to identify a certain time by way of such properties—for example, its connection to a particular event or action.[16] We can call such a determination "chronotypological." While numerical, quantitative chronometry aims to treat all times as equal, chronotypology precisely pertains to the divergent attributes of different times. Such determination is often aesthetically grounded: We distinguish between different times because they feel different. Dōgen provides an impressive example, again in his fascicle on "Sustained Practice," where he talks about the second Chinese patriarch standing in the snow in the cold of night: "Even when the sky is not full of snow, the winter nights in the deep mountains are, when you think of it, not a time for people to stand outside [lit.: before a window]. With the bamboo joints cracking [from the cold], it is [truly] a time to be feared."[17] One may argue that it is the climatic conditions and not the time itself that are to be feared, but that is not how the text is written: and our topic in this chapter is chronography, not its epistemological critique.

The fourth and final group of categories in Kant's survey, **modality**, is concerned with gauging and expressing the attitude of the subject toward the proposition it is making: Is that proposition hypothetical, venturing an (informed) opinion? Is it assertive, stating an affirmed conviction? Or is it, finally, apodictic, the expression of a judgment that something must necessarily be the case and cannot be otherwise? Most statements on time are assertive, as is the poem on the "Original Face." But there are exceptions to be found in Dōgen's writings: For instance, in "The Heart, Inapprehensible," he offers the following hypothetical statement about the Tang period master Deshan Xuanjian 德山宣鑒 (Jp. Tokusan Senkan 德山宣鑑, 780–865): "Had he stayed for a longer while with Longtan [lit: "Dragon-Depth"], he might have twisted his whiskers; *there might have been a time* when he would have rightly transmitted the [dragon's] chin pearl."[18] Furthermore, in "What Is:Time," Dōgen explains passing as a "virtue" or "merit" (*kudoku* 功德) of time with the following apodictic statement: "For example, the passing of spring inevitably passes through the phases of spring."[19]

In the following sections, we will use the above matrix of temporal determinations to investigate Dōgen's chronography in more detail. The aim is to better understand the relative weight and function of each of these modes of expressing time in his writings. While this concerns both implicit and explicit modes of chronography, evidently, the explicit chronographical statements will also shed light on his notion of time—thus preparing the ground for the conceptual analysis in part II.

Chronothesis

Implicit chronothetic determination is pervasive in Dōgen and elsewhere because every proposition that contains information about some temporal aspect of an event or thing is also implicitly chronothetic. By the same token, explicit chronothetic statements are rare. On the theoretical plane, they become necessary only in two types of cases: (a) when the connection between an event or a phenomenon and a certain time, or time in general, is in doubt; or (b) to counter the assumption that something is somehow outside the realm of time. As we have seen in chapter 1, Dōgen famously makes use of this exceptional form of chronography in the "What Is:Time" fascicle to boldly express the general proposition: "Said [word] *uji* means that time is altogether [what] there is, and that everything there is, is [also] time." The more obvious reason for this statement is to deny that the Buddhas exist outside of time; he therefore first specifies in another explicit chronothetic statement: "The golden body of one *jō* six is time, and because it is time, there is the sublime light of time." This connects to equally salient propositions in other writings, such as "Buddha nature is impermanent"[20]—all of which seem to deny a time-transcendent realm or the existence of some eternal, unchanging substance. But it is remarkable how quickly Dōgen in "What Is:Time" moves on to make similar, explicit chronothetic statements about ordinary things such as pine trees or bamboo. Apparently he feels the need to remind his disciples that these things are not substances accidentally undergoing temporal change. As he further explains through the example of spring and the notion of "passing through stations" (*kyōryaku* 経歴), they are the aggregate of the states and phases they are going through. The full meaning of these statements is scrutinized in chapter 6; suffice it here to say that their function is to contradict assumptions that something is on some level above temporal change or belongs to a realm outside time.

In terms of chronography, it deserves mention that Dōgen's use of temporal expressions rhetorically supports his generalized chronothetic statement that everything that exists is also time. "Time-laden" fascicles of the composite-vernacular *Treasury,* such as "Buddha Nature" (*Busshō* 佛性), overwhelmingly use expressions containing the character 時 (*ji/toki;* "time") in the affirmative: Of the fifty occurrences of such terms in this fascicle, only one is connected to an explicitly negative expression, and one more implicitly so.[21] Furthermore, the one explicitly negative expression conveys a view that Dōgen refutes as a misunderstanding. In discussing an attributed saying of the Buddha, "when the temporal occasion (*jisetsu* 時節) arrives, the Buddha nature shall appear,"[22] he insists it was wrong to infer from this that "if the temporal occasion had not yet arrived," Buddhist practice would not and could not make Buddha nature apparent.[23]

Notably, the term *jisetsu* mentioned here, which indicates an occasion or period, is among the compounds most often used by Dōgen in relation to time (twenty-six times in "Buddha Nature"). Another salient expression is "right at this time" (*shōtō immo ji* 正當恁麼時), which is used five times in "Buddha Nature." Both imply that the time in question is related to a specific event or period.

Chronometrics and Chronotypology

The Lexicon of Time

This brings us directly to the relationship between quantitative and relative determinations of time—which, as indicated above, are intricately intertwined. To start with the pertinent lexicon, terms like "temporal occasion" (*jisetsu*) or "right at this time" (*shōtō immo ji*), mentioned above, point to Dōgen's tendency to use temporal expressions that reference specific times. In quantitative terms, they relate to individual elements of a plurality. As Rolf Elberfeld has argued, this is in line with the general use of the lexem 時 in old Chinese, and up until late medieval Japanese.[24]

Accordingly, "time" is rarely used as a hyperonym or summary expression. When Dōgen refers to the totality of time(s), he usually does so by enumerating a complete series of phases. We have already encountered this mode of expression in his poem on the "Original Face," which indicates all of time by enumerating the full cycle of the seasons. To indicate not the completeness of a cycle, but the total expanse of time, Dōgen uses the series of past, present, and future, as in the following quote from the composite vernacular *Treasury* fascicle "Plum Blossom" (*Baika* 梅花): "My late master, the old Buddha, by virtue of having clarified the treasury of the true dharma eye, rightly transmitted it to all the Buddha-ancestors assembled in all ten directions in the past, present, and future."[25] Past, present, and future can further be summarily referred to as the "three times" (*sanji* 三時). An example is the title of the fascicle "The Karma in the Three Times" (*Sanji gō* 三時業).[26] Yet another equivalent term is the more traditional Buddhist expression "three periods/worlds" (*sanze* 三世). According to Kim, it again expresses the inextricable relation between time and particular events.[27] An earlier passage in the "Plum Blossom" fascicle, however, indicates that these three times only comprise the present cosmic eon. Alluding to the Buddha King of Majestic Voice, who according to the Lotus Sutra lived "infinite, boundless, inconceivable" eons ago,²⁸ Dōgen states: "The myriad things are not only those in the past, present, and future, but also those before the King of Majestic Voice, and up until those yet to come."²⁹

This demonstrates that Dōgen is not incapable of thinking or referencing the totality of time beyond the confines of a given event, situation, period, or age; however, he rarely finds reason to mention time in this sense. When he does, as in the above quote, the totality of time implied is not necessarily given an explicit term of its own. It is as if he consciously sought to avoid expressions that would foster the notion of time as an all-encompassing container, separate from things, events, or distinct periods. This is also supported by his cautious use of the attribute *jin* 盡 (modern Japanese: 尽), which indicates exhaustiveness. While this attribute appears quite regularly in conjunction with spatial terms (thirteen times with *kai* 界 "sphere" or *chi* 地 "ground" in "What Is:Time" alone), Dōgen rarely combines it with "time." The expression "all of time" (*jinji* 盡時) appears only twice in this text. Both instances refer back to the plurality of what there is, and to an exploration of everything that is, as time: "Because everything is only 'right at this [its] time,' each and every 'what is:time' is 'all of time.' The grass there is and the phenomena there are, are all time. [. . .] This is exploring to the full all time[s] as all there is."³⁰ The use of the indefinite plural marker *sho* 諸 in combination with *ji/toki* is also rare. Again, when it occurs, it points to distinct times with individual characteristics, as in the "Emptiness Flowers" fascicle: "The various times further have colors such as blue, yellow, red, and white."³¹ Full conceptual analysis of these passages follows later, in chapter 6, but these examples on first sight appear to support the received view that Dōgen prefers a "concrete," "phenomenal" view of time over an "abstract," "general" one.

The lexems for "time," then, primarily refer not to time in general but to specified times: for example, the occasion of a certain event or period. Relevant occurrences of the lexem *ji/toki* or its compounds can therefore often be aptly translated with the English conjunction "when." This is both true for passages in Literary Sinitic and for those written in the composite vernacular style. Compare the following quote in Literary Sinitic: "At the time/when [the emperor] Wu of Wei first met with Bodhidharma, he asked of him: 'What is the first and foremost meaning of the sacred truth?,'"³² with a passage written in the composite vernacular style: "At the time/when he [Zen master Zhixian, a disciple of Linji] later appeared in the world [as a religious teacher], he instructed his assembly."³³

It deserves mention, however, that the lexems for "time" only rarely refer to such singular, individual events. More frequently, they point to situations or actions of a certain type. The famous initial sentences of "Actualizing the *kōan*" are exemplary in this regard. They refer to the "time when all dharmas are the *Buddha Dharma*" and the "time when all dharmas are without substance," respectively.[34] The words for "time," when used in this manner, indicate a plurality of like situations, and they do include some degree of generalization. This stands in marked contrast to the received view, recently reiterated by Rein Raud, that Dōgen identifies time primarily and dominantly with the individual present moment, right here and now.[35]

Material vs. Formal Chronometry

Notwithstanding, it is equally remarkable that Dōgen apparently prefers to describe specific times in terms of material attributes, such as by linking them to a certain (type of) action, perspective, or constellation of characteristics, instead of using numeric indicators and time units. This is at least true for the main body of the instructions in the composite vernacular *Treasury*, where formal numeric chronography is rarely to be found. Instead, the temporal position of an event is most often determined by indicating its place in a sequence. For example, where Dōgen quotes and discusses sayings by the Zen patriarchs, the latter are often introduced by their names and their number in the traditional sequence of the twenty-eight Indian and six Chinese patriarchs (up to Huineng, after whom the lineages divided), as in "The twelfth ancestor, the venerable Aśvaghoṣa, in explaining the sea of the Buddha nature told the thirteenth ancestor [. . .]."[36] Where this is not applicable, a hint like "the National teacher Qian of Yanguan prefecture in Hangzhou was an esteemed member of Mazu's assembly" may be given to provide some orientation.[37] Furthermore, the masters are often quoted in chronological order.

As we shall see in more detail in the following chapter 4 on chronopolitics, this technique of temporal localization by sequence is matched in Dōgen's practical instructions. Here as well, the prescribed actions are primarily ordered by indicating which action follows or precedes another; for example: "Upon hearing the evening bell, monks don their *kesa*, enter the cloud hall, reach their place and do seated meditation."[38] Such localization via sequence is "absolute," since it does not indicate the position of the event in question in relation to that of the writer/reader, but it is also precise enough as a practical instruction. In contrast, the numerical identification of the patriarchs is fully relational in the context of the composite vernacular *Treasury*, as it does contain a complete list of the ancestors of Dōgen's line until his time in its fascicle on "Buddha Ancestors" (*Busso* 佛祖).[39]

Evidently, in the absence of additional information, such sequential positioning does not allow for the exact calculation of temporal distance. However, the orientation it provides about temporal location and consecution seems to have been sufficient and more important to Dōgen than that afforded by formal numerical chronography.

This approach to expressing time was a matter of choice, since he did on occasion use the latter mode: such as to indicate with some exactness (although incorrectly, according to modern-day calculations) the time that had passed since the days of Śākyamuni Buddha. In the "Transmission of the Robe" fascicle, he contents himself with specifying the time span as "more than 2,000 years," which he remarkably compares to the "much longer time" that the "country's divine treasures"—that is, the imperial regalia—have been transmitted.[40] In the fascicle "Summer Retreat" (*Ango* 安居), however, he gives a precise, fully relational date of the first institution of that event: "Since then, already 2,194 years have passed (until this third year of Kangen [1245] in Japan)."[41] Note that in both cases, the numerical measure of the distance to Śākyamuni is explicitly linked to local conditions, hinting at comparison between distant spatiotemporal spheres as a motif for formal, numeric chronography. We shall return to the forms and functions of this mode of chronography in the next section.

The above-quoted example concerning the numbered sequence of the patriarchs has shown how material chronography may be combined with a formal operation such as counting. Conversely, formal chronography is often connected with material attributes, as exemplified by the "Original Face" poem. Another of Dōgen's poems in classical Japanese uses the medieval poetic technique of "allusive variation" (*honka dori* 本歌取り) to impart feelings of laborious movement to the time unit of the night—which here stands for the blindness of the unawakened:

Ashibiki no / yamadori no o no / shidari o no / naganagashi yo mo / aketekeru kana[42]

(The foot-dragging / mountain-pheasant's / dangling tail / long, long night as well / has lifted and gone for good)

The variation is on a famous poem by the seventh-century court poet Kakinomoto no Hitomaro 柿本人麻呂:

Ashibiki no / yamadori no o no / shidari o no / naganaga shi yo o / hitori kamo nemu[43]

The foot-dragging / mountain-pheasant's / dangling tail / long, long night / am I to spend alone?

Dōgen's twist on the original is highly significant in several respects: on the textual level, the dubitative, open-ended aspect (expressed in the auxiliary verb *-mu*) of the final line in Hitomaro's poem is replaced with a completive aspect (marked by the combination of the auxiliary verbs *-te* and *-keri*): the poem is no longer about a long night to be expected, but about a night that has ended already. It is also transposed from the secular context of waiting in vain for a loved one, where the time unit of the night has a literal meaning, to the spiritual plane, where it stands metaphorically for ignorance and delusion. And where the technique of allusive variation is usually associated with a pessimistic view of the present and the longing for an idealized past, Dōgen subverts such sentimentalism by turning a poem about loneliness into one on the achievement of insight and liberation.

Now, both this and the "Original Face" poem refer to time units that have a certain basis in environmental phenomena and might be conceived of as "natural" (and therefore "material") rather than "formal." However, as Haruo Shirane has pointed out for the case of the seasons in Japan, it was a cultural choice to accommodate the Chinese patterning of the year and deny the rainy season a status on a par with spring or summer.[44] Similarly, "day" and "night" appear as natural units, but there is no natural determination of the start and end of a day. As we shall see in the next chapter, Dōgen starts his description of daily routines with the sound of the evening bell (with the passage quoted above), while Keizan Jōkin 瑩山紹瑾 (1268?–1325),the "second founder" of the Sōtō school in Japan, starts in the morning with the zodiacal hour of the dragon (beginning at roughly 7:00 a.m.). Neither of them thus sets the limit of the day at sunrise or sunset. These questions of delimitation may be of no consequence to the unit of the night as it is addressed in the above poem; but then again, the night in that poem is not a literal or natural night at all: It is a metaphorical night, which stands for a spiritual state of being.

An inscription celebrating the "inception of spring" (*risshun* 立春) of 1247 further exemplifies how formal, and in this case even numerical, chronography accompanies material attributes that convey a strong aesthetic aspect. The "inception of spring" is the first of twenty-four equidistant sections of the solar year and therefore is associated with the beginning of the new year in the lunisolar calendar (even though it can occur during the final month of the old year). Compare the following lines: "Salutations to the Buddha, the dharma, the congregation, greatly auspicious! The inception of spring, greatly auspicious! The one house, the ancestor-teacher, the ancestors' teaching, greatly auspicious! The *Buddha Dharma* widely spreading, greatly auspicious! [. . .] The fifth year of Kangen, yin-fire-sheep, inception of spring, greatly auspicious, greatly auspicious!"[45] To reiterate, "inception of spring" may sound like a "natural" turning point in time. But it is a technical term tied to twenty-four phases of the solar year that are calculated to be of equal length. These phases carry names that point to climatic phenomena associated with the course of the solar year on the continent, not in Japan. "Yin-fire-sheep" locates the year in the sexagenarian cycle built by combining the five element-phases (Chin. *wuxing*, Jp. *gogyō* 五行) in their yin and yang phases ("ten celestial stems") with the twelve "terrestrial branches," the Sinitic zodiacal signs. Because their sequence in the cycle is fixed, indication of the "stem" and "branch" also functions as an ordinal number—in this case, it identifies the forty-fourth year within the sixty-year cycle.

The formal system of time-reckoning Dōgen inherited thus combines calculation and attribution of certain material characteristics. The quoted inscription adds its celebratory epithets to these. There is no stark opposition between formal numerical and material descriptive or evaluative-emotive chronography. Instead, the quantitative, metrical determination of time and its typological and emotive characterization are regularly intertwined.

Numerical Chronometry and Its Uses

The above considerations have already led us to discuss some of the formats Dōgen used to record date and time. We shall now explore these in a more systematic fashion and examine the distribution of such formal numerical chronography in his texts, as well as the functions it serves. In terms of the overall argument of this book, this will provide us with a clearer picture of the status and relative weight of quantitative determinations of time within our corpus.

Formats

Formal numerical chronography is intricately linked to the extant methods and formats of chronometry. In early medieval Japan, the most relevant system in this regard was the Sinitic lunisolar calendar, which combined lunar months with the solar year by way of the regular interposition of extra, intercalary months. As noted above, each year was identified first by an ordinal number combined with an era name (combined with the unit sign *nen/toshi* 年); and, second, by its position in the sexagenary cycle of celestial stems and terrestrial branches (sometimes combined with the unit sign *sai/toshi* 歳). The new year began with the second new moon after the winter solstice. The lunar month started at new moon. As a consequence, the days of the month were tied to phases of the moon, and the fifteenth day was always full moon.

The day was divided into twelve zodiacal hours (derived from the position of the sun in relation to the constellations of the zodiac) comprising four sub-units, called "points" (*ten* 点) or "incisions" (*koku* 刻, also used for the mid-hour). Contrary to statements in the literature,[46] this was originally a system of equal hours, which required elaborate and well-calibrated water-clocks for time-reckoning.[47] In the capital and other administrative centers, these were provided at the courts, and the hours were announced by acoustic signs—drums and bells—in adjacent regions. In more remote areas without access to this socio-technical infrastructure, the zodiacal hours were often measured as units equally divided between sunrise and sunset during the day, and sunset and sunrise during the night. Their length accordingly changed with the seasons. The ambiguity produced by equal and seasonal hours was highlighted by the fact that outside the highly regulated social environments of the imperial court and of Buddhist monasteries, subdivisions of the hour were rarely used. While Dōgen requires the presence of a water-clock in his monastic rules[48]—which would indicate the use of equal hours—it is unclear whether his monasteries actually possessed one.

In parallel to the system of the hours, a system of five night-watches (*kō* 更), again subdivided into four "points," was also in use. This was a seasonal system, with the first watch starting after sunset and the last one ending before sunrise.

Within this system of time units, the standard format of formal numerical chronography used to identify the temporal location of an event first mentions the ordinal number of a year together with its era, then its position in the sexagenary cycle, then the number of the month, and, finally, the number of the day. This format is not specific to Dōgen, but conventionally used in a wide array of sources.

In the fascicle on "Sustained Practice," Dōgen reports on the meeting between the Emperor Wu of Wei and the 28th Indian/first Chinese ancestor Bodhidharma, stating: "This happened during the time of the Wei, in the year Putong 8, yin-fire-sheep, 9th month, 21st day."[49] As indicated above, however, this way of localizing events in time is an exception in the main text of his instructions. On the other hand, it is regularly used in paratexts, for example, in the colophones of the composite-vernacular *Treasury*, or in prefatory parts of ritual texts dedicated to specific occasions. Compare the following examples, from the *Treasury* (1) and a memorial for Dōgen's master Rujing (2):

(1) Informal instruction to the assembly at Kannon dōri Kōshō hōrin ji, Ninji, 2nd year [1241], yin-metal ox, 9th month, 9th day.[50]

(2) Japan, Kangen, 2nd year [1244], yang-wood dragon, 7th month, 17th day, on the occasion of the memorial for the late teacher, the late 30th abbot of the Tiandong monastery in the Great Song Empire's Qingyuan prefecture.[51]

As in the first case from the tale of Bodhidharma, example (2) specifies the era by relating it to a country because two regions with different era names are involved.

Sometimes further information is added to the "standard form." For example, the colophones to the vernacular "Treasury's" fascicles "Great Insight" (*Daigo* 大悟) and "Reading Sutras" (*Kankin* 看經) name the season after the year's position in the sexagenarian cycle, making explicit temporal information that could otherwise be inferred from the ordinal number of the month.[52] Conversely, the number of the month and day may be replaced by nominal expressions containing the same information, such as by specifying one of the twenty-four sections of the solar year, or an annual event with a fixed date, such as *tango* 端午, the fifth day of the fifth month.[53] This nominal format (which has a precise numerical meaning and is based on astronomical calculation) is often used in the *Extensive Record*. New information is added where the hour of instruction or writing is mentioned after the day, as in the "Mountain and Water Sutra" fascicle: "At the time of Ninji, 1st year [1240], yin-metal rat, 10th month, 18th day, hour of the rat, instruction to the assembly while being at Kannon dōri Kōshō hōrinji."[54] The information about the hour reveals that the instruction happened in the middle of the night, and this may explain why it is explicitly recorded. The only other instruction where the information is equally—or, to be precise, even more—specific about the time when it was given is that on "Shining Light." According to its colophone, it was delivered "in the night, at the fourth point of the third watch"—that is, long after midnight and probably at the end of a prolonged session of evening *zazen*.[55]

Notably, the colophones of the composite vernacular treasury are less precise where they pertain to when a certain instruction was copied. Here, often only the year and month or some other indication of a longer period are mentioned. This difference immediately connects to the function of numerical chronography or the indication of a precise date and time.

Distribution and Functions

As there is no explicit reflection concerning chronographical choices in our corpus, we can only infer the function of a particular mode from its uses. What follows is an analysis of the textual evidence.

Formal dates and times are given regularly as part of the colophones of informal instructions and only rarely within their main text. In contrast, they are rarely given for his formal instructions collected in the *Extensive Record*. This is, however, simply in line with the genre conventions for such "Recorded Sayings." Still, a precise date is given in formal numerical chronography for the first formal instruction Dōgen presented at Kōshōji in late 1236—or, according to the source, "on Katei, 2nd year, yang-fire monkey, 10th month, 15th day"—that is, on a full moon day.[56] The next full numerical dates are those recorded for his taking up residence at Daibutsuji in 1244, and then for instruction no. 177, on the occasion of renaming Daibutsuji as Eiheiji in 1246, or "Kangen 4th year, yang-fire horse, 6th month, 15th day" (full moon, again).[57] Next is no. 251, given upon Dōgen's return from Kamakura in the spring of 1248 and dated "Hōji 2nd year, yang-wood dog, 3rd month, 14th day."[58] In other words, of the 531 entries in the *Extensive Record*, only three provide a full numerical date, and they all indicate beginnings: the first formal instructions in Kōshōji, after the renaming of Eiheiji, and after the return from Kamakura. The same goes for commencing residence in Daibutsuji, although it is not connected to a formal instruction. The largest number of entries, in contrast, lack any date. Fewer than 20 percent (92 of 531) use formal nominal chronography; these are the instructions given on named regular annual occasions, such as the winter solstice or the celebration of Śākyamuni Buddha's enlightenment.[59] Finally, there are fourteen instructions (<3 percent) with incomplete numerical dates (no year, but month and day). Five of these (nos. 193, 279, 347, 389, and 451) pertain to the first day of the ninth month. They mark a break with the relaxed schedule for seated meditation during this month that was apparently common in many monasteries; in contrast, Dōgen insisted on implementing the full schedule and regularly used the day to expound on the merits of seated meditation.[60] Others mark extraordinary occasions, such as a one-time memorial for the second Chinese patriarch Dazu Huike, who according to legend cut off his arm to prove his dedication to Bodhidharma (no. 392);[61] or a special ceremony to stop a period of prolonged rainfall that threatened the harvest, and the livelihoods, of the people around Eiheiji (no. 379, DZZ II, 90).[62] Only 5 of 531 (fewer than 1 percent) appear to give a numerical record of month and day without such a special reason.

This is in stark contrast to the informal instructions of the 75-fascicle composite-vernacular *Treasury*, which regularly include full (and mostly numerical) dates in their colophons. Even the eight exceptions mostly specify at least a period within the year,[63] the month,[64] or a period within the month.[65] One example may have accidentally omitted the number of the day, as the unit itself is mentioned.[66] This leaves one fascicle that gives only the year.[67] Consequently, there is no completely undated part in the 75-fascicle *Treasury*.

This contrast between the *Extensive Record* and the 75-fascicle *Treasury* may be explained by a difference in the character of their content. The *Extensive Record* was intended as a public documentation of official, formal instructions that ideally followed a regular schedule (see the next chapter) and were, again ideally, presented in chronological order. It records the precise dates of a few institutional turning points. The temporal location of most instructions can then be roughly inferred from this framework and the regular annual events that are marked with nominal chronography ("Winter Solstice," "New Year," "Enlightenment Day," and so forth). The *Treasury*, on the other hand, contains informal teachings that were entrusted to the congregation of those who had accepted Dōgen as their personal teacher. They are not organized chronologically, and they present a more intimate and convoluted mode of discourse. As the subsequent history of the *Treasury* shows, access to its contents was perceived as a privileged sign of lineage—of partaking in the wisdom of the master. It was therefore important to document their authenticity. The colophones of the *Treasury*, with their precise dates (and, we may add, locations), have this testimonial function. They produce, to use a term by Roland Barthes, a "reality effect."[68] The same holds for the rare use of numerical dates within the main body of the *Treasury* texts or in the *Extensive Record*.

The above-quoted example of Bodhidharma's meeting with the emperor of Wei is a case in point. The same fascicle contains three other numerical dates, all related to the actions of emperors involved with Zen Buddhism. An especially notable case is that of Xuanzong, who as a prince allegedly became a monastic and fellow-monk of master Huangbo Xiyun (Jp. Ōbaku Kiun 黃檗希運, d. 850), the teacher of Linji. This and one other case also contain tales of resurrection, and their exceptional character may have motivated the mention of a specific, numerical date.[69] There are only five more cases of numerical dates for years within the main texts of the composite vernacular *Treasury*.[70] Three pertain to things heard and seen by Dōgen in China: In "Transmitting the Robe," he reports how two Korean monks had come to China during the year Jiading 17 (1224), the second year of his sojourn.[71] In "Buddha Nature" and "Washing the Face," he speaks of his own experiences in Chinese monasteries in the first months after his arrival during Jiading 16 (1223).[72] Finally, in two instances Dōgen measures the time since a decisive moment of institution in the past—the first summer retreat and Śākyamuni's final transmission of the teaching—by giving the number of years passed and the current date.[73]

Based on this survey, we can say that the various modes of formal chronography serve the following functions:

1. Numerical chronography primarily underlines the factuality of a given event. Full numerical dates in the colophones of the 75-fascicle *Treasury* confirm that a certain instruction was in fact given by the master himself. In the main text, they emphasize the historicity of events that connect the Zen tradition with imperial patronage or contain exceptional phenomena such as apparent resurrection of the dead, or they accentuate the fact that Dōgen had witnessed certain things himself during his sojourn in China.

2. An additional function of numerical chronography is to establish a framework of reference for certain turning points in time. In the *Extensive Record*, numerical dates record the moments of institution when the master held his first formal instruction at a certain monastery, when he moved or returned to a certain place of teaching, or when this place received a new name. In a similar fashion, two cases in the composite-vernacular *Treasury* identify the point in time when certain important elements of the Buddhist tradition were first instituted, along with the temporal distance to these events. The colophones of the 75-fascicle *Treasury* certainly also serve this function of temporal orientation regarding when exactly Dōgen composed or gave a certain instruction.

3. Formal nominal chronography is often used in the *Extensive Record* to connect a certain ritual or instruction to the regular annual events of the religious and secular calendars. In this fashion, an individual occasion is integrated into a virtually unending cycle of iterative events, and the moment "just now" is linked with the dimension of metric time—a metric, however, that is primarily represented by nominal rather than numerical designations.

Taken together, these points confirm an observation we have already made in the previous section of this chapter: that in Dōgen's writings there is no stark opposition between an "empty," homogeneous, numerical time, on the one hand, and the time of particular actions, events, or phenomena, laden with specific characteristics, on the other. The opposition created in parts of the literature between the "twelve hours"—time counted—and the "living moment" is a projection of later, modern concerns. This is not because "time as number" is absent from Dōgen's texts. On the contrary, numerical chronography is an important means of accentuating the reality and importance of certain events. The examples of the memorial for Rujing or the celebration of the new year further demonstrate how strong emotional qualities (or their expression) can be attached to "rational" numerical chronography.

One further aspect of the use of formal chronography deserves mention: this is the absence, by and large, of dates in describing duration.

The salient counter-example is the first formal instruction upon Dōgen's return from Kamakura. The pertinent passage runs as follows:

> Dharma Hall Discourse on the Fourteenth Day of the Third Month of the Second Year of Hōji [1248]
> On the third day of the eight month of last year, this mountain monk departed from this mountain and went to the Kamakura District of Sagami Prefecture to expound the Dharma for patrons and lay students. On this month of this year, just last night, I came home to this temple, and this morning I have ascended this seat.[74]

Otherwise, the use of dates to define precise time spans is conspicuously absent, and durational expressions in general are comparatively rare. At first sight, this supports the view that Dōgen emphasizes occasions or moments over longer periods of time. A closer view, however, complicates this picture.

As we have already seen in the passage from "Summer Retreat" quoted above, Dōgen sometimes accentuates the length of time a certain tradition or teaching has been transmitted by numerical chronographic expressions. A further case of this usage comes from the fascicle "Transmitting the Robe": "Because of this, ever since the ancestor came from the West, during the several hundred years from the Great Tang to the Great Song, there were many accomplished lecturers who thoroughly mastered their own profession, and many of the likes of experts in doctrinal studies or monastic rules, who, upon [truly] entering the Buddha Dharma, discarded their old robes in the received style and correctly accepted the *kesa* as rightly transmitted in the Buddha Way."[75] On a slightly smaller temporal scale, Dōgen often records a given number of years to highlight the sincerity and perseverance of a person's engagement with Buddhist practice. In the 75- and 12-fascicle *Treasury* combined, the word "year" (*nen/toshi* 年) appears a total of 125 times in the durational sense.[76] Among these, seventy-two cases are from the fascicle "Sustained Practice," fourteen are from "Attaining Expression" (*Dōte* 道得), seven from "Transmitting the Robe," six each from "Constants of the House" (*Kajō* 家常) and "Pervasive Exploration" (*Hensan* 遍参), and five from "Washing the Face." There is none in "What Is:Time"—which may explain in part why readers focusing on this fascicle tend to underrate the component of duration in Dōgen's concept of time.

The typical instances from "Sustained Practice" involve description of a prolonged period of dedicated religious exertion. To give just one example, from a sequence extolling monks who sacrificed sleep in favor of seated meditation: "The venerable Yunyan and Daowu both trained under Yaoshan, and both pledged that they would not lie down for forty years, perfecting their single-minded practice. They transmitted the dharma to the Great Teacher Wuben of Dongshan. Dongshan said, 'Since I started to wish for single-minded practice, I have negotiated the way in seated meditation for twenty years.' This way has now been transmitted extensively."[77] Another fairly frequent type is the injunction to study and practice a certain understanding for an extended amount of time, as in the following saying from "Buddha Nature": "The Buddha nature always goes together with becoming a Buddha. We should thoroughly investigate and make efforts according to this way of understanding; we make efforts and study it in practice for thirty or twenty years."[78] An expression often used in such cases of durational prescriptive chronography is the indeterminate "for some time" (Jp. *shibaraku*).[79] While this word in general usage points to a rather short time span, there is one passage revealing that in Dōgen's case, it can actually mean several years—nine, in the case in question.[80]

The expression of duration therefore has two main functions: First, it highlights the length of time a certain tradition has been followed. Second, it pertains to perseverance in Buddhist practice as both a token of commitment and a necessary element in maturing and deepening one's insight. Given the close connection between practice and enlightenment in Dōgen's thought, we should not lightly discard this chronographical evidence.

Conclusion

The main findings of our investigation into the ways time is expressed in Dōgen's writings may be summarized as follows.

1. His salient chronothetic statement in "What Is:Time" that everything there is is also time is supported by the pervasive use of affirmative expressions and the absence, more or less, of negative and limitative clauses pertaining to time.

2. At the same time, Dōgen avoids using the *words* for time as general nouns or hyperonyms, although he has a *notion* of time as a general, comprehensive concept.

3. Conversely, he predominantly uses the words for time to address specific occasions or, more often, types of events.

4. Within the main body of his instructions, the temporal relation between events or between a recounted event and the present is determined preferably by way of sequence and not by giving numerical coordinates or dates. However, numbers may be involved in establishing a sequence, such as for the sequence of the "ancestors" in the line of transmission.

5. Conversely, formal chronography is often connected with material attributes that describe the character and emotional quality of a certain date or occasion. Time counted or calculated is therefore not necessarily homogeneous or "empty" time.

6. Numerical chronography is regularly used in the paratexts of the 75-fascicle composite vernacular *Treasury* to state the time when the instructions collected therein were first composed or delivered. Within the main body of its text, and in the *Extensive Record,* it is used only rarely. The few cases accentuate the factuality of outstanding events and/or establish a temporal frame of reference.

7. Durational expressions are comparatively rare, but they do play a role in emphasizing dedication to Buddhist practice and the time devoted to the culmination of insight.

On the whole, the evidence presented shows that Dōgen generally selects a mode of chronography that highlights the material and emotive attributes of the time so described. Different events and actions are predominantly ordered in a sequence instead of being localized in a system of coordinates with numerical variables. However, temporal localization by means of coordinates is not entirely absent and does have an important role to play in his writings; it may be conjoined with typological attributes. Numerical chronography is also often employed to indicate the duration of Buddhist practice as a sign of dedication and to indicate the time spent in deepening and maturing insight. Its use therefore does not imply a contrast between an abstract "time as number" and a perceptually or emotionally charged "lived time."

In terms of morphology, the calculation of temporal distance and duration by the number of years past or spent, and the sequential mode of relating events, involve a strong element of linearity. On the other hand, the nominal chronography that is often used in the *Extensive Record* to establish the time and occasion of a certain formal instruction emphasizes the cyclical character of recurring events. Overall, the chronographic evidence reviewed here does not support the thesis that Dōgen denies linear time or pictures time predominantly in terms of individual, isolated moments or situations.

On yet another level of analysis, in terms established by sociologist Günter Dux, we can say that Dōgen predominantly uses a "time of action" mode in his description of actions and events. But this is a matter of choice and does not spring from the lack of the concept of "abstract world-time." A notion conforming to the latter type (and the concomitant numerical chronography) is occasionally employed to establish a frame of reference, especially where events or situations are connected that are far removed from each other in space and time. What the chronographical evidence suggests is that Dōgen commands a rich repertoire in the description of time and selects his modes of expression according to the primary aims of a given communication.

4

Chronopolitics

Time Regimes and the Social Language of Time

In this chapter, we move from the ways in which time was expressed in Dōgen's writings to the more practical question of how it was meant to be lived in the monasteries that he founded. I have chosen the title "chronopolitics" for this chapter because the sources that are available to us today are almost exclusively prescriptive in character—namely, Dōgen's monastic rules that were posthumously collected in the *Pure Rules of Eternal Peace* (*Eihei shingi*, 永平清規); texts on rituals and other practical matters of monastic life from the *Treasury*, and formal talks from the *Extensive Record*, plus various administrative documents. Another reason for speaking of "chronopolitics" is that Dōgen used temporal determinants to accentuate the identity of his community and decide positions in its hierarchy. In other words, he was not only shaping the time of the community, but also shaping the community through time.

To delineate the relevant features of these processes, the following analysis operates in three dimensions. The first is the semantic dimension, that is, the *content* of temporal organization; here, I examine the actions and events in monastic life that are the object of temporal regulation, the ebbs and flows of monastic life, and the way temporal order is achieved on a cognitive, symbolic, and practical level. A specific question in this regard is which aspects of time are the primary subject of regulation. I show how Dōgen realizes a primarily "task-oriented" organization of daily life for the majority of his community. This aspect immediately relates to the second, pragmatic dimension, which pertains to the social relations that inform the monastic time regime and are in turn expressed by it. Who is in control of time? What does temporal order tell us about the evaluation of different groups of people? How is the time of each of these groups appreciated and treated? Third, I examine the syntactic dimension, which here sheds light on how the religious aspect of life relates to other perspectives and issues, such as economic or political ones. Dōgen's monasteries and medieval monasteries in general were in themselves arenas of power, and they were part of a broader landscape of political exchanges. To secure their existence and that of their inhabitants, they needed to cater to economic aspects and the provisioning of resources necessary for survival. The question is how Dōgen and his followers organized monastic life to integrate these perspectives while preserving the monastery's raison d'être. Notably, in all these dimensions we will deal preeminently with temporal distinctions. On a conceptual level, the critical question follows: What weight is accorded to these distinctions? Are they treated as mere technical exigencies, as (in Buddhist terms) "expedient means" (*hōben*) that serve a higher aim—possibly one that, in itself, is beyond such distinctions? Or are they afforded a religious significance of their own, which contributes to the religious ideal?

In pursuing these questions, I move from daily life to the intermediate scales of the month and the year, with larger perspectives woven into the fabric of these diurnal, mensal, and annual cycles. Aspects of the pragmatic and syntactic dimensions are already palpable in this exploration of the rhythms of monastic life, but they are also explored in shorter, dedicated paragraphs at the end of the chapter. Finally, to evaluate whether and to what extent Dōgen's rules and instructions exhibit a vision of monastic life and religious practice that is specific to him, and where they represent standard views of his time, I calibrate my analysis of his texts through comparison with other sources. Three groups of texts are relevant in this regard. First, there are those he himself relied on, such as monastic regulations from the continent. The most important here are two Song period documents: the *Pure Rules for Zen Monasteries* (*Chanyuan qinggui*, Jp. *Zen'en shingi* 禅苑清規),[1] which are the famous monastic rules drafted by Changlu Zongze 長蘆宗賾 (d. 1107 CE), and the *Daily Essentials for Members of the Congregation* (*Ruzhong riyong*, Jp. *Nisshū nichiyō* 入衆日用). These texts formed the basic point of reference for Dōgen's instructions on monastic life.[2] Second, texts from the early Sōtō school, such as Keizan Jōkin's monastic rules, in turn used Dōgen's instructions as a reference; they show how his vision was followed or altered in subsequent generations. Third, documents written by other contemporary monastic leaders from the Zen and other schools will help us to understand where Dōgen's vision of monastic life and its temporal organization conformed to general ideas of the era and where he departed from such consensus to install temporal routines according to his own, possibly unique, ideas about time.

The Diurnal Rhythm in Monastic Life

The Method of Negotiating the Way

The best starting point for discovering how Dōgen envisioned the temporal structure and characteristics of daily life in his monastery is the text *The Method of Negotiating the Way* (*Bendō hō* 辨道法; short: *Method*).[3] It was probably written as an instruction for newcomers to his Daibutsuji monastery in Echizen, which started to attract larger numbers of monks in 1245.[4] *Method* outlines in some detail the daily activities of monks living together in the monks' hall (*sōdō* 僧堂) and how they are to be performed. Its aim is to ensure that members of this core group of the monastic community act in accord with each other and with the way of the Buddhas and ancestors. This, the introductions states, equals the state of "body and mind dropped off" (*datsuraku shinjin* 脱落身心)—Dōgen's signature phrase for the complete realization of supreme insight. Since life in the *sōdō* was to be centered around communal seated meditation (*zazen*), this equation is but an expansion of Dōgen's earlier equation of "dropping off / dropped off body and mind" with seated meditation.

Method does not aim at providing a comprehensive schedule for monastic life, but confines itself to the quotidian activities of the core community. Within this scope, however, conveying temporal information is essential to its objective. This is already clear from the organization of the text, which mainly follows the successive course of daily actions and events in the monks' hall, starting with communal evening *zazen*. Each action is described in itself as a whole, and the text then turns to the next action in the daily progression of events. This "time of action" mode subordinates chronology to topical organization and on occasion leads to temporal loops that make the text somewhat confusing to the modern reader. *Method* thus exemplifies a cognitive order that fits the term "task orientation," which was famously introduced by Thompson to describe pre-capitalist or pre-industrial social time regimes.[5] "Time" in this framework of practical orientation is subordinate to the "substance" of an action and appears mainly in the succession of the phases that make up its parts or as a succession of main events and actions. The "task orientation" mode of ordering tends to emphasize the integrity of each action, and the concomitant quality associated with its time. This stands in contrast to a framework where "time" serves as an overarching system of coordination in which each action is assigned its proper place and duration.

The ensuing passage about evening *zazen*—the first ritual activity described in *Method*—exemplifies this "task" mode of operation. It is quoted in some detail here to convey the style of the text and its priorities concerning temporal determination.

> Evening *zazen*. When you hear the evening bell, put on the *kesa*, enter the cloud hall, reach your place and do *zazen*. The abbot does *zazen* on his chair, facing the [statue of the] holy monk,[6] the head monk (*shuso* 首座) does *zazen* facing the wooden edge [of the platform], and the assembly does *zazen* facing the wall. While the abbot does *zazen*, a bench is set up outside the screen behind his seat, and either an attendant cleric (*jisha* 侍者) or a lay observant (*anja* 行者) is waiting on him there. At the time of *zazen*, the abbot enters from the northern pillar of the front portal. He walks up to the holy monk, bows with folded hands in greeting, and burns incense. When his obeisance to the holy monk is finished, he circumambulates the hall one time with hands clasped in front of his chest (*shashu* 叉手). When he reaches the holy monk, he bows in greeting, walks to his chair, bows to it, turns around and bows [once more] to the holy monk, then tucks his sleeves and mounts the chair, taking off his sandals and settling into the lotus position. The attendant cleric or observant stands still at the inside of the front portal close to the southern pillar and does not follow the abbot in his circumambulation. Once the abbot has settled into his seat, the attendant cleric or observant takes his position, pays obeisance to the holy monk and quietly sits down on the bench behind the seat. The attendant cleric or observant keeps the abbot's incense container.
>
> Should the abbot sleep in the cloud hall, he does so on a place provided to the upper side of the head monk. When

he gets up, he returns to his seat and does *zazen*. (During late night *zazen*, the assembly does not wear the *kesa*. The abbot does *zazen* with his *kesa* hung over the chair. This is the method.)

When evening *zazen* is supposed to end, the wooden board is sounded. This will be during the second or third watch, at the first, second or third point, depending on the direction of the abbot. After the sounding of the board, the assembly does *gasshō*,[7] folds their *kesa*, wraps it in its cloth and places it on the top of their storage chest. The abbot does not take off the *kesa*, but rises from his seat, goes in front of the holy monk, and, having paid obeisance, leaves via the north side of the front portal. The attendant cleric or observant leave first and wait for him outside the monks' hall. One attendant helps him and lifts the curtain. This is also done when entering the hall.[8]

A first feature that is remarkable (and typical of *Method* as a whole) is the absence of information about clock-time. The only numeric time unit mentioned in our passage is the "night watch" (*kō* 更, Chin. *geng*). As noted in the previous chapter, the length of this unit depends on the season, and this may to some extent explain the degree of latitude that is given above in determining the end of evening *zazen*. There are only two instances in *Method* that mention hours of the clock, but this happens in glosses and with the derogative qualifier "secular" (*sezoku no* 世俗の).[9]

One possible practical reason for such scarcity of references to the hours of the day is that at the time of writing, the recently founded Daibutsuji may not (yet) have possessed a water clock. The *Pure Rules for Temple Officers* (*Chiji shingi* 知事清規), written roughly one year later in summer 1246, stipulate that the officer in charge of infrastructure (*chissui* 直歳) would oversee the handling of such a device.[10] This implies that Dōgen wanted such clocks to be a regular part of his monasteries. Remarkably, he went beyond the *Pure Rules for Zen Monasteries* in this point, which indicates that he did, to say the least, not oppose, but embraced the options made available by measuring time by the clock, although he employed the tool in a distinct fashion.

While "task orientation" seems the dominant temporal perspective in "Method," this occurs within a given framework, with certain anchor points in time. The first of these is the evening bell, which initiates preparation for evening *zazen*. While Dōgen does not explicitly tie the signal to a numerical time unit, according to Kosaka et al., it was customarily sounded at the first point of the first night watch.[11] Explicit, numerical time units are mentioned in conjunction with the scheduling of daily personal hygiene, which happens, according to Chinese sources, during the fifth watch,[12] in mid-afternoon *zazen*, during the hour of the monkey, and "release from study" (or, by inference, verbal instruction by the abbot) at the mid-hour of the rooster.[13] We also see a certain degree of planning with regard to the end of evening *zazen*. Significantly, numerical time units again come into play at this point: While the text is not entirely clear about the exact procedures, apparently, the abbot was to decide on the length of ritual evening meditation and to have its end announced at a time he had indicated beforehand.[14] One can see how the use of a clock would have been integrated in this mode of temporal organization and decision-making.

That said, most of the time markers referenced in *Method* do not signal a numerically measured location in time, but a specific time of/for action. The sounding of the wooden board marked the end of evening *zazen*. Another board in front of the head monk's quarters was used for the wake-up call, followed by a coordinated sounding of the boards of all halls to signal the "breaking of the silence" (*kaijō* 開靜, ibid.) during the fifth watch and the beginning of daily activities.[15] The wooden board in front of the monks' hall was once again used to initiate morning *zazen* after breakfast, which ended upon the "fire plate" (*kohan* 火鈑) signal—a sounding of the metal "cloud plate" in front of the kitchen, indicating that lunch was ready.[16] This is a typical example of how the beginning of one action marked the end of another, without mediation by numerical time indicators. An intricate system of acoustic signals thus served to coordinate activities within the core group of tonsured practitioners, and between them and other groups in the monastic community. Within this system, the average member of the community could negotiate daily tasks and activities without taking note of clock-time (or any other numerical time unit). The length of the signals contributed to this effect: The "evening bell" for example consisted of 108 tolls, and the "breaking of the silence" was initiated by a sequence of three soundings of the board in front of the head monk's quarters, followed after some time by a synchronous sounding of the boards in front of all halls. According to an explanatory note by

Kosaka et al., each such "sounding" consisted of 36 beats that increased in speed. In other words, there was a first sequence of 108 beats in three groups of 36 beats on one board, followed some time later by a second, similar sequence, now using the metal "cloud plates" in front of all halls.[17] *Method* thus implies a division of labor regarding the quantitative cognition of time: Keeping track of time units was the duty of select temple officers. *Pure Rules for Temple Officers* explicitly states that it is the task of the *shissui* 直歳 officer to "know the time and discriminate what is favorable [to the monastery]."[18] The major part of the monastic community could simply follow the various signals initiating distinct sequences of action.

When *Method* calls the core community's attention to time, it is in respect to the attributes of an occasion or action. For example, concerning personal hygiene, the text says: "Looking out for the right time, you should head towards the washrooms and wash your face. 'Looking out for the right time' means to catch an interval when the washroom is not so crowded."[19] The intention behind this injunction clearly is that things should go as smoothly and quietly as possible. Similarly, when prescribing the mode of walking that is appropriate in the monks' hall, the document states:

> When you wish to get up from your seat, rise slowly. Get down softly from the platform. Do not raise your feet, do not make large steps, do not walk hurriedly or run about. Without fail fold your hands before your chest and cover them with your sleeves. Don't let them dangle down. Don't turn your head. Keep your eyes on your feet. Walk softly and in a refined manner. Do not rush, raising noise. Do everything diligently together with its time, and in accord with the dharma follow the assembly. This is the defining measure of negotiating the way.[20]

As argued in detail later, the injunctions to "do everything diligently together with its time" and "to follow the assembly in accord with the dharma" can be read as a transferal of Dōgen's concept of "what is:time" to the realm of monastic life. For the ordinary members of the monastery's core community, the chronopolitical focus is on doing things at the appropriate, indicated time, synchronizing their actions with the community, and, generally, on behaving in a quiet manner that avoids any disturbance to contemplative monastic practice. The focus on the mindful performance of each task accords well with the traditional view of Dōgen, but the strict emphasis on "following the community" also deserves to be noted. Furthermore, full concentration on keeping in synchrony with the community and on the appropriate temporal mode of action is made possible by a division of labor that leaves the planning, measurement, and announcement of proper time to designated temple officers and their attendants. For them, living in accord with time means to "know the time and judge what is appropriate."[21] They were to employ their tools—including, we may assume, the water clock, once it was installed—and their judgment to secure the unimpeded course of monastic life.

The schedule that can be collated from *Method* is clearly organized around communal and highly ritualized *zazen* sessions to be held at four of the six traditional Buddhist "times of the day."[22]

1. Evening *zazen* (*kōkon zazen* 黄昏坐禅)
2. Late-night *zazen* (*goya zazen* 後夜坐禅)
3. Morning *zazen* (*sōshin zazen* 早晨坐禅)
4. Late-afternoon *zazen* (*hoji zazen* 晡時坐禅)

Method thus pictures a day of ritual activities that starts in the evening, after sunset, with the night bell, as shown in table 4.1:

Table 4.1. Daily Schedule Extrapolated from *Method*

Time of day/time marker	Modern clock-time (approximate)	Communal meditation	Other activities
Evening/night bell (45–60 minutes after sunset)	6:00–8:00 p.m.	Start of evening *zazen*	
Night (2nd to 3rd watch)/sounding of monks' hall board	~10:00 p.m.	End of formal *zazen*	Monks take off *kesa*, continue informal meditation, take out bedding and quilts, start of sleep-time
Late night (3rd to 4th watch)/ sounding of monks' hall board	~2:00 a.m.	Start of late-night *zazen*	End of sleep-time: wake up

Time of day/time marker	Modern clock-time (approximate)	Communal meditation	Other activities
Late night (5th watch)/sounding of head monk's residence board	3:00–4:00 a.m.	Late-night *zazen*	While monks do *zazen*, the abbot and head monk enter the hall; monks also leave individually for personal hygiene (face washing and cleaning teeth); return to the hall
Morning/breaking of silence/ sounding of all halls' boards	(Some time after beginning of 5th watch)	End of late-night *zazen*	Monks clear away sleeping utensils, put on *kesa*
Morning	(After breaking of silence)		Breakfast and break
Morning/sounding of monks' hall board		Morning *zazen*	Formal meditation; individual excursion to bathroom allowed
Noon (?)/signal from kitchen "fire plate"	11:00 a.m.–12:00 noon (?)		Lunch
Early afternoon (until end of hour of sheep)	~ 3:00 p.m.		Rest and study time
Late afternoon/ after hour of sheep	3:00–6:00 p.m.	Late afternoon *zazen*	
Evening/mid-hour of the rooster	~6:00 p.m.		"Release from study" (tea break, rest, or individual study time) or (implicit): verbal instructions by the abbot

Table 4.1 explanation: Approximations for the night are based on data for sunset and sunrise in Echizen and made on the assumption that the rules are meant to provide a steady schedule throughout the year (see discussion below). Estimates for daytime are calculated on the assumption that Dōgen referred to equal (not seasonal) hours because of his mention of a water-clock as measuring device in *Pure Rules for Temple Officers*. Time for breakfast inferred from *Method of Taking Gruel and Rice* (*Fushuku hanpō* 赴粥飯法); see DZZ II, 348.

This schedule shows that communal *zazen* was indeed at the center of monastic life. With each session lasting at least two, but mostly closer to three modern hours, it was by far the activity accorded the most time, between ten and twelve hours on an average day. Periods of study or individual reading (at most three to four hours) were short in comparison, as was the time for all other activities. The length of time committed to the practice clearly indicates its pre-eminent weight.[23]

A special note is required about sleep time. Theoretically—in terms of the rules laid down in *Method*—sleep time could start as early as the first point of the second night watch and as late as the third point of the third watch. It was to end between the fourth point of the third watch and the third point of the fourth watch. If the regulations had been taken to the extreme, the abbot could have decided to have everyone do *zazen* until the third point of the third watch in midsummer (about 12:05 a.m.), then go to sleep for just about fifteen minutes, only to be woken up again at the fourth point of the third watch (12:20 a.m.). In reality, it seems more likely that the latitude in the rules was given to maintain an even rhythm and adjust for seasonal differences: 9:50 p.m. corresponds to the first point of the second watch in summer and to the fourth point of the second watch in winter (~9:35–10:05 p.m.). Similarly, in summer, the third point of the fourth watch equals about 2:00 a.m., while in winter, this hour would be during the second point of the third watch. If an even rhythm was indeed the intention of these regulations, sleep time would have been roughly between 10:00 p.m. and 2:00 a.m., that is, a total of four hours. This was to some extent complemented by the lengthy rest and study period after lunch and a shorter optional rest and study period early in the evening on days, without verbal instruction by the abbot. Dōgen's rules for the study hall, however, prevented monks from "lying down or leaning against the boards at the end of the platform, or exposing [. . .] legs and body." Complete physical rest was therefore indeed confined to four hours per day.

The Daily Schedule in Keizan's Monastic Rules

To contextualize the analysis of the rules for daily monastic life laid down in "Method," it is helpful to consider the way they were received and further developed in the *Pure Rules of Keizan* (*Keizan shingi* 瑩山清規), the monastic regulations laid down by the Japanese Sōtō school's "second founder," Keizan Jōkin 瑩山紹瑾 (1268–1325).[24] Its original title, "Sequence of rituals for Tōkoku Yōkō ji in Nōshū,"[25] indicates the document's concern for the proper order and progression of ritual activities in Keizan's monastic mainstay. At the end of the chapter on daily observances, Keizan explicitly references *Method* and various other works by Dōgen that detail proper procedure, including the "Washing the Face" and "Cleansing" (*Senjō* 洗浄) fascicles from the *Treasury*.[26] In spite of these references to precedent, his rules deviate in some aspects from Dōgen's. The first relates to chronography: *Pure Rules of Keizan* is organized around formal temporal units. In its chapter on daily observances (*nitchū gyōji* 日中行事), the text follows the progression of the zodiacal hours, with paragraphs often headed by their name. Similarly, the chapters on monthly and yearly rituals list events according to calendar dates. On the surface of the text, Keizan's rules therefore appear more modern, or at least more conducive in respect to modern reading habits. Their format, however, is not new—a similar document detailing the daily activities of the imperial court exists from the late Heian period.[27] Moreover, Keizan's time units cannot be equated with the homogeneous, metrical units of modern clock-time. In contradistinction to the older Heian court manual just mentioned, we have no evidence that the hours were indeed tied to a specific mode and instrument of measuring. Keizan's was a provincial monastery that in all probability did not command intricate devices like a water clock. This is evident from the way hours are referenced in his text: In two instances, Keizan mentions that during each hour, time is measured by way of burning incense ("when the snake hour's incense comes to its end"; "from half the incense of the monkey until half the incense of the rooster"[28]). Another passage ties the evening hour to the remaining light of day: "The 'hour of the dog' is [begins at?] the time when one can still see the waist of an ant."[29] This points to the use of seasonal hours. In fact, Keizan also correlates the hours with the night watches (*kō*), which are tied to the seasonally changing times of sunset and sunrise. He indicates these correlations with apparent precision: The third point of the first, second, and fourth watch coincides with the mid-hours of the dog, boar, and tiger, respectively. However, this precision is somewhat offset by the fact that the five *kō* are of uneven length: The first watch starts sometime after the beginning of the hour of the dog; the second and fourth are coeval with the hours of the boar and tiger; and the third watch lasts for two zodiacal hours, those of the rat and the ox. These are the designated hours of sleep, where no other activity is supposed to happen.[30] We may conclude that formal time units are not conceived as an independent metric; they are tied to environmental conditions and human actions. In that sense, they do not contradict the "task orientation" that was evident in Dōgen's *Method*; rather, they embody it.

84 | Zen Time

Table 4.2 presents the schedule that can be extrapolated from Keizan's rules. The modern clock-times given below should be read as mere approximations primarily intended to convey the scale of seasonal

Table 4.2. Monastic Daily Schedule according to the *Pure Rules of Keizan*

Zodiacal hour	Other time units	Modern clock-time (approximation)	Activities
Dragon	Morning 早晨	e. 7:00–9:00 a.m. s. 6:30–9:00 w. 8:00–9:50	Presentation of morning meal and offering, breakfast; afterward: recess or formal teaching of abbot in the monks' hall (1st, 5th, 10th, 15th, 20th, and 25th day of the month) and/or sutra chanting (2nd, 3rd, 8th, 13th, 16th, 18th, 28th day).
Snake		e. 9:00–11:00 a.m. s. 9:00–11:40 w. 9:50–11:40	Morning *zazen*
Horse	Lunchtime 斎の時	e. 11:00 a.m.–1:00 p.m. s. 11:40–2:20 w. 11:40–1:30	Midday sutra chanting [= *dharani* chanting] followed by lunch and rest time
Sheep		e. 1:00–3:00 p.m. s. 2:20–5:00 w. 1:30–3:20	*dharma* session: lecture and question and answer with the abbot; [or free/study time]
Monkey	Afternoon 晡時	e. 3:00–5:00 p.m. s. 5:00–7:30 w. 3:20–5:10	Afternoon *zazen* starting after midpoint of the hour of the monkey [~4:00 p.m.].
Rooster		e. 5:00–7:00 p.m. s. 7:30–9:00 w. 5:10–7:20	Afternoon *zazen* continued [around mid-hour of the rooster, ~6:00 p.m.]: formal calling-off of the evening's teaching session with the abbot [or teaching session] followed by sutra [= *dharani*] chanting (~30 minutes; in summer: shorter *dharani* are selected)
Dog	First night watch	e. 7:00–9:00 p.m. s. 9:00–10:20 w. 7:20–9:20	Evening bell, then evening *zazen*; at mid-hour (~8:00 p.m.): concentration bell, monks continue *zazen* or leave the hall

Zodiacal hour	Other time units	Modern clock-time (approximation)	Activities
Boar	Second night watch	e. 9:00–11:00 p.m. s. 10:20–11:40 w. 9:20–11:40	Ringing of fire bell/temple rounds, preparations for sleep-time; by mid-hour (~10:00 p.m.)/3rd point of 2nd watch, monks should be sleeping in the hall (until half-hour of the tiger)
Rat		e. 11:00 p.m.–1:00 a.m. s. 11:40–1:05 w. 11:40–1:50	Sleep; on select days, abbot makes a round of the hall to control for presence
Ox		e. 1:00–3:00 a.m. s. 1:05–2:30 w. 1:50–4:00	Sleep
Tiger	Fourth night watch	e. 3:00–5:00 a.m. s. 2:30–3:50 w. 4:00–6:10	After half-hour of the tiger = 3rd point of 4th watch (from ~4:00 p.m.): rounds of the fire-warning bell, followed by wooden board soundings: monks wake up and start *zazen*, with individual excursions to the washroom; a series of bell and board soundings signals the small breaking of silence; lay practitioners get up
Hare	~Fifth night watch	e. 5:00–7:00 a.m. s. 3:50–6:30 w. 6:10:00–8:00	*Zazen*, abbot enters the hall and makes round, during the end (= final third) of the hour of the hare, after the 5th point of the 5th night watch: great breaking of silence, monks fold their bedding and don the *kesa* and sit facing the isle, get up individually for excursions to the washroom

Table 4.2 explanation: e. = time at equinoctia; s. = time at summer solstice; w. = time at winter solstice; calculation of s. and w. See https://keisan.casio.jp/exec/system/1216973738, March 26, 2019; dates for formal lectures and sutra readings supplemented according to the chapter on monthly observances. Keizan, "Keizan oshō shingi," 265–72.

shifts. Any attempt to be precise in terms of modern clock-time would be anachronistic in relation to a temporal environment that was organized to coordinate actions without reference to an exact measuring device and without demanding that the average inhabitant of a monastery pay attention to smaller units of time. In Keizan's, as in Dōgen's monasteries, signals of considerable duration allowed the monks to prepare and arrive in time at the appropriate place for the scheduled actions.

The time for breakfast, formal lectures (*jōdō* 上堂), and informal evening talks by the abbot are part of this schedule, but are not found in "Method." Since these activities clearly also had their place in Dōgen's monastery, this information may simply be regarded as complementary, showing us how these events were fitted into the daily course of activities. Other items, such as the regular sutra chanting after lunch and the dharma talks in the early afternoon, can be considered an innovation vis-à-vis Dōgen—or, as we will see below, a return to older, more commonly shared traditions. In part, they allot more time for rituals that serve to connect the temple with its patrons. This is in line with the traditional picture of Keizan, who is said to have modified Dōgen's strict *zen* orientation to accommodate popular practices and expectations.[31] On the other hand, the additional dharma talks allow time for the direct encounter between the master and his disciples that was so central to Dōgen. Furthermore, communal seated meditation remains the preeminent ritual practice. If we take the estimates for spring and autumn as a basis, a monk at Keizan's monastery would participate in seven to ten hours of seated meditation every day: from 4:30 to 7:00 a.m., 9:00 to 11:00 a.m., 4:00 to 6:00 p.m., and 7:00 to 8:00 p.m. or 7:00 to 9:30 p.m., with some room for individual discretion in the hours of the early morning and the evening. This is certainly less than in Dōgen's schedule, but it hardly amounts to a dilution of *zazen* practice.

OTHER MONASTIC SCHEDULES

Both Dōgen's and Keizan's rules in general build on earlier documents that were imported from China, most prominently the already mentioned *Pure Rules for Zen Monasteries* by Zongze. The latter's brief chapter on "Signals to the Assembly" (Jp. *keishū* 警衆) shows that the general progression of the day's activities in Dōgen and Keizan is in line with earlier Chinese models.[32] There are, however, slight differences regarding the signals used and the exact timing of certain activities. Significantly, both Dōgen and Keizan are more restrictive on sleep time: The *Pure Rules for Zen Monasteries* has monks get up only at the sounding of the morning bell at the start of the fifth watch (roughly, between 4:00 and 6:00 a.m., depending on the season).³³ However, the *Daily Essentials for Members of the Congregation*—a text in the tradition of Chan master Dahui Zonggao that was compiled in 1209 by Wuliang Zongshou—already states that monks should get up "before the bell of the fifth watch sounds."³⁴ The text further emphasizes that restricting sleep is a hallmark of renunciant life.³⁵ This conforms to what Myōan Eisai in his *Promotion of Zen for the Protection of the Country* reports about the daily schedules in Song period Chan monasteries.³⁶ Keizan's rules may be more relaxed on sleep time than Dōgen's, but they are well within the frame of Zen tradition. The same holds for his instruction that during evening *zazen*, monks are allowed to leave the hall after the sounding of the concentration bell; this rule is also mentioned in the Chinese text.³⁷

The *Daily Essentials for Members of the Congregation* thus proves to be an important source on details of daily activities for Dōgen and Keizan.³⁸ Several injunctions in *Method*—such as to bend one's hip and lower the head when washing the face and not to stand up straight in front of the basin so as to not splash water—are quoted verbatim, others with only minimal changes.³⁹ Ishii Shūdō notes that the Chinese text also strongly informed Dōgen's rules on monastic meals.⁴⁰ A further parallel consists in the repeated prohibitions against laughter, loud voices, or hurried running; and the admonitions to walk softly and speak in a low voice emphasize aesthetic temporal attributes.⁴¹ Notably, references to numerical units of time increase in Dōgen and Keizan, accompanied by a higher degree of specificity in their instructions.

Two other Kamakura-era texts allow us to further assess how representative the chronopolitics in Dōgen's and Keizan's monasteries were for their time. The first was drafted by the Rinzai Zen monk Rankei Dōryū 蘭溪道隆 (Chin. Lanxi Daolong). Rankei belonged to a group of immigrant Zen masters from China who came to prominence in Japan. Under the patronage of the Shōgunal regent Hōjō Tokiyori, he was installed as the founding abbot of Kenchōji in Kamakura.⁴² The document in question bears the (apocryphal) title *Pure Rules for Negotiating the Way by Daikaku zenji, founder of Kenchō*.⁴³ After some introductory words, it succinctly lays out the framework of activities for one diurnal cycle. These instructions are given in full below:

> —During the hour of the tiger, get up and recite the *gāthā*,⁴⁴ then get down from the platform to wash. Dress, burn incense and pay homage to the Buddha. This is to renounce and

repent your karmic hindrances. (This is auxiliary practice.) After that, reach your place and free your spirit.[45] (This is the main practice.[46])—When at dawn it has become possible to discern colors, take your bowl and drink gruel. When the gruel has ended, drink tea. When tea has ended, recite sutras and *dharani* in front of the Buddha. (This is auxiliary practice.) During the hours of the dragon and the snake, reach your place and do *zazen*. (This is the main practice.)—At noon, eat your meal and when that has ended, drink tea. Meet with guests or wash your clothes or have everyone attend together to clean the ground. You may also take up the needle to repair or supplement clothing and other fabrics. When it has turned late afternoon, put on your attire and do *zazen*.—When the sun has gone down, recite sutras for the meals' donors. (This is auxiliary practice.) When darkness has arrived, pay homage before the Buddha. (This is self-practice.) When the obeisances are finished, do *zazen* as before. (This is the main practice.) When the mid-hour of the boar has come, turn your body to face outside, and recite sutras and *dharani*. This may be the chapter on all-sidedness,[47] or the eight-line *dharani*. Turn over the merit according to your wishes. After that, go to sleep, lying on your right side. This is the overall framework of practice for one day and night.[48]

Since Rankei Dōryū is traditionally credited with establishing "pure" Zen, over and against the allegedly more syncretic practices of Enni Ben'en,[49] it is worth noting here how well his time regime for daily activities accords with that of Keizan. In contrast, Dōgen's *Method*, if taken literally, appears as something of an outlier concerning the amount of time it reserves for *zazen*, at the expense of what is described by Rankei as "auxiliary practices." Nonetheless, all sources establish four periods of extensive *zazen*: during the small hours of the morning, between breakfast and lunch, in the late afternoon, and after dark in the evening. It is furthermore remarkable that the Rinzai monk Rankei does not establish a fixed time slot for meetings with the master, although that is an important part of the *kōan* practice traditionally regarded as the hallmark of that school.[50] On the other hand, Rankei offers several options for activities in the early afternoon that are important for the sustenance of monastic life. Some of these, such as washing one's clothes, are also described in the *Daily Essentials for Members of the Congregation*.[51] Perhaps we may conclude that similar activities would take place during this time of day in Dōgen's monasteries as well, as *Method* does not provide detailed prescriptions for the time between lunch and late afternoon *zazen*.

Equally brief texts on daily observances by the Kegon monk Myōe 明恵, famous for his record of dreams, and by *Vinaya*[52] master Shunjō 俊芿, an important member of the Esoteric Precepts School (*Shingon risshū* 真言律宗),[53] allow us to relate the Zen rules considered so far to the practices of other Kamakura-era Buddhist institutions. Myōe's text is the first part of injunctions about appropriate behavior in his monastery Kōzanji. It is titled with his signature expression *arubeki yōwa* ("appropriate conduct") and was originally written on a wooden tablet hung in the Sekisui-in building at Kōzanji.[54] The injunctions are organized around the zodiacal hours starting with the hour of the rooster around sunset. Table 4.3 reconstructs the corresponding schedule.

Table 4.3. Myōe's Daily Schedule

Zodiacal hour	Modern clock-time (approx.)	Activities
Rooster	5:00–7:00 p.m.	Liturgy: *Yuishin kangyō shiki* (Manual on the Practice of Contemplating the Mind-Only)
Dog	7:00–9:00 p.m.	One dharma practice. Chant the *Sambōrai* (Revering the Three Treasures)
Boar	9:00–11:00 p.m.	*Zazen* (seated meditation). Count breaths
Rat, ox, tiger	11:00 p.m.–5:00 a.m.	Rest for three [double-]hours
Hare	5:00–7:00 a.m.	One dharma practice. Perform or omit according to the occasion/time. Liturgy: e.g., *Rishukyō raisan* (Ritual Repentance Based on the Sutra of the Ultimate Meaning of Principle)
Dragon	7:00–9:00 a.m.	*Sambōrai* (veneration of the three treasures). During breakfast, chant sutras and the like and intone the *Kōmyō Shingon* (Mantra of Light) forty-nine times
Snake	9:00–11:00 a.m.	*Zazen*. Count breaths
Horse	11:00 a.m.–1:00 p.m.	Lunch. Chant the *Goji Shingon* (Mantra of the Five Syllables) five hundred times
Sheep	1:00–3:00 p.m.	Study or copy scriptures
Monkey	3:00–5:00 p.m.	Meet with the master and resolve essential matters

Comparing Myōe's rules with the documents discussed reveals a general daily schedule for monastic life that was shared across denominations. Roughly structured by the Buddhist "six times of day," it concerns the sleep-time/wake-time cycle, the timing of meals, and four main practice periods (late night to daybreak, late morning, midday, and evening) that were dedicated to shared ritual activities. Furthermore, *zazen* (seated meditation) was not an exclusive practice of the Zen school. The technique mentioned by Myōe, "counting breath" (*sūsokukan* 数息観), is widely used across Buddhist schools to calm and purify the mind.[55] Myōe here identifies the late morning and late evening as appropriate times for that practice, which coincides with two of the four periods of communal meditation according to the Zen school regulations considered. Similarly, his designation of early afternoon as time for study or the copying of scriptures seems to match in part with Dōgen's and Keizan's ideas, and there is a similar match with Keizan in respect to the time allotted for the recitation of sutras (after breakfast, around lunch) and meetings with the master (late afternoon).

Shunjō's instructions, which are part of his endeavor to reinstate life according to the rules of the *vinaya*, further corroborate these findings. He likewise refers to four practice periods, dedicating the morning to repentance rituals, the midday period to the recitation of sutras (the "Peace and Delight" chapter of the Lotus Sutra or a chapter from the *Ryōgon kyō* 楞厳経[56]), the evening period to sutra contemplation (*junen* 誦念; contemplation of Amida's paradise as depicted in the Amida Sutra), and the two late-night/early morning hours to seated meditation.[57]

These texts thus show a certain common ground in the time regimes of monastic institutions, at least those participating in the general movement of the era, to reinstate monastic discipline. On the other hand, they indicate that the dedication of four extended practice periods per day to communal seated meditation was indeed specific to Zen monasteries.[58] The latter were also—and perhaps by the same token—more restrictive on sleep time. Again, Dōgen's rules appear to take this to an extreme that may have proven unsustainable in the long run. Or, since other texts indicate that Dōgen regularly made space for ritual activities that were not part of its framework,[59] we should read *Method* as picturing a kind of default schedule that was not necessarily implemented on a day-to-day basis and was perhaps followed most strictly during the summer retreat.[60] Before we turn to this kind of evidence and move beyond the diurnal rhythm to the monthly and annual cycles, one further point deserves to be highlighted once more. This is the emphasis in *Method* (and already indicated in the *Daily Essentials for Members of the Congregation*) on timing individual actions in accord with the monastic community. "Zen action," to use the title phrase of a monograph dedicated to its philosophical interpretation,[61] is, in spite of Suzuki Daisetz's famous claim that Zen was "absolutely individualistic,"[62] first and foremost communal action, or action guided by communal rules and synchronized with the actions of fellow practitioners. And this is most strictly the case in Dōgen, with Keizan's and Rankei's rules allowing a little more scope for individual discretion, especially in the early afternoon and late evening. Whatever transcendence of clock-time may be implied in Dōgen's teachings, on a practical level it had to be realized and lived in a strictly defined temporal framework, and while keeping one's movements aligned with those of the monastic community.

The Monthly Cycle

We do not have a document by Dōgen that explicitly spells out regular activities and events during the monthly and yearly cycles. However, inferences can be drawn from his extensive reliance on the *Pure Rules for Zen Monasteries,* from references in his recorded sayings to significant calendar dates, and from his various writings commenting on monastic rules and ritual actions customary in reclusive life. As T. Griffith Foulk has argued, Dōgen's innovation vis-à-vis established rules lay not so much in changing them (*pace* the minor shifts we have seen above) as in tying them up with references to Zen lore and adding comments that imbued them with "spiritual significance."[63] Taken together, this body of evidence indicates that Dōgen strove to implement what was, at the time, regarded as a standard cycle of ritual monastic events: namely, combining Song period Chinese models with established Japanese custom. At the same time, he made certain choices that emphasized his priorities regarding monastic practice and his understanding of orthodoxy and proper lineage in the Buddhist tradition. Furthermore, regular monthly and annual rituals were used to strengthen links between the monastery and its (mostly aristocratic) patrons and to embed the religious institution in the body politic in general. In all these aspects, the monthly and annual schedules reveal strategies of differentiation between "ordinary and extraordinary times" that fit well with the pertinent analysis by sociologist Eviatar Zerubavel. His seminal article "The Language of Time" describes how social order and collective identities are expressed and embedded in day-to-day life by using the combined semantics and syntax of practical chronometry and chronotypology.[64]

An example from Dōgen's informal lecture on "Reading Sutras" illustrates how an annual event of high political significance and extended duration was accommodated into the regular monthly and daily schedule. It further sheds light on the synchronization of these cycles of different scales. Dōgen remarks on the ritual of sutra recitation on the occasion of the emperor's birthday.[65] This ritual had already been introduced to Japan in Myōan Eisai's *Promotion of Zen for the Protection of the Country*, where Eisai lists it as the first of sixteen rituals specific to Zen monasteries.[66] In line with Eisai's provisions, Dōgen explains that the ritual starts one month before the actual birthday. Should that fall on the fifteenth day of the first month, the ritual accordingly would begin on the fifteenth day of the twelfth month. In that case, the formal lecture regularly scheduled for the fifteenth of each month would be canceled.[67] This points to the regular cycle of formal lectures and how it could be superseded, on occasion, by a more important ritual—in this case, one that directly connected monastic religious activities with the political order of the day. For thirty days, from breakfast to lunchtime, a select group of monks was to recite sutras for the sake of the emperor, implying that they did not participate in morning communal *zazen*. A plaque was displayed in the monastery, linking that ritual to the name of the abbot, who would also hold a special congratulatory lecture on the final day, the emperor's birthday. The ritual is identified by Dōgen as an "ancient custom that is unbroken until today."[68] In Keizan's rules, prayers and sutra chanting for imperial longevity are scheduled for the first, second, and fifteenth day of each month, followed by prayers and praise for the monastery's chief patrons on the third and seventeenth days.[69] Keizan thus significantly increased the frequency of rituals that connected the monastic community to its patrons and the body politic, making them a regular part of monthly activities.

The *Pure Rules for Zen Monasteries* stipulate that the formal lectures should be held on the days of the month that are a multiple of five (including the first day).[70] This provision is mirrored in Keizan's rules. Keizan further stresses that the formal lectures on the first and fifteenth day of the month are of particular importance. In contrast, the lectures on the fifth and tenth days may be omitted if required by circumstance.[71] There is consequently a regular five-day rhythm of formal lectures, with accents on the first and fifteenth days of the month. This schedule ensures that there will always be a formal lecture around new moon and on full moon days. That gives occasion to references to the moon as a symbol of enlightenment and helps to tie transcendent truth to the course of natural events. In a lecture given on the fifteenth day of the fifth month in 1246, Dōgen explicitly draws a connection between the lunar cycle and the stages of Buddhist life, with the waxing moon symbolizing aspiration for enlightenment, the full moon enlightenment proper, and the waning moon practice after enlightenment: "Before the fifteenth day (the full moon), if we do not sleep alike at our places in the monks' hall, how can we know that our quilt covering is worn through? After the fifteenth day, when the pivotal wheel has not yet turned, if it turns it certainly will proceed including both sides. Right on the fifteenth day, no matter how green or red the ancient wall, waiting for autumn the crickets sing."[72] Another lecture celebrating the full moon was held on the mid-autumn day in 1251: "Yunmen's sesame cake hangs up in the sky, called the circle of the full moon of autumn. The heavenly lord in blue robes now sits upright. The purity of the clear light will never surpass this splendid occasion."[73] Most lectures in the *Extensive Record* are undated.[74] We therefore cannot be absolutely sure whether the five-day rhythm for formal lectures was ever fully implemented by Dōgen. At least, however, from summer 1246, when his monastery in Echizen was renamed Eiheiji, the number of formal lectures recorded support this assumption.[75]

In *Pure Rules for Zen Monasteries* and *Pure Rules of Keizan*, the five-day metric further applies to the informal lectures. They were scheduled for the days with a three or an eight in their number. *Pure Rules of Keizan* use the same rhythm for head shaving and bathing, to occur on the days with a four and a nine. In the absence of the formal time unit of the week, this metric thus generally served to schedule events that needed to occur regularly four to six times a month (hence leeway is given for omissions on "lesser" iterations of the cycle). Rituals and events to be implemented twice a month—for instance, sutra chanting for imperial longevity, for local deities, or for patrons and donors—followed a fourteen-day cycle (i.e., first and fifteenth, second and sixteenth, third and seventeenth day, respectively).[76]

Taken together, the metric of five- and fourteen-day cycles in Keizan's rules combined to create a rhythm of events with peaks of ritual activities at the beginning and during the middle of the month, and a couple of more or less "empty" days mostly at the end of the month (the sixth, the ninth, the nineteenth, the twenty-third, twenty-sixth, twenty-seventh, and, in long months, the twenty-ninth).[77] This policy not only answered to the basic human need to alternate between activity/significance and rest/triviality. It also emphasized coordination of the religious, the political, and the natural order; as well as a skillful use of the "language of time" to support the religious goals of the institution, its long-term viability, and its embeddedness in the body politic.

The Annual Cycle

In Dōgen's works, links to the secular order are infrequent, although by no means absent. This becomes evident when we turn to the annual cycle. Again, there is no specific document detailing a yearly schedule, but dated lectures on recurring events from the *Extensive Record* provide evidence of the annual rhythm of monastic life. Some of these tied the religious to the mundane annual cycle, imbuing the latter with spiritual significance. Others, such as on Buddhist holidays and select memorial days, served to set out and enact Dōgen's view of the tradition.

Turning Points

To start with a mundane topic, eight formal sermons are recorded with specific reference to the "opening of the fireplace" (*kairo* 開炉) on the first day of the tenth month (roughly: late October to early November). The first two of these sermons were apparently held in 1240 and 1242 at Kōshōji in Kyōto. The remaining six were recorded for every autumn Dōgen spent at Eiheiji.

From this day on and until the beginning of the third month of the following year, the monk's hall was heated by an open hearth fire. As Ōtani Tetsuo remarks, the fire in the hall held special significance in a building style that did almost nothing to protect its inhabitants from the cold outside.[78] It also was a practical measure in line with Dōgen's injunction to shield the place where one sat in meditation from strong external stimuli, such as cold, heat, strong winds, light, full darkness, or noise.[79] Ōtani further observes that Dōgen makes explicit the link between the occasion, practice, and realization in each of the six sermons.[80] The first one he gave at Eiheiji in 1246 may serve as an example:

> In his formal sermon on opening the fireplace, [the master] said: Dig in the earth to search for heaven; meet with sun face and moon face [Buddhas]. Dig a hole in the sky to plant the seed of a lotus that will blossom neither red nor white. Play with Linji's lump of red flesh, and penetrate the width of Xuefeng's ancient mirror. Furthermore, burn up Danxia's wooden buddha, and smelt a hundred times the iron ox at Shanfu. Don't laugh when the cold ash is revived. Return for a while to a warm place and deliberate about this.[81]

In displaying and using Dōgen's command of the tradition to imbue an apparently mundane occasion with highest spiritual significance, this brief discourse is a truly masterful exercise of Zen rhetoric. It also has a strong chronopolitical aspect, as it ties the economical[82] function of the furnace to the continuation of rigorous religious practice while highlighting the current moment's connection to traditional expressions of the quest for enlightenment.

By the very nature of the event, the closing of the fireplace provides less inspiration for such lofty imagery. There accordingly are only two pertinent instructions recorded in the *Extensive Record* (1:122/1243 and 7.489/1252). Nonetheless, the occasion was marked as a special event. Meals on this day would be served personally by the chief temple supervisor (*kan'in* 監院).[83]

Both the opening and closing of the furnace are economical measures; they adjust the built environment to human needs and seasonal climatic conditions. Dōgen takes up the aspect of cyclicity in the second discourse on closing the fireplace, which I have cited at the beginning of this book. A closer look at the original shows that the instruction takes the poetic form of a quatrain with seven characters per line:

一枚圓相向春至 Ichimai no ensō haru ni mukaite itaru
開閉臨時似畫圖 kaihei toki ni nozonde gazu ni nitari
添炭見灰兼點雪 sumi o soe hai o mite, kanete yuki o tenzu
衲僧喚作是紅爐 nōsō yonde, kore, kōro to nasu, to.[84]

(One full circle sheet approaches spring, and arrives
Opening and closing according to the times, it resembles a picture

Stoking with char, watching the ashes, adding a snowflake on top
Patch-robed monks call out, declaring it a furnace.)

The "full circle" addressed in the first line is matched by the complete regularity of the poem's form—but the emphasis on cyclicity is balanced with the paradoxical reference to "adding a snowflake on top": Reaction to the occasion is not limited to simply "going along" with the conditions of the time.

Other turning points in the cycle of the seasons and associated constellations were equally accentuated by Dōgen's designated formal or informal sermons and with personal servings of food by the chief administrator. They included:

- *tango* 端午 / "first horse [day]"[85] (the fifth day of the fifth month), close to the summer solstice (four sermons);

- "mid-autumn day" (*chūshū* 中秋, on the fifteenth day of the eighth month, the day of the traditional moon-viewing festival, nine sermons); as Ōtani remarks, *Extensive Record* vol. 10 further contains several poems by Dōgen on this occasion;[86]

- winter solstice (*tōji* 冬至; five formal and four informal sermons); and, obviously;

- New Year (*saitan* 歳旦; six formal sermons plus five informal sermons on New Year's Eve).

All of these occasions, including the opening and closing of the fireplace, are also mentioned in Keizan's rules. Keizan elaborates on them, often with much detail, in the pertinent chapter on annual ritual performances.[87] We may further add to the list the *tanabata* and *chōkyū* festivals on the seventh day of the seventh month and the ninth day of the ninth month. On these dates, meals were again personally served by the chief supervisor.[88]

In the pertinent discourses recorded in the *Extensive Record*, Dōgen regularly uses his command of Zen rhetoric to connect the mundane to spiritual ends. A typical example is the lecture on the occasion of the winter solstice in 1245. Dōgen first recites an episode from the record of Hongzhi Zhengjue that starts with the observation that on this day, "yin is consummated and yang arises."[89] He continues with several allusions to Chinese Chan lore. Finally he adds his own comments:

This month's auspicious occasion of the first yang is [commonly likened to the way] a noble person reaches maturity. Even though this is an auspicious period for secular people, it is in truth also a joyful support for Buddhas and ancestors. Yesterday, the line of the shortest day passed. Yin reached completion and grindingly came to a halt. This morning, the [cycle toward] the line of the longest day arrived.[90] Yang emerged, bustling and making a lot of noise. This is a happy support for patch-robed monks. Correspondingly, Buddhas and ancestors dance in congratulation. At once, they transcend the realms of the King of Emptiness and Awesome Sound[91]—how could they be tied to the seasons of spring and autumn, winter and summer? To achieve this way of seeing things is the life vein of the wise and holy, and the liver and kidneys of humans and heavenly beings. But it does not yet capture the nostrils of Śākyamuni's sermons or the eyeballs of Mahākaśyapa entering nirvana. You people, do you want to understand the occasion of this auspicious morning?" Drawing a circle with his whisk, he said: "Look!" And after a good while: "Even if plum blossoms amid the snow are clear, here we further inquire into the arrival of the first yang."[92]

A master conductor of mental time travel, within the space of a few lines, Dōgen has led his assembly from the current occasion to transcendent realms and back. We will come back to the doctrinal implications later. In practical terms, the gist of this discourse seems again to be an exhortation to heed the conditions of the time but not to let oneself be caught up in them, while also avoiding aloofness. This is certainly not a sermon that simply teaches living in harmony with the rhythms of nature. It breaks synchrony by anticipating the result (summer solstice) in the first instance of movement (the first day of growing light after the winter solstice). It furthermore ties the result (enlightenment) back to the conditions of the moment (plum blossoms amid snow, meaning continued practice in the harsh conditions of the wintery mountains, and sustained engagement with the spiritual meaning of natural cycles). Furthermore, this integrative movement allowed the monastic community to coordinate its rituals with the secular calendar. In this fashion, monastic life retained its distinctions while synchronizing its rhythm with the community of lay supporters, who would expect elevated ritual on certain occasions.

Memorial Days

Seasonal turning points and occasions like the opening and closing of the fireplace accentuated the natural and social cycle of the year. To these were added a number of dates of particular religious significance. Some of them commemorated events of importance to all Buddhist communities, such as the pivotal dates of Śākyamuni's life: "bathing the Buddha" (*yokubutsu* 浴仏), in celebration of his birth on the eighth day of the fourth month; "enlightenment day assembly" (*jōdōe* 成道会), named after its date, the eighth day of the twelfth month as *rōhatsu* 臘八;[93] and the "Parinirvana assembly" (*nehan e* 涅槃会), the day of Buddha's passing, on the fifteenth day of the second month.[94] The opening and closing days of the summer retreat (fifteenth day of the fourth and seventh months) may also be counted among dates of general importance to Buddhist monastic communities.[95] They framed the arguably most important period in annual monastic life, which we will return to later.

There also were a small number of memorial days dedicated to teachers with whom the abbot, and by extension the monastery, claimed a special connection. Here we can see a politics of memory that located the community within the ideological and social space of Buddhist schools. The *Extensive Record* records formal sermons on memorial days for Dōgen's own teachers Myōzen (on the twenty-seventh day of the fifth month) and Rujing (on the seventeenth day of the seventh month), as well as for Myōzen's teacher Eisai (on the fifth day of the seventh month), all of which coincided with their recorded death days.[96] The decision to memorialize Myōzen and Eisai—both of whom belonged to a Rinzai lineage—is significant because it provides counter-evidence to the literature that has criticized Dōgen for championing Sōtō sectarianism in his later years. It also fits well with discourses such as 7.493, held in the spring of 1252, which states that the designation "Zen school" (and, by implication, subdivisions within it) is meaningless and exhorts monks to refrain from ranking Buddhist schools.[97]

Keizan's rules retain the annual memorial for Rujing[98] but omit those for Myōzen and Eisai. Instead, Keizan established monthly memorials for Dōgen (on the twenty-eighth) and Ejō (on the twenty-fourth). His own teacher Tettsu Gikai received a monthly memorial on the fourteenth and a more elaborate annual memorial on the same day of the ninth month.[99] These memorial days traced a direct, single line from Rujing, via the founder of Eiheiji and his two earliest successors, to Keizan. As a consequence, they elevated the status of Keizan and his monastery as proper continuations of this line, even though Keizan never became abbot of Eiheiji.[100] Also, and in contrast to Dōgen, no patriarchs from the Linji/Rinzai lines received such ritual attention. This reinforced on a ritual level the establishment of a Japanese Sōtō school with a distinct and exclusive lineage consciousness.

CENTERING PRACTICE

To return to Dōgen, there are two groups of formal sermons in the *Extensive Record* that shed further light on his chronopolitics. The first are six lectures given on the first day of the ninth month, all of which emphasize continued practice of seated meditation.[101] The initial one was held in 1246. It explains (possibly with an eye to the large number of newcomers) that Dōgen's Eiheiji does not conform to the custom of relaxing the meditation schedule in the late eighth month or on the fifth day of each month. This is in line with the above evidence concerning the time dedicated to seated meditation in the daily schedule. On all three temporal scales of the day, month, and year, these time regimes echo Dōgen's view that seated meditation is not just a means to achieve enlightenment, but the actual performance of highest insight.[102] The last sermon of the group makes this connection explicit by taking up Dōgen's signature phrase "body and mind dropped off" (*datsuraku shinjin* 脱落身心) and thus points to full realization of enlightenment in seated meditation.[103]

The second group consists of formal and informal sermons that Dōgen held after Enlightenment Day in the twelfth month. They express gratitude to outgoing officers or welcome newly appointed ones[104] and indicate that important functions in the monastery were usually limited to a one-year term. Ishii Seijun, who has highlighted this group of texts, has connected them to passages from *Pure Rules of Eternal Peace* that emphasize collective decision-making among the temple officers and a spiritual rather than political role of the abbot. This, Ishii argues, is in contrast to Chinese monastic regulations, where temple officers, including abbots, held more individual discretionary power, and appointments were made by the government; this gave especially the abbot's office a more political character. Ishii concludes that Dōgen carefully revised customary practices to shield monastic affairs from political interference and to avoid individual accumulation of power in the monastery. Ishii's point is pertinent, even if his labeling of Eiheiji's mode of organization as "democratic" (*minshuteki* 民主的) may be exaggerated, since we have no evidence that officers were selected by community vote.¹⁰⁵ We can therefore see annual terms of office as a chronopolitical element in an effort to establish the monastery as a social space centered on religious practice and free from secular hierarchies and power wrangling.

As mentioned above, the change of offices was scheduled in the twelfth month between Enlightenment Day and New Year. It was part of a peak period of events with particular significance, which started with the winter solstice and celebrated both completion (Enlightenment Day) and rejuvenation (growth of yang, changes of office, New Year).¹⁰⁶ The second peak was mid-term and consisted of the summer retreat and associated events, which lasted from the first half of the fourth month to the second half of the seventh month.

THE SUMMER RETREAT

For Dōgen, this latter period was even more important than the series of events connected to the change of seasons and years in winter. He placed the retreat on a par with "the ancient turning of the dharma wheel" and the "ancient Buddhas and ancestors"¹⁰⁷ and discussed its details extensively in the *Treasury* chapter "Summer Retreat" (*Ango* 安居). The duration of the retreat was ninety days, from the fifteenth day of the fourth month to the fifteenth day of the seventh month, but preparations started earlier. "Summer Retreat" explains that clerics who wanted to participate in the retreat needed to arrive during the last days of the third month. From the first day of the fourth month onward, renunciants should no longer go on pilgrimages or visit other temples, and the monastery closed its gates. The community was to live in reclusion from that day on.¹⁰⁸ Conversely, this tells us that new members would regularly join the community during the third month, some only for the retreat and others to stay more permanently. Incidentally, in the final part of the fascicle, Dōgen mentions that not only ordained renunciants, but also lay practitioners of both sexes were invited to join the community for the summer retreat.¹⁰⁹ This constitutes further evidence against a more sectarian/cleric-centered approach in his final years.

During the next days of the preparatory period, temple officials were to examine the clerical participants' certificates to establish their legitimacy and dharma age (counting from the year in which they received the precepts).¹¹⁰ A preliminary list ("precept year roster," *kairō* 戒臘) in regular script was to be displayed at mealtime and in the afternoon of the third to fifth days, giving participants the time to verify, add previously held positions, and point out necessary corrections. The emended final roster was to be displayed on the fifteenth day.[111] The degree of precision with which these procedures and documents are described in "Summer Retreat" (and further detailed in Keizan's rules) points to the importance of establishing everyone's proper position in the community, which was organized as a hierarchy based on dharma age and rank.[112] Note, however, that Dōgen discouraged those who had held offices in insignificant temples from using their titles and pointed to precedents where such persons contented themselves with subaltern functions.[113] His paradigm for the list shows that, in accordance with monastic customs already in place in India,[114] dharma age took precedence over the track record of clerical offices. Notwithstanding the universalistic appeal to male and female renunciants and lay practitioners alike to join the retreat, the community during that event was by no means a community of equals. Hierarchy was important and determined the behavior expected of everyone. In spatial terms, it translated into the location of one's allotted place in the monks' hall. Primarily, one's position was determined by the number of dharma years completed (i.e., a numerical temporal factor requiring the counting of time). This was in contrast to other Kamakura-era monasteries, which placed more weight on descent or previous office and rank.

The following parts of "Summer Retreat" describe in detail the rituals performed leading up to the formal start of the retreat and at its end. These include[115] in the fourth month, on the eighth day, the celebration of the birth of the Buddha; on the thirteenth day, in the afternoon, a tea ceremony and sutra recitation in the respective dormitories (*shuryō* 衆寮); in the evening, a ritual offering with incantation at the shrine of the local guardian deity, followed by a serving of hot water or tea (*tentō* 点湯; *sentō* 煎湯) in the monks' hall; on the fifteenth day, a formal visit to the abbot's quarters by senior temple officials, incantations of Buddha names, and a formal sermon by the abbot, followed by a ritual exchange of greetings and entreaties between the abbot, supporting monastic officials, and various groups of followers and disciples. Here again, differentiation according to status and affiliation determines proper procedure. Furthermore, a comment on the location of the various groups in the hall reveals that lay patrons were invited to the ceremony, which they witnessed from a section in the hall that was separated by bamboo curtains.[116] The day closed with a formal visitation of all monastic quarters by the abbot and mutual visits and greetings between officials and practitioners who shared the same dharma lineage or had previously spent summer retreats together. Senior monks and monastic officials offered tea and refreshments on this occasion.

As indicated above, the main part of the retreat is not described in "Summer Retreat," but we may assume that the days followed the schedule described in "Method," probably with meditation periods extended to their maximum. The closing of the event involved basically the same sequence of rituals as the opening, with changes of wording where appropriate. Hence, on the thirteenth day of the seventh month, the heads of the dormitories served an offering of tea/hot water to the respective assemblies and oversaw a sutra recitation ceremony. On the evening of the fourteenth, an incantation was held at the shrine of the local guardian deity; and on the fifteenth, the formal lecture, followed by the exchange of greetings, the abbot's visitation of the various quarters, and tea offerings with mutual felicitations. In chronographical as well as chronopolitical terms, it is important to note that the words of greeting by the abbot contained a formula stating that the dharma year had now "come full circle" (*hassui shuen* 法歲周圓).[117] As we have seen above, this implies that all participants had moved up one year in rank.

The remainder of the fascicle restates an argument already made in its introduction: that the practice of the summer retreat contains and preserves the essence of the Buddha's teaching and insight. Both in the beginning and the end of the fascicle, this is connected to contemplations on its temporality. The first part of "Summer Retreat" reflects on the retreat's duration of ninety days and its relation to cosmic time; here, Dōgen emphasizes that the number of days is simply a technical device; the substance of that period, however, transcends that measure and allows quantitative comparisons even with cosmic eons: "The rest of times is submerged in the waves of hundreds, thousands, immeasurable eons. However, since the ninety days exhaust the waves of hundreds, thousands, immeasurable eons, they may come to see Buddha in the ninety days, but the ninety days do not depend on their waves."[118] The final part of the fascicle in turn emphasizes the continuity of practice and transmission. The summer period of intensive seated meditation in reclusion was observed by all Buddhas and patriarchs, including the Buddhas of past eons, and all the patriarchs that constitute the line of transmission up to Dōgen.[119] He concludes:

> In all truth, the retreat was shared by every heir in personal encounter from those during Buddha's time in this world

onwards. Therefore, the face of the Buddha and the faces of the ancestors came to be directly and rightly transmitted, and their bodies and minds were bound and witnessed. This is why we say to see the retreat is to see Buddha, to witness the retreat is to witness Buddha, to practice the retreat is to practice Buddha, to sense the retreat is to sense Buddha, to undergo the retreat is to explore Buddha.[120]

The above-mentioned ranked list of participants expresses this identity of the actual community of practitioners with those of the Buddhas and patriarchs: The first name in the list, preceding the abbot, is Jinnyo sonja 陣如尊者, the "Venerable Ājñātakauṇḍinya," who was purportedly the first disciple of Śākyamuni.[121] The list, however, also reminds us that, even if the identity in essence with Buddhas and patriarchs was reached within the retreat, social distinctions between practitioners remained. In ideological terms, this somewhat paradoxical stratification among persons who were supposedly one with the Buddhas and patriarchs can be connected to Dōgen's simile in "Actualizing the *kōan*," which equates enlightenment to the reflection of moonlight in the water:

Enlightenment is like the moon reflected on the water. The moon does not get wet, nor is the water broken. Although its light is wide and great, the moon is reflected even in a puddle an inch wide. The whole moon and the entire sky are reflected in dewdrops on the grass, or even in one drop of water. Enlightenment does not divide you, just as the moon does not break the water. [The limit of the] human person does not restrict enlightenment, just as [limits of the] drops and dew do not restrict the moon in the sky. Still, the depth [of the water] may be seen as the measure of the height [of the moon]. The length or shortness of time probes the large or small quantity of the water, and distinguishes the broad or narrow width of the moon and the sky.[122]

The Social Meaning of Time

The topic of stratification according to "dharma age" brings us to the subject of the social meaning of time or, in other words, the question of how time in Dōgen's community served to establish and express distinct social relations. The "precept year roster" in "Summer Retreat" can serve as a starting point because it exemplifies both aspects: First, the practice, traditionally shared by Buddhist monastic communities, of ranking members according to the number of years since they received the precepts.[123] Second, the mode of expressing this rank by spatio-temporal sequence; in this case, by mentioning successive groups in descending order of rank.[124] Note that important temple offices are apparently held by those high in dharma age, indicating that the principle of seniority applied, at least as a principle of eligibility, in the selection of higher-ranking monastics.

Other passages in "Summer Retreat" reveal how distinctions in rank translated into temporal (mostly chronometric) aspects of behavior. For example, the principle "temporal precedence equals seniority in rank" was embodied by the order in which monks entered the hall during the formal opening of the retreat. "The head monk leads the assembly into the hall, they circumambulate it and stand at their place [in order] according to the precept year roster."[125] The same ritual, however, also exemplifies the reverse principle of "augmentation by succession": the chief officers enter, once again according to rank, after the assembly has settled in their places. The abbot enters last, when everyone else has assumed their position. As a whole, these seemingly conflicting principles of temporal ordering are in line with an observation made by Zerubavel in his above-mentioned article on the "language of time": "While we normally regard temporal precedence as virtually synonymous with priority (and would indeed be quite correct in assuming that the leading stories in radio and television news magazines are also the most important ones), the order in which speakers are usually introduced at formal ceremonies seems to suggest that last is not always least."[126] The apparent paradox is easily explained when the characteristics of the actions in question are taken into account. To once more quote Zerubavel: "Just as we associate long 'positive' stretches of time (such as interacting with desirable others) with high priority and importance, we tend to associate long 'negative' stretches of time with insignificance. *Waiting*, for example (which, given the modern utilitarian approach to time [. . .] is generally regarded as an ordeal), is normally associated with worthlessness, and making others wait is often regarded as a symbolic display of degradation."[127] In other words, and relating to our example: Within the group of the general monastic assembly, the more important, higher-ranking members will enter the ritual space first, while the others are made to wait outside. Once everyone is at their place, the group as a whole is made to wait for the senior officials. The ritual proper starts when the abbot (the highest-ranking person) has assumed his proper position in the hall.[128]

Variations of this principle are evident in another document related to the summer retreat, the *Rules for Facing Senior Expert Practitioners of More than Five Summers*.[129] This document, drafted one year before the *Treasury*'s "Summer Retreat" in the late spring of 1243, enumerates, in fairly unsystematic fashion, sixty-two rules for behavior toward senior monks. Rule 15 explains who falls into that category: "Those who have completed five summer retreats or more are ranked as *ajari* [instructors], and those who underwent ten or more are ranked as *oshō* [personal teachers]."[130] Note that the principle of social ranking used here is similar to that of the "dharma age," but instead of the *duration* of time passed since ordination, the criterion now is the *iteration* of summer training periods. Formally, this points to a third chronometric element (besides duration and sequence) that may be used in establishing and expressing social distinctions.[131] On a material level, the criterion served to establish a hierarchy based on commitment to sustained meditative practice and not simply on the mere passing of time. This was a pertinent and dexterous choice with regard to the makeup of Dōgen's assembly because prior to the move to Echizen, the community had been joined by a significant number of followers from the lineage of Dainichibō Nōnin, who allegedly identified enlightenment with the ordinary workings of the mind and thus denied the necessity of adherence to monastic rules and practice.[132] In this situation, the ranking of Dōgen's community members according to their actual experience (quantified by the number of iterations of the summer retreat) had three functions: First, it ensured that those in a position to instruct junior monks were indeed committed to sustained meditative practice and adherence to monastic rules. Second, as a corollary, Daruma shū adherents who had not participated in summer retreats before joining Dōgen would be excluded from such positions. Third, the rule demonstrated to outsiders that the community was serious in its spiritual and ethical commitments and not a bunch of happy-go-lucky antinomians.[133]

As for the temporal details of proper behavior toward seniors, Rule 30 most clearly expresses the principle of adequately correlating the attributes of an action and its proper sequencing with respect to the social ranking of those involved: "When in the presence of a senior, precede them in attending to disagreeable tasks and let them go first in those things that are pleasant."[134] Rules 38 to 41 spell out that principle in detail, preventing juniors from sleeping, eating, bathing, and sitting before seniors do.[135] Rules 48 and 49, which prohibit finishing one's meal and standing up earlier than the senior,[136] do not contradict this principle. Instead, they point to a complementary one: seniors take precedence (which would in itself also explain Rules 38 to 41) and can make juniors wait.

Other rules demand proper posture and demeanor. Several (Rules 3, 4, 6) instruct acolytes to stand at attention until granted permission to sit down (which may be seen as an application of the principle expressed in Rule 30) and to maintain a dignified position when seated (Rules 16, 22, 50, 55). Others ensure that seniors are spared potentially unpleasant sights such as having to watch monks pick lice, blow their noses, or yawn; even necessary activities such as cleaning one's mouth or shaving one's head should be avoided in the presence of superiors (Rules 9–11, 37). Similarly, several rules aim to prevent exposure to noise (including loud sutra reading, Rule 24) or untoward talk (Rules 34, 44). Incidentally, some employ a "language of space" to express deference, which translates universal metaphors such as "higher is mightier, lower is inferior"[137] into embodied performance (Rules 14, 16, 56). Taken together, they characterize time spent in the presence of a senior as time demanding special composure and painstakingly "pure" conduct, in contrast to "ordinary" time spent among peers. Conversely, this meant that seniors needed to ensure they left junior members of the assembly to themselves at times so that they could relax and perform certain necessary but aesthetically unfavorable activities.

A contrasting issue is that of access to seniors and, most importantly, to the abbot. After all, the abbot in Zen monasteries claimed legitimation as a "dharma heir," which placed him in a direct, uninterrupted line of transmission to the patriarchs and the Buddhas of the past. This was eminently so for Dōgen, as expressed in his "document of succession," which displays the names of all patriarchs in a circle around that of Śākyamuni, with those of the first and the latest patriarchs (Kaśyapa and, in this case, Dōgen) side by side at the bottom.[138] Note that the document visualizes both temporal succession and the immediate, intimate, and time-transcending relation of each patriarch with the Buddha. It is thus an important expression of the way in which Dōgen strove to configure history and the perception of his own relation to the past.

Time and again, Dōgen stressed the importance of face-to-face meetings with an authorized master (like himself) as a means to probe and validate any claims to insight. His emphasis on this issue is again closely connected to the presence of Daruma shū followers in his congregation because the founder of that lineage, Dainichibō Nōnin, had not had direct contact with a legitimate Zen master. In the same year when he wrote the *Rules for Facing Senior Practitioners* discussed above, Dōgen drafted the main text of "Conferral of the Face-to-Face Transmission" (*Menju* 面授, short: "Conferral") of the *Treasury*. Further additions were made in the following year. They conveyed a considerably polemical tone, which indicates that this continued to be a contested issue in his community.[139] The following passage, which links the topic both to Dōgen's personal record and to a tradition of purportedly cosmic dimensions, perhaps best exemplifies the essence of his view:

> On the first day of the fifth month in the first year of the Baoqing era, a yin-wood rooster year, [I,] Dōgen first offered incense and prostrations to the late master Tiantong [= Rujing], the old Buddha, at the abbot's quarters, and the late master, the old Buddha, first saw [me,] Dōgen. Conferring his teaching face-to-face, he spoke: "The Buddhas and patriarchs have actualized access to the dharma in face-to-face conferral. It is identical with holding up a flower at Vulture Peak, attaining the marrow at Songshan, transmitting the robe at Huangmei, and Dongshan's conferring of the face.[140] This is the Buddhas' and patriarchs' face-to-face conferral of the treasury of the eye. It only exists in my house. Other people haven't even seen or heard of it in their dreams."
>
> This norm of face-to-face conferral entails that Shākyamuni received and preserved the face-to-face transmission from the assembly of Kaśyapa Buddha, which is why it is the face of the Buddhas and patriarchs. If it weren't transmission from the Buddha's face, it wouldn't be [the face of] all Buddhas.[141]

Once more, we see how the essentially linear notion of transmission through an unbroken succession of generations turns back on itself to emphasize the identity of each instance with the essence of the Buddha and his insight. All this means that for the aspiring acolyte, the opportunity for face-to-face meetings with a master who was a legitimate heir to the dharma was of paramount importance. Attendance at his formal and informal lectures would not suffice, because these were collective events and would not normally provide occasion for the master to "see" the disciple. How, then, was access to individual meetings regulated and organized? Again, we do not have a document from Dōgen or the monasteries directly associated with him. Some inferences, however, may be drawn from the *Pure Rules for Zen Monasteries*, which he referred to extensively in other matters, and from Keizan's rules, which in any case open a window on later Sōtō school practices.

The pertinent section on "Entering the [abbot's] quarters" (Chin. *rushi*, Jp. *nisshitsu* 入室) in the former indicates that interviews with the abbot were to be scheduled on a regular basis. Nevertheless, the text leaves a good deal of discretion concerning the way this was organized: "Appointments to meet with the abbot in his quarters are sometimes arranged section by section [i.e., the various daises in the monks' hall] or quarter by quarter. Sometimes they are scheduled for every other day or fixed on a certain day, with some appointments in the morning and some in the evening. Whatever arrangement is chosen depends on the abbot."[142] Disciples thus gained access to the abbot as part of a group. While they entered the abbot's room individually, time allotted to each individual was confined to the exchange of one question and answer, and they were exhorted to not make the other members of the group wait by unnecessarily prolonging the conversation. Furthermore, the frequency of such an interview depended on the size of the monastery's population. But the overall idea in *Pure Rules for Zen Monasteries* is that accepted members of the congregation should receive regular individual guidance and monitoring of their spiritual progress.

Keizan's rules convey a similar arrangement. In his monthly schedule, he enters individual interviews on the seventh, twelfth, and twenty-second day of each month, with group interviews (where the leading monks of the groups conduct the dialogue with the abbot) on the preceding days. However, he also remarks in the entry on the twelfth day that individual interviews may be set up only once per month (probably on the twelfth day) on a regular basis and three times per month during the summer retreat.[143] In any case, the formal scheduling and tight temporal frame of these interviews underlined their importance.[144] Note also that there was a three- to four-day succession of formal lecture, group meetings, individual interviews, and perhaps also informal instructions (*jishū*, scheduled in *Pure Rules for Zen Monasteries* on the days including the numbers 3 or 8). This succession would give the abbot the chance to establish a topic for reflection and discussion, emphasize its general points, receive individual thoughts and questions, and then possibly expand on selected aspects in an informal lecture.

While ordinary members of the community thus were allowed to speak to the master individually one to three times per month and for a couple of minutes only, select disciples would get access on a less restricted basis. The maximum—free access irrespective of the time of day and night—is a privilege Dōgen himself claims to have received from his teacher Rujing on the grounds of a formal, written application.[145] It is conceivable that he granted similar access to trusted disciples such as Kōun Ejō or Yōkō Senne 永興詮慧, who later became his dharma heirs, and that such permission established a relation of intimacy that would foreshadow eventual succession in the dharma.

Control and Commitment

If we apply the information on the time regimes in place in Dōgen's and early Sōtō monasteries to the question of control over monastics' time, it follows that the core community of ordained renunciants would command a considerable degree of cognitive control but only a low degree of actual discretion. In other words, they would (or at least could) know what general course of events to expect in the course of a day, a month, and a year, but the details of the schedule would be mostly decided for them. A system of written announcements and acoustic signals then ensured that they knew what was immediately ahead. Some room for variation (and, thus, surprise) existed regarding the actual length of *zazen* sessions and the scheduling of individual interviews with the abbot. In Dōgen's monasteries—especially in Eiheiji, where his ideas on monastic organization were most fully developed—individual discretion on the use of time during an ordinary day mostly extended to the roughly three-hour period between lunch and afternoon *zazen*. Keizan's monasteries, as well as those of Rankei Dōryū, allowed additional room for discretion in the evening. In all cases, when collective action, ritual or otherwise, was called for, temporally extended acoustic signals ensured that ordinary practitioners could be in place without a large amount of previous planning—this being the prerogative and duty of senior temple officers.

To be part of the monastic community thus required commitment to a rhythm of activities that was to a large degree fixed beforehand. Its details were mostly decided by temple authorities and not by individual renunciants themselves. On the other hand, it was possible to know the general course of events ahead of time. Furthermore, the spiritual meaning of each action, and of commitment to the schedule, would be repeatedly explained and emphasized. Once they had memorialized the pertinent routines, practitioners could simply react to the various acoustic signals and follow the movements of the community these called for by focusing on the action at hand. Ideally (and this was clearly the vision Dōgen wanted his community to share) this would incite them to be aware in each moment that they were leading the lives of Buddhas and patriarchs. Each action was meant to be understood as a realization of enlightened insight, an opportunity to perpetuate and deepen its presence in the world. Once again, we find here the practical application of the concept of "what is:time"—in terms of negotiating each instance as part of the life-course of an enlightened being.

To enable this spiritual orientation, a clear boundary had to be drawn between monastic life and all secular aspirations, actions, and modes of thought; on a political plane, this meant establishing Eiheiji unambiguously as a monastery for reclusive monks and nuns (*tonseisō* 遁世僧/*tonseini* 遁世尼).[146] This aspect is highly visible in a document on nine fundamental restrictions that applied to members of Eiheiji's monastic congregation.[147] Its articles serve to ensure that resident renunciants were engaged neither in secular affairs nor in religious functions that demanded their presence in places outside the monastery, be they secular or sacred. The document was apparently submitted to the court and the Kamakura military government in 1250 to receive official permission concerning its content.[148] Specifically, it forbade Eiheiji's monks from acting as guardian monks (*gojisō* 護持僧) for high-ranking persons, to initiate or participate in litigation, to promote patronage for their own or other temples, or to associate with other renunciants for economic gain.[149] Apart from precluding a commitment to secular gain and profit, the aim of the provisions was to protect and prevent members of the community from time-consuming engagements that would necessitate separation from the activities of the congregation. An official sanctioning of the articles—which is not documented—would have shielded Eiheiji residents from any such demands.

These measures are perhaps best understood as the outward defense in Dōgen's attempt to establish Eiheiji as a temporal sphere where life was completely in accord with his vision of the life of Buddhas and patriarchs. A similar intention is visible in various internal regulations prohibiting engagement in secular affairs within the monastery. His admonitions for the study hall/dormitory (*shuryō* 衆寮)[150] are exemplary in this regard.

Having exhorted students to consult and live in accord with the *vinaya* tradition and the rules of the Zen school, it contains numerous provisions on matters of propriety for communal life in the hall, where monks studied, copied sutras, and perhaps also slept on occasion. Notably, Dōgen found it necessary to exhort members of the congregation to not store weapons or treasuries and to refrain from consumption of alcohol, meat, and other prohibited foods.[151] Further injunctions specifically prohibit all involvement with secular affairs: Monks should not "hold meetings with traders, doctors, experts of divination or other disciplines,"[152] "stick their heads together for idle talk or shameless laughter,"[153] "discuss social affairs, matters of fame and gain, political disturbances, or the rough or polished [habitus] of their companions in the assembly,"[154] or "keep secular literature, books on astronomy and geomancy, the treatises of outlying ways, or handscrolls of Chinese or Japanese poetry."[155]

A short document containing five "Rules for Eiheiji's Kitchen"[156] is illuminating in its attempt to prevent the encroachment of profit seeking on monastic life. Its first and fourth rules state:

- If a patron donates meals for the *sangha*, the money should be used to buy rice; if rice from the monastery's stores is used, measure the amount used and quickly buy the same amount of rice to replace it. You should not use the money for other purposes.

- Do not use the community's rice for giving loans to this or that person.

In other words, the persons in charge should not treat donations as an economic means from which to gain a maximum of utility. They should not attempt to buy rice when it was cheap, but simply accept the current price at the time of the donation. Similarly, they should not lend out rice from the monastery's storehouses. Taking advantage of the change in price or the accumulation of interest over time would mean to treat time as an economic resource. This manner of using time for economic gain was well established in medieval monasteries,[157] or else Dōgen would not have had to impose the prohibition in question. Eiheiji, however, was not meant to become an affluent institution; it was meant to entrust itself to support from donors and patrons attracted by its single-minded dedication to spiritual purposes. Even if the heading of the document displays the intention to regulate future behavior by stating that the following are "items to be firmly adhered to from now on,"[158] this was done precisely to prevent even the slightest profit-seeking "colonization of the future" from structuring monastic attitudes toward time.

Conclusion

In the preceding pages, we have reviewed the daily, monthly, and annual rhythms of renunciant life in Dōgen's monasteries, in comparison to those of his contemporaries and successors, along with the interpretation they received in the relevant sources. We have further explored the social and political language of time that was employed in this context. We are now well prepared to return to our initial questions concerning the temporal orientation and perspective prevalent in Dōgen's organization and doctrinal explanation of monastic life.

To start with a point that is striking in light of the prescriptive character of many of the sources reviewed, it seems remarkable how little concern they have exhibited for the future. Naturally, all setting of rules is an attempt to bind what lies ahead to present intentions or, to put it differently, to tie the future to its past. As we have seen in Dōgen's rules for Eiheiji's kitchen, cited above, this goal was clearly acknowledged and even firmly stated along with the content of the regulation in question. Apart from that, however, and in terms of content, the future does not figure prominently in the documents explored. Specifically, there appears a certain tendency to discourage planning for the future, which is also visible in the general division of labor regarding the cognitive and practical keeping of time. Planning was the duty of higher monastic officials. They were expected to "know the time" in a larger perspective, including oversight of clocks, and to decide on the details of the congregation's schedule. Ordinary renunciants, in contrast, were encouraged to focus on the activities present at hand and their spiritual significance; these were to be carried out according to preestablished patterns. By living life according to the precedents set by Buddhas and patriarchs, renunciants would apply and actualize their insight and thus participate in their enlightenment. Dedicating themselves to the negotiation of examples set in the past, they would, in this sense, find in them the model of their own future. At least, that is the salvific vision entertained by Dōgen and extolled in his winter solstice lecture of 1245.

In contrast to the future, the past therefore dominates the temporal imagination and guides practical activities in the monastery. This is most visible in Dōgen's formal lectures. Here we see him time and again connect the actual occasion to the words and actions of past masters in order to imbue it with a trans-temporal meaning. Looking to the past and actualizing what was instituted within it as the right dharma is, therefore, the practically dominant temporal orientation. In terms of time's morphology, this results in an ever-expanding circle where every moment is in direct contact with the center. This morphology is graphically expressed in Dōgen's document of succession. Its red line, running from Śākyamuni in the center through the names of the first and all following "ancestors" to Dōgen and back to the center, exemplifies how the trans-temporality of the Buddha Dharma is practically sustained through its instance-to-instance actualization.

On the other hand, the imagination of history is not completely absorbed in this even, circular pattern. The selection of memorial days highlights specific events and, as a politics of memory, maintains a shared core with other Buddhist schools while underlining specific lineage connections. Furthermore, commemoration of the turning points in Śākyamuni Buddha's life was shared among Buddhist institutions. Other memorials Dōgen introduced late in his life emphasize his personal connections to certain teachers, independent of their respective lineage affiliations. With Keizan, we have seen a growing sense of Sōtō school identity, highlighting the line extending from Rujing via Dōgen and subsequent abbots of the Eiheiji.

The importance of the past notwithstanding, the present is the locus where the past is to be actualized by aligning each activity at hand with established precedent. Within the division of labor mentioned above, the ordinary members of the community are enjoined to concentrate on performing the prescribed action of the moment in accord with each other. As we have seen in the analysis of "Method," this attitude is expressed in a "task-oriented" mode of writing that was designed to translate into a corresponding orientation in daily monastic life. The aspects of time that matter within this orientation are typological rather than metrical. Given that the schedule and progression of activities were already decided and announced by acoustic signals of considerable duration, attention was directed toward appropriate timing, speed, and, in general, the creation of a calm and smooth flow to support the community as a whole. To reiterate, this does not mean that formal, numeric chronometry was absent from monastic time and temporal imagination. However, it was the task of monastic superiors to be in command of this aspect and to put it into the service of the highly ritualized communal life. Knowledge of the clock and the calendar was therefore used to ensure coherence within the community and to synchronize its actions with the natural and social environment. The formal lectures recorded in *Extensive Record* contain numerous examples of how this coordination could be employed to enhance and deepen the religious significance of the moment at hand while at the same time embedding the monastic community in a larger social space. It is thus probably no mere coincidence that we found in Keizan an increase both in numeric metrical chronography and in the number of rituals that served to connect the monastery with its community of lay patrons.

Nevertheless, communal seated meditation remained at the center of monastic activities. Dōgen took this to an extreme in the amount of time he reserved for it in his daily schedule and in his reluctance to relax that schedule on certain days of the month or in the late eighth month, as was apparently customary in other Zen monasteries. Keizan's rules were slightly less stringent, conceding more sleep time and individual discretion during later evening hours. However, they retained a clearly preeminent position for the practice, which was conducted four times a day, as opposed to twice in Myōe's Kōzanji and once with the *vinaya* master Shunjō. In practical terms, there is thus no evidence that Dōgen or the generations following him ever recanted from the views he divulged in *Discourses* on the "unity of practice and attainment." He admitted lay practitioners (both male and female) to his summer retreats in Eiheiji, displaying an undiminished concern for acolytes from secular walks of life as long as they showed what he saw as the necessary degree of dedication. He also continued to use his signature phrase "body and mind dropped off" to describe the essence of seated meditation in his later formal sermons.

In spite of its transcendental and even mystical implications, "unity of practice and attainment" did not, however, mean an absence of all distinctions, temporally or socially. Dōgen argued in "Actualizing the *kōan*" that the moon would be mirrored in its entirety by a drop of water or a pond, but that the depth and width of the water would still make a difference; similarly, the accumulation of practice—especially through reiterated summer retreats—translated into rank within the community and influenced the details of participation in ritual (including meditation) and other monastic activities. At the same time, limitations in office duration were used to prevent an accumulation of power. Dōgen furthermore attempted to shield members of his congregation from external demands on their time, be it for secular or spiritual purposes. The practical ideal was to exploit changing occasions to connect with different instances in the lives of Buddhas and the patriarchs, and with utterances highlighting various aspects of insight. The "unity of practice and attainment" was to be lived through, and not beyond, distinctions as presented by the varying moments of monastic life, with its daily schedules, seasonal changes, and the phases of each renunciant's progress on the path and within monastic hierarchy. It was realized, so to speak, in each step on the ground, and not in a leap beyond the clouds—because each step, no matter how humble, was conceived and, ideally, lived, like a step in the life of the Buddha-ancestors.

Part II

Chrononoetics

Understanding Time

In the previous chapters, we saw how, over the course of his life, Dōgen masterfully expressed and used time for his own purposes. Examining his operational references to time revealed the rich tapestry of temporal determinations that Dōgen employed, with profound implications for theory, aesthetics, and practice. Time served him as a powerful tool in several ways. It was a means to articulate his soteriological convictions, to underline the authenticity of his teachings, and to bring out his competence as an enlightened teacher. Furthermore, it played a crucial role in organizing his monastic congregation in accord with his religious vision. To all these ends, Dōgen skillfully intertwined time's quantitative and metrical aspects with its respective qualitative and typological attributes.

Having laid this foundation, we now turn to those writings where time takes center stage as a subject for contemplation and explore Dōgen's understanding of time, or his chrononoetics. The goal is to construct a compelling interpretation of his time-related notions by probing their conceptual depths and the doctrinal implications they hold. Given the results of the previous chapters, I assume as a premise for my reconstruction a fundamental consistency in Dōgen's works. This means in particular that I do not follow readings based on the Lotus Sutra's famous chapter on "expedient means," or on the "two truths" tradition,[1] as these texts relegate those passages that emphasize temporal distinctions and so forth to the level of mere didactics; they regard them as provisional expressions directed at lay followers and beginners in training, or to be used for merely pragmatic reasons. I believe that we do not need to make this separation. It is possible to construct an interpretation that is hermeneutically sound as well as complex, content rich, and compelling. In particular, by integrating the content of Dōgen's pragmatic instructions for monastic routines or lay believers with his arcane disquisitions for his closest adepts, we can understand what the latter implied in practical terms—that is, what difference they were meant to make within the dimension of everyday experience and life. This in turn greatly contributes to appreciating their overall significance.

For obvious reasons, the "What Is:Time" fascicle of the 75-fascicle *Treasury* will hold a prominent place in the following discussion, as it is the single text in his works where time is the central topic of contemplation (chapter 6 elucidates its argument in detail). However, "What Is:Time" is by no means an outlier or isolated text. Dōgen's first doctrinal exposition, the *Discourses on Negotiating the Way,* already contains key passages concerning his understanding of time in relation to practice and enlightened insight, and other writings leading up to "What Is:Time" elaborate on further temporal aspects. Moreover, Dōgen's deliberations on the subject build on some of the various temporal concepts that had been developed in the tradition. Chapter 5 reviews these "building blocks" that "What Is:Time" brings to a synthesis and culmination. However, while Dōgen curiously did not return to the expression "what is:time" in later writings, he revisited certain themes, such as the notion of a "consummate now" comprising past, present, and future; and the relation of time and causality or karmic retribution (e.g., the "Karma in the Three Times" fascicle from the 12-fascicle redaction of the *Treasury*). Chapter 7 explores these later writings to clarify some of the more enigmatic passages and open questions from "What Is:Time" and prepares the conclusive reconstruction of Dōgen's intricate and complex conception of time. I consider each of the pertinent texts in terms of the time-related argument that it makes, its pragmatic context, and its intertextual relations. There is a certain emphasis on writings from the corpus of the composite vernacular *Treasury* because of their more discursive character, but other sources are introduced wherever pertinent and appropriate. As indicated above, the argument is organized in roughly chronological order, starting with a survey of concepts Dōgen received from the tradition and his early engagements with the subject of time. In this manner, it will be possible to follow the way Dōgen's ideas unfolded over the course of his career as a thinker and spiritual guide.

5

Building Blocks and Early Approaches

Conceptual Heritage: Dōgen and the Tradition of Buddhist Thought on Time

As a religious author who claimed to express nothing but the correct teaching transmitted between Buddhas and ancestors, it is unsurprising that Dōgen's doctrinal explanations regarding time used terms and concepts he found within the tradition. Indeed, it is difficult to identify anything that was entirely new in his ideas at the time of his writing. However, in his pioneering 1975 study on Dōgen, Kim correctly emphasized "the fact that although the problem of time was an integral part of Buddhist thought, it had never been treated as central, but was instead subordinated to such issues as nonsubstantiality, causation, emptiness, Buddha-nature, and so forth."[1] The originality of Dōgen, if we are to apply such a modern notion, lay in attributing a key soteriological function to the proper engagement with time that included, but also went beyond, emphasizing contemplation of the impermanence of worldly things.

Building on previous research by Yanagida Seizan, Guido Rappe, and Rolf Elberfeld,[2] I proceed to briefly review some of the seminal conceptual elements of Dōgen's notion of time that he was able to extract from the tradition and identify their historical origins. Notably, the sources of his ideas were much broader than the Zen tradition with which he later came to be identified. They include elements of "old" Nara Buddhism (especially Kegon) as well as Tendai and Esoteric thought. This points to the formative influences he received in his early years of monastic training before coming into contact with Zen teaching and practice.

Yanagida Seizan has observed that Buddhist thought in general, and Buddhist thought on time in particular, originated in agricultural societies and remained firmly embedded in their modes of thinking. This extends even to such a fundamental notion as impermanence, which, in his words, "refers to the periodicity (*shūki* 周期) of things with sensual form that come forth and are extinguished within boundlessly recurring time. Time then means the segmentation of the limitless recurrence of birth and death of living beings, i.e., the 'temporal occasions and their causes and conditions' (*jisetsu in'en* 時節因縁)."³ Ideas about transmigration or moral causation (*karma*) are similarly modeled after processes and patterns of agricultural production. Harvesting, storage, and the sowing of seeds reaped in previous years are frequently used as metaphors in this regard. Dharmakṣema's translation of the *Nirvana Sutra* likewise links the notion of a Buddha nature inherent in all sentient beings to a seed that grew over time and under the right conditions.⁴ Dōgen embraced much of this metaphorical language but also grappled with the naturalist ideas it suggested.

A further time-related element that Dōgen inherited from the continent concerned the periodization of the Buddha's teachings. Various teachings that had developed over time in India were synchronically accessible in China and Japan. This posed the problem of creating coherence between contrasting doctrines, which was addressed by a procedure known as the "classification of doctrines" (*kyōsō hanjaku* 経相判釈). A pertinent and widely employed strategy was to allocate doctrines and canonical texts to specific periods in the Buddha's life.⁵ Zhiyi 智顗 (538–597 CE), the founder of the Tiantai (Jp. Tendai) school, was clearly important for Dōgen in that he placed the Kegon (Avatamsaka) Sutra at the beginning and the Lotus and Nirvana Sutras at the end.⁶ As Yanagida remarks, the Kegon Sutra is thereby identified as an immediate reflection of the Buddha's self-understanding and enlightenment. It is further labeled as a classic formulation of a "sudden teaching";⁷ that is, one that reveals the totality of insight in one instance. Yanagida also points to passages in its *Shōki* 性器 fascicle, which report that the Buddha's first utterance after enlightenment was to say that he realized that his body was endowed with consummate insight from the start. This is extended to imply that all beings achieved realization together with the Buddha, an idea Dōgen takes up in "What Is:Time." On the other hand, the sutra also posits a prolonged process of completion of that realization in a defined number of steps.⁸ As we shall see later in the next section, Dōgen will integrate all of these elements in his temporal configuring of the "unity of practice and attainment" (*shushō ittō* 修証一等).

Kim, Rappe, and Elberfeld have all pointed to the importance of the Kegon teaching in the development of East Asian Buddhist thought on time. They unanimously singled out Fazang 法藏 (643–712), the third patriarch of the Chinese Huayan school, as a seminal author in this regard.⁹ Elberfeld, who between them gave the most lucid presentation of Fazang's thought, emphasized that this author moved beyond the negation of substantialist views, which had dominated earlier phases of Buddhist thought, to develop a fully relational concept of time.¹⁰

This relational approach is put into strong relief in Fazang's treatment of the series of past, present, and future in the "Chapter on the Ten Periods" from his commentary on the Avatamsaka Sutra.¹¹ Fazang here starts by considering the present as seen from the past; he observes that what is present now was future in the past, while what is now past was present at that time. The same thought holds for the present: There is the present as seen from the present, the past as seen from the present, and the future of the present. The present will further be the past if seen from the future, and so on. These considerations can be applied to the stages of past, present, and future, amounting to nine "periods" (Chin. *shi* 世). To this is added the time of reflection, when all nine are seen together. The resulting total of ten periods is not understood as an aggregate of self-contained temporal entities, but as a totality of temporal configurations that mutually imply each other.¹² The phase that unites all times in a vision of their totality is further identified as a "dynamic function" (Jp. *rikiyō* 力用). Fazang emphasizes that within this phase the distinctions between different times are maintained.¹³ This further implies that "not all times can simultaneously appear as present."¹⁴ Rappe gives an important further clue with a quote from the "Essay on the Golden Lion" (*Jin shizi zang* 金師子章). Here, Fazang explains that all is one because everything (including the one) is without self-contained essence. The one unfolds as everything through karma, or the distinct segmentation of causes and effects, and the correlation between causes and effects enfolds segmented phenomena into one totality. In the dynamic function, "enfolding and lining up are free and without obstruction."¹⁵

The above-mentioned paragraph from Fazang's "Golden Lion" essay further suggests a mutual implication of motion and stasis. This element may be traced back even several centuries earlier to Sengzhao 僧肇 (374–414), a disciple of the famous translator and scholar-monk Kumārajīva (343–413). Sengzhao's collected essays contain a brief treatise titled "Things Do Not Shift" (*Wu bu qian lun* 物不遷論).[16] Here, Sengzhao posits that movement or change is possible only if it is seen in its inseparable connection to stasis. A phase of movement or change has to remain in a fixed temporal position for another one to occur. If what happened yesterday moved into today, today would be the same as yesterday, and there would be no change. Stasis and movement are not the same, but inseparable.[17] Importantly, this means that the present also never simply goes away;[18] it retains its own position. Dōgen will later address this motif in "What Is:Time" against the one-sided view that time only passes. Other than Fazang, Sengzhao is also mentioned several times in Dōgen's formal instructions and lauded as a recipient of the authentic teaching.[19]

Elberfeld observes that Sengzhao in his treatise spoke only of the past and the present, but not of the future. Accordingly, the notion that the present is fixed seems to preclude the mutability of the future.[20] Fazang presented a more inclusive and certainly more complex view; but his thought remained on a highly abstract level.[21] As we have seen already in the previous chapter, Dōgen in contrast proposed an engagement with time that included each and every moment of (monastic) life as an occasion to emulate the enlightened ones. Yanagida Seizan has pointed to an element from the Zen tradition that may have served as an important bridge from earlier teachers' abstract principles to this method, which unites theory and practice in a unique way. The Zen school strongly emphasized teaching for an individual, accommodated to a specific situation. Its particular modes of communication between masters and disciples were all developed to cater to this end. According to Yanagida, the tradition's famous aversion to abstract, generalizing forms of argumentation mirrors the conviction that any such demonstration would compromise the individual's search for insight. Nonetheless, Zen dialogues were recorded precisely because they purportedly entailed a communication of insight in accord with the conditions in play at the time.[22]

This tradition of teaching provided a conceptual bridge for Dōgen to move from intellectual reflections on time to the idea that insight is present in every instance of practice that follows the precedent set by the enlightened ones. In the next section, we will follow the development of this thought in Dōgen's writings.

Setting the Stage: Trans-Temporal Unity in a Transient World

There is no text among Dōgen's writings before "What Is:Time" in which time or one of its aspects is the central topic. However, his first doctrinal exposition, the *Discourses on Negotiating the Way* of 1231, already highlights two temporal aspects of Buddhist insight and practice that he will continue to emphasize and clarify in subsequent writings. One is the promise of trans-temporal unity of practitioners with the enlightened ones; the other is the inexorable transiency of all aspects of human life, which imbues this promise with relevance and urgency. Logically speaking, it is the impermanence of everything in life, and the associated suffering, which sustain the quest for insight and liberation from this condition. Therefore, Dōgen later famously even equated impermanence with Buddha nature (*busshō* 仏性).[23] Significantly, however, he started his teaching with the promise that liberation is not just a faraway goal, but one that is already present within every instance of practice. This seminal passage reads, in Nearman's translation:

> Even though it may be merely for a moment [RST: lit: "for one time," *ichiji* 一時], when someone, whilst sitting upright in meditation, puts the mark of the Buddha seal upon his three types of volitional actions—namely, those of body, speech and thought—the whole physical universe and everything in it becomes and is the Buddha seal; all of space, throughout, becomes and is enlightenment. As a result, all Buddhas, as embodiments of Truth, experience a compounding of Their delight in the Dharma of Their own Original Nature, and the awesome splendor of Their realization of the Way is refreshed for Them.[24]

While space is emphasized more explicitly here, these sentences also imply that the actual practice of meditation "refreshes" or, more literally, "renews" (*arata ni su*) the enlightenment of all Buddhas. Dōgen goes on to insist that by virtue of this accord and synchrony of meditation with the enlightenment of all Buddhas, the sacred "truth" is omnipresent in living beings as well as in insentient matter.[25] In conclusion, he states: "In this manner, even the seated meditation of merely one person at one time imperceptibly merges with all that exists and tranquilly permeates all times. For this reason, this meditation continues to perform the work of Buddhas to transform and guide beings to the way in the inexhaustible worlds across the past, present, and future."[26] There is, in other words, according to Dōgen, an eminent "pervasiveness" to Buddhist practice, and one that mysteriously extends not only into the future, but also into the past. All times of enlightened practice come together in every instance of seated meditation. Meditation in this fashion not only "refreshes" the insight of previous enlightened ones, but also "guides" sentient beings from the past. No explanation of the precise meaning of this form of retroaction or of the way it works is given here, however, beyond the general idea of the fundamental unity (inseparability) of everything that exists. We shall therefore return to this question later in our discussion of "What Is:Time." Suffice it at this point to note that this mystical unity of all times is a way of explicating the omnipresence of the *Buddha Dharma*—which in turn explains why liberation from the karmic cycle of birth and death is always possible. This allows Dōgen to reject the pessimistic outlook engendered by the then-popular concept of the "Final Dharma Age."[27]

The notion of inseparability between the self and the world emerges again in the *Discourses* in a long passage in the question-and-answer section. Here, it serves to refute the notion of an unchanging, immortal self and to underline the ineluctable transience of both body and soul. This hints at an intrinsic link between the idea of a trans-temporal, mystical unity between practitioners and enlightened ones (and the present, past, and future) on the one hand, and the impermanence of all aspects of human life on the other. Dōgen will only arrive at explaining this link in "What Is:Time," but it is worth mentioning that it exists already in his first doctrinal exposition. The assumption of an immortal soul that he seeks to refute is couched much in the way of the Indian notion of an eternal self or *ātman*, which remains in its essence unaffected by its own thoughts and experiences in the world of illusion. Dōgen's main argument against it is simply that this is a non-Buddhist notion. Rejection of eternalism—that is, denying that things, and even more importantly, the human mind or soul, have a permanent substance—certainly is a core tenet of Buddhist teachings.[28] Even those schools that reintroduced some notion of eternity or eternal being had to rhetorically acknowledge this tenet, which is embodied in the Buddhist key term *anātman* (no-self, Jp. *muga* 無我).[29] In line with this core doctrine, Dōgen consistently repudiated any attempt to return to notions of a permanent self, however rhetorically adorned.[30]

According to Hee-Jin Kim, Dōgen's whole interest in time arose "out of existential concerns with the impermanence of life."[31] Karaki Junzō has collected the many instances in which Dōgen pointed to the importance of considering impermanence.³² However, there is a notable difference in emphasis within the literature. Interpretations building on the perceived analogies between Dōgen and Heidegger or existentialism in general tend to present such meditation on impermanence as a means toward developing an "authentic experience of time"—an experience that reveals, in Gereon Kopf's words, "the ontological priority of the *immediate now*"³³ and is identified by Steven Heine with overcoming a "sequential view of temporality."³⁴ Authors such as Kopf, Heine, or Stambaugh may mention Dōgen's insistence on exertion "through sustained meditative practice," but they tend to prioritize achieving what Heine calls "a genuine sense of detachment that enables full engagement with all aspects of reality."³⁵ Joan Stambaugh makes this most explicit by stating: "Other examples of sustained exertion might be found in an actor performing in a play, a musician playing in a concert or an athlete engaging in a competition."³⁶ In contrast, Dōgen referred to contemplation of impermanence specifically as a contemplation on the inevitable sequence of origination and cessation, birth and death, and as a prime motivator for exertion in Buddhist practice. He also expressly disavowed any engagement with the world that was not part of the latter, including study of the arts and sciences.³⁷

The *Collection of Essentials in the Study of the Way*, written three years after the *Discourses*, is a case in point. Its initial chapter emphasizes contemplation of impermanence as the source of the "*bodhi*-mind" (*bodaishin* 菩提心), that is, the intention to seek enlightenment that is the first step on the path of the *bodhisattva*. Referring to an undocumented statement by the eminent Indian Buddhist scholar and purported ancestor of nearly every East Asian Mahāyāna school, Nāgārjuna, it states:

> The requirement to bring forth the *bodhi*-mind
>
> What is here called "*bodhi*-mind" has many names, but they all refer to the same. The ancestor Nāgārjuna said: "Simply, the mind contemplating origination, cessation and transience of the secular world is called the *bodhi*-mind." When we rely for now on this mind, we will certainly realize *bodhi*-mind. Indeed, when contemplating impermanence, the thought of a [permanent] self or ideas about fame and gain will not arise. Fear of the lightning speed of time will cause us to practice the way as if we had to brush away a fire on our heads.³⁸

The motif is taken up repeatedly in the "informal lectures or *shosan*"[39] (小参) that Dōgen's leading disciple Ejō recorded in his *Record of Things Heard* between 1235 and 1237 or 1238.[40] In one lecture, Dōgen states that contemplation of impermanence is a superior way of motivating diligent practice because it is "not like a teaching among others one may consider, or something one has to fabricate out of nothing and then think about it: It is the principle of what really happens before our eyes."[41] The attitude that such contemplation is supposed to foster is characterized in another lecture by a sense of urgency, which translates into the determination to "not let days and nights go by while vainly doing useless things."[42] An example from a later writing gives evidence to the consistency of this pattern throughout his career. In the "The Merits of Leaving Home" (*Shukke kudoku* 出家功徳) we read: "Those already born as human beings should make haste to shave their hair, don the robe of the three dharmas, and exercise the path of the Buddha. [. . .] It would be the height of stupidity to vainly crave for a career, to waste one's whole life as minister to a prince, traversing in delusions, only to sink into darkness in the next existence because one has not yet sought after it."[43]

An essential aspect visible in these passages is that time as impermanence is not neutral. It is laden with urgency and essentially linked to the Buddhist path of liberation. The emotional and pragmatic quality of urgency is not conceived of as external evaluation of time/impermanence but as one of its intrinsic features: impermanence *is* urgency and *necessitates* practical consequences. Time as impermanence thus has an important aesthetic attribute, which, according to Dōgen, is not a subjective feature, but an objective characteristic. Or, to be more precise, it is a feature of time as a mode of a fundamentally non-dual reality, in which the observer and the observed can never be fully separated. There is no "god's eye view" of the world, no view of a virtually unaffected observer.[44] Stated in the affirmative, Dōgen—with a large part of Buddhist tradition—posits that the world, and reality for that matter, is interdependent of the self, or, as a consequence, of any and all selves.[45] Time to Dōgen is exactly that mode of reality that can serve to clarify and explain this interdependence. Hee-Jin Kim dexterously adduces the following passage from "Comprehensive Occasion" (*Zenki* 全機) to illustrate what this means:

> Life is, for example, like people sailing in a boat. Although we set a sail, steer our course, and pole the boat along, the boat carries us and we do not exist apart from the boat. By sailing

in the boat, we make the boat what it is. Study assiduously this very time. At such a time, there is nothing but the world of the boat. The heavens, the water, and the shore—all become the boat's time (*fune no jisetsu*); they are not the same as the time that is not the boat. Hence, I make life what it is; life makes me what I am. In riding the boat, one's body and mind, the self and the world are together the dynamic function of the boat (*fune no kikan*). The entire earth and the whole empty sky are in company with the boat's vigorous exertion. Such is the I that is life, the life that is I.[46]

Returning to the *Discourses*, there is one more important temporal aspect that Dōgen highlights in his repudiation of teachings that separate body and mind, or mutable form from immutable essence. Specifically, if the notion of non-duality is taken seriously, predicates such as "persistence" or "cessation" apply to each and every component of human life: "[I]n Buddhist instruction that speaks of what is persistent, all things are said to have persistence without their ever being separated into categories of 'body' and 'mind.' In instruction that talks about cessation, all things are said to be subject to cessation without differentiating whether they are of some particular nature or have some particular form."[47] This implies a notion of "persistence" that is inseparably connected to "cessation." As Nearman remarks: "all phenomena, physical and non-physical, arise and continue on ('persist') for an unspecified period before disintegrating and disappearing." This stands in contrast to the notion of a permanent spiritual substance that is "thought to remain ('abide') unchanged and unchanging forever."[48]

The theme of persistence and cessation is also addressed in a well-known paragraph from another seminal early text, "Actualizing the *Kōan*" (from 1233), which Ueda Shizuteru characterized as the "Alpha and Omega of Dōgen's teaching."[49] The passage considers the transience of all that exists and the absence of a permanent substance. It further introduces the technical term *hōi* 法位, translated by Kim as "Dharma-position," and, alternatively, by Raud as "dharma-configuration."[50] Dōgen takes the expression probably from a passage in the Lotus Sutra, where according to Jacqueline Stone it described "the nonsubstantiality of the dharmas that arise through dependent origination."[51] Dōgen introduces it to describe the relationship between life and death. The simile he uses is that of firewood and ash:

> Firewood becomes ashes and it cannot become firewood again. Although this is so, we should not see ashes as "after" and firewood as "before." You should know that firewood abides in the dharma-configuration of firewood, for which there is a "before" and "after." But although there is "before" and "after," before and after are cut off. Ashes abide in the dharma-configuration of ashes, and there is a "before," and there is an "after." Just like this firewood, which will not become firewood again after it has become ashes, a human being will not return to life again after death. It is the decisive custom of the *Buddha Dharma* not to state this in the way that life becomes death, and therefore, we speak of "no birth/origination." Death does not become life—this is the Buddha's decisive turning of the dharma-wheel, and therefore, we speak of "no extinction." Life is a configuration of one time, and so is death a configuration of one time. This is like, for example, winter and spring. We do not think that winter becomes spring, we do not say that spring becomes summer.[52]

Raud, whose translation I have followed here, lucidly explains one aspect of the expression "abiding in the dharma-configuration" (*jūhōi* 住法位), as well as his choice of translation, by saying:

> We can understand *jūhōi* ["abiding in the dharma-configuration"] [. . .] as the relation in which the constituent particles of reality are to each other: in one specific mode of organization they are perceived as "firewood," in another as "ashes;" the notion of "firewood" abides in a particular configuration of dharmas just as the notion of "offside" abides in a particular configuration of players on a football field. In a photograph that depicts an offside situation, the images of the players stand absolutely still [. . .], but each of them has a certain speed and direction (past, present, and future) that may, in a next moment, place them in some other configuration that can be described by some other technical term.[53]

One can easily see how understanding individual occasions such as the above-mentioned boat, firewood, or ash as "configurations" implicates the self, as well as every other part of the environment. There is no barrier, gap, or bubble that separates individual "things" or "selves" from each other. Similarly, there is no conceivable way to separate "what they are" completely from "how they are perceived" by those to whom they appear. "Time" in Dōgen may stand for such "occasions" that involve specific "configurations" of self and world in mutual interaction.

Rein Raud has connected this idea of a reality composed of "dharma-configurations" to a strictly momentarist view of time, suggesting "that it does more justice to Dōgen's thinking to translate his *ji* 時 primarily as 'moment' [. . .] and not as 'time' (*toki*)."[54] "Momentarism," the theory of instantaneous arising and cessation (*setsuna shōmetsu* 剎那消滅), has a long tradition in Buddhist thought and is extensively discussed in the literature.[55] Several authors have noticed that Dōgen's thought embraces elements of this tradition.[56] According to Hee-Jin Kim, his ideas in this regard resemble the thoughts of the Sautrāntika school, which maintained that only the present moment was real and that it contained the totality of the past and future.[57] While some authors seem to downplay this momentarist background,[58] there is to my knowledge none who explicitly denies it.

A certain contention exists, however, concerning the concept of the "moment" or "instant" itself. Raud argued that moments are "without duration" and belong to "a different register of being than *time*,"[59] separate from the "measurable time-system," on the grounds that "time has duration, but moments do not."[60] Echoing a pattern of thought already established by Akiyama, Raud further posited a co-incidence of the moment with eternity: "[T]he 'moment' as understood here does not have dimensions at all and is thus simultaneously unmeasurably brief and everlasting, always present."[61]

In contrast, Hee-Jin Kim and, more recently, Steven Heine, have pointed to a passage from "The Merits of Leaving Home" where the length of the moment (*setsuna*, Skt. *kṣaṇa*) is calculated in relation to the length of day and night to illustrate how everything that exists arises and perishes within an instant:

> Life arises and perishes instantaneously from moment to moment, and does not abide at all [. . .] there are sixty-five *setsunas* being born and annihilated in one *tanji* [snap of the fingers, RST], yet ordinary worldly persons do not yet realize this owing to their own ignorance. Although one day and one night is comprised of 6.400.099.980 *setsuna,* and the five skandhas [constituents of the human body and mind, RST]

appear and disappear, they do not know it. Pity those who are altogether unaware of their own births and deaths!⁶²

Such calculation, although clearly not a primary concern in Dōgen's texts, indicates that the moments (*setsuna*) in question are minimal quanta of time that can, in fact, be added up to longer periods of duration—although there is no "real substance" persisting beyond each quantum.⁶³

This brings us to the next questions: Are individual moments entirely separate from each other, or are they interconnected? Is there a legitimate notion of "duration"? Does Dōgen further accept a progression of or in time or does he deny it? In the literature, opinions on these questions are strongly divided. The discussion hinges on the expression *zengo saidan* 前後際断 ("before and after are cut off"), which appears in the above-quoted paragraph on firewood and ashes.

Rein Raud again takes the extreme position that denies any connection between moments and, as a consequence, all duration and linear progression. This view was already proposed by Kazue Kyōichi in a lengthy article published in 1959, and by Heinrich Dumoulin, who first translated "Actualizing the *Kōan*" into a Western language. It is also partly embraced by Hee-Jin Kim and Abe Masao.⁶⁴ In such a reading, the expression "before and after are cut off" means that each dharma-configuration is, in Abe's words, "beyond before and after."⁶⁵ As Dumoulin explains concerning firewood and ashes:

> The physical process of burning is not denied, but it does not affect the essence of reality. All dharmas exist from moment to moment, i.e., always only this moment, their way of existing is not in the flux of time. The temporal continuity with its before and after comes from our subjective way of looking (*Anschauung*) and does not touch the dharmas existing moment to moment (*augenblicksweise*). Firewood is firewood, and ashes are ashes, in every moment each a dharma and independent of the other.⁶⁶

Raud avoids such openly metaphysical language, but implies this in making the distinction between "ontological and linguistic existence."⁶⁷ Using the terms of his translation, his view acknowledges a "shifting" from one "dharma-configuration" to another, but no entity that actually "shifts." This is certainly in line with the above-mentioned tenet of instantaneous arising and perishing (*setsuna shōmetsu*), which refutes the assumption of a material substance persisting beyond the measure of the moment. It is generally accepted that Dōgen expressed this latter view.[68] But this does not necessarily lead to the conclusion that, to use Kim's words, Dōgen "denies duration," that his view of time is characterized by "an absence of coming and going as well," and that it "entails a denial of the present as an instance of the linear conception of time."[69]

We will return to this topic in the discussion of "What Is:Time." Suffice it to notice here that Raud's simile of the sports game is open to a less extreme interpretation. Few people would assume that a soccer game is a "thing" sustained by its "substance." This, however, does not mean that it has only "linguistic existence." The game is an apt example of an "occasion" and is perhaps even more intuitive than Dōgen's above-mentioned simile of the boat: Soccer consists of players, running on a field, kicking a ball, getting hurt when running into each other, and arousing powerful feelings in their team and their fans whenever they manage to drive or narrowly fail to drive the ball into the opponent side's goal. We need not assume that a single one of these participating entities is supported by an unchanging material substance during the time of the game to understand that they are real. No one can kick a "linguistic entity," but that does not mean we believe that the ball remains materially completely identical for the ninety minutes of the game. What players and fans need to see is that it shows a certain consistent shape and behavior. It cannot be on the penalty point one second and then, suddenly, outside the field without anyone having touched it; nor can it become heavy like iron one moment and light as a feather the next, or morph into a kitchen pot or golden Buddha statue in an instant. Such events would interrupt, or completely stop, the game. Similarly, the players of one team can change to some extent, but as a team they must consistently attempt to move the ball into their opponent team's goal, and vice versa. Only then does a real match come to pass—and this is different from a fictional one in a novel or movie or the definition of the game in a textbook. While numerous changes are taking place during one match, it is the order and coherence between the changing moments that make possible its (always fragile) existence.[70] Without this coherence, it would not even make sense to speak of "configurations" on the playing field, such as Raud's offside—first, because the offside rule itself entails a relation of the moment a player receives the ball to the moment when it was passed on to them, and second, because there would be no "directions" of movements to speak of if there were only isolated moments.

To return from sports to Dōgen, and to Dumoulin's phrasing, there must be some consistent relation between the different instances of a dharma such as firewood to allow us to say that it exists "from moment to moment," or even speak of firewood at all. As Ishii Kiyozumi has pointed out, Dōgen appears to employ the notion of "dharma-configuration" (*hōi* 法位) precisely in this fashion to express a situation or state that maintains some essential features over a limited period of time without assuming that it is free from change or is supported by an underlying substance. Dōgen further seems to argue that not only living human beings, firewood, or ashes, but also the Buddhas, are to be conceived as such states.[71]

John Maraldo has offered a helpful paraphrase of the passage in question that accords well with this interpretation. His words further help to clarify Dōgen's ensuing, somewhat puzzling statements, that within the Buddhist purview of things there is "no birth/origination" and "no annihilation":

> We speak of firewood turning to ashes, and not returning again to firewood. But it is not quite right to say something is first firewood and afterwards ashes. There is a "before" the firewood and an "after." What is before is not firewood and what is after is not firewood. [. . .] While we speak of there being a "before" and an "after," for the time being "before" and "after" are divided. [. . .] Analogously, after a person dies she does not return to life. But it is not quite right to put it this way. [. . .] The right way is not to say that life becomes death, that something that was alive is now dead. The right way is to say "all is arising"; there is nothing but arising, being born, living. [. . .] The right way is to say that death does not become life, that something that was dead is not alive again. So we say "all is perishing"; there is nothing but perishing, dying.[72]

From this perspective, the statements on origination/arising and annihilation/perishing say that birth does not mean the origin of something that would abide beyond the stage of life. Similarly, death does not indicate that such a something has been extinguished, leaving nothing behind. Neither are we to think of "origination" and "cessation" as metaphysical states with a substance or essence of their own, independent of each other and independent from that which comes into being or ceases to be.[73] The advantage of this reading is that it does not force us to abandon temporal succession, let alone logical consistency—as, for example, Akiyama Hanji did when he wrote that individual occasions result from a self-determination of nothingness "without reason and in an irrational fashion."[74]

The "case" cited at the end of the fascicle further corroborates a rational reading. Its subject is the "nature" of the wind, a metaphor for enlightened activity. The dialogue significantly modifies the notion of "permanence" or "persistence": Master Baozhe, asked by a monk why he was using a fan to cool himself when the nature of the wind was "permanently abiding," responds: "You may know that the nature of the wind is permanently abiding, but you do not know the reason why there is no place that it does not reach." As the monk further inquires about this reason, he simply fans himself. Against the assumption of a realm where the nature of the wind permanently exists, Dōgen, with Baozhe, points out that it is only through and within activities such as fanning oneself that the wind manifests its persistent nature.

Like the paragraph on firewood, the Baozhe episode explains an expression from the Lotus Sutra's verse about the permanence of the dharma. The firewood passage illustrates the term "dharma-position" or "dharma-configuration," and the Baozhe story the expression "permanently abiding."[75] Dōgen will again use the expression "dwelling in the dharma-position" in "What Is:Time," but will no longer speak of "permanently abiding."

At the end of the firewood paragraph, Dōgen further uses the simile of the seasons to illustrate his understanding of the way things exist. Together with the notion of the "dharma-position" or "dharma-configuration," he will return to this simile in "What Is:Time"—this time to explain his concept of temporal passage, which is intimately connected to that of "dwelling in a dharma-position." It seems that these ideas were to some extent already in his mind when he wrote "Actualizing the *Kōan*," unless he inserted them later, when revising the 1233 text. In any case, there is a strong intertextual connection between "Actualizing the *Kōan*" and "What Is:Time."

Most thematic statements on time between 1234 and the winter of 1240 reiterate the theme of urgency as arising from a due consideration of impermanence. This may because at the time Dōgen was slowly building his first monastery and educating its congregation on basic matters, from monastic rules to meditation practice, doctrine, and acquaintance with the Zen tradition. As mentioned above, impermanence and urgency are dealt with repeatedly in the informal lectures that form the body of the *Record of Things Heard*.⁷⁶ The admonitions there notably involve an objectification of time. Consider the following words from the lecture given on the occasion of Ejō's first formal instruction in 1237: "Will time stop flashing by because you cherish it?"⁷⁷ The implication is, once more, "to study and practice the way, and not spend time in vain."⁷⁸

In practical terms, this translates into an argument against two common modes of facing the future: procrastination and planning for future convenience. Several lectures warn against postponing practice in favor of first taking care of one's secular affairs or curing an illness. They cite examples of people who did so and then died before they could realize their wish to take up monastic life.⁷⁹ Planning for future provisions is discouraged as a preoccupation that leads the mind away from practice and insight.⁸⁰ Furthermore, one lecture insists, what is made available in this fashion is impure and unfit for consumption by monastics.⁸¹ These statements foreshadow the instructions for Eiheiji's kitchen that we discussed in the previous chapter.⁸² They clearly exhibit the difference (and conflict) between Dōgen's religious rationality, which is oriented toward salvation from ordinary human life, and secular economic rationality, concerned with providing for the needs and wants of this life only.

Nevertheless, there is room for rational planning and reckoning with time in Dōgen's vision of religious life. Another oft-cited document from the period under investigation, the *Instructions for the Head Cook*,⁸³ is pertinent in this regard. Relying strongly on the "Regulations for Zen Monasteries," the text first establishes the high importance of the office, which is to be given to an experienced, senior monk. The "Instructions" then describe in detail how the person in charge should plan each meal for the community carefully and in consultation with other temple officers. The greatest efforts should be made in its diligent preparation and preservation until consumption.⁸⁴ The difference in relation to secular economic planning is that monastic cooks operate with provisions given by voluntary and unsolicited donations; they must, the text insists, remain unconcerned with judgments concerning their quality or quantity.⁸⁵ The planning in question is thus different in scope and intent from that of secular economic activity. It does not involve the exchange of equivalent values and the concomitant calculation of monetary gain and loss. Instead, the head cook is admonished to carefully consider the conditions of the present and to take precautions for the future, such as to protect food against rodents and other damages. The goal is to make the best use possible of what has been made available.

If performed in this manner, the actions of the head cook are appreciated as expressions of highest insight. Thus, Dōgen lavishes praise on the master cooks he met in China and on more distant precedents. To his mind, only the uncomprehending eye would regard their chores as mundane tasks in opposition to the lofty religious activities, such as studying *kōan* or engaging in seated meditation.[86] Notably, as Nagai Kenryū explains, the attitude described here as "uncomprehending" was common among Japanese monastics at the time, since most of them were descended from aristocratic families.[87] The importance of seated meditation notwithstanding, Dōgen posited that there were different modes of expressing insight and adherence to the Buddha's path according to circumstance. In fact, this can be seen as a central message of "What Is:Time," which we shall turn to presently.

To summarize, in Dōgen's writings before "What Is:Time," time is addressed first and foremost as part of an analysis of the general conditions of human life, a consideration that motivates the decision to discard secular life. Dōgen identifies impermanence as an inevitable condition of human existence and highlights contemplation of impermanence as a prime force for turning to and staying on the Buddha's path. In this context, time assumes the quality of an external agent. This implies a certain reification of time.

A second aspect that emerges from this rigorous acknowledgement of impermanence concerns the primacy of action over knowledge or subjective experience. In the absence of a permanent substance such as the Brahmanist *ātman*, enlightenment cannot consist in an experience or awareness of it; therefore, the right way to understand and realize insight is by performing actions in accordance with the Buddha's way. Insight is transtemporal in that it becomes a reality whenever practiced in this manner, but it does not have a separate substance or nature that exists apart from this realization.

Finally, as indicated by the *Instructions for the Head Cook*, what action is called for depends on the conditions of the time. Where the *Discourses* highlight seated meditation as the supreme medium of insight, later texts like the "Instructions" widen the spectrum of actions that may fulfill the same function if conducted according to the model set by the enlightened ones. Every one of these actions can realize the trans-temporal mystical unity, which complements the sense of urgency (derived from contemplation of impermanence) with the promise of time-transcending perfection.

As we shall see in the following chapter, "What Is:Time" brings concepts and ideas developed in these contexts together and carries them further toward a multifaceted notion of time that supports Buddhist teaching and practice. It also offers answers to questions that were left open in earlier texts: Are we to understand the notion that "before and after are cut off" in a strictly momentarist fashion? Is there a place for continuity, and therefore duration, in Dōgen's concept of time? Does he accept or deny the idea of temporal sequence, and if he accepts it, how does this fit with the notion of trans-temporal unity or even retroaction ("sustaining" sentient beings in previous ages?) that we found in the *Discourses*?

6

Time in "What Is:Time"

We are now fully prepared to engage with Dōgen's most famous and enigmatic text on time, the fascicle "What Is:Time" in the composite vernacular *Treasury*. Because of its well-deserved prominence in the reception of his ideas, the text deserves close scrutiny. In the following, I first give a brief account of its origin and context and then present an overview of its argument. This provides the basis for the discussion of the new concepts that Dōgen introduces in "What is:Time." In contradistinction to previous interpretations, I demonstrate that these concepts serve to build a complex notion of time that integrates temporal distinctions and measures with the notion that each present moment comprises the totality of time.

According to its colophone, "What Is:Time" was "written" (*sho* 書) in Dōgen's first monastery, Kōshō hōrinji (referred to as Shōbōji 聖寶寺), in the vicinity of the capital in the first year of Ninji (1240 CE) during the "beginning of winter"[1] — an alternative name for the tenth lunar month (late October to late November). The expression here probably indicates its first day.[2] In any case, the text was written during the upsurge of Kōshōji and in a highly productive period; indeed, the "Transmitting the Robe" fascicle in the 75-fascicle redaction and its variant in the 12-fascicle redaction "The Virtues of the Robe" carry the same date.[3] If "What Is:Time" was written on the first day of the tenth lunar month, then Dōgen also delivered a formal lecture on "Opening the Fireplace" on that day.[4] Furthermore, the *Extensive Record* lists eleven formal instructions between the first day of the tenth month and the winter solstice, which means that Dōgen more or less implemented the schedule of formal instructions according to the *Pure Rules for Zen Monasteries* discussed in the previous chapter.⁵ In addition, Dōgen also drafted the "Mountain and Water Sutra" fascicle from the vernacular *Treasury* during this time. These vernacular texts are probably among the earliest fascicles written with the idea of a comprehensive vernacular *Treasury* in mind.⁶

"What Is:Time": Structure and Argument

Dōgen's earlier references to time have firmly placed his engagement with the subject within the symbolic form of religion: To him, time was of interest with respect to its relevance to the goal of salvation: that is, liberation from the cycle of birth and death. That cycle is characterized first and foremost by suffering. Its main causes are ignorance and attachment to the misconception of an enduring, substantial self. Elucidation of impermanence as an ineluctable condition of human existence was therefore the prime theme of Dōgen's earlier disquisitions on time, where it regularly supported the call to renounce secular life and take up or sustain Buddhist practice. "What Is:Time" expands on this theme, complementing it with the perspective of fulfillment within impermanence. The text can therefore be understood as an elaboration of the two foremost temporal notions that were already present in Dōgen's earliest doctrinal work, the *Discourses*.

To ensure that the multifaceted propositions of this complex text become visible in their proper context, I first examine the problems Dōgen explicitly seeks to address in it. This will help to identify the chief assertions of "What Is:Time." I then survey the text's thematic units and elucidate their function in its argument.

The misconception that Dōgen seeks to rebut in "What Is:Time" is the belief in an ontological gap between the state of the practitioner seeking insight and that of the perfectly enlightened beings. By extension, this view implies an ontological separation between different situations and actions within human existence. Such separation is supported by the notion that time "flies past," or the opinion that what is present goes out of existence because of the passing of time. These notions further connect to the view that individual things, like individual situations, are separate from each other—which in turn promotes the idea that things have no intrinsic connection to time and that change is merely accidental.

Soteriologically, this complex of notions engenders a disconnect between individuals, their past and present actions, and the future that is conditioned by these actions—and, most importantly, a disconnect between the present of an aspiring practitioner, who may err and fail, and the state of accomplished insight, the "golden Buddha body."

Against this received and, to his mind, delusional view, Dōgen posits his notion of "what is:time," which entails the unity of things and time, and a complex view of temporal passage. The whole text can be read as an argument in this regard: It seeks to support both the intrinsic temporality of everything that is and the prospect of liberation. Liberating insight is, first, an element already present in current religious practice. Second, on a fundamental level, its driving moment—"the sublime light of time"—is present in everything that exists.

Table 6.1 presents an overview of the texts' thematic units, their position in the traditional Sinitic four-part scheme of development (*kishōtenketsu* 起承転結, "exposition, expansion, turning, conclusion"),[7] and their function in the overall argument. In addition to the page numbers in Ōkubo's "Collected Works," I refer to the section numbering used by Elberfeld (*Phänomenologie der Zeit*, 2004, 385–94, abbreviated here as E) and to the page numbers in the open-access translation by Nearman (Nearman, *The Shōbōgenzō*, abbreviated as N). Concerning the functional parts of the argumentative sequence, I follow Swiss linguist Jean-Michel Adam's analysis, which builds on Steven Toulmin and others.[8]

To explain in detail, the text's topic and thesis are indicated somewhat enigmatically in paragraph (1) by the eight-line stanza attributed to an "old Buddha," already described in chapter 1.[9] This stanza builds on words of Yaoshan Weiyan, who, however, is not named at this point. It enumerates contrasting phases of the "old Buddha's" existence and expressions of insight, including pointers to ordinary existence and unity with the cosmos. (2) The thesis is then spelled out in the following, famous paragraph that turns the reading of the compound *uji* at the beginning of each of these lines around to point to the inextricable unity of "what there is" and time.[10] This second paragraph also makes a connection to clock-time, which it characterizes as being poorly understood by ordinary people. (3) A further introductory section strings together a number of propositions concerning (a) the intrinsic seriality of the self; (b) its being of the same mind *and* the same time with the Buddhas and ancestors in the dedication to the Buddha's path; (c) the mutual non-obstruction

Table 6.1. Overview of "What Is:Time"

Part of fourfold scheme	Thematic Unit	Part of Argumentative Sequence	Reference
Exposition *ki* 起	(1) Eight-line stanza (2) "Time is what there is" (3) Seriality of the self, synchrony with Buddhas and ancestors	Thesis	DZZ I, 189; E I; N 108 DZZ I, 189; E II; N 109 DZZ I, 190; E III–IV; N 109–10
Expansion *shō* 承	(4) The common view that time flies by is incorrect, as the past is present to the observer	Antithesis + Counterevidence	DZZ I, 190; E V–VIII; N 110–12
	(5) Change means "passage through phases":	Additional support	DZZ I, 191; E IX–X; N 112–13
	(5.1) Passage is multidirectional (present becomes past, now moves on from what was past to what is present, future comes into present), holistic character of each phase	First affirmative conceptual support for thesis	
	(5.2) Up and down of abiding in dharma-positions; connection between phase of the unenlightened and that of the Buddha (by virtue of its position within the temporal/causal sequence, each situation comprises the whole of time)	Second affirmative conceptual support for thesis	DZZ I, 191–92; E XI; N 113–14
	(5.3) Time not flying away, but also arriving: the future of the yet-unenlightened practitioner	Negative conceptual support (against antithesis)	DZZ I, 192; E XII; N 114
	(5.4) Fetters/barriers to insight are phases of enlightenment	Reevaluation/consequences of thesis	DZZ I, 192; E XIII; N 114

Part of fourfold scheme	Thematic Unit	Part of Argumentative Sequence	Reference
Expansion *shō* 承	(5.5) "Passing" not like wind, but like the seasons	First stabilizer: illustration by intuitive image	DZZ I, 192; E XIV; N 114–15
Turning *ten* 転	(6) Yaoshan case and explanation	Second stabilizer	DZZ I, 193; E XV–XVI; N 115–16
	(7) Guisheng case and explanation	Third stabilizer	DZZ I, 193–94; E XVIII; N 117–18
Conclusion *ketsu* 結	(8) Half, failed, and failed times are *uji*	Conclusion/ evaluation	DZZ I, 194; E XIX–XXI; N 118

Table 6.1 explanation: E + Roman number = paragraph numbering according to Elberfeld, *Phänomenologie der Zeit*, 2004, 385–94; N + Arabic number: page numbers in the open-access translation by Nearman, *The Shōbōgenzō*.

of things if seen as time; and (d) the holistic aspect of each thing/time, which comprises the totality of time.[11] While apparently presented as implications of the identity of "what there is" with time, none of these propositions is immediately self-evident, and the remainder of the text can be understood as an elucidation of their content. In the traditional four-part scheme of ordering extensive symbolic expressions, these first three units may therefore be seen as the "exposition" (*ki* 起).

(4) The next unit contrasts what has been said so far with the common, secular view of time, in which things are seen as separate from time, and different situations appear as separate from each other. Thus, the time of the deity (or demon) with three heads and eight arms is separate from the time of the Buddha, just as when one crosses a river and then scales a mountain to reach a vermilion palace on top. When in the palace, the river and the effort of crossing it seem far away and without any intrinsic connection to dwelling in the palace.[12] This view forms the antithesis of Dōgen's argument. It is challenged as being not so much simply wrong, but incomplete: In a reformulation of what was said in section (3), the text states that the "I" that remembers previous actions must have been there as it is in the present, and its past is present with it. In this sense, each instance comprises the totality of time. Time therefore cannot simply be said to pass or fly away.[13] Dōgen appropriates the otherwise inconspicuous Literary Sinitic expression *nikon/shikin* ("now")[14] to indicate this pervasive comprehensiveness of each present situation, described by Heine as "holistic and dynamic situational context."[15] Where the word is used in this sense, it will be rendered in the following as "consummate now."

(5) The text goes on to offer additional conceptional support for its thesis by replacing the problematic view of a unidirectional "flow of time" with the notion of "transiting through phases" (*kyōryaku* 経歴). This notion is explained in some detail (5.1). The "transiting" of time is declared to be multidirectional, and it connects each moment or situation with all others. As a consequence, the time of delusional, ordinary persons and that of fully fledged insight or enlightenment are inseparably connected. Dōgen here once more emphasizes the holistic character of each and every moment/situation.[16]

(5.2) Dōgen then revisits the notion of "abiding in dharma positions" he had already addressed in "Actualizing the *kōan*," but this time connects it to the dynamism of change. His example is the incessant progression ("up and down") of the hours of the day in their sequence. As a phase that is positioned within these connections, each time/hour is said to both exhaust and confirm the whole world. This finding is once more related to the case of the unenlightened practitioner: Even a situation in which one fails to grasp the Buddha's teaching is depicted as part of "what is:time," and therefore one phase in the realization of the golden Buddha body.[17]

(5.3) In further elucidation of the meaning of "transiting through phases," Dōgen points out that time is not simply flying away; each moment and each period of time is followed by another. Otherwise, there would be a gap where there is no time. Time therefore not only passes, but also arrives. Likewise, each time maintains its position in the series. Again, the point is about the relationship between delusion and insight: If time is seen simply flying past, one loses sight of the time when insight will arrive; and likewise, bodhi and nirvana would merely be transient states.[18] (5.4) In truth, the fetters keeping one from full realization of insight are phases of precisely that realization. Because of the holistic character of each situation, everything, including the Buddhas and heavenly protectors of the teaching, appear as the exertion of the self as time. Nothing, the text goes on to posit, could come to pass without that exertion.[19] (5.5) Finally, Dōgen illustrates the meaning of "transiting through phases" with a pair of contrasting similes: It is not like the wind going from east to west, but like spring, which may be seen as a larger phase realized by transition through a series of smaller phases. A one-directional view of passing that ignores the multidirectional movements making up this process is not the right way of studying the Buddhist teaching.[20]

Paragraphs (4) and (5) together may be allocated to the "expansion" part (*shō* 承) of the traditional fourfold scheme. They present evidence and conceptual support in favor of the text's main idea. The part ends with a simile that serves to anchor this novel notion by way of an intuitive image of strong cultural significance.

Next in the traditional fourfold structure is a "turning" (*ten* 転), which here comes in the form of reference to two authoritative cases from the Zen canon. (6) The first case translates a dialogue that reportedly provoked "great insight" (*daigo* 大悟) in Yaoshan Weiyan (referred to as Yakusan Kudō 藥山弘道), the unnamed "old Buddha" of the fascicle's beginning.[21] Yaoshan was a disciple of Shitou Xiqian (Jp. Sekitō Kisen 石頭希遷, 700–790), one of the primary ancestors of the Caodong/Sōtō line of Zen. Shitou here is said to have sent him to Mazu Daoyi (Jp. Baso Dōitsu 馬祖道一; 709–788, referred to by his alternative designation as Kōzei Daijaku/Chin. Jiangxi Daji 江西大寂), who counted among the ancestors of the Linji/Rinzai tradition. Yaoshan tells Mazu that he thinks he has mastered traditional doctrines but has not yet understood "why the ancestral teacher [Bodhidharma, the legendary founder of Zen] came from the West [from India to China]"—that is, the meaning of the Zen teaching. The answer, which is rendered in Literary Sinitic and defies summing up, is translated by Nearman as follows: "There are times when we make That One's eyebrows rise and His eyes twinkle, and there are times when we do not make His eyebrows rise and His eyes twinkle. There are times when we who make That One's eyebrows rise and His eyes twinkle are right, and there are times when we who make His eyebrows rise and His eyes twinkle are not right."[22] What Nearman translates here as "there are times" is again *uji* in the original. Dōgen in his ensuing discussion equates eyebrows and eyes with mountains and the ocean, and insists that both the time of "being right" and "not being right" are *uji* ("what is:time"); and so are mountains and oceans. Mountains and oceans, like everything else, exist only as/with time; they would perish if time were to perish, and they will not perish if time does not perish. He posits this as a "principle" (*dōri* 道理) from which the Buddha's enlightenment and the Zen tradition originate.[23]

(7) The second confirmatory case directly (that is, in Literary Sinitic) quotes another master from Linji's line of tradition. It renders some lines from an instruction of Guisheng (Jp. Kisei 帰省 ?–?) to his congregation, which reflect on the relation of verbal expressions and the meaning/insight they seek to convey: As Guisheng states, "sometimes" such a statement has been reached, but not the meaning/intention (*i* 意), or vice versa; or both have arrived, or none.[24] "Sometimes" is *uji* in the Literary Sinitic text. Dōgen accordingly reads this to mean that each of these phases signifies "what is:time;" including the ones where one is still groping for an insight or has an intuitive grasp of something but not yet arrived at a way to express it. He then proceeds to somewhat enigmatically distinguish arriving from coming and, as a consequence, also not arriving from not yet having arrived. The explanation offered is that each phase in being "what is:time" restricts (*keige* 罣礙) itself, but is not restricted by its negation. The meaning thus restricts itself, and in this manner also "sees" itself, and the same goes for verbal expression. Meaning is further equated with the "actualization of the *kōan*" 現成公安, and verbal expression with "the time when one looks up and unbolts the barrier gate."[25]

(8) The concluding section (*ketsu/musubi* 結 in the four-part scheme), which consists mainly of a number of seven-character lines in Literary Sinitic, sums up and extends what has been said already. Dōgen once

more insists that all phases in the process of generating and expressing insight, including those that apparently fail to do so, are "what is:time." To emphasize, he restates Yaoshan's words by introducing the expressions "half," "failed," and "failed what is:time," respectively. Every instance of practice, regardless of its apparent success, can count as a fully fledged realization of the Buddha Way and shares the "same time" with the Buddhas and ancestors.[26]

Central Concepts and Propositions

What Is:Time

Based on the above outline of the overall argument in "What Is:Time," we can now review in more detail the meaning of its central concepts and propositions. As we noted in passing in chapter 1, the word *uji* itself was coined by upgrading a standard compound that would normally be read to mean "at one time." Dōgen treats the expression not as a conjunction, but as a stand-alone term, analogous in form (but obviously not in meaning) to the English expression "the how and the why." Unlike that expression, however, *uji* is used both as a noun and a verb. The term embodies four of the seven rhetorical strategies that Hee-Jin Kim identified as typical of Dōgen's use of language as a means of generating insight: "semantic reconstruction through syntactic change," "explication of semantic attributes," "upgrading commonplace notions and using neglected metaphors," and finally, as we shall see later on, "reinterpretation based on the principle of nonduality."[27] Ultimately, all of them serve to exemplify how the *Buddha Dharma* may be found both in inconspicuous passages of canonical texts and in trivial elements of everyday experience. As Dōgen says in relation to "what is:time": "One is to study this in/according to the present twelve [zodiacal] hours."

As a concept, *uji* implies a complex view of time with important soteriological consequences. It serves to explain the unity of actual practice with the Buddhas' consummate insight and achievement of liberation, and, on a deeper level, the omnipresence of the *Buddha Dharma* (both already themes in the *Discourses*; see above, regarding section 2). The following central propositions can be extracted from the paragraphs of the exposition:

(1) What there is exists not "in" time but "as" time. This is generally accepted to be the philosophically most relevant intervention of "What

Is:Time" because the term posits that everything real is also temporal. In the words of Joan Stambaugh: "anything whatsoever that is happening is not *in* time, but is time itself. Time is the taking place (passage, *kyōryaku* 經歷) of all beings. It is the way they *are*."[28] Dōgen's teaching is thus placed in opposition to all views, Buddhist or not, which consider time as something projected on things from the outside—be it by way of a human mode of perception (as in Kant's idea of time as the form of the "inner sense" or contemporary ideas of "time as illusion"[29]) or by way of cognitive action (as in Norbert Elias's or Niklas Luhmann's ideas about time as a result of human efforts at "timing"[30]). Further phrases from "What Is:Time," such as "Thus, a pine tree is time, bamboo is time," confirm this position.[31]

(2) As Elberfeld observes in his interlinear commentary, this entails being "a" time that can be distinguished from others, but also being "time" tout court.[32]

(3) Both aspects are connected by positing seriality or situative ordering as a fundamental principle of being: Each "thing" establishes itself as a situation with a certain temporal ordering, which ultimately involves the whole world, including the practitioner's self. Elberfeld speaks of a process of "configuring factors of existence, which is at the same time a configuring of the world's interrelations."[33]

(4) Ultimately, this results in the thesis that practitioners (and, possibly, everything) share the same time with Buddhas. Practice is coeval with consummate attainment of the way. This aspect of universal synchrony obviously involves questions about time's ordering and directionality; hence, its relation to the aspect of seriality or situative ordering needs further clarification.

Further central concepts and terms of the fascicle—such as "transition through phases," "abiding in the dharma position," and "consummate now"—are introduced to explicate and support these central propositions. Their close inspection will help to answer at least some of the questions that have been raised.

The major point of contention in the research literature concerning the above propositions is how they deal with temporal distinctions. As mentioned above, the idea of synchrony or coevality of religious practice here and now with the supreme enlightenment of all Buddhas and Bodhisattvas across the ages calls into question the direction of time and the status of duration and causality. As a consequence, the question arises of how "what is:time" relates to chronometry and chronology, addressed in terms of the "twelve [zodiacal] hours" in the fascicle's first paragraphs.

Generally, the literature has emphasized the "concrete," "existential," and "subjective" aspects of *uji* over and against "abstract," "objective" notions of "measurable" time, often identified with the "modern" view of time: Kim contrasted Dōgen's "highly personal and existential emphasis" with a view where "temporal units are represented only quantitatively, abstracted from their experiential contact with felt qualities of life."[34] In a similar vein, Yorizumi stated that Dōgen "developed a subjective theory of time."[35] Sometimes this juxtaposition simply works to negate the idea that time exists independently of things and human experience. Consider the following statement from Tsujiguchi Yūichirō's insightful study of Dōgen's thought: "Modern people generally think of time and space as containers in which various events occur, and which have their own, uniform measure. But since this understanding posits time and space as independent from dharma*s* (=existents), it can only get in the way of thinking about Dōgen's theory of time, who taught that dharma*s* and time are one."[36] However, the opposition between "subjective," "concrete," and "existential" time on the one hand, and "objective," "abstract," and "measurable" time on the other, is often taken further. Many readers of Dōgen think that the notion of "what is:time" is incompatible with any form of objectification—and, especially, quantification. Thus, Elberfeld succinctly states: " 'Time' in Dōgen's sense is *not* measurable."[37] Heine speaks of Dōgen's intention to "overcome any assumption about sequential time, which is calculated."[38]

In her recent book, Shinshū Roberts explains the reasoning behind this opposition to thinking of time in terms of sequence from the aspect of Zen practice:

> When you view your practice in this way, you think, "Oh, well, I left behind those mistakes because I'm here on the path to enlightenment." You have arrived at the vermilion palace, the place of imagined enlightenment. When we view practice as a means to attain realization, we tend to view our previous stage as behind us, and our attainment as not yet arrived. [. . .] Your struggles, the difficulties that you had, are something in the past, and they are not currently in your present situation. [. . .] Being caught in thinking of time as three sequential time periods—past, present, and future—we [. . .] are cutting ourselves

off from our own life as well as the life of all being(s). [. . .] We adhere to this notion of time out of a kind of anxiety to protect the self. The desire to define realization as something outside of ourselves, only attainable at some future date and better than our current ordinary life, will only take us further from our true experience.³⁹

There is little room for doubt that Dōgen, with his concept of "what is:time," refutes the view of practice as a stage apart from enlightenment, and the concomitant notion of time as a three-part container that exists outside of things and the self. But these stronger statements in the literature—which posit that his concept of time denies the validity of temporal sequence and measure, and that he rejects the reality (however understood) of duration—stand in contrast to our findings in the previous chapters. They further seem to rely on a one-sided notion of nonduality, in which, in the words of Hee-Jin Kim "the deconstructive function of emptiness as ultimate truth lacks a dynamic, dialectical relationship with worldly truth."⁴⁰ I therefore explore below whether the core notions and propositions of "What Is:Time" can be interpreted in a way that integrates the objective, measurable, and possibly even the abstract aspects of time, while addressing the concerns voiced by Heine, Roberts, and others.⁴¹ In doing so, I apply Dōgen's above-quoted injunction to study the concept "within the twelve hours" on the conceptual plane—including his admonition not to take time's measure for granted.⁴² In light of Dōgen's use of chronography and the time regimes he installed, it makes sense to investigate how measuring or other "objective" ways of grasping time may find their place within his view of time. The challenge for such an interpretation is to account for those propositions in "What Is:Time" that state that practitioners share the "same time" with enlightened beings, since this idea appears to defy notions of temporal sequence and measurable distance.

THE CONSUMMATE NOW

Nikon 而今 (literally, simply "now") is the first of the explanatory terms introduced in "What Is:Time" and brings us right to the heart of this matter. A compound built from the conjunctive *ni/ji* ("so; and, and then; and yet, but")⁴³ and the character for "now," it is yet another case where a common word is upgraded by Dōgen to take on deeper significance. In its ordinary use, the expression simply points to what is happening presently as a continuation of the past or in opposition to it.⁴⁴ Within "What Is:Time," the term first appears at the beginning of the expansion (thematic unit 4) when Dōgen employs the simile of crossing a river, scaling a mountain, and then residing in a bright vermilion palace on top to counter the view that time simply flies past. The "now" of each of these situations must, he argues, contain the other times that led up to it as well as those following from it. Each such "now" contains in some way all times, and each is perfect in the sense that no time is lacking from it. This is why I have chosen the translation "consummate now."

Other commentaries and translations render *nikon* with expressions such as "eternal now" or "absolute now," which have strong mystical connotations.⁴⁵ Yorizumi Mitsuko, for example, writes: "This 'present moment right now' has attained 'emptiness' and is the 'one moment' that lets the world appear. It is a time based on the timeless (*mujikan* 無時間), namely 'emptiness.' In terms of the philosophy of religion, we can call it the 'now of eternity.'"⁴⁶ Read in this vein, the term *nikon* implies that temporal distinctions fall away on a fundamental level that is consequently addressed as "timeless." A closer inspection of Dōgen's words in question, however, opens up a path to a fully non-dual understanding, which integrates the "objective," measured side of time instead of emptying time of its distinctions. Dōgen first states that the earlier stages cannot simply have vanished into nothing, because "I" was there crossing the river and scaling the mountain, as "I" am here now. "'I' was there at that time of scaling the mountain and crossing the river. There must be time for that 'I.' That 'I' was necessarily there, and time cannot have gone away."⁴⁷ In that sense, the present time is all-comprehensive, and this is what Dōgen first designates with the term "consummate now": "Should time not have the property of leaving and arriving, then the time of scaling the mountain is what is:time's consummate now."⁴⁸

This latter sentence is often read in isolation, which explains why many authors take it to signify a denial of linear time. Holbrook, for example, says in a statement reiterated by Rein Raud that Dōgen "is postulating not a presentness that exists without any reference to a past or future but rather a presentness in which time does not have a linear meaning."⁴⁹ In this view, each moment presents the totality of time in the fashion of a holistic engram. One has to comprehend the "absolute now" as a compact whole, without dividing it into parts connected by linear movements. Hee-Jin Kim expresses this view as follows: "the structure of the absolute now is such that the past, present, and future [. . .] are not arranged in a linear fashion but realized simultaneously in the manner of mutual identity and mutual penetration (*sōsoku sōnyū*)."[50]

Others, starting with Akiyama, have devised ways to integrate some notion of linearity between past, present, and future into the idea of a holistic present. Notably, such reconstructions also allow for the integration of the concept of karma, the principle of moral retribution. A somewhat rationalistic reconstruction, which I have proposed earlier,[51] would argue that the present contains the past precisely because it is the causal result of previous events and actions. Similarly, the causal vectors in place or initialized in the present entail their future outcomes. Heine seems to indicate a similar idea when he writes about the "unrepeatable stage of a thing's existence at any given moment, which encompasses everything that caused its current status and, in turn, it helps generate."[52] Paradoxically, Heine connects this to a rejection of the sequence of before and after.[53]

Dōgen, however, continues his explanation of the consummate now with a sentence that explicitly grants the notion of passage (and thereby, sequence): "If time retains the property of coming and going, then there is together with me the consummate now of what is:time, and that is what is:time."[54]

The apparent contradiction in the passage quoted above can be resolved if we take into account that both views are formulated as hypothetical propositions. In other words, they stand for possible, legitimate perspectives on time. Further, they converge in stating that what is usually seen as the past has to be accepted as part of the present. The first passage starts from the hypothesis that "coming and going" are not properties of time. This proposition accounts for the fundamental fact that any time we speak of must be there for us; no time can ever be lost or vanish completely. Therefore, all times are always (also) part of the present. This may sound strange and invoke mystical connotations, but it is in line with a fundamental observation made by the famous sociologist Niklas Luhmann, who was certainly not a mysticist:

> Time is in a much deeper sense constituted in paradoxical fashion: as the synchrony of the asynchronous. [. . .] Therefore, past and future are complementary horizons of time which can only be given in synchrony. They are always horizons of the present, a present past and a present future [. . .] This is only an alternative way of saying that everything that happens,

happens at the same time, even if within that happening we can discover movement or change, and therefore, the horizons of the past and the future.[55]

Notably, this fundamental presence of all times does not preclude temporal distinctions. On the contrary, it is their necessary foundation. Dōgen uses different language but follows a similar logic in applying the "consummate now" to a temporal perspective that sustains the distinctions of coming and going, past and future. These distinctions are tied to a point of observation, a center around which the temporal order is crystallized. Dōgen refers to this center with the expression *ware*, which here clearly references the "I" that climbed the mountain and crossed the river. But *ware* is also his translation term for the Sanskrit *ātman*, which traditionally indicates the notions of a permanent self and substantiality. We will have to consider how far these aspects come into play for Dōgen, insofar as he accepts the perspective of "coming and going" as one where the "now" of "what is:time" is there "for" or "together with" *ware*. In any case, the past belongs to the present. The distinction between them is tied to a temporal occasion (*jisetsu* 時節) when that distinction is made, similar to the moment where someone who has wandered from afar and climbed a mountain range then surveys "a thousand and myriad peaks." Finally, Dōgen links the argument back to matters of soteriology. His point is that one may think of the Buddha's body as a far-off goal of religious practice, but in reality it "transits its course within the I's is:time; it looks as if it was in a different place, but it is the consummate now."[56] In that sense, the vermilion "palace on top of the mountain" in Dōgen's text is not so much a symbol of "idle hopes and expectations" for a "secure and triumphant" position outside the inexorable dynamic of change, as Heine believed it to be.[57] Instead, Dōgen in his explanation of the "consummate now" integrates the holistic perspective from the top of the mountain, which unites past, present, and future, as a given aspect of every single moment.

This brings us back to the idea that the time of the practitioner is fundamentally synchronous to that of enlightened beings, an idea we have already met with in the *Discourses*. "What Is:Time" introduces it early on with a thetic expression, following the explanation that things, seen as occasions, can each be one with the whole (including past, present, and future) and still coexist without impeding each other: "For this reason, there is same-time origination of the intention [to obtain enlightenment], which is bringing forth time from the same intention." The Japanese original makes use of the option to cluster Chinese characters into quadruples that may then undergo permutation: *kono yue ni dōji hosshin ari, dōshin hotsuji nari* このゆゑに同時発心あり、同心発時なり.[58] *Hosshin* 発心, the initial aspiration for enlightenment, or more literally the "bringing forth of the [*bodhi-*] mind," is a technical term that indicates the first stage on the path to enlightenment (see above, pp. 125–26). In the Mahāyāna interpretation, it means to open the mind to the truth of suffering and decide to seek a way to liberate all sentient (and therefore suffering) beings. The parallelism between the four-character clusters *dōji hosshin* 同時発心 and *dōshin hotsuji* 同心発時 implies that the "time" in question is not time in general, but the time of enlightenment. Then again, because of the fundamental unity of every "thing" with the whole, every time/occasion/thing is already the time of enlightenment. On a primary level, the formula indicates that when practitioners bring forth the wish for liberation, they do so in synchrony with all the Buddhas and Bodhisattvas. On a second, expanded level, it says that each and every occasion, whatever its apparent attributes, has the same quality of being one with Buddha's enlightenment. From this perspective, everything that happens is perfect as it is.

Transiting through Phases/Lining up in Order

How is this notion possible? According to "What Is:Time," a close attention to time reveals that synchrony across temporal distances is indeed compatible with the process of temporal passage, if correctly understood. As Tsujiguchi has pointed out, the expression "transpires in my what is:time," from the conclusion of the paragraph on the consummate now, already looks forward to the next explanatory term Dōgen introduces, which is *kyōryaku* 經歷 (more commonly pronounced *keireki*).[59] Previous translations of this term already indicate the spectrum of interpretations: "flowing," "shifting," "event-like running" (*ereignishaftes Verlaufen*), "passage," "seriatim passage," "[totalistic] passage," and even "passageless passage."[60] I propose to render it as "transition through phases" for the following reasons. First, very often, and even in other passages of the *Treasury,* the expression simply denotes the passing or spending of time. From this are derived lexical usages that entail wandering, visiting, and passing through various places, or experiencing something. Finally, the term may denote the sum of what one has experienced or the stations in life and society one has gone through.[61] Dōgen's use of the term in

"What Is:Time" apparently harvests these meanings to counter the idea that time simply passes or flies away. It is notable in this regard that the few paragraphs in "What Is:Time" dedicated to the explication of the "transition through phases" (section 5 in Table 1, DZZ I, 191–92) also make prominent use of the expressions "dharma-position" (*hōi* 法位) and "dwelling in the dharma-position."

The term *kyōryaku* itself is used a total of twenty-two times in "What Is:Time," including nineteen occasions in the two paragraphs quoted below. They frame a series of statements on the notions of "abiding in the dharma-position," "lining up in order" (*hairetsu su* 配列す), and "exhausting" (*jin* 尽・盡):

> What is:time possesses the virtue of transiting through phases. It transits from what we call today to tomorrow, it transits from today to yesterday, it transits from yesterday to today. It transits from today to today, it transits from tomorrow to tomorrow. And this is because transiting through phases is a virtue of time.[62]
>
> [. . .]
>
> What is called transition through phases cannot be studied in the usual way[63] as if it were like wind and rain moving from east to west. [Exhausting] the whole world[64] is not something without movement, something that neither progresses nor recedes, it is transiting through phases. This transition through phases is something like spring. There are many diverse states in spring, and that is what we call transition through phases. This is to be studied as a transition that has nothing external to it. In our example, spring's transition through phases transits inevitably through spring. The transition through phases is not identical with spring, but since spring is a transition through phases, the transition through phases is for now completing its course in the time of spring. One must probe this in detail, approaching it, leaving it alone, and coming back to it again. When speaking of transiting through phases, the study of the Buddha Way does not simply imagine the realm [of transition] as something external and the dharma that is the agent of the transition through phases as something that moves eastward through hundreds and thousands of spheres, passing hundreds and thousands of eons.[65]

Commentators who read the first paragraph in isolation have often understood it as a rejection of the directional passing of time. Tsunoda Tairyū, for example, writes: " 'Time' does not mean the passing of time, but 'being' (existence) and *kyōryaku* (way of being)."[66] To others, it has appeared as a description of the temporal dynamism that is designed to leave one, in the words of Joan Stambaugh, "with nothing to hold on to."[67] The simile of spring that appears in the second paragraph, however, opens up a different perspective. I concur with Tsujiguchi, who insisted that it precludes the view that temporal distinctions are merely subjective and therefore possibly delusional.[68] Like the soccer game analogy by Rein Raud—but in contrast to Raud's momentarist interpretation—spring is certainly a reality, but not one defined by a solid substance with changing attributes. It consists entirely of diverse states and phases, and it is realized in transiting through all of them, with some happening at the same time, some in sequence. In the beginning of spring, shoots rise from the earth and buds grow on trees. Later on, shoots and buds may turn into flowers. In doing so, they become a thing of the past. From this image of spring, one can understand the somewhat paradoxical statement that time moves from yesterday to today as much as from today to yesterday: Tomorrow's flower will be that of today when tomorrow has arrived, while then "tomorrow" will have moved another day ahead.[69] Dōgen is not denying the passing of time here. Instead, he points to the complexity of the "shifts," to use Raud's term, which are revealed by a full appreciation of temporal change.

In the text between the two paragraphs quoted above, Dōgen states that considering time as something that only flies past means overlooking the time that has not yet arrived.[70] He further explains that, because of the "transition through phases," the past and present do not "pile up" or "accumulate by lining up."[71] As time, they belong together, while as so many times, they remain distinct and do not stand in each other's way. Likewise, practice belongs to enlightenment, even if full insight has not yet been obtained. The past "dharma-configuration" gives way to the present. Both mutually "line up in order," just like the hours "arise" and "decline" in their given sequence.[72] The important point, as Dōgen emphasizes, is to be aware of how these phases or "dharma-configurations" form a unity. Consequently, even when one feels totally distant from the golden Buddha body, this is just a part or phase of the very process of attaining it: "When people try to get away with thinking that they are not the golden body of one *jō* six, these are really just fragments of what is:time; they are the ideations of those who have not yet realized [insight]."[73]

Exhausting

Also notable is the conjunction, here and in the introductory paragraphs of "What Is:Time," of "lining up in order" (*hairetsu su* 排列す) with various compounds using the character 盡 (modern: 尽; "to exhaust, exhausting, exhaustive"). For example, Dōgen writes at one point: "At this time, one realizes exhausting all worlds with three heads and eight arms, one realizes exhausting all worlds with the golden body of one *jō* six. The world-exhausting of all worlds with all worlds is called fully exhausting."[74] The following sentence makes clear how this "golden Buddha body" is realized by going through the series of life-phases of a Buddha or Bodhisattva: The ordinary sentient being awakens to the truth of suffering, submits to the path of practice, and arrives at full realization: "The one *jō* six golden body is embodied in a one *jō* six golden fashion by bringing forth the intention, practicing, obtaining enlightenment, and nirvana, *and it is precisely what is, and it is time*"[75] [emphasis mine].

In general terms, each "self" entails a certain configuration of the whole world, of everything else. This much was already stated in the introductory section of "What Is:Time":

> When one lines up the self-identical in order and takes that to exhaust the world, one has to look at all living beings and all things of this exhaustive world as so many times. Things do not obstruct one another just like times do not obstruct one another. For this reason, there is same-time origination of the intention [to obtain enlightenment], which is bringing forth time from the same intention. Practice and realization of the way are also like this. Lining up the self-identical in order, the self-identical looks at this. This is the way to understand how the self is time.[76]

"The self-identical" here translates *ware*. As noted above, this word can function as a first-person pronoun, but it can also stand for the Sanskrit *ātman*, the trans-personal, eternal cosmic self. The substantialist and eternalist aspects of the latter notion are obviously anathema to Dōgen. Nonetheless, he retains the aspect of a self that encompasses the whole world, configuring it in a particular way. This holistic aspect with Dōgen does not imply an eternal substance. To use a description from Ishii Kiyozumi, *ware* in this context refers to anything that maintains a certain identity, a set of defining characteristics, over a certain time. Ishii mainly argues against readings of Dōgen that equate "what is:time" with the present moment, and which deny that his concept of time allows for duration. He emphasizes that time in Dōgen "attaches individually to particular things and phenomena, and refers to the period in which they continue to retain their specific attributes."[77] This observation matches well with our findings on Dōgen's chronography; especially concerning his frequent references to *types* of situations, when things happen in a certain way.[78]

In light of these findings, the point of the above passage is precisely that, as such a self, each *ware* is a dynamic configuration of everything and is thus in a certain sense one with everything. As a specific configuration of the whole, it however remains distinct from everything else. This may explain why Dōgen says that things, by being distinct "is:times," are not obstructed by each other, but restrict (*keige* 罣礙) themselves.

Identifying time as the way things are further serves to explain how an infinite number of such exhaustive totalities may coexist without getting in each other's way. Dōgen here clearly alludes to the tenet of the "mutual non-obstruction of things" from the Kegon school. He offers an explanation for this enigmatic phrase by way of clarifying the relation of "things" and "time."[79] To illustrate, one can imagine how his most trusted disciple, Ejō, supervised a morning's meditation session in the monks' hall while (and knowing that) the head cook was preparing lunch in the kitchen hall—provided by a donor, because the peasants on her landholdings had obtained a good harvest due to favorable weather that year. The head cook may have been scolding a novice who had spilled some of the soaked rice, causing worries about whether there would be enough for all to eat, and both may have been reminded of the faces of exhausted peasants they knew from home, and so forth. All of this transpired within a social structure that had developed from strategies to cope with the requirements of the centralist administrative system envisioned in the founding laws of the Japanese empire under conditions of highly limited productivity. These laws in turn had been formulated as a reaction to perceived military challenges from the continent.

This example serves to illustrate how the configuration of elements that make up a given something extends far beyond its immediate present location. In Dōgen's view, this involves the whole universe of things, affairs, and events—all of which may be described in a like manner. This helps to explain why Dōgen links "lining up in order" with expressions of "exhausting." From here, one can understand the following, possibly most cryptic statement in "What Is:Time": "One should study in practice how not a single dharma or a single thing could neither actually come to pass nor transit through phases if it were not for my transiting through the phases of exhausting my powers right now."[80]

As Awaya Ryōdō has shown in a series of articles on "The Idea of Exhausting in the 'Treasury,'"[81] "exhaustion" combines two perspectives: the inclusion and affirmation of complete reality, *and* the equation of everything with Buddhas, ancestors, and also emptiness.[82] Awaya discusses "What Is:Time" only in passing, and he perceives these perspectives to stand in contradiction. But it seems to me that Dōgen's concept of "what is:time," in joining the "consummate now" with the "transition through phases" and the exhaustive "lining up in order," offers a way to understand how—for Dōgen at least—they actually imply each other. If every time is a configuration of the whole world and all times, one may as a first step argue that this configuration must include the Buddhas of the present as well as those of the past and the future. In soteriological terms, however, such an argument would still seem to fall flat: What would be the use of telling a suffering being that all is well, since their actual suffering is a configuration of the world that includes all enlightened beings?

The same statement, however, acquires a fuller meaning when combined with the perspective of transiting through phases in accord and synchrony with the Buddhas and ancestors. Now the current suffering becomes part of the path of enlightenment as it is realized by the "golden body of one *jō* six." Suffering beings are not alone, but one with the Buddhas and ancestors in their struggle—even if their own perspective remains limited, and only the "exhaustive exploration of half of what is:time."[83] There would be no Buddhas without this kind of exhausting all the phases of their path, including the suffering that prompts awakening.

Finally, given the presupposition that there is no ontological hiatus between self and world, it is again only logical to extend this to non-sentient entities such as "mountains and seas." Dōgen does so in the "turning" part of "What Is:Time" when he discusses Mazu's statement about making the Buddha's eyebrows rise and his eyes twinkle in practice: "'Making him raise' must see mountains, 'making him blink' must instruct the sea. [. . .] Mountains are also time, as is the sea. If they weren't time, there couldn't be mountains and sea. It is not possible that there is no time in the consummate now of mountains and sea."[84] Mazu's quote is linked in the text to Yaoshan and therefore may be referred back to the latter's words about "standing on top of the mountain, walking on the bottom of the sea," which form the initial lines of "What Is:Time." This would give the passage an ontologically somewhat less provocative meaning. It would then simply appear to rephrase what Dōgen has already said about other phases in the life of a Buddha or ancestor. But even if one insists on reading "mountains" literally, it is possible to understand how, in the conceptual framework laid out above, mountains and seas are part of the configurations called "Buddhas" or "sentient beings" and vice versa, once all of them are seen as "what is:time."

A first interpretation is offered by phenomenology; this states that "mountains" as objects are constituted in subjective experience, which gives them their specific *gestalt*.[85] I believe, however, that this is only part of what Dōgen is implying here. The exhaustive "lining up in order" that is inherent in "what is:time" means that to be something involves a mutual configuration of everything: The mountains literally shape the self that climbs them or looks at them (or has climbed or looked at them, or must climb or look at them at some point), much as the mountains are configured by the grasses and trees growing on them, the birds and beasts inhabiting them, and the people who walk them or exploit their riches for a living. To extend this proposition beyond the sphere of immediate contact is a strong holistic hypothesis, but still an intelligible one; to further infer that everything else depends on the exhaustive dynamic activity of the "self" is taking this proposition to its extreme, but again, in an intelligible fashion.

Conclusion

"What Is:Time," with its central explanatory terms "consummate now," "transition through phases," and "lining up in order," does not leave us with a notion of separate, individual times that are congruent with particular things or occasions. Even less does it force us to assume the notion of isolated, dimensionless (but nevertheless holistic) moments, as was recently proposed by Rein Raud. There is certainly the notion that everything has, and is, its own time. This time is composed of moments, understood as minimal temporal quanta, and there is no material component enduring beyond the temporal space of one such moment or minimal quantum. The moments, however, aggregate into phases that display certain common characteristics: A new boat will not suddenly morph into a butterfly; this is Ishii's point. Furthermore, analogous to Dōgen's example of spring transiting through its phases, there will come a time when this boat is still a boat, but a well-used one; a time when it needs repair; and a further time when it is beyond repair, perhaps because it has been abandoned. This then connects to another seminal conceptual component of "what is:time." Each "thing" involves the exhaustive "lining up" of the whole world. For the configuration "boat" to exist, there must be people who use it and dedicate themselves to its maintenance, plus water, a geological formation, and so on. At some point, the necessary conditions for the configuration of this specific boat will no longer exist, and then it will go out of existence. This illustrates how no single "thing," conceived as "what is:time," stands in isolation. If each of them is a configuration that exhausts the whole world, these "things" mutually permeate each other. In this regard, my interpretation goes beyond that of Ishii.

From the mutual permeation of holistic orderings, one can further derive the notion of "objective" time, including ordered sequence and the quantified time of clocks. Consider the example given above, of Ejō presiding over morning *zazen* while the head cook prepares the midday meal. "Ejō presiding" as a configuration of the whole world includes the head cook, and vice versa, and both configurations include the sun slowly moving from one stellar constellation in the sky to the other—which is what the monastery's water clock, supervised by another monastic officer, is supposed to measure. The clock is an indicator of movements inherent in each configuration in question. As these configurations permeate each other, each can refer to the clock, or the celestial movements it represents, as a common denominator to coordinate their actions. Clock-time, then, is not external to things, but emerges from their holistic being as time, where every present moment of their existence includes a configuration of the whole world and all time, and these configurations mutually include each other. Seen in this manner, clock-time does have its conceptual place in Dōgen's idea of time. It may not be a primary one, but neither is it a mere "expedient means" that one must discard to gain the "higher truth" of time.

To sum up in relation to the soteriological agenda in "What Is:Time": The concepts that Dōgen presents here call on his followers to understand their present situation as a distinct phase in the overall process of transition through phases that constitutes the realization of consummate insight. The current state of the practitioner can be identified and described as a configuration of the whole world, including the past, present, and future. It has its stable position in a series of events. By virtue of this position, it may be understood as a phase integral to the realization of insight. "Transition through phases" and "abiding in the dharma position" thus do not stand in opposition to the "consummate now," which emphasizes the aspects of exhaustive totality and synchrony with the Buddha-ancestors. On the contrary: Transition through phases, abiding in position, lining up in order, and exhausting the whole world describe the modality of the "consummate now." Together, they elucidate how what there is, by virtue of being time, is the realization of the *Buddha Dharma*. Importantly, this remains true while distinctions, temporal and otherwise, are being maintained. To err or to fail in practice are phases belonging to the path to full liberation and insight, even if they are not, in themselves, enlightened behavior. In this manner, Dōgen in "What Is:Time" combines the assurance that present practice, including present failures, is the realization of enlightenment on the one hand while emphasizing the necessity to continuously strive for right practice on the other. We can now understand how his "unity of practice and enlightenment" allows for distinctions within practice, temporal and otherwise. The differentiation among practitioners we have seen at work in his chronopolitics thus has a firm doctrinal basis in the concept of "what is:time."

Certain aspects, however, continue to remain obscure. Perhaps most importantly, the above interpretation downplays the implications of the idea that practitioners act together and in synchrony with the enlightened ones—which, if taken literally, strongly challenges the idea of temporal directionality. Giving up directionality, however, would call into question the whole concept of cause and effect. But that concept, or so I argue, is indispensable in providing the links between past, present, and future that support Dōgen's holistic notion that each "what is:time" is a "lining up in order," a configuration of the whole world. It thus seems that the soteriological promise held by the concept of "what is:time" may, on a conceptual level, be self-defeating. In the following chapter, I therefore focus on textual evidence regarding aspects of synchrony and causality found in other fascicles of the *Treasury* and pertinent formal instructions from the *Extensive Record* that were written after "What Is:Time."

7

Karma and the "Consummate Now"

Synchrony and Sequence

After "What Is:Time," time does not again become the main topic of instructions in the *Treasury* until the undated "Karma in the Three Periods"—a text belonging to the 12-fascicle redaction that was first copied by Ejō in April 1253 CE. However, Dōgen returns to the subject of time in a number of instructions written in the months and years after "What Is:Time." Several of them deal with seminal concepts such as the "consummate now" in a fashion that adds new nuances to their understanding. Given the open questions remaining after investigating "What Is:Time," the pertinent texts help to reconstruct Dōgen's ideas on karma, temporal sequence, and the meaning of synchrony for practitioners and enlightened ones. I loosely follow the order in which Dōgen wrote these instructions, to acknowledge their respective contexts, but I sometimes deviate from chronology where the passages in question are closely connected thematically.

In spring 1241, a couple of months after "What Is:Time," Dōgen makes a statement about the correct line of Zen ancestors in the instruction "Buddha Ancestors." The main body of that instruction simply presents a chronological list of names.[1] The introductory paragraph, however, contains a phrase explaining how the Buddhas and ancestors are "actualized" or "realized in the present" (*genjō* 現成): "The present realization of the Buddha ancestors consists in upholding and honoring Buddha ancestors. This not only pertains to the past, present, and future; it certainly goes beyond Buddha's going beyond. One twirls in one's hand[2] the fact of being entrusted with the face of Buddha ancestors, venerates it, exchanges glances with it. By actually upholding the Buddha ancestors' meritorious powers, they are kept constant and bodily realized."[3] This paragraph can be read to imply that Buddha ancestors are present because those following their path "uphold" them in veneration, invoking and practicing their virtues. While denying any separate, self-contained trans-temporal existence of Buddhas and ancestors, the passage in this interpretation upholds the promise that their merits and power accrue for practitioners.

Various passages from the fascicle "Old Mirror" (*Kokyō* 古鏡), first presented in the fall of 1241, point in a similar direction. In this instruction, Dōgen takes the legend of the eighteenth ancestor Gayaśata 伽耶舍多, who was said to have been born with a mirror showing "all Buddha affairs from the past, present and future,"[4] as an occasion to review mirror-related lore. One story he discusses concerns the legendary Yellow Emperor of China, who possessed twelve mirrors. According to his teacher, they represented the twelve stellar hours. The teacher is further quoted as saying: "If the twelve hours were not mirrors, how could one now enlighten the past? If they were not mirrors, how could one enlighten the present? The twelve hours are twelve faces, and the twelve faces are the twelve mirrors, and the present and past are the result of using the twelve hours."[5] This is a rare case where Dōgen mentions non-Buddhist teachings. While he remarks on the fact, he still finds this saying instructive. It certainly aligns with the position that the totality of time is to be found in the changes of every present hour—a central theme of "What Is:Time." This position is reinforced later in "Old Mirror" by discussing a dialogue between the Zen masters Xuefeng and Xuansha, in which Xuefeng (in this dialogue, the teacher) claims to have within himself an old mirror similar to Gayashata's. Xuansha responds that the truth of this mirror is "one hundred broken pieces."[6]

Dōgen endorses this expression and expands on it with the words "We can speak of a clear mirror because it can burst into a hundred pieces. The clear mirror is where a hundred pieces are hanging. Do not limit your view to thinking that previously there was a time when it was not yet sprung into pieces and later there may come a time when it becomes un-sprung again. It is just a hundred pieces."[7] The mirror's fractured pieces reflect the truth. There is, Dōgen insists, no separate instance of (unbroken) wholeness apart from these fractions. To put it in the conceptual language of Mahāyāna Buddhist metaphysics, "emptiness"

空 is not a separate realm, but is present precisely in and through myriad "distinct forms" 色. Furthermore, there is no sphere of eternity or timelessness beyond temporal existence. As Steven Heine writes, awakening has to be realized "through the particular circumstances of evanescence or in the midst of the process of living and dying on all levels of human and natural existence."[8]

At the end of the fascicle, Dōgen discusses the famous *kōan* in which Mazu likens seated meditation to the polishing of a tile to make a mirror. This was traditionally understood as an intervention against seeing seated meditation as the means to achieve enlightenment. Dōgen gives Mazu's saying yet another twist: meditation is not the means to this end; it is the way in which enlightenment is realized. Again we are reminded that in "What Is:Time," it is the moment of striving that realizes synchrony with the enlightened ones because it accords with their pattern of the continuous realization of insight.

This passage further serves to remind us that Dōgen does indeed reject the notion that practice comes first and realization follows later. Practice embodies realization and occurs in synchrony with Buddha ancestors. In this sense, it is true that Dōgen denies an order of temporal sequence, as Steven Heine and others have emphasized.[9] But Dōgen also repeatedly points out that realization as practice is realization in the course of distinct actions, and the course of events and actions is, in any case, irreversible. The denial of sequence specifically refers to the relation of practice and realization. It is not a general refutation of temporal progression.

In the instruction "Thus" (*Inmo* 恁麼), which was given in spring 1242, Dōgen resorts to traditional Buddhist rhetoric to drive home the point that "life is transported by days and nights and cannot stop and pause anywhere. The rosy face [of youth] has gone, and if you search for it, there is nothing of it left behind. When you look at it closely, there are so many past things that you cannot encounter again."[10] The same, he says, holds for the "pure mind" (*sekishin* 赤心): "Neither does the pure mind stop and pause; it goes and comes in fragments. Even what accords with truth is not something lingering in the sphere of a self."[11] In a similar vein, instructing on "Sustained Practice" a couple of days later, Dōgen exhorts his disciples to make good use of their time by unceasing practice, asking "what good skill, what expedient means could there be to bring back a day that is gone?"[12] Time, as he explained in "What Is:Time," means transiting through phases. The direction of this transiting cannot be reversed.

The initial lines of the fascicle echo those of "Buddha Ancestors." They once more present the image of a circular movement to explain how the unity of practice and realization, or of acolytes and Buddhas, is realized:

> Regarding the great way of the Buddha ancestors, there is, without fail, the unsurpassed sustained practice, which turns the cycle of the way and never ceases. There are no gaps between bringing forth the mind, practice, insight, and nirvana. They are sustained practice/way circulation. Therefore, they are untainted sustained practice, neither forced by oneself, nor by another. The merit of this sustained practice entrusts me, and entrusts others. [. . .] Accordingly, by each and every Buddha's and ancestor's sustained practice, our sustained practice actualizes, and our great way arrives at completion. By our sustained practice, the sustained practice of all Buddhas actualizes, and their great way arrives at completion. This merit of the way-circuit exists because of our sustained practice.[13]

The image of cyclical movement without gaps here conjoins both practice with realization and Buddha ancestors with those who emulate them. In a rhetorical move reminiscent of what he says about "exhausting" in "What Is:Time," Dōgen then expands this idea of sustained, revolving practice to comprehend everything that exists, including the earth, the sky, the elements, and the various components that make up the human body and mind.[14] This suggests once more that the "circle" of the way is realized by going through its various phases and their concomitant configurations of the world.

Similarly, Dōgen insists in "Sustained Practice" that a day that is used for practice after the model of the Buddha ancestors "is the seed of all Buddhas, the sustaining in practice of all Buddhas."[15] This statement echoes the idea of the "consummate now," applying it directly to the moment of practice. It further provides us with a link between the idea of transition and that of the "consummate now," because Dōgen insists that "the now of practice is not something residing in the self from the beginning, as its original being. Nor does it go and come, leave and enter the self. The expression 'now' does not exist before sustained practice. Actualizing sustained practice is what is called 'now.'"[16] We have seen in chapter 3 how this "now" may be extended over several years.[17]

The informal instruction "Confirmation" from 1242 further elucidates the holistic dimension of this "revolving circle of the way," even if it uses a different expression to make the point. Incidentally, it is placed directly after "What Is:Time" in the 75-fascicle redaction of the *Treasury*.[18] The title "Confirmation" (*juki* 授記) takes up the technical term for predictions made by the Buddha about someone's future attainment of enlightenment. Expanding its meaning in a fashion that is again reminiscent of his use of "exhausting" in "What Is:Time," Dōgen emphasizes that the Buddha Way confirms everything. Accordingly, everything is affirmed as an "aspect of enlightenment."[19] The latter expression is taken from the Vimalakirti Sutra, where it refers only to sentient beings;[20] however, Dōgen mentions not only "one or half of the third child of Zhang, or the fourth child of Li" (who also figure in the introductory lines of "What Is:Time"), but also "mountains, rivers, earth, Mount Sumeru, or great oceans."[21]

Again, this leads us to question the meaning of temporal distinctions once it is suggested that all is already confirmed as part of consummate enlightenment. At the end of the fascicle, Dōgen seems to expressly deny the distinctions that constitute tensed time, saying: "The past has not necessarily already perished, the future has not necessarily not yet arrived, and the present not necessarily does not abide. Non-abiding/not yet arrived/already gone, etc., are studied as past, future, and present, but it is necessary to express the principle that not arrived is past, present, and future."[22] This statement, however, should be read in light of an earlier paragraph that emphasizes the notion of continuous succession. Quoting an unnamed "old Buddha" who speaks of "successively attaining Buddhahood," Dōgen posits that the "attainment of Buddhahood spoken of here is always successive."[23] Moreover, in "What Is:Time," the expression "not arrived" was used to explain the "transition through phases" and the "consummate now." The context thus favors an interpretation that maintains temporal sequence and distinction. The passage invites disciples to think about time as "what is:time," where each temporal segment comprises a configuration of past, present, and future, and temporal shifting includes the transition from today to today, and so forth.

Some have argued, however, that "succession" for Dōgen did not necessarily imply linearity. Yorizumi Mitsuko[24] has pointed to the final passage of the instruction on "Documents of Heritage" (*Shisho* 嗣書), written a couple of months after "What Is:Time." Dōgen here quotes his teacher Rujing's comment on the correct understanding of transmission between Buddha ancestors. The problem Rujing addresses is how it was possible for Śākyamuni to receive transmission from the Buddha of a previous cosmic eon, Kāśyapa, since they could not have met in person. In his explanation, Rujing insists not only that direct transmission between the two did occur, but also that it went both ways:

> We have learned that Śākyamuni truly received the dharma from Kāśyapa. This is to be understood and studied in the sense that Kāśyapa entered nirvana after Śākyamuni received the dharma from him. [. . .] The dharma has reached us by being transmitted in this manner between the Buddhas, and each and every Buddha is its rightful heir. They do not line up in a row or come together in groups. [. . .] If the dharma had been initiated by Śākyamuni, it would exist for only 2,000 years until now. It would not be old. [. . .] But succession between the Buddhas is not to be understood in this way. It is to be studied in the fashion that Śākyamuni inherited the dharma from Kāśyapa, and that Kāśyapa inherited it from Śākyamuni. Only when studied in this way, it is truly the dharma succession between all Buddha ancestors.[25]

This idea of a mutual transmission between Buddha ancestors is repeated in other fascicles such as "Old Buddha Mind" (*Kobusshin* 古佛心).[26] As indicated by Yorizumi, it appears to call into question the notion of linear progression.

A passage in the instruction "Pervasive Exploration," however, points to an explanation that acknowledges both mutual transmission and temporal sequence. The instruction originates from the time of transition in a "grass thatched hut at the foot of Yamashi peak" in January 1244. It returns to the notion of shared practice and synchrony between Buddha ancestors (and, by extension, practitioners and enlightened beings).[27] Dōgen once more emphasizes that the true practice is the same between enlightened ones. Then he goes on to state that this precisely makes Śākyamuni the "old Buddha" and Xuansha his "descendant," and exhorts his disciples to understand this by way of studying the "period in which they practice the same at the same time."[28] The mutual interaction is, in other words, not so much one in two directions of time, but a result of the fundamental synchrony and identity of all true practice. Dōgen elaborates further on this three months later in the fascicle on "Arousing the Aspiration for the Unsurpassable" (*Hotsu mujōshin* 發無上心).²⁹ Here, he refers to a canonical saying where the Buddha states that when he attained enlightenment, all sentient beings and the "great earth" attained it with him at the same time. Dōgen infers from this, first, that aspiration, practice, enlightenment, and nirvana happen at the same time for Śākyamuni and everything that exists. With aspiration, the world is configured in a way that makes every part of it an element of the Buddha Way.³⁰ Second, he posits an identity between each one of these phases in each and every being: "Arousing the aspiration for enlightenment one thousand times, one billion times, is none other than arousing the aspiration for enlightenment one time. Arousing the aspiration for enlightenment by one thousand billion people is not other than arousing one aspiration. [. . .] Practice, realization, and the turning of the dharma are also like this."³¹ There are two ways to understand this passage. Either one takes it like Yorizumi (and, following her, Heine) to indicate that there is a realm (or perspective) where temporal distinctions fall away, where everything exists simultaneously, in an absolute "eternal now."³² Or, as I would suggest, one connects this passage to a reading of "What Is:Time" that emphasizes the aspect of chronotypology. As Dōgen insists that every realization of the Buddha Way (as expressed through the fourfold expression of aspiration, practice, enlightenment, and nirvana) is identical, each instance of aspiration, practice, enlightenment, and nirvana (re)creates or, to be more precise, actualizes "the same time." In doing so, it communicates with all other actualizations. In this reading, Dōgen's above quote from Rujing indicates that Kāśyapa Buddha attained nirvana after transmitting the dharma to Śākyamuni because at that time, the configuration of events where Śākyamuni appeared and attained enlightenment was already present. It further indicates that each actualization of aspiration and enlightenment enriches all previous ones, while this enrichment is, however, already preconfigured in the previous instances.

Notably, while retaining the notion of temporal sequence, this is a strongly holistic position that raises questions about determinism and human freedom. Dōgen's repeated polemics against the "naturalist heresy" demonstrate, however, his emphasis on individual effort and decision-making. In other words, Dōgen takes Śākyamuni's words about sentient beings attaining enlightenment "at the same time" as a promise about universal salvation, but not as a prediction concerning the exact when and where of this event for every being. In this interpretation, the expression "the same time" assures the occurrence of the fact and the quality of the event. However, the temporal location depends on when individual beings let it happen by actualizing aspiration and practice.

The notion of "synchrony" and sharing the "same practice" with the enlightened ones further implies differentiation into the various acts and events that fill insight with life—similarly to how the "consummate now" in "What Is:Time" implies "transition through phases." That is why the instruction on "Arousing the Aspiration for the Unsurpassable" points toward the multifarious acts that participate in this "same practice" at the "same time"—from building Buddha statues or stupas as objects of veneration, to seated meditation. Similarly, in an instruction on "The Constants of the House," Dōgen identifies the "golden, wondrous form" of Buddha with "getting dressed and eating meals."[33]

These statements do not instruct monastics to simply attend to daily matters at hand. They imply procedures he has laid out in detail in his monastic regulations. These include, in the case of meals, a temporal sequence reflecting the social distinctions between monks, which are based on their dharma age and record of participation in summer retreats. As we have seen in chapter 4, similar rules obtain for many other daily activities. One may downplay such instructions as mere corollaries for dealing with practical needs, in opposition to the higher truth in a dimension beyond all temporal distinction. But the evidence assembled here suggests otherwise: Dōgen does insist that the "same practice" at the "same time" with Buddha ancestors is realized precisely by assiduously attending to the distinct demands and affordances of each time and situation, following the model set by the Buddha ancestors.

Karma and the "Final Dharma Age"

Further clarification comes from considering Dōgen's treatment of the notion of karma after "What Is:Time." Investigation of this subject additionally connects his ideas on time to the larger contexts of the Buddhist traditions and religiosity in medieval Japan.

Yorizumi Mitsuko has provided a useful review of the conceptual history of karma in Buddhism up to Dōgen. As she explains, a straightforward, commonsense reading of this notion implies a straight vector of time. Specifically, the current conditions of someone's existence are seen as consequences of their acts in previous lives, and the conditions and events of their future existence will depend on the cumulative effects of their past and present actions.[34]

The question arises of how such a vector of cause and effect is possible in mortal beings, given the absence of a persistent soul. Yorizumi Mitsuko points to an intuitive simile from the "Questions of King Milinda," an early introduction to Buddhism in the form of a dialogue between a Greco-Indian king and a Buddhist monk:[35] Like a fire from one lamp lighting another, karma causes a new psycho-physical complex to arise that then receives the effects accumulated in previous existences.[36] This time-honored Buddhist doctrine was very much in line with Dōgen's teachings, but, as Yorizumi further explains, it also prompted probing questions. One reason was the central position that the notion of "emptiness" had acquired over time, as it was increasingly understood to negate fixed essences as well as persistent substance. If things are entirely without essence, there is nothing intrinsically "good" or "bad." As a consequence, there is no reason why certain actions should necessarily cause beneficial or detrimental effects on future existences. This extended idea of emptiness may appear self-defeating to the project of liberation from suffering through "right insight" and "right practice," as endorsed in early Buddhism. However, it served to counter doubts regarding whether enlightenment was at all possible in the present existence. It was additionally important in countering the kind of formalism and Pharisean attitude that could easily attach itself to the elaborate system of monastic rules that had developed in Buddhism over time.[37] Within the Zen school in particular, the notion of karma was largely understood as a provisional doctrine, used to emphasize the necessity of living according to Buddhist teachings.[38] On a higher plane of insight, the concept was put in parentheses to assure practitioners that enlightenment was possible at any given moment.[39]

Dōgen's work contains both passages that embrace the linear understanding of karma and those that move beyond its commonsense interpretation. There is a long-standing discussion in the literature regarding how to understand this.[40] The subject was also at the center of the debate on the periodization of his work, triggered by the Critical Buddhism movement. In many cases, the apparent contradiction was explained by assumptions that Dōgen moved, for better (according to Critical Buddhists) or worse (decline theorists), from the traditional Zen position of higher insight to the more restricted, linear view. We have seen in chapter 2 that such biographical explanations are historically inaccurate, as both positions are to be found in works from various stages of his career.[41] Another explanation works with the two-truth model. Dōgen's repeated insistence on the linear effects of karma is, in this view, addressing lay believers, beginners on the path, and know-it-all "Zennists" who believe that practice is beneath them. His expressions of a non-linear outlook are directed at the smaller circle of advanced and diligent students.[42] They operate on a higher level of understanding, where all distinctions are left behind. Yorizumi and Heine accordingly think that commitment to the linear view arises from the distortions of a limited perspective. The ordinary human mind cannot move beyond it. The enlightened mind has left it behind, but freely returns to it to realize "a productive reentry into the world of intricate particularities."[43]

Yorizumi and Heine have a point in linking the linear and the non-linear perspectives to different concerns in guiding a mixed body of disciples. On a logical or philosophical plane, however, the distinction between two levels of insight leaves open the question of their connection. Why is it that enlightened insight has to return to the sphere of linear temporality? How is the higher level of truth beyond distinctions the truth of the provisional level as well? To express it in the terms of Buddhist ontology: Can we find in Dōgen—as repeatedly suggested by Hee-Jin Kim[44]—a truly "non-dual" outlook, and how would that extend to the topics of time and karma? Clarification of these questions will lead us to understand how, in Dōgen's view, causally conditioned, linear transiency is precisely the realization of "emptiness"—how, in other words, emptiness (with all its soteriological implications) is realized, factually and cognitively, through differentiation, and not apart from it.

The two *Treasury* texts that are at the center of the debate on Dōgen's stance on karma—namely, "Great Practice" (*Daishugyō* 大修行) and "Deep Certitude about Cause and Effect" (*Jinshin inga* 深信因果)—provide seminal answers to these questions.[45] Both are commentaries on a famous episode[46] in which the Zen master Baizhang Huaihai (749–814)—according to tradition, the author of the first Zen school monastic rules[47]—reacts to the request from an old man in his assembly who claims to have fallen into the form of a fox for five hundred lifetimes because he wrongly stated that those who had realized consummate practice would "not fall into cause and effect" in the previous eon of the Buddha Kāśyapa. When asked for a word of liberation on the same topic of consummate practice, Baizhang responds, "Not obscuring cause and effect." This sparks great insight on the part of the old man. He thanks the master for liberating him from his existence as a fox and asks to be buried as a monk. Later on, the body of a dead fox is found on the monastery's grounds, and Baizhang, granting the old man's wish, arranges a funeral with the proper ceremonies for a deceased monastic. When he asks his assembly about a comment on the significance of this event, his preeminent disciple Huangbo Xiyun (died 850; Baizhang's later dharma heir and a proponent of a monistic mystical interpretation of Zen[48]) comes up to him and slaps his face.

In the instruction on "Great Practice," delivered at a transitional dwelling in Echizen in spring 1244, Dōgen follows Zen tradition, and in the words of Heine's useful review, "supports an equalization of karmic causality and the transcendence of karma in accord with standard Sung commentaries."[49] In contrast, the instruction "Deep Certitude about Cause and Effect," which was drafted in the last years of Dōgen's life, explores Baizhang's expression "not obscuring cause and effect" as an "all-encompassing principle [. . .] with a distinct moral imperative based on a commitment to the principle of karmic conditioning and retribution."[50] As mentioned above, the received explanation for these contrasting attitudes is that Dōgen addressed different segments of his assembly with each text: While "Great Practice" was directed at disciples with a higher degree of insight, "Deep Certitude about Cause and Effect" spoke to beginners and those with an antinomian understanding of the Zen tradition.[51]

Heine helpfully goes beyond this juxtaposition and observes fundamental commonalities between the two instructions. Two points are especially relevant for our discussion. First, both texts refute the "naturalist" or eternalist position that was already an object of Dōgen's critique in *Discourses*.[52] Whatever Dōgen is arguing in "Great Practice," it is apparently not that one achieves awareness of an unchanging and peaceful core part of one's being by understanding that all distinctions are illusory. Second, after the passage in "Great Practice" that does seem to argue for a stance "beyond a discussion of falling or not falling, or considerations of ignoring or not ignoring,"[53] Dōgen extensively questions Baizhang's decision to grant a monk's funeral ceremony to the body of a dead fox. He insists on the fundamental distinction between renunciants, who have received the precepts and engaged in practice, and lay devotees of all ranks. This includes even tutelary deities (in the Buddhist understanding) such as the Vedic gods Brahma or Indra.[54] Furthermore, he reminds his audience that they have been lucky enough to meet the "authentically transmitted tradition from the Buddha ancestors" and should "celebrate this great fortune," or otherwise they would "not possess a single virtue or acquire any benefit even if they were to encounter the emanation of a thousand Buddhas."[55] In other words, whatever he wanted to say in the earlier paragraph does not amount to a negation of karma. Much like the instruction on "Deep Certitude about Cause and Effect," his instruction in "Great Practice" ultimately seeks to fortify the decision to take up, and follow through with, monastic life.

Having noted this much about the context, let us return to the propositions from "Great Practice" that apparently endorse a stance "beyond" commitment to the belief in the inexorable dynamic of karma. They are part of a line-by-line probing of the meaning of the fox case and explore the statement "not falling into cause and effect" and its reported consequence of assuming the body of a fox.

> To achieve investigation of great practice is precisely the great cause and effect. Because this cause and effect are without question the complete cause and consummate fruit, there was never a question of falling or not falling, and no talk about obscuring or not obscuring. If not falling into cause and effect was wrong, then not obscuring cause and effect should also be wrong. One speaks of overcoming one mistake and falling into the next, but there is assuming the body of a fox and shedding the body of a fox. There is also the principle that not falling into cause and effect was wrong at the time of Kāśyapa, but is not a mistake in Śākyamuni's time. There must be actualization of the principle that not obscuring cause and effect in this present age of Śākyamuni means to drop off the fox body, but it was not like that in the age of Kāśyapa. [. . .] The former Baizhang [from the time of Kāśyapa] was not originally a fox. To say that his soul left his body and entered the skin of a fox would be heterodoxy. [. . .] If one says that the former Baizhang later became a fox, he would first have to shed the body of the former Baizhang and then assume the body of a fox; it cannot be that one takes the body of Baizhang and replaces it with the body of a fox. Whatever cause and effect are, they do not work in this way. Cause and effect are neither something that is originally there, nor do they spring into existence for the first time. They do not idly exist, waiting for someone to meet them. Even if we assume that not falling into cause and effect was a mistaken answer,

this does not necessarily lead to assuming the body of a fox [. . . or] how many million cases from masters [in the lines of] Linji and Deshan and their followers assuming fox bodies would there have been in recent time? [. . .] It may so happen sometimes that not falling into cause and effect is not a mistaken answer, and there are many responses that are much more deranged than this. [56]

The premise of the passage is clearly that "great practice" is the "complete cause and consummate fruit." From this premise, the text questions the status of the "mistaken" answer and how it links to the subsequent fall into the existence as a fox. The expression "overcoming one mistake and falling into the next" echoes the final words of "What Is:Time," where Dōgen reassures his followers that errors on the path of practice are part and parcel of the complete way of Buddha ancestors. In this sense, the point is not to decide whether statements like "not falling into" or "not obscuring" karma—if given as part of the endeavor to practice and comprehend the Buddha's teaching—are right or wrong. Another part of the passage is directed against notions of a permanent soul, apparently here associated with the Linji and Deshan lines. With its repeated twists and turns, the complex statement therefore does not amount to a strong endorsement of a stance "beyond" cause and effect. Heine takes it to represent "a novel way of bypassing—rather than collapsing—the basic hermeneutic dilemma of choosing between causality and noncausality."[57]

Nonetheless, authors such as Yorizumi have connected this passage to others from the 75-fascicle *Treasury* to demonstrate that Dōgen does embrace a standpoint beyond the linear view of cause and effect. Yorizumi quotes the instruction "Non-Production of Evil" (*Shoaku makusa* 諸惡莫作),[58] first presented one and a half months before "What Is:Time." Here, both cause and effect are seen as completion. Dōgen furthermore expressly denies that "cause is before and fruit is afterwards," because "there is the saying that before and after are one."[59] Much in line with what we have seen in "What Is:Time," Yorizumi explains this to mean that good action and its beneficial effects are equal as manifestations in practice. Because Dōgen posits that practice is based on insight, but insight is also only realized fully in practice, there is a circle of mutual support. Going one step further, Yorizumi then offers the interpretation that through practice, one comes in contact with the "world of truth,"[60] which one realizes within the present world. This "world of truth" is an intended goal, but also the "principal basis,"[61] the starting point and the mainstay of practice. Insight, in this fashion, is both the cause of practice and its fruit. In temporal terms, this means that within practice, cause and effect happen at the same time.[62]

Comparing Dōgen's standpoint in "Great Practice" with that of "Deep Certitude about Cause and Effect," Yorizumi further posits that once insight into and contact with the world of truth are achieved, "retribution, obligation, and all normative discourse is rendered obsolete."[63] Therefore, an expression such as "not falling into cause and effect" may arise. However, both standpoints remain connected through the realm of practice. Even with enlightened insight into the simultaneity of cause and effect, the two are actualized at different times. Practice, in its unity with enlightenment, links the provisional, linear grasp of cause and effect with the higher insight into their simultaneity.

Yorizumi certainly has a point. In the passage in question from "Non-Production of Evil," Dōgen does endorse a non-linear perspective on cause and effect, at least as regards religious practice. Furthermore, Yorizumi's explanation is for the most part in line with the results from our analysis of "what is:time" as a complex notion combining "transition through phases" with the "consummate now."

However, I find problematic Yorizumi's notion of an "eternal world of truth" that is separate from "the relative world of delusion."[64] Her interpretation may offer a way to understand how religious practice achieves a connection between the linear and non-linear views. On the level of insight, however, the contention remains that contact with the "eternal world of truth" renders irrelevant or even annihilates all differentiation and, consequently, the linear view of time. But if the "world of truth" is to be understood as "absolute" in the strong sense that it also contains the truth of the relative world—and this is clearly what Yorizumi suggests—then what she calls the "relative" must inherently have some grounding in the absolute truth itself and cannot be merely deficient.

Fortunately, the quote Yorizumi adduces from "Non-Production of Evil" offers a way out of this dilemma. Dōgen here concedes that, generally, the "effect is awaited by the cause" (and, thus, there is temporal dilation between them). But such dilation is irrelevant in the case of practice and insight, because cause and effect are both realizations of the same. In other words, the attribute they share, in terms of being so many "realizations of enlightenment," makes metrical distinctions between them redundant. Seen in this light, passages that speak of the "same time" of cause and effect, or practice and attainment, or Buddha ancestors and practitioners, do not concern themselves with chronometry. They are chronotypological, describing the kind of time in question. Thus, they do not deny the linear perspective, but complement it with a non-metrical, non-linear one—which, to Dōgen, holds more weight where religious practice and insight are concerned. The emphasis on the linear perspective we find in texts from Dōgen's final years, then, was intended to clarify that metrically, the linear perspective remained valid and was not made obsolete by a higher, non-linear point of view.

This interpretation gives full credit to the passages in "What Is:Time" and other works where Dōgen insists that transiency is a necessary characteristic of insight, and even of "Buddha nature," because only by way of the "transition through phases" can the full abundance of enlightened insight and its merits be actualized. I would further argue that only such a view, in which the linear and non-linear perspectives are understood to coexist and complement each other, can truly be called "non-dual."

While the above differentiation between typological and metrical statements regarding the "same time" solves a logical conundrum, it should not be taken as an attempt to unduly "rationalize" Dōgen's teaching on time or reduce it to something more amenable to modern common sense. The complementary view I suggest here fully accounts for the mystical dynamics Dōgen ascribes to the aspect of the "consummate now," where the totality of the Buddhas' and ancestors' power and merit supports and sustains the struggling practitioner and, ultimately, everything that exists. Furthermore, maintaining the linear perspective as an indispensable part of the "enlightened" view requires us to take seriously what Dōgen has to say about karma and retribution over time in the one other instruction from the *Treasury* that bears the character for "time" in its title: "Karma in the Three Times."

This instruction, which follows "Deep Certitude about Cause and Effect" in the 12-fascicle redaction of the *Treasury*, explains how the apparent well-being of wrongdoers in present life is compatible with the notion of karma and the inexorable dynamics of retribution for good and bad actions. Adducing pertinent lore from the tradition, Dōgen illustrates how actions may receive their commensurate retribution in the present life, the next life, or a later existence (this is what the "three times" here refer to). The selected examples are all clearly legendary. They speak of talking animals, supra- and sub-mundane worlds, and the like. On a theoretical level, they suggest a correlation between the qualities and significance of the action and the time of retribution. Thus, minor good and evil actions receive retribution in the present life, while major offenses lead to rebirth in hell and hence affect the locus and quality of one's next existence. Finally, actions that display either correct and compassionate insight into the Buddha's teaching or its opposite, egotistic delusion, come to fruition often in later existences. Metrical and typological aspects are clearly conjoined in this vision of the workings of karma. To prevent a fatalistic interpretation of these tenets, Dōgen posits that the effects of any action may be changed for better or worse by the attitude one later takes toward it. Specifically, repentance (and commensurate wholesome action) will help to ameliorate the effects of previous harmful deeds.[65] Again, this statement does not merely address beginners and those of smaller intellectual capacity,[66] but reflects monastic practice, where ritual repentance is performed several times per day, for instance as part of the ceremonies accompanying meals.[67] In terms of causal dynamics, the belief in the liberating power of repentance connects to the position, already expounded in *Discourses,* that authentic practice realizes an accord with the enlightened ones, which actualizes their meritorious power. Moreover, the possibility of such actualization is ever-present precisely because it is intrinsic to the temporal character of everything that exists. As explained in "What Is:Time," everything is a configuration of the whole world and all times by way of the transition through phases. Therefore, nothing is ever completely separate from Buddha ancestors and the realization of insight. Nonetheless, the decision has to be made to "make it happen" here and now. Actualization does not come about without dedicated participation by the individual. To assume as much would be, as Dōgen never tires of pointing out, to fall into the "naturalist heresy."

Incidentally, the complementary perspectives on karma and their grounding in the concept of "what is:time" also serve to explain Dōgen's stance toward the idea that the world had entered the "Final Dharma Age."[68] This idea, which originated in China in the fifth century and had become pervasive in Japan by Dōgen's lifetime, is an application of the central Buddhist concept of impermanence to the teaching itself.[69] Generally, the notion is understood to express a pessimistic feeling about the possibilities for salvation;[70] it involves a tripartite periodization of the presence of Buddha's teaching in the world, deteriorating from the age of the "True Dharma" through that of "Semblance Dharma" to the "Final Dharma Age." The length of the previous two periods is calculated differently, but the "Final Dharma Age" is usually said to last for ten thousand years.⁷¹ In medieval Japan, the world was usually thought to have already entered the Final Dharma Age in the year corresponding to 1052. Prominent Kamakura-era figures such as Hōnen and Shinran (see above, pp. 31–34) emphasized the catastrophic conditions of the Final Dharma Age as a reason for seeking salvation through faith in an external power, and their thought has dominated the received view of the topic.⁷² In contrast, Dōgen's remarks on the idea are few and far between, and they reflect the opinion, present already in the concept's formative stage,⁷³ that the age called for strict adherence to monastic rules.

In *Discourses*, Dōgen stated that the scheme of True, Semblance, and Final Dharma Ages was not part of the "true Mahāyāna teaching." He thus relegated this periodization to a provisional teaching at best.⁷⁴ In other places—for example, in "Transmission of the Robe," which bears the same date as "What Is:Time"—reference to the concept functions as a rhetorical device to emphasize that disciples should seize their opportunity to have met with the *Buddha Dharma* or one of its tokens.⁷⁵ One of the more systematic engagements with the concept occurs in an extended formal instruction given in the summer of 1250, possibly around the end of the summer retreat.⁷⁶ Notably, Dōgen here links karmic retribution to the Final Dharma Age. He starts out by stating that his assembly has received the opportunity to "encounter Buddha Dharma" as "a reward for seeds of *prajñā* planted in previous lives" and that they are "without hindrance." However, he continues, the conditions in his day are much less favorable than those in previous ages of the "True Dharma Age and the Semblance Dharma Age." But although they are operating under conditions "as difficult to compare as gold and sand" with those of earlier days, Dōgen advises his audience that they "have no serious obstructions and have received superior connections" and enjoins them to "not slacken and regress."⁷⁷ The remainder of the instruction argues against the idea of a fundamental unity of the three teachings of Confucius, Laozi, and Buddha (which would, again, obscure the notion of karma). In conclusion, Dōgen admonishes the monastic community to adhere to the precepts, discard selfish desires, and commit earnestly to practice.⁷⁸

This argument is, again, very much aligned with that of "What Is:-Time": Dōgen acknowledges that practitioners find themselves in specific situations, which they may perceive as unfavorable for attaining enlightenment. Against this, he essentially sends a message of hope, combined with encouragement to commit to the Buddha Way. The effects of actions in previous lives have their bearing on the present situation but do not preclude diligent practice. Practice realizes unity with the enlightened ones. This unity deepens over time with the continuation and iteration of actions that are modeled after their precedent.

Conclusion

Dōgen did not return to the expression "what is:time" in later writings. This is in itself remarkable, considering the attention that this phrase has received since the twentieth century. However, his subsequent writings expand on various related themes and conceptual questions. Concerning the subject of synchrony between practitioners and enlightened beings, later instructions show that this notion is best understood primarily in a typological and not in a metrical sense. Practitioners share the same kind of time with enlightened beings. Furthermore, they are supported by the enlightened ones' soteriological power, which is actualized in every instant of practice. Finally, their enlightenment consists in the Buddhas' attainment of consummate insight. These elements of synchrony and the consummate now transcend the limits of a narrowly defined present. They do not, however, stand in the way of transience (and therefore linearity) or the working of karma, which Dōgen consistently upholds as an inexorable condition of existence. The distinction between chronotypology and chronometry has proven to be essential for building an interpretation that acknowledges the holistic mystical unity of each time of practice with all enlightened time without denying the role of chronology and causal sequence.

Part III
Conclusions and After-Thoughts

8

Dōgen's Concept of Time in Context

Our investigation into Dōgen's thematic expositions on the subject of time has revealed a complex, but also remarkably consistent, set of notions. In the following sections, I first summarize the findings of the preceding chapters into a brief reconstruction and analysis of Dōgen's concept of time, highlighting continuities and differences from earlier interpretations. Next, I place his concepts against the background of early medieval religion. I show that his more elaborate ideas were not well understood even by his immediate disciples and successors. They were, however, built from elements that were well accepted and, in some cases, pervasive in medieval society. Finally, I discuss Dōgen's concept with regard to the general history of the understanding of time, showing how it serves to challenge the still broadly accepted paradigm of contrasting modern hegemonic "Western" ideas with those of previous eras and—from the hegemonic standpoint—"peripheral" regions.

What is:Time: A Brief Reconstruction and Conceptual Analysis

Recognition of impermanence forms the pedal point[1] of Dōgen's complex notion of time. In its inexorable connection to the finitude of the human lifespan, impermanence defines the tone and modality of his engagement with the subject. "Impermanence" here is not simply an observational predicate; it is imbued with the aesthetic sense of existential urgency and wedded to the practical call for salvific action. These aesthetic and religious aspects have their ontological basis in the recognition of impermanence as a universal predicate, which precludes any notion of an eternal substance. We have seen how Dōgen time and again criticized ideas about an unchanging, immortal soul or psychic essence—notions that had seeped into contemporary Buddhist thought, and Zen thought specifically. Again, his polemic is not merely theoretical, but carries aesthetic and pragmatic overtones. Its intention is to warn against unquestioning acceptance of one's current way of being.

Recognition of impermanence does not, however, preclude acceptance of duration—and this is where our findings part with strictly momentarist interpretations, such as the recent one by Rein Raud. Duration is, we found, not reduced to mere linguistic convention, but accepted as part of reality. Its foundation, however, is not material continuity over time. On a material level, Dōgen states that everything arises and perishes within the space of a minimal temporal quantum, the *setsuna* (Skt. *kṣaṇa*), for which he calculates a value corresponding to 0.0000135 modern seconds. Continuity results from the display of similar characteristics over limited periods of time. These characteristics are, again, not "properties" belonging to an independent "essence"; they are modalities consistently displayed in like interactions with other things. Everything, from insentient matter to living beings, is in this paradigm inherently temporal. A thing exists as the continued, dynamic unfolding of its defining characteristics through various phases. Spring, and not a stone, a tree, or a statue, is therefore Dōgen's prototype for everything there is. This "seasonal" paradigm of things that persist for a limited time, by way of displaying a consistent set of characteristics, conforms with our findings regarding the frequent chronographical references to "temporal occasions" (*jisetsu*) of a certain type in Dōgen's works.

Conversely, time is not a mere cognitive framework. Nor is it a reality of its own that somehow affects otherwise atemporal things. Time inheres in things and is integral to what and how they are. This view of time accords with Dōgen's chronographical practice to avoid using the word as a hyperonym. Instead, we have his ingenious adaptation of the phrase *uji* (there was/is at a time . . .) to indicate that "what is" is also "time." This intrinsic link between "things" (understood, to reiterate, according to the model of the "season") and time can further serve to explain surprising chronotypological statements like the one quoted earlier about times having colors "such as blue, yellow, red, and white."[2]

To understand time as intrinsic to things also affects the understanding of its measure. Dōgen does not take issue so much with measuring time as such, but with taking temporal measures for granted—that is, as measures of an entity separate from things and, more importantly, from oneself. There is, in his inventory of images, no clock hidden away in a separate dimension that provides apportionate measures of absolute time on a universal scale. Time is measurable, but measured time should not be reified into something external to oneself and the objects of one's desires and actions. In this respect, our findings do accord with the concerns voiced by authors such as Steven Heine or Shinshū Roberts about calculated time. The upshot of Dōgen's deliberations on time is that time's measure is properly understood as the result of comparison of relative durations. All objects "transit through phases," and certain phases of one object are held as reference points to measure the duration of the phases of another. The draft manuscript of *Discourses* expresses as much when it says that flowers and frost changed nine times in describing how long Dōgen studied as a monk before he went to China. Each temporal measure is therefore relative, but that does not mean that time's measure is merely a matter of convention or subjective projection. Being neither an astronomer nor a moneylender, Dōgen did not seek the truth of time in number, and he often preferred to localize events in time through a sequence of actions or events. Nevertheless, he valued numerical chronometry and used it in a variety of contexts to emphasize objectivity and significance. The examples in his writings are numerous and multifold: For instance, calendar dates underline the factual character of events of special importance and secure the authenticity of his works. The length of time since ordination and the iterations of summer retreats serve to impartially distinguish levels of hierarchy and proper procedure in the monastery. Furthermore, the number of years spent in practice indicates commitment to the Buddha Way and maturing of insight, and the numbered sequence of ancestors serves to delineate proper tradition. A unified chronology accentuates the length (or shortness) of the presence of Buddha's teaching in the world. In conceptual terms, there is no indication that Dōgen accorded less validity to quantitative measurement over and against typological characterization; both accordingly often went hand in hand to correctly define and exploit the specifics of an occasion, mostly in connection to diligent religious practice. In acknowledging these essential functions of chronometry in Dōgen's works and understanding how they relate to his concept of time, the findings presented here are again distinguished from earlier interpretations, which tended to associate chronometry with an "inauthentic" view of time and at best accepted it as a conventional tool to organize life.[3]

Measured time as it appears in Dōgen's texts is therefore not "empty," homogeneous time. It is the time of a specific occasion, event, or activity, even though it may be located and quantitatively compared in its relation to other times with different characteristics. In other words, time is neither reified as a separate being of its own nor understood as a mere mental construct. What, then, makes it possible to count and compare different times? Dōgen did not expressly concern himself with that question, but an answer may still be construed from his discourses on the subject. I believe that it precisely corresponds with the aspect that may appear, on first sight, the most mystical in his conception of time: namely, the "consummate now."

To recall, the notion of the "consummate now" indicates that the present of an action or event comprises a configuration of the whole world. Dōgen states that each "consummate now" exhausts all places and times. Some of these are "lined up" synchronically, and others diachronically. In this manner, each present action, state, or event is a totality comprising its relations to all other occasions, events, or processes. Close inspection of those other occasions and events reveals them to be equally all-inclusive configurations. The relations between them may be described in terms of "lining up in order" and "transiting through phases," which together with every element's "abiding in its dharma position" make up the "consummate now." The mutual permeation of all these distinct, holistic event-configurations ensures that they form one reality. Their structure, as a totality of relations between discernible parts, allows the counting and comparing of quantities among them, and this extends to counting and comparing in terms of time. Witness the old man in the fox *kōan*, who could say that, between the two eons of Kāśyapa and Śākyamuni Buddha, he had fallen into the shape of a fox for five hundred lives. The "eon of Śākyamuni," however conceived, is certainly different in many essential characteristics from the lifetime of a fox, yet their differences do not make them incommensurable.

Nevertheless, the logical relation between chronometric and chronotypological attributes is not the topic of concern when Dōgen speaks of the consummate now. The notion is introduced for soteriological purposes, to argue against a stance that separates the current state of affairs from the past that led up to it, and from the future it may bring forth. Past actions are not simply carried away by the flow of time; they remain as conditions of the present state and accompany the agent as causes that will, sooner or later, lead to retribution according to the law of karma. In particular, previous instances of Buddhist practice, and even accidental links formed with the teaching in earlier lives, result in opportunities for further correct practice and the generation of insight. Present diligent practice after the model set by the enlightened ones generates a synchronization of patterns that transcends temporal distance; practice inserts the present into the process of realizing enlightenment through the phases of bringing forth the mind, practice, insight, and nirvana, all of which thereby become part of the consummate now.

Much has been made in the literature of how this "circle of sustained practice" (*gyōji dōkan* 行持道環) contradicts the linear view of time.[4] This understanding again ultimately relies on a "two truths" view of Dōgen's texts. Hoshi Shundō's suggestion to instead combine the circular with the linear element into the image of a spiral movement points toward another possibility of interpretation, one that seems to be more in line with the complexity of Dōgen's view of time. Hoshi's argument is basically that Dōgen does *not* indicate that each practitioner simply repeats actions strictly identical to those of previous Buddhas and ancestors. He infers this from the analysis of Dōgen's graphic representation of the "circle" of Buddha ancestors.[5] The reason is that each new instance of practice and insight also enriches the circle of enlightenment with new elements as it negotiates a unique situation. This is what Dōgen describes by saying that Buddhas and ancestors "move beyond" (*kōjō* 向上) from Buddha to Buddha.[6] The "same time" Dōgen speaks of when addressing the relation of current practice and the Buddha ancestors refers to a type, not a token or instance of time—even if it involves, according to him, a resonance that imbues the moment of practice with the power and merits accrued by all Buddhas and ancestors through the ages.

In terms of the morphology of time, we can take Hoshi's suggestion one step further to include the full complexity of the "geometry" of time hinted at by Dōgen. A major point of the discussion in "What Is:Time" concerns the fact that the linear movement of time is represented inadequately by the notion that time flies past. Undeniably, the present "now" will become a thing of the past, but by then a different time—now in the future—will have arrived. The "transition through phases" therefore includes the movement from the present now to the future now, as much as the shifts from the present now to the past, and from the future to the now. When stated as the paradox that the now stays, and moves both forward and backward in time, this only expresses the inadequacy of reducing the dynamic of time to the graphic projection of one simple, two-dimensional movement of whatever shape. Hoshi's spiral, then, is a valid but still reductive three-dimensional projection. It aptly captures and illustrates an important aspect of Dōgen's soteriology of time as applied to a single individual. From another angle, this spiral may be projected as an ever-expanding circle.[7] If applied to subsequent individuals, the time of practice may thereby be imagined like ripples on the water, caused by the repeated fall of drops on the same spot.

In the final analysis, however, such contemplation of chronometry and the geometrical shape of time springs more from a modern concern than from Dōgen's own agenda. The fundamental distinction at the center of his discourses is typological and inexorably wedded to aesthetic evaluation and practical injunction. Specifically, it is the religious distinction between the time of secular existence, and that of religious practice modeled after the precedent of Buddhas and ancestors. Time spent in the pursuit of secular goals and obligations is futile; time passed practicing according to Buddhist teachings is salvific. His instructions on time mainly fulfill three purposes depending on the audience: They enjoin his addressees to choose monastic life; they fortify that choice in those who have already made it; and they explain its significance by way of its temporal relation to the attainment of enlightenment. Returning to the issue of morphology, this means that the decision to give up secular life forms a tipping point, after which the previous, otherwise endlessly repeating cycle of transmigration becomes the first part of a sequence leading up to enlightenment. This sequence is, as we have seen, always already complete. However, its completion is actualized by consecutively living through all its phases, just as Dōgen illustrated in his poem on the "Original Face." Beyond the tipping point, then, all times, including those spent in the cycle of suffering, are moments belonging to enlightenment. Nothing has ever gone wrong; but this is only true when the present time is committed to practice.

The injunctions to make that choice raise a final question, which brings us back to the topic of karma and its place in Dōgen's doctrine. In modern philosophical terms, it may be called the question of freedom or, conversely, determinism. Using Dōgen's own terms, we can formulate it in the following way: If the workings of karma are inescapable and determine one's present condition, capacity for insight, and the opportunities to meet with the Buddhas' teachings, can one then speak of a choice to be made between secular and religious life? On an operative level, the answer is obvious: Dōgen consistently argued against "naturalism," the idea that enlightenment will come in and of itself. He also repeatedly insinuated that his audiences needed to decide first to take up monastic life and then, in every moment, to follow the model set by previous enlightened ones. "Seeds" of karma from previous lives are mentioned in his texts as supporting that decision or generating opportunities to become a monastic (which required a certain amount of wealth to begin with)—but apparently they are not thought to guarantee a determination for diligent practice; nor is the choice to follow the Buddha Way itself presented as depending on such conditions.

Thus, the question (again one that Dōgen himself does not systematically address) is how both elements—the inexorable causal dynamism of karma and the possibility and necessity to choose monastic life—fit together.

Again, I believe an answer may be construed from Dōgen's idea of the "consummate now." The consummate now is the temporal articulation of non-duality or, in soteriological terms, the idea that there is no separation between Buddhas and ordinary, deluded beings. Consequently, every instance of reality is always already connected to the dynamism of enlightenment, which may break through at any moment when given room in life through religious practice.

The consummate now can be understood as such a totality of all there is precisely because of its causal links to the past and future. The past conditions the present and the present conditions the future, but these causal links do not completely determine what happens. This is evident from those stories Dōgen presents where the effects of conditions leading to rebirth in a certain realm are changed for the better or worse depending on how the affected person reflects on them. In Dōgen's scheme of things, the karma of an action is generally sufficient to generate repercussions of commensurate scale and quality. However, this is not totally deterministic; it may be moderated by insight and meritorious practice—and vice versa: a lack of insight may cancel benefic effects of karma. Insight is always available, as the merit of right practice extends through the whole universe, and reality at every moment actualizes and confirms the truth of the Buddha's teaching. This is why the chronoaesthetic perspectives conveyed by Dōgen's texts are clearly divided along the line that separates secular from religious/monastic life. Secular life is fleeting, its merits are illusory, and its pleasures mainly the cause of future suffering; its chronomorphology is that of an endless spiral of painful existences.[8] Religious life may be arduous but is carried by the reassurance of unity with Buddhas and ancestors; its morphology combines immediate completion in the consummate now with progress on a vector of deepening insight. Conforming to a pattern we already found in our analysis of Dōgen's chronopolitics, modeling the present after the precedent set by Buddhas and ancestors is thought to actualize their insight and merits. While this may not be fully experienced immediately, it is nevertheless real and will make itself felt eventually as full enlightenment, the liberation from the remaining bonds of karma. This message of hope and reassurance, however, rests on the belief in the infinite merits of right practice that are always accessible in the "consummate now." On the whole, the emphasis in Dōgen's thematic discussions of time is more on the virtues of living in the present according to the model set by the enlightened ones than on the promises this holds for the future.

Integrating Distinctions

I believe that the above reconstruction of Dōgen's thought on time is not only consistent with the way he expressed, explained, and regulated time; it also addresses the critical concerns behind modern authors' previous arguments regarding his ideas. Furthermore, it integrates and explains most of the conceptual elements that these authors have highlighted, albeit in a fashion that avoids relegating ordinary experience to a secondary level of reality or resorting to contradiction. At the same time, it stays true to Dōgen's soteriological agenda and the commitments he made to Buddhist metaphysics. The following paragraphs briefly elucidate these claims.

A critical point that makes Dōgen relevant to many modern authors is his refutation of a set of three interdependent notions: First, that the self and the things it encounters in the world have at their basis a material, durable substance that ensures their persistence over time. Second, that they possess an essence that makes them what they are, independent of the relations they enter into with the self or other objects. Third, that change is not intrinsic to things, but accidental; something inflicted on them by the workings of an external force called time. This critical impetus against what is often perceived as an entrenched, commonsense metaphysics, associated with the Western philosophical tradition,[9] has led authors to deny (or at least vastly downplay) temporal sequence, linearity, and the reality of duration, and to accord ontological primacy to the instantaneous present. Rein Raud has strongly emphasized this ontological primacy of the present moment by rejecting the reality of any form of durational being and proposing to "look at 'firewood' and 'ashes' as solely linguistic entities, names of things the existence of which we posit with our language, but which are without their own self-nature (similar to what is designated by the words 'spring' and 'autumn,' in which case it is easier to see that there are no objective thing-referents to which they could refer)."[10] Steven Heine mainly denies clock-time and temporal sequence as merely "derivative" notions, positing that "*Uji* (as *muga*) is fully detached from the daily time of twenty-four hours derivatively conceived as sequential, and yet is found nowhere else but right within daily time when penetrated as the insubstantiality and impermanence of all factors of experience here-and-now and at all occasions."[11] Heine's argument against clock-time and sequence is related to two further motifs that other authors have taken up and elaborated upon: First, the spiritual concern that thinking of time as sequence leads to seeing enlightened insight as a faraway goal, and second, the connection between clock-time and the reification and commodification of time.

Shinshū Roberts articulates the reservations about the sequential view of practice and enlightenment with direct reference to Heine:

> When we view practice as a means to attain realization, we tend to view our previous stage as behind us, and our attainment as not yet arrived. [. . .] Steven Heine likens this belief in sequential time to creating a gulf between oneself and one's experience. [. . .] To understand that delusion is something to be discarded and enlightenment something to be picked up is really missing the point. [. . .] heaven and earth are not separate and the way back is only a matter of hearing and understanding. [. . .] It is all here, in us and of us, all the time. We must come back to what is unfolding right now.[12]

This argument is obviously motivated by the belief that the notion of temporal sequence implies the separation of insight from practice. As a consequence, thinking in terms of temporal progression and, indeed, goal-directed behavior, is considered detrimental: Practice and exertion have to be, in Heine's words, "purposeless" to be aligned with Dōgen's idea of the unity of resolve, practice, and realization.[13] Authors inspired by the metaphysics of Nishida Kitarō have taken this issue with goal-directed behavior or any form of "positional attitude" even further: Akiyama Hanji declared that time must be understood as the result of the "self-determination of nothingness" into individual moments, "without reason and in an irrational fashion." Gereon Kopf conjoined the "authentic" view of time with acceptance of a "contradictory self-identity of existence and awareness."[14] These somewhat extreme conceptual moves can be understood as efforts to think through the consequences of finding truth in the negation of all forms of determination and distinction.

The second motif, which links clock-time to the "objectification" and "commodification" of time, has been most strongly emphasized by Goodhew and Loy: "Even as accelerating economic globalization commodifies the earth into resources, human life is commodified into labor (work time), also bought and sold according to supply and demand. Today that applies to our understanding of time generally, the most precious 'resource' of all because we can never have too much of it. [. . .] time is a commodity that can be saved and invested. The commodification of time was made possible, perhaps inevitable, by the clock."[15] The belief underlying this argument is obviously that measuring time with some degree of necessity leads to treating it as a resource or commodity. Once time is measured according to the clock, it is naturally understood as a self-subsistent entity that can and will be exploited in terms of monetary gain. This, then, creates the time pressures and alienation that are ubiquitous in contemporary society.

These critical perspectives on duration/persistence, sequence, and the quantification of time have without doubt helped to elucidate the relevance of Dōgen's thought on time for the world of today and to clarify essential aspects of his ideas. To radically refute substantialist and essentialist ontologies of the self and reality in general and replace them with an understanding of the intrinsically temporal character of everything real was certainly one of Dōgen's primary concerns. We have seen how he insisted that there is only a highly limited quantum of solid material duration; that things display particular attributes as part of their "lining up in order" of the world, dependent on their mutual interaction; and that their very existence consists in a "transition through phases"—all to explain how sustained religious practice is a necessity *and* a sufficient condition for liberation from the cycle of suffering. He also highlighted the present moment as the primary occasion to realize that aim and posited that it includes the past and future with his notion of the "consummate now."

However, the conceptual analysis I have presented in the preceding chapters differs in crucial aspects from the positions cited above. On the theoretical plane, it does not relegate durational existence to the level of mere linguistic convention; it allows and even demands the acceptance of temporal sequence, and it includes rather than excludes temporal distinctions and time's measure among the essential aspects of time. On the practical and spiritual plane, this translates into accepting purposive, goal-directed behavior as part of enlightened action, and a fine-tuned integration of calendar and clock-time into the organization of communal life.

The close inspection of Dōgen's concepts has thus provided us with critical responses to metaphysical substantialism and essentialism that integrate basic elements of ordinary experience—such as limited temporal continuity, sequence, and linearity—instead of downgrading them to the sphere of mere convention or even delusion. Furthermore, these responses do not demand acceptance of some higher-order logic where the laws of identity and non-contradiction do not count. Dōgen's texts show that it is possible to think of things (and oneself) as meta-stable configurations of the world, whose existence unfolds as a "transition through phases." Similarly, it is possible to envision an ethical or religious ideal such as Buddhist enlightenment not as the final stage that follows after the process of its achievement, and is separate from the efforts and exertion it demands, but as a driving principle present within these efforts, which has no reality apart from them.[16] Finally, clock-time, if correctly understood, can be an essential instrument for grasping reality and coordinating human actions toward shared goals. The reification of clock-time into a commodity is not a logical necessity, but the result of social processes of expropriation and domination that are mutable in principle at least. There is no need to abandon the division of labor and revert to elementary forms of communal life to overcome the alienation inherent in the commodification of time and human life. Dōgen's monasteries may not provide a viable template for the organization of human society, but, as I discuss in the final chapter of this volume, their time regimes still contain important lessons for a mode of coordinating human actions that is beneficial for everyone involved.

Dōgen and Time in Medieval Japan

Returning to the historical plane, a first question is whether and how far Dōgen's thoughts on time and his time regimes represent commonly shared notions and practices of medieval Japan. It is safe to say that his idea of "what is:time" was not widely shared and understood in the medieval period, but this does not mean that it was a complete outlier. Even if not connected to his name, his emphasis on unceasing practice and the constant deepening of insight found its way into Noh, the most salient performative art of the later medieval period, and permeated from there to other arts as well.[17] Moreover, most elements of Dōgen's chronography, chronopolitics, and chrononoetics were not his inventions; they were shared, albeit to varying degrees, by his contemporaries. The originality and lasting value of his ideas lie in the manner in which he interpreted, selected, combined, and connected them into an engagement with time that was as practical as it was conceptually consistent and imbued with deep religious meaning. The resulting elaborate complex of ideas I have reconstructed above was, for all its richness and complexity, difficult to grasp. As a consequence, its intricacies may have been lost even on his own disciples: For instance, the earliest commentary on "What Is:Time," by Dōgen's erstwhile personal attendant Senne, completely glosses over notions like "lining up in order" or "transiting through phases" in favor of a simplified monistic reading.[18] The second commentary, by Senne's disciple Kyōgō 經豪, only exacerbates this tendency,[19] while the third, the verse commentary by Giun 義雲 (1253–1333), does not enter into extensive conceptual discussion at all.[20] These adjustments on the conceptual level may have been motivated partly by the necessity of gaining acceptance and prestige for the fledgling Sōtō school vis-à-vis its more established competitors, including the Rinzai school. In that respect, Dōgen shared the fate of other founding figures of the period, whose teachings were accommodated over the following generations to dominant ways of thinking and practice. Satō Hiroo has described in some detail how all new schools of the Kamakura period followed this path, to some extent simply in response to the pressure from older and more powerful institutions.[21]

In light of these historical developments, the following paragraphs serve to elucidate the position of Dōgen's ideas on time in relation to concepts and paradigms that were commonly accepted in his era. They demonstrate how strongly the complex array of temporal notions indicated by his signature term "what is:time" was embedded in the medieval intellectual repertoire, even if its specifics were not shared by his contemporaries.

First and foremost among the elements common to Dōgen and larger parts of medieval Japanese society was the chronometric system used to measure, record, announce, and regulate time. Its central components were the zodiacal hours and the lunisolar calendar. Both were based on the system of five elementary phases and twelve zodiacal animals, combined into the sexagenary cycle. This cycle could be applied to all basic units of time. Furthermore, beyond its metric function, it imparted each given unit with certain qualitative attributes. Era names were additionally used in the counting of years; these were tied to the political realm and were employed to disambiguate and localize temporal events. Their frequent changes made the establishment of overarching chronologies a challenging task; nonetheless, this task was increasingly undertaken in the medieval period, as is visible in Dōgen's references to the timeline of the Buddhist tradition.

As we have seen in chapters 3 and 4, Dōgen made use of these chronometric elements to underline the facticity of seminal events—and, on a practical and political level, to schedule monthly and annual events in his monasteries. Monastic life was meant to constitute a sphere of its own, but by organizing its schedule through the civil calendar, it maintained a fundamental synchrony with society. Both shared certain festive events in the course of the year, the most important of which was the New Year, an occasion also used to pray for the well-being of the emperor and the realm. This serves to demonstrate that Dōgen's monasteries were in no way meant to constitute a challenge to the social and political order. They formed a social sphere that was dominated by religious aims, manifesting a "pure" religious realm, but one that was intended to coexist with the order of the day.

Conversely, certain Buddhist memorial days (such as "Buddha's birthday" on the eighth day of the fourth month) were observed by all Buddhist monasteries and larger parts of society. Monasteries furthermore all used the same system of six periods of the day to schedule sleep, meals, and ritual activities. In other words, on the practical level of the organization of daily life, there was a large degree of synchrony among monasteries. Differentiation existed with respect to the number of periods allotted to specific religious practices and in the identification and distribution of memorial days that cemented adherence to a certain lineage. Notably, the memorial days instituted by Dōgen transcended the boundaries of the two dominant Zen schools of the day. A distinct Sōtō school identity would only be accentuated with dedicated memorial days by his successors, who all used a chronopolitical method that was widely shared at the time.

One further important chrononoetic element is the attention given to environmental rhythms such as the lunar cycle and the cycle of the seasons. As we have seen in chapter 4, the monthly schedule ensured, for example, that there was always a formal instruction on full moon days. This chronopolitical and chrononoetic tool had already developed in Chinese Zen monastic rules; however, Dōgen used it to both connect to the continental tradition and to express his views on insight realized within impermanence.

References to seasonal specifics, which formed an important part of the common literary repertoire (and, of course, of the agricultural and economic calendar),[22] were employed for similar ends. Their characteristics were noticed and given elaborate, often poetic, expression. However, Dōgen did not instruct his disciples to simply go along with natural rhythms; instead, his words often included a moment of reversal. Like calendar dates, seasonal conditions to him were stepping stones for exploring specific aspects of trans-temporal truth. His successors often glossed over this incisive way of relating to natural cycles. This in turn was facilitated by the fact that Dōgen's ideas and modes of expression were so deeply embedded in the cultural traditions he inherited.

The same holds for his approach to impermanence. The notion that nothing in the mundane world could possibly persist was a common conceptual denominator with a reach far beyond the religious field. It is famously expressed in the initial lines of the "Tale of the Heike," the epic about the internecine strife between the Minamoto and Taira that resulted in the establishment of the Shogunate in Kamakura:

> The Jetavana Temple bells / ring the passing of all things. Twinned sal trees, white in full flower / declare the great man's certain fate. / The arrogant do not long endure: / They are like a dream one night in spring. / The bold and brave perish in the end. / They are as dust before the wind.[23]

The ontological conviction underlying this pervasive notion was that things are inherently "empty," that is, without a self-sustaining substance. This Buddhist concept had assumed the character of a widely shared worldview at the time. In the succinct formula of the "Heart Sutra," an oft-quoted and copied text, this meant that "forms are empty."[24]

This formula, however, not only negatively stated that things had neither a stable substance nor a fixed essence. "Emptiness" also stood for the salvific, liberating aspect of reality and insight. The second part of the formula, which conversely posits that emptiness is identical with forms, therefore also means that liberation is present in the realm of forms, that there is no metaphysical gap between the realms of suffering (form) and liberation (emptiness): The two may be distinguished, but they are not to thought of as separate.

This "non-dual" relationship was conceived of in various ways. As we have seen above, one widely accepted way of understanding was a kind of perspectivism in which emptiness came to stand for salvific insight and higher truth, while form and its recognition were relegated to the lesser status of, at best, "provisional truth." This notion was further accentuated by the idea that, qua emptiness, sentient and even non-sentient beings possessed "original awakening" or, to use a term with similar implications, "Buddha nature."

We have seen in the previous chapters how Dōgen took issue with possible eternalist and quietist implications of these ideas. His elucidations concerning time form an important part of that endeavor. They point to a mode of non-dualism in which "forms" (and the distinctions by which they may be grasped) are understood as precisely the way in which emptiness is, just as emptiness designates the way forms are. There is, then, for Dōgen no hierarchy between the two sides of the formula; both are to be taken as implying each other. The more common form of delusion may be to remain entangled in forms without seeing emptiness. But to cling to emptiness and to refuse to accept forms in their distinctions would be just another mode of delusory "discriminatory thinking," a thinking that divides and isolates what needs to be seen in conjunction. Steven Heine, in his recent book on Giun's verse commentary of the *Treasury*, has indicated how the above, strictly complementary interpretation of non-dualism, has inspired literary production in the Sōtō school since the Chinese master Hongzhi Zhengjue 宏智正覺 (Jp. Wanshi Shōgaku, 1091–1157).[25]

In line with this non-dualist mode of thinking that places the finite and its conceptual apprehension in conjunction with emptiness, Dōgen also insisted on continued engagement with terms such as "Buddha nature" and what they stood for.[26] This certainly ensured a common ground for debates within his community. However, as detailed above, this ground also enabled his texts and ideas to be accommodated to more widely shared notions once he was no longer there to point out the differences. On the one hand, this development turned out to be detrimental to the study of Dōgen's more specific and elaborate thoughts on time. On the other hand, it points to the fact that, all in all, the central elements of his discourse were representative of (at least) Buddhist thinking and practice in medieval Japan.

This may even be true, to some extent, in the case of what appears to be the major pièce de résistance in this regard—that is, his deprecation of the concept of the "Final Dharma Age." As we saw in chapter 7,

Dōgen did accept the idea that two thousand years after the purported demise of Śākyamuni, the world had entered an age of decay, much as he accepted that Japan was on the periphery of civilization. But ultimately, he insisted, such ideas were of a provisional nature and were valid only insofar as they incited people to practice the Buddha Way. This certainly makes his evaluation of the "Final Dharma Age" a very restricted one in relation to popular notions of the time. By the same token, his guarded rejection of strongly pessimistic views of this matter places him in the middle ground between those who, like Hōnen or Shinran (see above, p. 177), would argue in favor of abandoning the quest for salvation through efforts on one's own part, and an optimistic reversal like Nichiren's, who celebrated this time as the period when the superior teaching of the Lotus Sutra was destined to reign supreme.[27] Dōgen was certainly not alone in responding to the "Final Dharma Age" concept with an insistence on rigorous practice and monastic discipline. His attitude was shared by other movements of the time, such as the Esoteric Precepts School (see above, p. 89), albeit with different soteriological underpinnings. Again, the details of his position may not have been widely known or accepted, but its components are representative of the discourse at the time. When placed properly in the context of shared and contested ideas, forms of expression, and practices, Dōgen's practical injunctions and contemplative musings on time therefore open a window on the way time was felt, understood, and lived in medieval Japan.

Dōgen and the History of Time

The history of time, as far as it concerns the history of human engagement with time, emerged as a topic in the second half of the twentieth century and has so far largely been written from an evolutionary perspective that is firmly rooted in Western modernity. In this perspective, a concept of time described by the attributes "abstract," "homogeneous," "quantitative," "linear," and "global" is considered to be the fully developed standard for contemplating pre-modern European and non-Western notions of time. Authors such as Norbert Elias[28] and Günter Dux have emphasized the advances in the "operational" concept of time (a term coined by developmental psychologist Jean Piaget) that were gained through science, technology, and capitalist methods of production and connected to the concept of "abstract global time."[29] Rudolf Wendorff described the progress toward a "systematic discovery of time and its creative potential" in detail, including modern reactions "against linear time-consciousness."[30] Gerhard Dohrn-van Rossum showed how the technological development of mechanical clocks that measured equal hours supported the implementation of abstract, homogeneous time.[31] Others, among them Japanese sociologist Maki Yūsuke, have pointed to the existential anxiety that co-originated with the notion of an empty, infinitely progressing time.[32]

As indicated above, in this grand scheme of things, pre-modern times and non-Western regions appear predominantly as alternatives to "abstract global time"—alternatives that may be evaluated as less developed or elevated as remedies for the ills of modernity. Dōgen is often cited in this latter context.[33] Accordingly, the implementation of abstract global time in places such as Japan has often been described as part and parcel of a process of Westernization,[34] and the time consciousness and time regimes of earlier periods are placed in simple opposition to the modern, "Westernized" standard.[35] This general tendency is even followed by Maki Yūsuke, despite his strong awareness of the link between capitalist relations of production—which are basically the same in Japan and Europe—and the implementation of modern time regimes.[36] Maki also notes that already in ancient Imperial Japan, the centralized political system was based on abstract time regimes that created a strong awareness of time's inexorable linear progression. However, he then chooses to describe the changes wrought by the growth and eventual ubiquitous dominance of capitalist relations of production purely as a Western development.

In this historiographical paradigm, there is an apparent evolution from limited, event- or action-bound, local and intuitive notions toward an abstract, comprehensive, linear, transitive, homogeneous concept of time. This evolution is often described as a growing consciousness of time itself. Within a framework of analysis that focuses on Europe as the center and motor of historical progress, the idea of such an evolution connects to the notion of the early medieval period (roughly 600–1100 CE) as an intermediate age in which developments that had begun in Greek and Roman antiquity (including early Christianity) came to a halt. From Whitrow to Dux and Wendorff, authors have described how the evolutionary path was resumed again in the late medieval and Renaissance periods and accelerated in the ensuing centuries.[37]

Medieval Japan provides many opportunities to complement and question this perspective, and the notions and practices embraced by Dōgen and his followers are just one case in point. For instance, it seems difficult to argue that Dōgen's concept of time is deficient in terms of complexity or does not support full operational competence. It positively allows for infinite, global, and transitive linear sequencing, which Dōgen employs where he addresses the chronology of the Buddhist teaching (also in comparison to other worldviews) or emphasizes the facticity of certain core events by providing their date.[38] It also entails, via the notions of karma and "lining up in order," an interest in the future and how it is shaped by current action.[39] This interest was shared, for different reasons, by many of his contemporaries: Aristocrats wrote records of daily affairs at court to preserve ritual and procedural knowledge for succeeding generations; bureaucrats in the military administration disputed how judicial decisions might turn into precedents and affect future handling of disputes; monasteries offered advance sale for memorial rituals; historiographers sought to align the chronology of Indian, Chinese, and Japanese mythohistories and mused about the number of generations left for the Japanese empire; and so on.[40]

To return to Dōgen: Physics or any other natural science, as well as mathematical calculation, were certainly not among his concerns, and he repudiated the reduction of time to the quantitative determination of motions or velocities. However, this does not amount to relegating time's measure to the level of mere convention. His notion of "what is:time" includes the basis for a concept of temporal measure through the mutual inclusion of distinct "dharma positions." This makes it possible to compare and relate motions of different speed, which form the operational basis of clock-time. Having grown up in court society, Dōgen was also familiar with the measurement of equal hours, and the water clocks he wanted to install in his monasteries were instruments devised for that end. When talking about the twelve hours of the zodiac, he was therefore including a system of timekeeping that was abstracted from the immediate perception of the length of day and night. He may or may not have known firsthand the elaborate mechanisms, including the mechanical escapement, which had developed several centuries earlier in China with the help of the Esoteric Buddhist mathematician Yixing, to ensure the measuring of equal temporal units.[41] In any case, his multiperspectival view of time was certainly able to accommodate such methods of timekeeping and to employ them for its own ends.

If we further depart from issues that Dōgen himself considered, the complex of notions condensed in the term "what is:time" could even serve as the basis for thinking about relativity because it treats time's measure as resulting from the comparison between the phases of transition of different objects. The point of this observation is not that Dōgen in some way anticipated modern physics: He certainly did not. The point is that, whatever the differences between his conception of time and those engendered by modern science, they are not differences at the level of complexity or logical capacity. This is not to deny the advances made in time measurement, the coordination of clocks, and, concomitantly, human actions; as well as in the exploration of the environment and the physical universe in general. However, this progress is a consequence not of the different level of logical complexity, but of underlying convictions, technological developments, and social conditions. I would contend, hypothetically, that if Dōgen were alive today, he would (and could) integrate modern chronometry into his doctrinal system, as he did with the state of the art in his day.

That said, there remains a fundamental difference in value orientation between the drive for scientific exploration and technological development on the one hand, and Dōgen's soteriological outlook on the other. Dōgen's single-minded dedication to the Buddha Way, in combination with his idea that insight is realized through assiduous adherence to the model behavior of Buddhas and ancestors, precluded a broad interest in the empirical investigation of the world and in matters of social and technological improvement. The literature of the Zen school that he turned to placed no weight either on expanding the knowledge of nature or on charitable efforts. There is a notable difference in this regard between Dōgen and other Japanese Buddhist figures such as Gyōki 行基 (668–749), Dōgen's contemporaries Eison 叡尊 (1201–1290) and Ninshō 忍性 (1217–1303), or, in a later era, the Sōtō Zen monk Suzuki Shōsan 鈴木正三 (1579–1655).[42] Shōsan's case is particularly compelling because his position that the benevolent pursuit of secular professions is a way to realize Buddhist insight inherits Dōgen's idea of the unity of practice and attainment, while resolving a contradiction inherent in the latter's singular commitment to the monastic path. Specifically, monastic life as realized in Dōgen's Kōshōji and Eiheiji depended on support through the production of wealth in the secular world. Therefore, Dōgen's lack of interest in matters of economic productivity and technological advancement constituted a blind spot that was at odds with his soteriological ambitions. Clearly, heightened productivity would offer more people the chance to pursue monastic life. Furthermore, improving productivity to better meet the needs of sentient beings could be seen as an expanded application of

Dōgen's instructions to senior monks in charge of monastic economy, to plan carefully and protect provisions against rodents or other causes of damage. This application is beyond Dōgen's purview, but is nevertheless in line with his principles.

One might criticize Dōgen's outlook on time, from a scientific, economic, or ethical perspective, for its lack of interest in exploring nature, technological advancement, and the improvement of society. However, from his point of view, the questions to ask would be: Do these endeavors, and more specifically, the quantification and homogenization of time, foster insight into impermanence and the Buddhist teaching? How far do they alleviate suffering, and where do they create pain and multiply its causes? Can we, for example, honestly say that the application of time regimes unilaterally based on the economization of quantified time are compatible with the well-being of a population? How do we weigh the interests of those who are subject to factory regimes, piece rates, and flexible work shifts against the interests of those who profit from increased productivity and higher rates of surplus value?

Reciprocal comparison in this manner reveals a fundamental point relevant to the historiography of time and the study of time in general: History or theory, when written from the standpoint of one symbolic form—such as technology, politics, or religion—alone will of necessity be biased. That is a fortiori true where the perspective is that of a specific historical formation—be it Dōgen's interpretation of Buddhism or today's mainstream economics.

A history that takes all symbolic forms into account is, however, much less likely to be a straightforward history of cultural progress or evolution; it will at any rate have to consider a larger number of criteria. In the case of time, it can no longer be written simply as a history of ever more exact chronometry and increasing "operational" competence, but has to account for the whole gamut of chronographical and chrononoetic determinations, as well as for the dimensions of chronopolitics and chronoaesthetics.

In this enhanced matrix, we find that Dōgen formulated a position that was able to account for and integrate his era's state of the art in chronometry, including reckoning with equal hours, infinite timelines, and global chronology. In line with his religious orientation and goals, however, he restricted the application of abstract chronometry in the organization of monastic life. In practical as well as in theoretical matters, typological determination often assumed primary importance. This enabled him to articulate a view that emphasized, on the one hand, responsibility for past and present actions, but opened, on the other, the present and future up to the promise of attaining full liberation. In that regard, he countered antinomian as well as pessimistic and fatalistic tendencies, which were all present in his day. The chronoaesthetic nature of his view is one that combines urgency and reassurance: urgency to take up monastic life and reassurance that following this mode of life will result, or indeed, immediately realize, attainment of the ultimate religious goal. This realization, in turn, would connect one via communal practice and iteration with the trans-temporal community of those following the Buddha Way, but it also necessitates the ever-renewed effort to move beyond extant expressions of insight. This openness and dynamism are features that continue to resonate today. However, one should not overlook the fact that they are restricted to the field of religious practice in accord with the Buddhist tradition, which is placed beyond critical questioning. This includes belief in the moral causality of karma, miraculous events, the superhuman powers of sacred beings, the existence of demons and deities, and other elements that were more readily acceptable at a time when the knowledge of the physical universe and its laws was still much more limited than today. Addressing Dōgen as a critical thinker in a generalized sense, as has been common in the literature, is not only problematic in terms of hermeneutics, as it attributes to him an openness that he explicitly repudiated. It is also anachronistic, because it imputes to him an awareness of problems that arose only later, when a plurality of political and ideological systems on the one hand and theoretical paradigms on the other were broadly available for public discussion.

9

After-Thoughts

Dimensions of Contemporary Significance

What can secular (or more generally, non-Buddhist) readers today take away from Dōgen's ideas on time and time-related practices, as I have reconstructed them in the previous chapters? The following reflections are dedicated to answering this question in the dimensions of the theoretical, the practical, and the spiritual. They move the discussion back to a philosophical engagement with his thought, based on reciprocal comparison. Instead of assimilating Dōgen into contemporary philosophical discourse, this mode of comparison accepts that his orientation differs fundamentally from modern philosophy with its emphasis on arguments about theoretical propositions. The question then is: What remains if we parenthesize the beliefs in karmic retribution or the omnipresence of enlightened insight that are fundamental to Dōgen's soteriology, but that cannot be proven by ordinary human means of knowledge?

Theoretical: Dōgen and the Concept of Time

The exploration of Dōgen's works has revealed several points that are generally relevant to the understanding of time. Concerning the morphology or "shape" of time, we found that Dōgen complemented the dominant notion of time's flow with a number of other images. Ultimately, he resisted the idea that time can be appropriately rendered by one single spatial form; rather, the adequate representation of time requires the use of multiple images. On a more abstract level, his approach to time illustrates how the quantitative and numerical determination of time can work hand in hand with typological characterization. Elaborate chronometry can be conducive to an existentially authentic stance and serve the creation of meaningful and beneficial structures of communal life.

The Morphology of Time and Things

"Time" is an abstract and complex notion that is made comprehensible by way of metaphors and mental images. In particular, "Most of our understanding of time is a metaphorical version of our understanding of motion in space."[1] The "flow" or "river" of time is a common example. It was employed early in the development of Japanese literature to picture time's passage, as in Harumichi no Tsuraki's poem: "Speaking of yesterday, today is spent, the Morrow River flows and quickly it's been months and years."[2]

We have seen how Dōgen employed images and metaphors that represent a variety of shapes and forms of movement to complement and enrich this image. Regarding linear movement, he prompted his audience and readers to turn around and face time's coming to show how time does not simply carry the present away; it also brings along what is yet to arrive. He further used linear imagery of a different kind—that of the genealogical lineage—to describe the history of Buddhist teaching. In contrast to the more locally confined image of a river, the line of generations in this particular case stretched far beyond the present world. It included Buddhas of past eons and reached into an open future, when current practitioners would become fully accomplished enlightened beings. These images bear witness to the fact that Dōgen did not simply deny or reject the notion of linear temporal sequence.

However, Dōgen also introduced images of a different kind to break the fixation with the idea of simple serial progression. A powerful example is his image of surveying a vast range of mountains while standing on a peak. Notably, this image is introduced to explain an element of any given moment. I have therefore argued that the "ruby palace on top of the mountain," which was identified by Steven Heine as a symbol of "idle hopes and expectations,"[3] should rather be understood as illustrating the fundamental holistic perspective inherent in the "consummate now." The slightly more abstract, but still metaphorical expression of "lining up in order" points in a similar direction: What is past is not simply lost. Such vanishing into oblivion was impossible for Dōgen, who insisted on the inexorable workings of karma. However, the chain of causation could, in his view, be transformed by religious insight and practice.

This image of "lining up in order" therefore also connects to the figure of the "cycle of sustained practice." Hoshi Shunya showed how that formula does not indicate a strictly circular movement: It translates best into the geometrical form of a spiral, which unites aspects of the circular with the linear. The planar projection in Dōgen's document of succession is a two-dimensional representation of this geometrical shape.[4] More fundamental in an ontological sense than all these images is, however, that of oscillation between existence and nonexistence—which happens, according to Dōgen, "sixty-five times within one snap of one's fingers."[5]

In conclusion, we find that all four of Maki Yūsuke's fundamental morphologies of time (oscillating, circular/cyclical, segmented linear, and infinite linear)[6] are present in Dōgen's work. To these, we may add the imagery of the mountain range (or "lining up in order"), which is static and therefore does not appear in Maki's typology. It is difficult to say which morphology is dominant in Dōgen's texts, but that may precisely be the point. The dense juxtaposition of different types of imagery in "What Is:Time" suggests that Dōgen intentionally sought to disrupt the fixation on the culturally pervasive notion of time's flow, as it invites the idea that things may somehow exist outside of time.

In this regard, and moving beyond his specific agenda, one can say that Dōgen's deliberate use of variation in the imagery of time is dexterous, even exemplary. It acknowledges the seminal role of intuition in guiding human cognition and action, but avoids the tendency of visual images to restrict and ossify the understanding of time. As George Lakoff and Mark Johnson have shown, no single visual form or metaphor for time can encompass the gamut of temporal relations and attributes, and all of them "can get us into silliness if we take them literally."[7] While every one of the images mentioned above (including that of the river) fosters the intuitive grasp of important aspects of time, regarding any one of them as its complete representation can only lead to mystification.

The same might be said about the images that are used to intuitively think about the real world. Here, the general prototype—whether in medieval Japan or the modern West—tends to be that of a solid object like Ōmori Shōzō's kitchen pot, Quine's Parthenon, Hume's mountain and horse, or Descartes' dressing gown and paper.[8] Objects that are, in essence, dynamic and unstable, like the wind, or living, animate things, are accordingly understood as belonging to more specific types.[9] This easily connects to the intuition that time is, normally at least, somehow extraneous to objects. Using the stone as a prototype, one may imagine that things exist without time and as self-contained entities independent of any relation to something else.

Like the image of time as a river, the image of a stable, independent object fulfills an important function in our dealings with the world. In many situations, we simply have to assume that the objects surrounding us will retain their essential characteristics throughout a certain action, process, or event.

However, to generalize the image of a stable object and consider it as the standard model for whatever is real is as problematic as it is common. In this regard, Dōgen's exploration of alternative imagery is once again helpful beyond his specific religious agenda. His reference to the season of spring as an alternative prototype to guide thinking about objects in their relation to time and, specifically, temporal passing is a case in point. By contemplating things in analogy to the prototype of the season, we intuitively understand that their existence and reality do not depend on a persistent, unchanging, self-contained substance. Where it exists, spring—the season of incipient growth—is certainly more than merely (to return to an expression of Rein Raud's) a "linguistic entity" or some sort of "conventional object" devoid of any attributes that are independent of human recognition. It is not because of convention that farmers in moderate climate zones plant the bulk of their crops in spring. As a consequence, the actual appearance of spring is shaped by activities that respond to its qualities. Spring is therefore a reality, but not a monolithic, static object. It comprises many states and changes to the extent that it has become the symbol of (upward) change, of renewed life and novelty. It is neither a mere figment of imagination or convention nor separate from our modes of interacting with its qualities. Furthermore, it is contingent on conditions that support and sustain their continued existence. These conditions extend in space and time far beyond what we perceive as the contours of the object in question: Even in medieval Japan, one would recognize how spring depended on the power of the sunlight reaching the earth (whatever the geographic and astronomical model used to explain it). Using the paradigm of the seasons instead of that of solid objects invites us to think of a "thing" as the focal point or center of a certain configuration of the world. As such, it is still distinct in its contours and well differentiated from other things. But we are led to see the changes it undergoes and the connections it has with other elements of the world as part and parcel of what it is, and not as accidental, extraneous to what the thing is in and of itself. It would certainly be an exaggeration to regard Dōgen as an ecological thinker avant la lettre, as his concerns were very different from ours, and he discouraged the empirical study of the natural environment. Nevertheless, the examples he presented as paradigms for thinking about reality may be useful beyond the bounds of his vision. This especially holds for the current era, where the old way of regarding the world as largely independent of human action is no longer applicable to the habitat of our species.[10]

Time's Measure and Attributes

Another topic where Dōgen's thoughts on time are relevant to philosophy is the relation between the quantitative determination of time (chronometry) and the determination of attributes or properties that specify particular times (chronotypology). Current discussions of time tend to regard the metric of time as most essential. For example, an essay contest conducted in 2008 by the Foundational Questions Institute on the "nature of time" revolved almost entirely around the question of whether the metric of time is a fundamental physical factor or whether, in the words of the winning essay, "intervals of time do not pre-exist but are created by what the universe does."[11] This emphasis on the geometry of time entails the ontological conviction that the fundamental truth about time lies in its measure, best grasped by physics, and that everything else about it is a matter of individual psychology or collective convention.[12] The contrasting, minority view is that measurement fails to grasp the essence of time. The ecologist David Woods, for example, recently posited: "Measuring time would be like investigating the swimming habits of fish by taking them out of the water to check more closely." Wood connected this to the Heideggerian "legacy of philosophers for whom calculation is something to be very suspicious of, especially when it seeks to substitute itself for *thinking*."[13] The idea behind this notion, as succinctly argued by Heidegger in his so-called "Natorp report" of 1923 and expanded on in *Being and Time*, is that the authentic sense of time originates with the human anticipation of death.[14] Calculation of time, as in relation to average life expectancy, in his view only obfuscates the existential confrontation at the heart of such anticipation: It is a way to avoid facing death squarely in its ever-looming imminence.[15] Dōgen's ideas on time constitute an alternative to this stark opposition between the reduction of time to number and the outright refutation of attempts to grasp time through its measure. They thus present an opportunity to rethink the premises on which the arguments on both sides are based.

On the one hand, it is an illusion to think that non-metrical determinations of time can be relegated to the realm of secondary, subjective attributes. Typological determinations of time are not simply subjective, and accepting their objectivity is not in every case an archaic notion. On the contrary, typological determination is indispensable in principle because, at a logical level, it is impossible to separate quantitative from attributive determination.[16] It is true that an hour spent by a sick person helplessly in pain in the middle of the night contains as many minutes and seconds as an hour flying by in lighthearted conversation. The measure of clock-time is independent of how one experiences its speed; that is, in a way, its point. Clocks are created to coordinate human actions among individuals and with the events in their environment. They are designed to transcend individual time perception. Nonetheless, one needs to be able to identify two different hours to compare their length, whether perceived or otherwise. Such identification cannot happen without reference to particular attributes, such as "that hour at night when I was sick and in pain," "that hour at lunch last week," or "between 9:00 and 10:00 a.m. on Wednesday, March 29, 2023." For the sake of social organization, attributes may be chosen with minimal reference to individual specifics. For instance, prevailing calendrical systems, which enable fully relational determination, are mostly tied to origin dates of presumably shared religious significance. The Julian dating system, which avoids religious commitment, entails another form of cultural positioning; it is based on the conjunction of the solar and the lunar with the fifteen-year Roman indiction cycles (used to reassess taxation). Even the definition of purely stereometric time units cannot occur without reference to material attributes. Witness the modern definition of the second as a multiple of "the unperturbed ground-state hyperfine transition frequency of the caesium 133 atom."[17]

Nonetheless, the quantitative determination of time can "forget" about this basis and be abstracted from virtually every specific material attribute. Modern clock-readers will rarely think of caesium when checking the time. This potential for abstraction is part of the clock's social and cognitive function. It is implicit wherever time is counted, as the series of numbers is infinite, and different numerical measures of time (for example, seasonal vs. equal hours, equal zodiacal hours vs. modern minutes, and so forth) may be compared and converted into each other once their material basis (the process of measurement) is understood.

Conversely, it is equally fallacious to believe in a sense of time that is completely independent of quantitative determination. This is evident even in the Heideggerian view of authenticity. To speak of the imminence of death as the true condition of human existence is already to quantify: It amounts to saying that death may come "soon" or "at any time." The quantity in question here is numerically indeterminate, but it is a quantity nonetheless. Semantically and logically, quantitative determination is different from typological determination, but that does not mean the two are fully separate or even separable in the actual perception of time.

Shifting the subject to the question of authenticity, one may argue that indeterminacy is essential when speaking of the imminence of death. Calculating time, in contrast, puts a number between a person and death and thus distracts them from the true sense of imminence. Calculation requires the identification of units that are posited as equal and interchangeable. In other words, when time is calculated, all attributes beyond those that define the unit are ignored. The calculation of time thus transcends the singularity that each given time has for the living individual. In Heideggerian terms and understanding, the singularity of "my time" as "being-unto-death" is leveled in the process.[18] "My time" becomes interchangeable with any other time. Thinking of time primarily in terms of numbers thus obscures the singularity of each existential moment. This is what Heideggerian readers of Dōgen seem to have in mind when they warn against the "preoccupation with the chronology and calculation of time."[19]

While time calculation may indeed be used consciously or unconsciously to keep the thought of death at bay, it can also be employed to the contrary. We saw how Dōgen illustrated the fundamental fragility of human existence by putting a number on the imperceptibly short duration of the "moment" in which the human body and mind materially persists. Taking this one step further, one may argue that without the calculation of one's position within linear time, the singularity of each moment of lived time would hardly come to the fore. In addition, the inexorable ephemerality and cosmic insignificance of individual life is also a truth of time and human existence. Life is built on anonymous processes that continue regardless and extend incalculably beyond the reach of any individual. Thus, individual lives are embedded in a world whose sheer vastness can inspire both awe and unfathomable fear. Each is an authentic human response to what Kant called the "mathematical sublime."

Moreover, as again exemplified in Dōgen's writings, calculation can also become a source of new meaning. It allows one to clarify one's position in the world and to form trans-temporal connections that work *against* the leveling of time. The creation of a ritual calendar that establishes meaningful connections beyond individual occasions depends on the ability to calculate time.

In sum, Dōgen's concept of time and his time regimes illustrate that the calculation of time does not necessarily lead to a process of alienation. There are alternatives to the outright rejection of clock-time in the name of authentic existence. In the final analysis, life "ruled by the clock" is a social phenomenon; it rests on a particular division of labor and power.[20] Alienation occurs when the discretion over time use is taken out of individuals' hands and disconnected from their sense of purpose. To blame the clock is an act of negative fetishism, where the cause of a social phenomenon is attributed to a thing instead of a social relationship.[21] Ultimately, the problem is not the calculation of time, but the way that calculation is factored into a particular social formation.

In his "Comparative Sociology of Time," the Japanese sociologist Maki Yūsuke observed that the relative weight of the quantitative determination of time is contingent on the cognitive and material outreach of a society.[22] Where actions and interactions remain within the boundaries of a region or country, there is little need to look beyond material attributes that are specific to the environment of the region or country in question. In studies of the history of time that focus on the European and Western world, emphasis is placed on the combined advancement of science and capitalism in the development of a universal, "abstract" system of global time.[23] This points to the inherent potential of numerical chronometry to increase cognitive freedom and social integration. However, it also overstates the uniqueness and achievements of so-called "Western modernity" and the ties between the capacity to calculate time and the specific social formation of capitalism.

The references to chronology in Dōgen's writings bear witness to the fact that, historically, the creation of integrated chronological systems was in some instances driven by religious motifs. In his case, this motif consisted in the identification of a line of tradition across cultural and political boundaries. To believe that pre-modern cultures were incapable of *thinking* an abstract universal metric of time is therefore a case of modern exceptionalism. Earlier societies' practical use for this mode of temporal determination, however, was very restricted, as were their technological abilities to *realize* it on both the larger and the smaller ends of the scale of temporal measures. Advancements in this regard have greatly increased, in principle at least, the spaces of human discretion. How this potential is used, however, and to whose gain, is a matter of social and political organization. In the balance of things, the ability to restrict the application of "abstracted" quantified time regimes, or to reintegrate numerical chronometry into a system that is meaningful (and respectful) to those subject to it, may turn out to be as important to human culture as the ability to perform ever more fine-grained chronometric determinations, or to implement a seamless stream of homogenized time.

The ritual calendar Dōgen installed in his monasteries demonstrates how quantitative determination can be used for material attributive characterization. This serves to infuse "abstract" units of time with meaning and to connect them to a shared sense of purpose. On the level of daily activities, his time regimes furthermore show how restricting the granularity of timekeeping in social organization can give members of a group the opportunity to concentrate on the action at hand. Whether one shares Dōgen's religious outlook or not, his works therefore hold lessons for the historical understanding of time, as well as for the creation of time regimes that benefit their participants.

Practical: Time- and Task-Orientation Combined

We live in an era when, because of pressures inherent in the capitalist mode of production,[24] nearly everyone in society is in one way or the other confronted with the imperative to "use" time "efficiently"; that is, in a way that produces the highest returns on investment. As Hartmut Rosa vividly described in his recent book on "social acceleration," this creates a trend toward the compartmentalization and speeding up of processes, which makes itself felt in virtually all areas of life and on all levels of society.[25] In this context, Dōgen's practical instructions concerning monastic life can serve to remind us of possible alternatives. Whatever we think about their attractiveness or viability for ourselves, it is important to preserve the knowledge of such alternative forms of organizing life to prevent a simplistic dualism in the critique of culture.

As mentioned in passing in chapter 4, the historian E. P. Thompson famously distinguished between two modes of organizing individual and collective human activity: first, task-orientation, and second, time-orientation. Task-orientation is that mode where the content of an action determines the time required and thus functions as its zeitgeber: The action is continued until its objective is completed, or circumstances make continuation impossible, or another action appears more pressing. Thompson highlighted two intrinsic characteristics: First, task orientation is intuitive and "humanly comprehensible." Second, it also, somewhat counterintuitively, allows us to mix or jointly pursue different tasks.[26] In the words of Japanologist Brigitte Steger, task-orientation is regularly associated with a "polychronic" mode of life, where several things are done simultaneously and each action can be interrupted should the need arise.[27] We saw an example of this task-oriented, polychronic mode in Dōgen's instructions for the late-night/early-morning hours in the monks' hall: Here, monks were supposed to sit in *zazen* while "looking for the right time" to leave for the washing rooms and perform their morning hygiene.[28]

Time-orientation, in contrast, is that mode of organizing human activities where actions are scheduled and performed according to a numerical measure. Time here functions as something external to the tasks at hand; this can create a friction that becomes systemic where time is monetized. Thompson, building on the insights of Karl Marx, observed that time-orientation becomes pervasive with the introduction of wage labor, where employers buy labor power for a given time. In such a system, time takes on the attributes of a resource that is divorced from the tasks at hand: "the employer must use the time of his labour, and see it is not wasted: not the task but the value of time when reduced to money is dominant. Time is now currency: it is not passed but spent."[29]

As critics of Thompson have noted, the link between time-orientation, temporal pressures, and wage labor is less exclusive to capitalist relations of production than it appears in his article.[30] Thompson himself indicated that the need to synchronize activities between individuals and groups not in direct contact is one of the drivers of time-orientation.[31] Such a need can arise from quite different motives, not all of which are economic, let alone monetary.

In Dōgen's case, the religious idea of modeling life after the precedent of previous enlightened ones supported the motivation to use an external time frame set by the tradition. Time-orientation here ensured a kind of "synchrony across time" by maintaining the same fundamental rhythms on the scale of the day, month, and year. Verbal instructions reminded the community of this shared metric and imbued it with religious significance.

We have further seen how Dōgen created within this time-oriented framework the opportunity for ordinary monks to live largely in a task-oriented mode. Negotiating external, numeric measures of time was the responsibility of senior temple officers, while the greater part of the congregation could simply proceed with the activities at hand. New tasks (e.g., moving from afternoon rest or study to late-afternoon meditation) were announced by extensive acoustic signals that left enough time to end one occupation and move to the right place for the next. Within the daily schedule, some actions were also timed in a task-bound mode. For example, monks were called to lunch not at a fixed hour, but when the kitchen had finished its preparations.

This mixed mode of time- and task-orientation holds a practical lesson beyond the scope of monastic, or religious, life. As Thompson noted, task-orientation is generally intuitive in that the timing of actions is aligned with their purpose and importance. Thompson's critics have observed that this does not mean that time pressures are absent; life is not idyllic in societies where task-orientation dominates.[32] But if time pressures do not originate, as they often will, in oppressive social dominance (with tasks and their timing being set at will by some superior), they usually "make sense" in and of themselves. Vanquishing such pressures therefore comes with a feeling of reward.

The time regime Dōgen devised for his monastery is thus an example of a dexterous combination of time- and task-orientation. It allowed for the synchronization of activities within a general scheme, while ordinary members of the community were able to focus on the action at hand without having to worry about timekeeping. Significantly, time-orientation was restricted to units on the scale of the zodiacal hour and beyond. Below that scale, actions were organized in task-oriented mode. This meant that the lived present was generally characterized by immersion into the action one was performing at the moment, as opposed to "running against the clock."

Time-orientation was further mitigated by giving external measures of time a clear connection to something that was meaningful to those performing the actions in question. Dōgen's formal instructions are masterful exercises in that regard. One may argue that practically, this, then, no longer represents a mode of pure time-orientation. But that is precisely the point: time-orientation can be infused with task-orientation when time's metric is associated with a typology that distinguishes the attributes of different times.³³ This gives significance to an occasion according to its numerical measure and creates meaningful connections between different times. The present moment is integrated into a larger framework of meaning, from which spiritual significance accrues to the present.

Restricting time-orientation to a scale beyond the hour and connecting time units with meaningful attributes are therefore efficient means for synthesizing time- and task-orientation. Under the right social conditions (that is, in the absence of oppressive social domination), they can prevent the alienation often associated with submission to clock-time. But they also restrict the gains in single-task efficiency realized by pure time-orientation, where "saving time" in the execution of a clearly defined task is the dominant imperative.

Spiritual: Trans-Temporal Synchrony, Holistic Connectedness

The word "spirituality" was revived in the early twentieth century in religious discourse, primarily to designate the personal aspect of transformative engagement with the sacred, as opposed to institutional religion and its public rituals.³⁴ It should be clear from the analysis of Dōgen's ways of engaging time that they do not fall neatly on either side. Their institutional and public aspects have been detailed in chapter 4. Here, I would like to discuss their spiritual side, focusing on their significance beyond the confines of (Sōtō) Zen Buddhism. Pierre Hadot's influential monograph on spiritual exercises has brought the subject of spirituality back into philosophical discussions.³⁵ Hadot complemented the earlier theological emphasis on the moral content of such exercises³⁶ with a broader spectrum of goals, comprising aspects such as learning to live, to enter into dialogue, to die, but also—perhaps most surprisingly—to read.³⁷ In recent decades, the subject of spirituality has gained attention in an even wider variety of fields, from health to management.³⁸

Two main defining elements may be derived from the multiple understandings that are by now present in this discourse:³⁹ First, spirituality is an attitude through which individuals relate their life, or events in their life, to something beyond the confines of their own limited perspective on the world. This relationship is supposed to give an individual's life its meaning. Second, spirituality involves the individual as a whole, including the intellectual, emotional, and corporeal aspects of human existence.

Spirituality in this understanding is a subset of possible general attitudes toward human existence that supports a certain way of leading one's life with transformative effects on one's personality or character. It can be bound to a socially instituted religion, with shared ideas about the sacred, an established set of rituals, and so forth, but it does not have to be—and this is why a discussion of the spiritual meaning of Dōgen's ideas on time can be meaningful beyond the confines of the Zen Buddhist community. Certainly, in our case it is best to leave it to members of the Sōtō school to express what Dōgen's instructions on time mean for their own religious life today.[40] A study of such expressions would cast light on the ways religious traditions survive by accommodating canonical texts to contemporary conditions and views, and be instructive about changes prompted by modern chronometry, chronopolitics, and the contemporary repertoire of knowledge—but it would also be a subject for another book. What I offer here instead are thoughts on the spiritual significance of Dōgen's engagement with time beyond the boundaries of this denomination.

Synchrony across Time

In chapter 6, we saw that Dōgen's view of time is oriented toward the goal of liberation from the cycle of suffering, and it bases itself on the Buddhist tradition. Two time-related elements stand out in this regard: First, the notion of "trans-temporal synchrony" in religious practice, whereby the practitioner acts, in Dōgen's words, in the "same time" with all enlightened beings and is supported by their accumulated merits. Second, the idea of karma, which is fundamental for explaining the holistic aspect of his concept of time. For those who accept the authority of the Buddhist tradition, these ideas may be carried over into the present since they do not contradict what we now know about the world. However, they are also not supported by commonly accessible empirical evidence. Neither do they derive logically from any commonly known fact about the world. According to Dōgen's own words, they are in principle unverifiable in this manner; only fully enlightened beings have access to that kind of knowledge. They must therefore remain a matter of faith for ordinary human beings.

The question concerning us here, then, is whether these ideas can have meaning for those who do not hold such faith. I believe they can, although in a much reduced fashion.

The idea of sharing the "same time" with enlightened beings, if taken as presented by Dōgen, is bound to particular religious doctrines. The calling forth of a unity with enlightened beings in every instance of practice and the concomitant transfer of merit defy ordinary empirical verification. However, even without belief in the real presence of enlightened ones or the transfer of their merit, sharing in the same activity across time creates a meaningful spiritual experience. In fact, this kind of symbolic repetition is to be found in many cultures. It was identified by Mircea Eliade as fundamental to the mythological engagement with time.[41] But it is not restricted to ritual reenactments of a mythic tale of origin. Any action of significance that can be ritually memorialized or repeated may be performed with an awareness of its past and future iterations and those involved in them. Furthermore, contra Eliade, it is sufficient to imagine unity with past and future participants without believing in their actual presence.[42] If performed with this idea in mind, the action creates a connection over time that integrates those currently engaged in the action into the trans-temporal community of all who have performed it in the past and will perform it in the future.

In other words, acts of trans-temporal synchronization are apt to invite a spiritual experience of being embedded in time, instead of being exposed to it. They thus offer an experiential way to transcend individual finitude, with powerful effects, especially if the experience is a communal one. Well-considered actions of this type can function as a way of making human life feel meaningful and foster resilience against its vicissitudes.

However, there is also the danger of exploiting the power of such experiences for nefarious ends.[43] Like all cultural performances, the enactment of trans-temporal synchrony must therefore be subject to critical scrutiny and reflection. Polemics against such scrutiny, or against critical reasoning in general, introduce a dualism of the intellect and whatever comes to stand on the other side that indicates, at best, an incomplete realization of the spiritual goal to integrate all aspects of human existence.

Karma and What Is:Time

Moving to the concept of karma, it is certainly not irrational to contemplate one's own situation as the result of one's previous actions. Notably, Dōgen's instructions restrict such contemplation to the first person. In his view, only enlightened beings have the knowledge to assess the situation for others. A commonsense truth implied in this is that contemplating the fate of others as karmic recompense can easily encourage hypocrisy, especially when applied to those born, in William Blake's famous words, to "endless night."[44]

When restricted to those actions one finds oneself responsible for in the present life, such contemplation may, however, help to identify the choices one has made that led to the present situation. This can work first as a reminder that one is not subject to a preordained fate. Second, when facing adverse attitudes or actions by others, examining one's past for the "seeds" that brought about such "fruit" can bring to light actions of a similar kind that one has committed at some time. Ideally, this will result in a more understanding attitude toward those against whom one might otherwise hold a grudge and open the path to resolving the situation in a way that placates adversity.

Applying the idea of karma to aspects of one's own life that cannot be affected by one's actions in this present existence requires a certain leap of faith. One would have to accept, however provisionally, the idea that there is some kind of moral causality that links beings across time and forms individual chains of existences. For those who are born to "sweet delight," such contemplation can serve to caution against thoughtless and egotistic use of the associated privileges. For others who are less gifted and in unhappier circumstances, it may strengthen them against resentfulness and spite.

Much less speculative investment is required to make the idea of karma significant for the future. It is not even necessary to assume some moral force that ensures apt retribution for one's deeds in another life. A metaphysically restrained but still consequential version of the idea can work from the undeniable facticity of our actions, placing them in connection with the consequences they entail. In Dōgen's terms, this means to contemplate the present action as a certain "lining up in order" of the world, including the time that will arrive. Simply put, what one has done cannot be undone, and oneself and everybody else will have to live with it. A lie told to a friend or spouse, even if for the supposedly benevolent reason of avoiding unnecessary bad feelings, may require additional lies or cause awkward silences that undermine mutual trust. The same generally holds for other acts that one may not wish the world to know—they entail consequences for oneself and one's relations with others, whether one manages to keep them a secret or not, simply because of the efforts to keep them a secret.

The notions of karma and trans-temporal synchrony come together in Dōgen's idea of "what is:time," which includes the concept of a holistic dynamic that actualizes the totality of enlightenment at every given moment. One may be skeptical about its soteriological implications and the underlying metaphysical holism, yet still find spiritual meaning in it. To contemplate oneself as the vantage point of a configuration that "lines up (the world) in order"—at least as far as one may identify causal and epistemological connections—makes palpable the manifold links that support one's individual existence, without dissolving the individual into the enfolding embrace of the whole. The element of "transiting through phases" forces one to recognize the inevitability of change, again without denying some form of consistency in patterns over time.

The idea of "transiting through phases" further supports active engagement with the present in light of the future it may bring forth. It means seeing initial or ongoing struggles as necessary parts of a process for realizing an ideal that has no existence apart from such efforts. Seen in this light, they become more than some preliminary stage to be overcome and forgotten: They are essential for the ideal to remain a part of reality.

The above notions connected to "what is:time" thus generate questions that hold meaning on an individual and communal or social level: How am I, how are we "lining up the world"? Which distinctions do we make; what kind of configurations are we inserting ourselves into; and what ideals and what type of agency are we realizing by "transiting through the phases" of our actions? While these questions serve to prevent feelings of isolation and futility, they are by no means part of an easygoing "feel-good" attitude. In the opening sequence to her novel *The Book of Form and Emptiness*, Ruth Ozeki has expressed part of the concomitant attitude in terms of "listening to things":

> [T]ry it with the pencil first. Pencils have stories inside them [. . .]. Can you hear the wood whisper? The ghost of the pine? The mutter of lead? Sometimes it's more than one voice. Sometimes it's a whole chorus of voices rising from a single thing, especially if it's a made thing with lots of different makers, but don't be scared. I think it depends on the kind of day they were having back in Guangdong or Laos or wherever, and if it was a good day at the old sweatshop, if they were enjoying a pleasant thought at the moment when that particular grommet came tumbling down the line and passed through their fingers, then that pleasant thought will cling to the whole. Sometimes it's not so much a thought as a feeling. A nice warm feeling, like love, for example. [. . .] But when it's a sad feeling or an angry one that gets laced into your shoe, then you'd better watch out.

Poetic licenses aside, contemplating ourselves as "what is: time" means to confront ourselves not only with our own finitude, the limited duration of our existence as living and sentient beings "transiting through phases." Observing how we "line up" the world "in order" reveals the manifold links that support our life and connect us with distant parts of the world. With these connections come responsibilities—or, to say the least, the question of what kind of world we are trying to shape and configure with our lives. What is our "consummate now"? A consummation of violence and destruction or one of mutual respect and solidarity with sentient beings? While such considerations are "spiritual" in the sense given above, they are by no means irrational. Indeed, they are arguably even more "realistic" than a positivistic attitude that refuses to acknowledge the meaningful connections between us and the human and non-human world we live in. Even if Dōgen's ideas defy easy integration into contemporary philosophical discourse, his time-related thoughts and practices thus posit a productive challenge that can enhance self-reflection in our time.

Appendix 1

Translation of *Uji* ("What Is:Time")

Prefatory Note

The following translation of *Uji* is based on Ōkubo's edition (DZZ I, 189–194). I have noted where Ōkubo's text differs from the Internet edition published by Shōmonji (http://www.shomonji.or.jp/soroku/genzou.htm), which provides an easy way to compare the translation with the Japanese original. Numbers in parentheses preceding a paragraph indicate the thematic section according to the overview of the text given in table 6.1, pp. 140–41.

Among the basic dimensions of equivalence a translation may hope to achieve, I have prioritized the semantic (denotative and, where possible, connotative) and formal over the functional and pragmatic.[1] For this reason, I render names in the way Dōgen gives them, even where he uses abbreviations or lesser known styles; I stick as closely to his metaphorical language as possible; and I use awkward constructions and composite expressions where he does the same. I also render in small capitals passages where Dōgen changes the linguistic register from the composite vernacular style to Literary Sinitic[2] to reciprocate as best as possible the "block-like" visual impression of these passages. The reason for this choice is that there are other translations available that prioritize the functional and pragmatic dimension, attempting to make his text more easily accessible to modern readers interested or invested in Zen Buddhism. I have consulted and am indebted to extant translations, especially the English ones by Heine, Nearman, Tanahashi, and Waddell and Abe; the German translation by Elberfeld; and the modern Japanese versions by Nakamura, Takahashi, and Tamaki.[3]

Translation

(1) A Buddha of old[4] said:
What is:time,[5] standing on top of a high, high mountain,
What is:time, walking the bottom of the deep, deep sea.
What is:time, three heads and eight arms,[6]
What is:time, one jō, six or eight shaku.[7]
What is:time, staff and fly whisk,[8]
What is:time, pillar and lantern.[9]
What is:time, Zhang's third and Li's fourth [son].[10]
What is:time, the great earth and empty sky.[11]

(2) "What is:time" here means that time is altogether what there is, and what there is, each and all of it, is time. The golden body of one *jō* six is time. Because it is time, there is the sublime light of time. Study and practice[12] this in the current twelve [zodiacal] hours.[13] The three-headed, eight-armed is time. Because it is time, it is one and the same as the current twelve hours. One calls them "twelve hours" without having measured the length or brevity of their duration. Since the traces of their going and coming are clear, people do not hold them in doubt. They may not hold them in doubt, but that does not mean they have come to know them. In their original state, sentient beings do not consistently doubt every single thing and affair they are ignorant about, so their previous doubts do not necessarily match with their present ones. Their doubting is just, for a little while, time, and that is all.

(3) When one lines up the self-identical[14] in order and takes that to exhaust the world,[15] one has to look at all living beings and all things of this exhaustive world as so many times. Things do not obstruct one another[16] just like times do not obstruct one another. For this reason, there is same-time origination of the intention [to obtain enlightenment],[17] which is bringing forth time from the same intention.[18] Practice and realization of the way are also like this.

Lining up the self-identical in order, the self-identical looks at this. This is the way to understand[19] how the self[20] is time. Because of this way of understanding, one should study in practice how there are myriad shapes and hundreds of grasses[21] on the whole earth and how each blade of grass and each shape is part of the whole earth. Going back and forth in this fashion[22] is the first step of practice. When one arrives at this field, it is one blade of grass, one shape, encountering the shape or not encountering the shape, encountering the grass, not encountering the grass.[23] Because each is:time is just right this time, it is the whole of time. There is grass, there is form—both are time. At the time of each time, there is all there is and the whole world. Consider for a moment: All there is, the whole world, has leaked into this very time[24]—is it here, or is it not?

(4) When they hear the words "what is: time," the understandings among those in the situation of ordinary people who haven't studied the Buddha dharma all amount to thinking: "At one time, one had become three-headed and eight-armed, at another time, one had become a golden body of one *jō* six. It is like having passed a river and a mountain. Even if mountain and river still exist, I[25] have passed them and am now placed in a vermilion tower of a jewel palace. The mountain and river are [as distant] to me as the sky is to earth."

That may be, but the way to understand things doesn't end with this one proposition alone. "I"[26] was there at that time of scaling the mountain and crossing the river. There must be time for that "I." That "I" was necessarily there, and time cannot have gone away. Should time not have the property of leaving and arriving, then the time of scaling the mountain is what is:time's consummate now.[27] If, however, time preserves the properties of leaving and coming, then for the "I" there is what is:time's consummate now, and that is what is:time. Doesn't the time of scaling the mountain and crossing the river gulp down the time of the jewel palace's vermilion tower? Doesn't it spit it out? The three-headed, eight-armed [being] was yesterday's time, [the Buddha's body standing at] one *jō* six or [sitting at] eight *shaku* are today's time. Nevertheless, the way to understand yesterday and today equals the occasion where one has entered the mountains and surveys thousands and myriads of peaks—they don't pass by and go away. The three-headed, eight-armed transits its course within the I's is:time; it looks as if it was over there but it is the consummate now. The [Buddha's body standing at] one *jō* six or [sitting at] eight *shaku* equally transits its course within the I's is:time; it looks as if it was in a different place, but it is the consummate now.

Because of this, pines, too, are time, bamboo is also time.[28]

One should not understand time as merely flying past, or study flying past as its only function. If time completely committed to flying past, gaps should have appeared. One fails to lend one's ear to the teaching of what is:time because one solely studies time as passing by. Briefly said, all [the things][29] that are in all spheres are, while cohering, so many times. By way of being what is:time, they are what is:time.[30]

(5.1) What is:time possesses the virtue[31] of transiting through phases.[32] It transits from what we call today to tomorrow, it transits from today to yesterday, it transits from yesterday to today. It transits from today to today, it transits from tomorrow to tomorrow. And this is because transiting through phases is a virtue of time.

The past and present time have neither piled up nor have they, in lining up, accumulated.[33] Nevertheless, Qingyuan is time, Huangbo is time, and Jiangxi and Shitou are also time.[34] Since self and other are inevitably time, practice and insight are so many times. Entering into the mud and entering into the water[35] are time in the same way. The above view of ordinary people and the conditions from which it arises are what these people see. However, they are not the dharma of ordinary people.[36] It is just that the dharma for a while conditions the arising of ordinary people. One assumes that the golden body of one *jō* six is not oneself because one learns that this time, and what is now, is not the dharma. When people try to get away with thinking that they are not the golden body of one *jō* six, these are really just fragments of what is:time; they are the ideations of those who have not yet realized [insight].

(5.2) Furthermore, this arising and decline, up and down of abiding in dharma-configurations[37] also makes appear the horse and sheep that are lined up in order in the present world.[38] Rats are time, tigers are time, being alive is time, and Buddhas are time. At this time, one realizes exhausting[39] all worlds with three heads and eight arms, one realizes exhausting all worlds with the golden body of one *jō* six. The world-exhausting of all worlds with all worlds is called fully exhausting.[40] The one *jō* six golden body is embodied in a one *jō* six golden fashion by bringing forth the intention, practicing, obtaining enlightenment, and nirvana, and it is precisely what is, and it is time. This is exploring to the full all time[s] as all there is. Beyond this, no dharma[41] remains, because such an excess dharma would be a redundant dharma. Even when what is:time is only a half-baked exploration, that is the exhaustive exploration of half of what is:time. The phase that looks like a misstep is also what is. If one commits oneself to this, it is—while appearing before or after the misstep—what is:time's abiding configuration. This is how abiding in the dharma-configuration is full of activity and buzzing with life, this is what is:time. One shouldn't mix this up with "absence" or pretentiously call it "being."[42]

(5.3) Those straining to plot time exclusively as passing in one direction fail to understand it as something that has not yet arrived. While understanding is time, there is otherwise no condition attached [to it].[43] No leather bag[44] who takes passing and coming [for time] will arrive at penetrating it as what is:time abiding in its configuration. How could there be for them the time of breaking through the barrier? Even if they accept [what is:time's] abiding in its configuration—how could they achieve the preservation of having attained this already? And even if they manage to achieve this for some time, they will without fail grope about for the actual appearance of the [true] face. As long as one commits oneself to the time of being an ordinary person, even *bodhi* and nirvana are an is:time with the property of passing and arriving for only a short while.

(5.4) In general, what is:time actualizes without stopping at weirs and traps. The celestial kings and retinues[45] who actualize right now to the right and left—this now is my is:time exhausting its powers.[46] The what is:time of all other hosts of beings living on the land and in the water [likewise] actualize because of my current complete exertion. All the species and individuals, hidden and apparent, being whatever is:time, are all the actualization of my full exertion, the transiting through phases of my full exertion. One should study in practice how not a single dharma or a single thing could neither actually come to pass nor transit through phases if it were not for my transiting through the phases of exhausting my powers right now.

(5.5) What is called transition through phases cannot be studied in the usual way[47] as if it were like wind and rain moving from east to west. [Exhausting] the whole world[48] is not something without movement, something that neither progresses nor recedes, it is transiting through phases. This transition through phases is something like spring. There are many diverse states in spring, and that is what we call transition through phases. This is to be studied as a transition that has nothing external to it. In our example, spring's transition through phases transits inevitably through spring. The transition through phases is not identical with spring, but since spring is a transition through phases, the transition through phases is for now completing its course in the time of spring. One must probe this in detail, approaching it, leaving it alone, and coming back to it again. When speaking of transiting through phases, the study of the Buddha Way does not simply imagine the realm [of transition] as something external and the dharma that is the agent of the transition through phases as something that moves eastward through hundreds and thousands of spheres, passing hundreds and thousands of eons.[49]

(6) Instructed by the Great Teacher Wuji,[50] the Great Teacher Yaoshan Guangdao[51] inquired with Zen Master Daji of Jiangxi:[52] "I have clarified the instructions of the three vehicles[53] and the twelve divisions of teachings. But why did the ancestor come from the West?"[54]

When he inquired like this, Zen Master Daji said:

"WHAT IS:TIME: MAKING[55] HIM RAISE HIS EYEBROWS AND BLINK HIS EYES.[56]

WHAT IS:TIME: NOT MAKING HIM RAISE HIS EYEBROWS AND BLINK HIS EYES.

WHAT IS:TIME: RIGHT IN MAKING HIM RAISE HIS EYEBROWS AND BLINK HIS EYES.

WHAT IS:TIME: NOT RIGHT IN MAKING HIM RAISE HIS EYEBROWS AND BLINK HIS EYES."

Hearing this, Yaoshan had great insight and said to Daji: "When I was staying with Shitou, it was like a mosquito scaling an iron bull."

What Daji expresses is not like the words of other people. Eyebrows and eyes must be mountains and sea, because mountains and sea are eyebrows and eyes.[57] "Making him raise" must see mountains, "making him blink" must instruct[58] the sea. What is right is to be learned from him, and he is invited by the "making." "Not right" is not "not making him," "not making him" is not "not right," as both are what is:time. Mountains are also time, as is the sea. If they weren't time, there couldn't be mountains and sea. It is not possible that there is no time in the consummate now of mountains and sea. If time were to collapse, mountains and sea would collapse as well. If time is not-collapsing, then mountains and sea are also not-collapsing. In accord with this way of understanding, the morning star appears,[59] the Tathāgata appears, the eyeball[60] appears, the turning of the flower[61] appears. That is time. If it weren't time, it wouldn't be like this.

(7) Zen Master Guisheng of Ye district[62] was a dharma descendant of Linji and the [dharma] heir of Shoushan. At one time he instructed the assembly:

"WHAT IS:TIME WHEN THE INTENTION[63] ARRIVES BUT A SAYING[64] DOES NOT ARRIVE.

WHAT IS:TIME WHEN A SAYING ARRIVES BUT THE INTENTION DOES NOT ARRIVE.

WHAT IS:TIME WHEN INTENTION AND SAYING ARRIVE TOGETHER.

WHAT IS:TIME WHEN BOTH INTENTION AND SAYING DO NOT ARRIVE."[65]

Both intention and saying are what is:time. Both arriving and not-arriving are what is:time. The arriving time may be incomplete, but that is the coming of not-arrived time. Intention is the donkey, saying the horse.[66] The horse has been called saying, the donkey intention. Arriving is not coming, not arriving is not not-yet. What is:time is like this. Arriving is restricted by arriving and not by not-arriving. Not-arriving is restricted by not-arriving and not by arriving.⁶⁷ The intention stands in the way of the intention and sees the intention. The saying stands in the way of the saying and sees the saying. The impediment stands in the way of the impediment and sees the impediment. Time is the impediment impeding the impediment. The impediment may be occasioned by another dharma, but there has never been an impediment that impedes another dharma. I go out and meet someone,⁶⁸ someone goes out and meets someone, I go out and meet myself, going out goes out and meets going out. If these things did not attain time, it couldn't be like this.

Furthermore, intention is the time of actualizing the *kōan*, the saying is the time of moving beyond and breaking through the barrier. Arriving is the time of substance falling off; not-arriving is the time of identifying with this [function] and leaving this [function]. One should differentiate and affirm things and perform what is:time⁶⁹ in this manner.

(8) While those previous venerables have conjointly spoken thus, there is, without doubt, more to be said. Like this:

INTENTION AND SAYING ARRIVING HALFWAY IS WHAT IS:TIME, AND

INTENTION AND SAYING NOT ARRIVING HALFWAY IS WHAT IS:TIME, AS WELL.⁷⁰

There should be study and practice in this manner.

HAVING HIM RAISE HIS EYEBROWS AND BLINK HIS EYES IS HALF IS:TIME, AND

HAVING HIM RAISE HIS EYEBROWS AND BLINK HIS EYES IS:TIME, FAILING, AND

NOT HAVING HIM RAISE HIS EYEBROWS AND BLINK HIS EYES IS:TIME, FAILING FAILING.

To approach and leave, to arrive and not arrive in this manner, that is the time of what is:time.

Treasury of the True Dharma Eye, chapter 20, "What Is:Time." Written in Kōshō hōrin monastery on the first day of winter⁷¹ in the first year of Ninji,⁷² yin-metal rat. Copied during the summer retreat of the yin-water hare year of Kangen⁷³—Ejō

Appendix 2

Titles of Dōgen's Writings and Other Original Sources

Japanese-English

Works by Dōgen

Bendōwa 辨道話 = *Discourses on Negotiating the Way*, short: *Discourses*
Bendō hō 辨道法 = *The Method of Negotiating the Way*, short: *Method*
Chiji shingi 知事清規 = *Pure Rules for Temple Officers*
Eihei kōroku 永平廣録 = *Extensive Record of Eternal Peace*, short: *Extensive Record*
Eihei shingi 永平清規 = *Pure Rules of Eternal Peace*
Fukan zazen gi 普勸坐禪儀 = *Manual for the Universal Promotion of Seated Meditation*, short *Manual of Seated Meditation* or *Manual*
Fushuku hanpō 赴粥飯法 = *Method of Taking Gruel and Rice*
Gakudō yōjin shū 學道用心集 = *Collection of Essentials in the Study of the Way*, short: *Essentials*
Hōkyō ki 寶慶記 = *Record from the Baojing Era*
Shōbō genzō 正法眼藏 = *Treasury of the True Dharma Eye*, short: *Treasury*, SBGZ
  "Ango" 安居 = "Summer Retreat" SBGZ 72/75
  "Baika" 梅花 = "Plum Blossom" SBGZ 53/75
  "Bukkyō" 佛經 = "Buddhist Sutras" SBGZ 47/75
  "Busshō" 佛性 = "Buddha Nature" SBGZ 3/75
  "Busso" 佛祖 = "Buddha Ancestors," SBGZ 52/75
  "Daigo" 大悟 = "Great Insight" SBGZ 10/75
  "Daishugyō" 大修行 = "Great Practice" SBGZ 68/75
  "Den'e" 傳衣 = "Transmitting the Robe," SBGZ 32/75

"Dōte" 道得 = "Attaining Expression" SBGZ 33/75
"Genjō kōan" 現成公案 = "Actualizing the *Kōan*" SBGZ 1/75
"Gyōbutsu igi" 行佛威儀 = "The Deportment of the Practicing Buddha" SBGZ 6/75
"Gyōji" 行持 = "Sustained Practice" SBGZ 16/75
"Hensan" 遍參 = "Pervasive Exploration" SBGZ 57/75
"Hotsu mujōshin" 發無上心 = "Arousing the Aspiration for the Unsurpassable" SBGZ 63/75
"Ikka Myōju" 一顆明珠 = "One Bright Pearl" SBGZ 7/75
"Inmo" 恁麼 = "Thus" SBGZ 17/75
"Jinshin inga" 深信因果 "Deep Certitude about Cause and Effect" SBGZ 7/12
"Jishō Zammai" 自證三昧 = "The Self-Realized Samādhi" SBGZ 69/75
"Juki" 授記 = "Confirmation" SBGZ 21/75
"Kajō" 家常 = "Constants of the House" SBGZ 59/75
"Kankin" 看經 = "Reading Sutras" SBGZ 30/75
"Keisei sanshiki" 谿聲山色 = "Valley Sounds, Mountain Colors" SBGZ 25/75
"Kesa kudoku" 袈裟功德 = "The Virtues of the *Kesa*" SBGZ 3/12
"Kobusshin" 古佛心 = "Old Buddha Mind" SBGZ 9/75
"Kokyō" 古鏡 = "Old Mirror" SBGZ 19/75
"Kōmyō" 光明 = "Shining Light" SBGZ 15/75
"Kūge" 空華 = "Emptiness Flowers" SBGZ 14/75
"Maka hannya haramitsu" 摩訶般若波羅蜜 = "Great Wisdom Perfection" SBGZ 2/75
"Menju" 面授 "Conferral of the Face-to-Face Transmission," short: "Conferral" SBGZ 51/75
"Raihai tokuzui" 礼拝得髓 "Paying Obeisance and Attaining the Mark" SBGZ 28/75
"Sanjigō" 三時業 = "The Karma in the Three Times" SBGZ 8/12
"Sansuikyō" 山水經 = "Mountain and Water Sutra" SBGZ 29/75
"Sanjūshichihon Bodai Bumpō" 三十七品菩提分法 = "37 Methods of Insight" SBGZ 60/75
"Senjō" 洗淨 = "Cleansing" SBGZ 54/75
"Senmen" 洗面 = "Washing the Face" SBGZ 50/75
"Sesshin sesshō" 説心説性 "Explaining the Heart, Explaining the Nature" SBGZ 42/75
"Shin fukatoku" 心不可得 = "The Heart, Inapprehensible" SBGZ 8/75
"Shisho" 嗣書 = "Documents of Heritage" SBGZ 39/75
"Shoaku makusa" 諸惡莫作 = "Non-Production of Evil" SBGZ 31/75

"Shohō jissō" 諸法實相 "The True Attributes of All Dharmas" SBGZ 43/75

"Shukke kudoku" 出家功徳 = "The Merits of Leaving Home" SBGZ 1/12

"Shunjū" 春秋 = "Spring and Autumn" SBGZ 66/75

"Uji" 有時 = "What Is:Time" SBGZ 20/75

"Zazen gi" 坐禪儀 = *Manual of Seated Meditation* SBGZ 11/75

"Zenki" 全機 = "Comprehensive Occasion" SBGZ 22/75

Shōbōgenzō sanbyaku soku 正法眼蔵三百則 = *Three Hundred Cases of the Treasury of the True Dharma Eye*, short: *300 Cases Treasury*

Shōbōgenzō zuimonki 正法眼蔵随聞記 = *Record of Things Heard about the Treasury of the True Dharma Eye*, short: *Record of Things Heard*

Taitaiko goge jari hō 對大己五夏闍梨法 = *Rules for Facing Senior Expert Practitioners of More Than Five Summers*, short: *Rules for Facing Senior Practitioners*

Tenzō kyōkun 典座教訓 = *Instructions for the Head Cook*

Works by Other Authors

Chanyuan qinggui, Jp. *Zen'en shingi* 禅苑清規 = *Pure Rules for Zen Monasteries*

Keizan shingi 瑩山清規 = *Pure Rules of Keizan*

Kenchō kaizan Daikaku zenji bendō shingi 建長開山大覚禅師弁道清規 = *Pure Rules for Negotiating the Way by Daikaku zenji, founder of Kenchō ji*

Kōzen gokoku ron 興禅護国論 = *Promotion of Zen for the Protection of the Country*

Kyō gyō shin shō 教行信証 = *Teaching, Practice, Faith, and Realization*

Ruzhong riyong, Jp. *Nisshū nichiyō* 入衆日用 = *Daily Essentials for Members of the Congregation*

Senjaku hongan nenbutsu shū 選択本願念仏集 = *Collection of Passages on the Nenbutsu Chosen in the Original Vow*

Wudeng huiyan (Jp. *Gotō egen* 五燈會元) = *Assembled Origins of the Five Lamps*

English-Japanese

Works by Dōgen

Collection of Essentials in the Study of the Way, short: *Essentials* = Gakudō yōjin shū 學道用心集

Discourses on Negotiating the Way, short: *Discourses* = Bendōwa 辨道話

Extensive Record of Eternal Peace, short: *Extensive Record* = *Eihei kōroku* 永平廣録
Instructions for the Head Cook = "*Tenzō kyōkun*" 典座教訓
Manual for the Universal Promotion of Seated Meditation, short: *Manual of Seated Meditation* or *Manual* = *Fukan zazen gi* 普勸坐禪儀
Method of Taking Gruel and Rice = *Fushuku hanpō* 赴粥飯法
Pure Rules for Temple Officers = *Chiji shingi* 知事清規
Pure Rules of Eternal Peace = *Eihei shingi* 永平清規
Record from the Baojing Era = *Hōkyō ki* 寶慶記
Record of Things Heard about the Treasury of the True Dharma Eye, short: *Record of Things Heard* = "*Shōbōgenzō zuimonki*" 正法眼蔵随聞記
Rules for Facing Senior Expert Practitioners of More Than Five Summers, short: *Rules for Facing Senior Practitioners* = *Taitaiko goge jari hō* 對大己五夏闍梨法 =
The Method of Negotiating the Way, short: *Method* = *Bendō hō* 辨道法
Treasury of the True Dharma Eye, short: *Treasury* = *Shōbō genzō* 正法眼蔵 SBGZ

    "Arousing the Aspiration for the Unsurpassable" = "Hotsu mujōshin" 發無上心 SBGZ 63/75
    "37 Methods of Insight" = "Sanjūshichihon Bodai Bumpō" 三十七品菩提分法 SBGZ 60/75
    "Actualizing the *kōan*" = "Genjō kōan" 現成公案 SBGZ 1/75
    "Attaining Expression" = "Dōte" 道得 SBGZ 33/75
    "Buddha Ancestors" = "Busso" 佛祖 SBGZ 52/75
    "Buddha Nature" = "Busshō" 佛性 SBGZ 3/75
    "Buddhist Sutras" = "Bukkyō" 佛經 SBGZ 47/75
    "Cleansing" = "Senjō" 洗浄 SBGZ 54/75
    "Comprehensive Occasion" = "Zenki" 全機 SBGZ 22/75
    "Conferral of the Face-to-Face Transmission," short: "Conferral" = "Menju" 面授 SBGZ 51/75
    "Confirmation" = "Juki" 授記 SBGZ 21/75
    "Constants of the House" = "Kajō" 家常 SBGZ 59/75
    "Deep Certitude about Cause and Effect" = "Jinshin inga" 深信因果 SBGZ 7/12
    "Documents of Heritage" = "Shisho" 嗣書 SBGZ 39/75
    "Emptiness Flowers" = "Kūge" 空華 SBGZ 14/75
    "Explaining the Heart, Explaining the Nature" = "Sesshin sesshō" 説心説性 SBGZ 42/75
    "Great Insight" = "Daigo" 大悟 SBGZ 10/75
    "Great Practice" "Daishugyō" 大修行 SBGZ 68/75

"Great Wisdom Perfection" = "Maka hannya haramitsu" 摩訶般若波羅蜜 SBGZ 2/75
Manual of Seated Meditation = "Zazen gi" 坐禪儀 SBGZ 11/75
"Mountain and Water Sutra" = "Sansuikyō" 山水經 SBGZ 29/75
"Non-Production of Evil" = "Shoaku makusa" 諸惡莫作 SBGZ 31/75
"Old Buddha Mind" = "Kobusshin" 古佛心 SBGZ 9/75
"Old Mirror" = "Kokyō" 古鏡 SBGZ 19/75
"One Bright Pearl" = "Ikka Myōju" 一顆明珠 SBGZ 7/75
"Paying Obeisance and Attaining the Mark" = "Raihai tokuzui" 礼拝得髓 SBGZ 28/75
"Pervasive Exploration" = "Hensan" 遍參 SBGZ 57/75
"Plum Blossom" "Baika" 梅花 = SBGZ 53/75
"Reading Sutras" = "Kankin" 看經 SBGZ 30/75
"Shining Light" = "Kōmyō" 光明 SBGZ 15/75
"Spring and Autumn" = "Shunjū" 春秋 SBGZ 66/75
"Summer Retreat" = "Ango" 安居 SBGZ 72/75
"Sustained Practice" = "Gyōji" 行持 SBGZ 16/75
"The Deportment of the Practicing Buddha" = "Gyōbutsu igi" 行佛威儀 SBGZ 6/75
"The Heart, Inapprehensible" = "Shin fukatoku" 心不可得 SBGZ 8/75
"The Karma in the Three Times" = "Sanjigō" 三時業 SBGZ 8/12
"The merits of leaving home" = "Shukke kudoku" 出家功德 SBGZ 1/12
"The Self-Realized Samādhi" = "Jishō Zammai" 自證三昧 SBGZ 69/75
"The True Attributes of All Dharmas" = "Shohō jissō" 諸法實相 SBGZ 43/75
"The Virtues of the *Kesa*" = "Kesa kudoku" 袈裟功德 SBGZ 3/12
"Three Hundred Cases of the Treasury of the True Dharma Eye," "Three Hundred Cases Treasury" = "Shōbōgenzō sanbyaku soku" 正法眼藏三百則
"Thus" = "Inmo" 恁麼 SBGZ 17/75
"Transmitting the Robe" = "Den'e" 傳衣 SBGZ 32/75
"Valley Sounds, Mountain Colors" = "Keisei sanshiki" 谿聲山色 SBGZ 25/75
"Washing the Face" = "Senmen" 洗面 SBGZ 50/75
"What Is:Time" = "Uji" 有時 SBGZ 20/75

WORKS BY OTHER AUTHORS

Assembled Origins of the Five Lamps = Wudeng huiyan (Jp. *Gotō egen*) 五燈會元

Collection of Passages on the Nenbutsu Chosen in the Original Vow = Senjaku hongan nenbutsu shū 選択本願念仏集
Daily Essentials for Members of the Congregation = Ruzhong riyong, Jp. *Nisshū nichiyō* 入衆日用
Promotion of Zen for the Protection of the Country = Kōzen gokoku ron 興禪護國論
Pure Rules for Negotiating the Way by Daikaku zenji, founder of Kenchō ji = Kenchō kaizan Daikaku zenji bendō shingi 建長開山大覚禅師弁道清規
Pure Rules for Zen Monasteries = Chanyuan qinggui, Jp. *Zen'en shingi* 禅苑清規
Pure Rules of Keizan = Keizan shingi 瑩山清規
Teaching, Practice, Faith, and Realization = Kyō gyō shin shō 教行信証

Notes

Introduction

1. Japanese original: DZZ II, 128; my translation builds on Leighton and Okumura, *Dōgen's Extensive Record: A Translation of the Eihei Koroku* (below: *Extensive Record*), 435.

2. *Shōbō genzō* 正法眼蔵, DZZ I. Below referred to as *Treasury*. There is also a *kōan* collection by the same title, to which I refer as the *300 Cases Treasury*.

3. Watsuji, "Shamon Dōgen," English translation: Bein, *Purifying Zen*. Tsujiguchi Yōichirō remarked on this work: "His book turned 'Dōgen' from the exclusive property of the Sōtō school into an intellectual resource shared among the Japanese." Tsujiguchi, *Shōbōgenzō no shisōteki kenkyū*, 218.

4. Akiyama, *Dōgen no kenkyū*. The volume has two main parts, dedicated to Dōgen's "theory of being" (*sonzairon* 存在論) and his "theory of practice" (*jissenron* 実践論), respectively. Akiyama was a Sōtō Zen priest who had studied philosophy with Nishida Kitarō, see Wakatsuki, "Shōwa zenki ni okeru shūgaku kenkyū no 'shūhen' (1): Akiyama Hanji cho 'Dōgen no kenkyū' ni tsuite."

5. Masunaga, "Dōgen zenji no tachiba to sono jikanron"; Takahashi, "Dōgen ni okeru sonzaijikan no ronri"; Nieda, " 'Nothing' in Zen"; Azuma, "Shūkyōteki shi to shūkyōteki jikan: Haideggā/Kirkegōru/Dōgen"; Sugio, "Haideggā saikin no nyōgai to Dōgen Zen"; Tellenbach and Kimura, "Some Meanings of the Concept 'Nature' in European Vernacular Languages and Their Correspondences in Japanese"; Olson, "The Leap of Thinking: A Comparison of Heidegger and the Zen Master Dōgen"; Takayanagi, "Jitsuzon tetsugaku to Dōgen 2: Jikanron o megutte"; Izutsu, "Tōyō tetsugaku no tame ni-4-sōzō fudan—tōyō-teki jikan ishiki no genkei-shita-Dōgen no ˋyūji' ni tsuite."

6. Heine, *Dimensions of Time*; Stambaugh, *Impermanence*.

7. Ōtsuka, "Dōgen to Meruro Ponti ni okeru jikan (<Tokushū> tōzai ni okeru jikanron)"; Foshay, "Denegation, Nonduality, and Language in Derrida and

Dōgen"; Holbrook, "Does Time Move? Dogen and the Art of Understanding the Moment"; Bredeson, "On Dōgen and Derrida"; Giles, "To Practise One Thing: Kierkegaard through the Eyes of Dogen"; Mills, "*Aeterno Modo*: The Expression of an Integral Consciousness in the Work of Kierkegaard and Dogen."

    8. *List der Vernunft*. For recent discussions of this concept, see Jaeschke, "Die List der Vernunft"; Nahm, "Hegels Begriff der List."

    9. See chapter 8, section "Dōgen in Time."

    10. Heine, *Dimensions of Time*, 1.

    11. *Butsudō* 仏道. This term may refer to the Buddha's enlightenment (*bodhi*) as well as to the path leading toward it. In the second sense, the term emphasizes the practical aspect, while the conceptual aspect is often referred to as "*Buddha Dharma*" (*buppō* 仏法).

    12. *Shiki soku ze kū, kū soku ze shiki* 色即是空、空即是色. Nakamura and Kino, *Hannyashingyō/Kongōhannyakyō*, 10.

    13. Notably, Dōgen's earliest recorded informal instruction after he established his first monastic congregation is a comment on the text's initial lines: see DZZ I, 11–13 and Nearman, *The Shōbōgenzō*, 25–30; Tanahashi, *Treasury*, 25–28.

    14. *Guhō gushō* 弘法救生, DZZ I, 730.

Chapter 1

    1. Aguessy, *Time and the Philosophies*.

    2. Ohe, "Time, Temporality, and Freedom," 81. According to the author, this is a modified version of the translation by Masunaga Reihō in his *The Soto Approach to Zen*.

    3. In fact, the first two lines are taken from the Chinese master, but the remaining six are probably Dōgen's own composition. See below for more detail.

    4. Yaoshan Weiyan (Jp. Yakusan Igen 藥山惟儼, 745–827 CE). The discourse reads, in Tanahashi's translation: "If you want to know human endeavors, then purify this noble form, hold a jar, and carry a monk's bowl. If you try to escape from falling into the lower realms, first of all you should not give up these practices. It is not easy. You should stand on the highest peak and go to the bottom of the deepest mountain. This is not easy practice, but you will have some realization." *Moon in a Dewdrop*, 246, n.2. For the Chinese original, see e.g., *Jingde chuan deng lu*, T 2056.51: 440b.

    5. Arifuku, *Dōgen no Sekai*, 233.

    6. Ōmori, *Jikan to sonzai*, 20.

    7. Ohe, "Time, Temporality, and Freedom," 83.

    8. Akiyama, *Dōgen no kenkyū*.

    9. Husserl, *Cartesian Meditations*, 20.

10. Husserl, *Cartesian Meditations*, 20.

11. Akiyama is rarely quoted in Western literature, although several writers propose ideas similar to his. Gereon Kopf, for example, applies the same pattern of argument: "Dōgen differentiates between two experiences of time, inauthentic experience of time, indicative of everyday awareness, and authentic experience of time, corresponding to the non-positional awareness attained in the experience of *satori*." *Beyond Personal Identity*, 178.

12. Husserl, *Cartesian Meditations*, 36.

13. Akiyama, *Dōgen no kenkyū*, 67.

14. *Eien no ima* 永遠の今. Akiyama observes: "Time is just the now of eternity—the now beyond of *uji*. The time yonder and the time now, each one of the specific times all originate in this now of eternity and perish in it." Akiyama, *Dōgen no kenkyū*, 140. *Eien no ima* is a term already used by Nishida in NKZ II, 284. I chose the translation "now of eternity" over and against the more common "eternal now" because the latter seems to indicate a "now" that is "always present"—in other words, one of eternal duration—whereas Nishida and Akiyama appear to envision an ever-changing "now" that is nonetheless the present realization of eternity.

15. Stambaugh, *Impermanence*, 32–33. The quote is from William Blake, "Auguries of Innocence"; see Stevenson, *Blake: The Complete Poems*, 612.

16. Stambaugh, *Impermanence*, 38.

17. Tanabe, *Shōbōgenzō no tetsugaku shikan*; Abe, "Dōgen no jikan-kūkan-ron"; Abe, *A Study of Dōgen: His Philosophy and Religion*; Heine, *Dimensions of Time*; Raud, "The Existential Moment: Rereading Dōgen's Theory of Time." See Steineck, "A Zen Philosopher?—Notes on the Philosophical Reading of Dōgen's Shōbōgenzō," and "From *Uji* to Being-time (and Back): Translating Dōgen into Philosophy" for more details and examples.

18. See above, p. 236, note 4.

19. *Shōbō genzō sanbyaku soku* 正法眼蔵三百則, quoted below as *300 Cases Treasury*; DZZ II, 101–252. See cases 1.1, 3.29, 3.56 (whisk); 1.91 (staff); 1.41, 3.101 (pillar); 3. 96 (lantern); 1.39 (Zhang and Li); 2.91 (sky). See also Loori and Tanahashi, *The True Dharma Eye*, 3, 313, 349; 121; 56; 401; 54; 259.

20. *Iwayuru uji wa, ji sude ni u nari, u wa mina ji nari.* いはゆる有時は、時すでにこれ有なり、有はみな時なり。DZZ I, 189. 有時 is glossed as *yūji* according to the Dōunji manuscript used as the main source by Ōkubo, but I follow the more common practice of reading it as *uji* to avoid confusion.

21. Elberfeld refers to the Chinese-German dictionary by Rüdenberg and Stange, and Ogawa Shinji's etymological lexicon of Chinese characters, which conjectures that the character initially depicted a hand giving out meat. His observation reads in full: "Zusammenfassend kann gesagt werden, daß mit diesem Zeichen konkret Gegebenes gemeint ist, was auch ganz dem Bild, welches dem Zeichen

zugrunde liegt, entspricht." Elberfeld, *Phänomenologie der Zeit im Buddhismus: Methoden interkulturellen Philosophierens*, 231.

22. See, for example, the contributions to the dedicated issue of *Synthese* 179/1 (2011), and Cornell and Panfilio, *Symbolic Forms for a New Humanity: Cultural and Racial Reconfigurations of Critical Theory*; Favuzzi, Endres, and Klattenhoff, "Cassirer, Globalized—Über Sinn und Zweck eines Neulesens."

23. Cassirer, *An Essay on Man: An Introduction to the Philosophy of Human Culture*, 42.

24. I do not discuss in detail the applicability of the term "religion" to historical, non-European culture here. This discussion was seminal and necessary for a critical reflection of the facile universalizations connected to the term "religion" in classical modern scholarship, informed as it was by an unquestioning acceptance of the superiority of its Protestant Christian variant. But, much as Pomeranz argued with respect to economic history, rather than abandon the term altogether, it makes sense to continually revisit our understanding of it by way of reciprocal comparisons. I have reviewed Dōgen's own statements concerning the "Buddha Way" that he endorsed, and reflected on how they relate to a notion of "religion" informed by the said discussion in my article "'Religion' and the Concept of the Buddha Way: Semantics of the Religious in Dōgen."

25. Cassirer observes that "in fact every basic form of spirit, in that it appears and develops, is a unique endeavor to give itself not just in part but as a whole and consequently to claim for itself not a merely relative validity but rather an absolute validity." Cassirer and Lofts, *Philosophy of Symbolic Forms* I, 10. Cf. the German original in Cassirer *Philosophie der symbolischen Formen I: Die Sprache*, 13.

26. Steineck, "'Religion' and the Concept of the Buddha Way"; Steineck, "A Zen Philosopher?"

27. For an extended discussion of this point, see Freudenthal, "Der fehlende Kern von Cassirers Philosophie: Homo faber in abstracto"; Steineck, *Kritik der symbolischen Formen I: Symbolische Form und Funktion*, and "Kritik der Kultur. Überlegungen zu Cassirers Konzept der symbolischen Form."

28. Paul Ricoeur pointed in a similar direction in his "The History of Religions and the Phenomenology of Time Consciousness," esp. 14–19.

29. Jakobson, "Closing Statement: Linguistics and Poetics." These factors obviously interact: The message can introduce new code, for example by proposing new definitions that change the lexicon. But it can do so only to a certain extent, as it needs to use established code to explicate its innovations. The quality of the channel determines the reach of the message and the levels of complexity afforded (think of Twitter (now X), or unrecorded, unamplified public speech). The social standing, attitude, and erudition of the addressees have similar effects. Last but not least, the environment is not a naked reality, but one conceived according to established paradigms of understanding, which in turn form part of the code.

30. Kaufmann and Steineck, "Another Discourse on the Method: Understanding Philosophy through Rhetorical Analysis."

31. "Chronography" is often equated with "chronometry," as in Harweg's magisterial comparative study *Zeit in Mythos und Geschichte*. I have proposed and explained an alternative model in Steineck, "Chronographical Analysis: An Essay in Methodology."

32. Lakoff and Johnson, *Philosophy in the Flesh: The Embodied Mind and Its Challenge to Western Thought*, 139.

33. Maki, *Jikan no hikaku shakaigaku*. For a brief description of Maki's theory and his "quadrant of temporal morphologies" in English, see Steineck, "Time in Old Japan: In Search of a Paradigm," 24–28.

34. For a useful overview of this concept and its analytical purchase on the history of politics and religion, see Hodgkin and Radstone, *Contested Pasts*.

35. Haas, *"Amida Buddha unsere Zuflucht": Urkunden zum Verständnis des japanischen Sukhāvatī-Buddhismus*.

36. Bloom, *Shinran's Gospel of Pure Grace*.

37. Otto, "Über Zazen als Extrem des numinosen Irrationalen."

38. Murphy, "Religionswissenschaft as Colonialist Discourse: The Case of Rudolf Otto."

39. *Guhō gushō* 弘法救生; *Discourses*, DZZ I, 730.

40. An instructive example in this regard is Garrett, "Getting Away from 'Religion' in Medieval Japan."

41. See above, and Steineck, "From *Uji* to Being-Time."

Chapter 2

1. See Bielefeldt, "Recarving the Dragon: History and Dogma in the Study of Dōgen," 31–39, for an overview of pertinent passages.

2. Dumoulin, *A History of Zen Buddhism*, 62, 104; Bielefeldt, "Recarving the Dragon," 28–39; Heine, "The Dōgen Canon. Dōgen's Pre-Shōbōgenzō Writings and the Question of Change in His Later Works," 42.

3. Rein Raud, personal communication at the 2018 ENOJP conference, September 2018.

4. Matsumoto, *Engi to kū: Nyoraizō shisō hihan*; Hakamaya, *Dōgen to Bukkyō*. And see Hubbard and Swanson, *Pruning the Bodhi Tree*.

5. Hakamaya, *Dōgen to bukkyō*, 107–9; 151–59. See also Heine, "The Dōgen Canon," 43; Tsunoda, *Dōgen zenji kenkyū ni okeru shomondai: kindai no shūgaku ronsō o chūshin toshite*, 23–26.

6. Hakamaya, *Dōgen to bukkyō*, 108.

7. William Bodiford has explored the context of this movement in his seminal article "Zen and the Art of Religious Prejudice: Efforts to Reform a Tradition of Social Discrimination."

8. Heine, "'Critical Buddhism' (*Hihan Bukkyō*) and the Debate Concerning the 75-Fascicle and 12-Fascicle Shōbōgenzō Texts," 41–42; Hakamaya, *Honkaku shisō hihan*, 142.

9. Kawamura, *Shōbōgenzō no seiritsushiteki kenkyū*; Heine, "The Dōgen Canon"; Heine, *Did Dōgen Go to China? What Dōgen Wrote and When He Wrote It*; Tsunoda, *Dōgen zenji kenkyū*; Bodiford, "Rewriting Dōgen."

10. Nakaseko, *Dōgen zenji den kenkyū*; Nakaseko, *Dōgen* zenji den *kenkyū*; Nakaseko, *Shin Dōgen zenji den kenkyū*.

11. Totman, *A History of Japan*, 176–79; Adolphson and Ramseyer, "The Competitive Enforcement of Property Rights in Medieval Japan."

12. Farris, *Japan to 1600: A Social and Economic History*, 113–22; Kamo and Ichiko, *Shintei Hōjōki*; Kamo and Sadler, *The Ten Foot Square Hut; And, Tales of the Heike*.

13. Müller, *Wirtschafts- und Technikgeschichte Japans*, 64–102.

14. Matsuo, *A History of Japanese Buddhism*, 175–90.

15. Satō, *Kamakura bukkyō*, 61–70.

16. I speak of *kanbun* and *wabun* as styles of writing here, and not as two different written languages, because *kanbun* was sometimes used to write a text according to the norms of Japanese word order/sentence structure. However, the larger part of the literature discussed in this section was written to conform to the grammatical rules of Literary Sinitic, even if Japanese reading techniques (*kundoku*) were sometimes employed to tease out meanings that clearly go against a "normal" reading of the Sinitic text. In other words, medieval *kanbun* was a mode of written expression that could represent a certain language (Literary Sinitic) or a Sino-Japanese creole. See Fraleigh, *Plucking Chrysanthemums: Narushima Ryūhoku and Sinitic Literary Traditions in Modern Japan*, 20–28, for a recent discussion of the terminological issues at stake here.

17. See Hōnen, *Collection of Passages on the Nenbutsu Chosen in the Original Vow* (*Senjaku hongan nenbutsu shū* 選択本願念仏集; T 2608), Shinran, *Teaching, Practice, Faith, and Realization* (*Kyō gyō shin shō* 教行信証, T 2646), Eisai, *Promotion of Zen for the Protection of the Country* (*Kōzen gokoku ron* 興禅護国論, T 2543), and Nichiren, *Treatise on Establishing the Right [Teaching] and Bringing Peace to the Land* (*Risshō ankoku ron* 立証安国論, T 2688).

18. Shirane, "Canon Formation in Japan: Genre, Gender, Popular Culture, and Nationalism"; Fraleigh, *Plucking Chrysanthemums*, 3–6. The composition of the first Iwanami *Canon of Classical Japanese Literature* (*Nihon koten bungaku taike i* 日本古典文学体系) clearly exemplifies these priorities. It follows, for example, the "School of National Learning" (*kokugaku* 国学) in selecting the *Record of Ancient Matters* (*Kojiki* 古事記) in preference to the first official Imperial chronicle *Documents and Records of Japan* (*Nihon shoki* 日本書紀).

19. Kornicki, *The Book in Japan: A Cultural History from the Beginnings to the Nineteenth Century*, 114–19.

20. Ibid., 87, 118–22.

21. Tajima, "Sōtōshū ni okeru tenseki kaihan no rekishi," 304–5.

22. Ibid., 306. The masters are Wuwai Yiyuan 無外義遠, a dharma heir of Rujing; Tuigeng Dening 退耕徳寧, abbot of Lingyinsi 霊隠寺; and Xutang Zhiyu 虚堂智愚, abbot of Jingcisi 浄慈寺. The latter monasteries belonged to the "Five Mountains," eminent monasteries where abbots were appointed by imperial decree. See Kagamishima, *Dōgen zenji goroku*, 18, 211, 212.

23. Tajima, "Sōtōshū ni okeru tenseki kaihan no rekishi," 303.

24. Ibid., 307. See also DZZ II, 253–60.

25. See Sango, "Buddhist Debate in Medieval Japan."

26. Satō, *Kamakura bukkyō*, 134–35. The Tendai School had established itself as the most powerful Buddhist school in the Heian period, and scholar-monks from its head monastery Enryakuji 延暦寺 were regularly consulted by the court on doctrinal matters. See Groner, *Saigyō, Ryōgen on Mount Hiei*, and *Precepts, Ordinations, and Practice in Medieval Japanese Tendai*, for detailed analyses of the monastery's role from its foundation to the medieval period.

27. This is evident in another contemporary complaint against the Pure Land school, spearheaded by the Kōfukuji in Nara, which listed "establishing a new school" (*shinshū o tatsuru* 新宗を立つる) as the first of its "mistakes" (*shitsu* 失). Satō, *Kamakura bukkyō*, 137.

28. Shinohara, *Gakudō yōjin shū*, 259.

29. Kuroda, "The Development of the Kenmitsu System as Japan's Medieval Orthodoxy."

30. Adolphson, *The Teeth and Claws of the Buddha: Monastic Warriors and Sōhei in Japanese History*.

31. On the Karoku disturbance (*Karoku no hōnan* 嘉禄の法難), see Satō, *Kamakura bukkyō*, 143–44.

32. On the Daruma shū, see Breugem, *From Dominance to Obscurity*; on its influence on Dōgen's career, see Faure, "The Daruma-Shū, Dōgen, and Sōtō Zen."

33. Satō, *Kamakura bukkyō*, 144–54.

34. And many modern researchers have followed them, at least in terms of identifying Michichika as his father; see, e.g., Ōkubo, *Dōgen zenji den no kenkyū* (Kaitei Zōho), 62; Satō, *Kamakura bukkyō*, 126; and implicitly also Heine, *Did Dōgen Go to China?*, 92.

The fictionalized biography of Dōgen (also the basis for the film *Zen*) by Ōtani Tetsuo—former president of Komazawa University and editor of the first *kakikudashi-bun* edition of the *Extensive Record of Eternal Peace* (*Eihei kōroku* 永平廣録; short: *Extensive Record*)—fully exploits all of Dōgen's alleged connections with prominent contemporaries, thus attesting to the vibrancy of this hagiographical tradition. Ōtani, *Eihei no kaze: Dōgen no shōgai*.

35. Nakaseko, *Dōgen zenji den kenkyū*, 50–57, 73–77; Nakaseko, *Shin Dōgen zenji den kenkyū*, 40–62.

36. Matsunami, *Kamakura bukkyō zenshū shisōshi no kenkyū: "Nihon zenshū" no keisei*, 55–56.

37. Ishikawa, "'Mappō Tōmyōki' to Dōgen Zen," 178.

38. Steiniger, "Manuscript Culture and Chinese Learning in Medieval Kamakura."

39. See the relevant quotations from *Sandaison gyōjō ki* and *Denkōroku* in Nakaseko, *Dōgen zenji den kenkyū*, 77.

40. Nakaseko, *Dōgen zenji den kenkyū*, 85, quoting *Sandaison gyōjō ki*.

41. Heine, *Did Dōgen go to China?*, 69.

42. Nakaseko, *Dōgen zenji den kenkyū*, 107–12.

43. Leighton, "Dōgen's Appropriation of Lotus Sutra Ground and Space"; Seino, "Dogen's Acceptance of the Lotus Sutra and Tendai Theology in the Bukkyo Chapter of His Shobogenzo."

44. Sueki, "Shisō/shisō shi/shisō shigaku: Futatsu no Nihon shisōshi kōza to Nihon shisōshi no toikata," 19.

45. Girard, "Did Huayan's Teachings Influence Dōgen's Thought?: Dōgen's Treatment of Huayan Concepts of Mind-Only and One-and-Allness," 241, 242. See also Winfield, *Icons and Iconoclasm in Japanese Buddhism: Kukai and Dogen on the Art of Enlightenment*, 48.

46. Kim, *Dōgen Kigen, Mystical Realist*, 19–22.

47. See the discussion and sources quoted in Dōgen: Girard, *Les dialogues de Dōgen en Chine*, 69–79. See also Tsunoda, "Dōgen zenji no daigitai to sono kaiketsu."

48. Nakaseko, *Dōgen zenjiden kenkyū*, 107–8. See also Masunaga, *A Primer of Sōtō Zen*, 66–67.

49. Nakaseko infers from pertinent statements in Ejō's *Record of Things Heard about the Treasury of the True Dharma Eye* (*Shōbōgenzō zuimonki* 正法眼蔵随聞記; short: *Record of Things Heard*) that Dōgen supported his studies at Mount Hiei and in Kenninji through the income from estates in his possession, which he traded to fund his trip to China. Nakaseko, *Dōgen zenjiden kenkyū*, 181. Heine, *Did Dōgen Go to China?*, 107–11, gives a useful overview of Dōgen's itinerary in China, separating fact from legend.

50. Compiled in the tenth volume of the *Extensive Record*, DZZ II, 189–93. See also Heine, *Did Dōgen Go to China?*, 121, for translations of two examples.

51. While this text was long treated as a journal, drafted during Dōgen's stay in China, researchers in the past decades have emphasized that in its extant form, it is more probably a product of later years (after 1242 or even after 1248). See Heine, *Did Dōgen Go to China?*, 36–38.

52. The various versions of these manuals and their chronology are exhaustively discussed in the seminal work by Bielefeldt, *Dōgen's Manuals of Zen Meditation*, which marks a turning point in Western Dōgen studies.

53. Nakaseko, *Dōgen zenji den kenkyū*, 279–81. Nakaseko further surmises that the Konoe, who had close ties to Dōgen's later chief patron Hatano Yoshishige, invited him to take up residence here. Nakaseko, *Dōgen zenji den kenkyū*, 288–91.

54. Collected (without dates) in the *Extensive Record*, vol. 8, cf. DZZ II, 151–64. English translation: Leighton and Okumura, *Extensive Record*. Heine surmises that six of the fourteen instructions assembled there are from this period, that is, nos. 1, 2, 4, 5, 9, 12; see Heine, *Did Dōgen Go to China?*, 123. No. 5 contains a date corresponding to 1235. Leighton and Okumura, *Extensive Record*, 508.

55. Dōgen and Girard, *Les dialogues de Dōgen en Chine*, 641–42.

In distinction to the much more famous composite vernacular (*kana* 仮名) *Shōbō genzō*, which contains the above-mentioned "What Is:Time," Dōgen's *kōan* collection later became known as the sinographic (*mana/shinji* 真字) *Shōbō genzō* or *Shōbō genzō sanbyakusoku* 正法眼蔵三百則 ("Three Hundred Cases of the Treasury of the True Dharma Eye"), below *300 Cases Treasury*.

56. Nakaseko, *Dōgen zenji den kenkyū*, 288.

57. Tanahashi, *Enlightenment Unfolds*, 47, 48. Cf. DZZ II, 400–1.

58. Vol. 1.1, DZZ II, 7; Leighton and Okumura, *Extensive Record*, 75.

59. DZZ II, 419–95. The colophone of the sixth fascicle mentions that these lectures were recorded by Ejō during the era Katei (1235–1237); see DZZ II, 495. Heine gives a broader time frame of 1234–1238, possibly allowing for some lectures to have taken place before the era name changed in 1238 (Heine, *Did Dōgen Go to China?*, 139). For a detailed discussion of the redaction of the document, see Hashimoto, "'Zuimonki' no seiritsu o kangaeru."

Note that the available English translation by Masunaga is based on the popular printed edition prepared by Menzan; in modern Japan, this was first edited and published by Watsuji Tetsurō. This version differs in the order of the fascicles and lectures from an earlier manuscript copy found in Chōonji, Aichi Prefecture, which is the basis of the text presented in Ōkubo's edition of the collected works cited here. Masunaga, *A Primer*, 1–2; DZZ II, 419.

60. Leighton and Okumura, *Extensive Record*, 140.

61. Imaeda, *Dōgen: Zazen hitosuji no shamon*, 194–95. Heine, *Did Dōgen Go to China?*, 151, has six for 1240 and nine for 1241 because he only counts the texts that went into the 75-fascicle redaction.

62. See table 31 in Heine, *Did Dōgen Go to China?*, 183.

63. Moriya, "Dōgen zenji to hokuetsu ishaku no shinsō—zenji no ketsudan to Hakusan tendai ni kikyō," 23–24; Heine, *Did Dōgen Go to China?*, 156–57.

64. Faure, "The Daruma-Shū"; Bielefeldt, *Dōgen's Manuals*, 28; Heine, *Did Dōgen Go to China?*, 34–35.

65. Heine, *Did Dōgen Go to China?*, 172–79.

66. Furuta, *Nihon Zenshū shi no nagare*, 50–52.

67. Nakaseko, *Dōgen zenji den kenkyū*, 292–98.

68. Heine, *Did Dōgen Go to China?*, 158.

69. On Dōgen and Hatano, see Nakaseko, *Dōgen zenji den kenkyū*, 277–78; Heine, *Did Dōgen Go to China?*, 159.

70. Moriya, "Dōgen zenji to hokuetsu ishaku no shinsō," 24. Heine also considers this option: Heine, *Did Dōgen Go to China?*, 170.

71. Heine, *Did Dōgen Go to China?*, 162–66.

72. Kim, *Dōgen Kigen*, 44.

73. Jp. *Keisei sanshoku* 谿聲山色 is the title of an informal instruction drafted in 1240 while at Kōshōji (later vol. 25 of the 75-fascicle *Treasury*). Heine quotes two later poems that indicate how Dōgen missed the environment in the vicinity of the capital. Heine, *Did Dōgen Go to China?*, 164.

74. See, once more, his *Instructions for the Head Cook* of 1237 and the vernacular *Treasury* fascicles "Washing the Face" and "Cleansing" (1239). See also below, chapter 4, "Chronopolitics."

75. See the table in Heine, *Did Dōgen Go to China?*, 243–44.

76. Heine, *Did Dōgen Go to China?*, 179.

77. See the tables in Nakaseko, *Dōgen zenji den kenkyū*, 365–66, and in Heine, *Did Dōgen Go to China?*, 242–44.

78. The status of the various redactions and their evaluation is, of course, a much belabored subject. See, e.g., Heine, "Critical Buddhism." William Bodiford has usefully summed up the pertinent research and textual evidence; see Bodiford, "Rewriting Dōgen.," esp. 246–64.

79. The pertinent passages are quoted in Nakaseko, *Dōgen zenji den kenkyū*, 380.

80. Ibid., 380–90.

81. DZZ II, 447.

82. See the table in Heine, *Did Dōgen Go to China?*, 84, and the discussion in the ensuing chapters of that book; also, Heine, *Readings of Dōgen's Treasury of the True Dharma Eye*, 68.

83. Tajima, "Sōtōshū ni okeru tenseki kaihan no rekishi," 304–5.

Chapter 3

1. *Honrai no menmoku o eizu* 詠ス_本来ノ面目ヲ_, DZZ II, 412.

2. Cf. the entry *honrai* 本来 in Zengaku Daijiten Hensanjo, *Zengaku daijiten*, 1169.

3. In the official translation of Kawabata's speech, the poem reads: "In the spring, cherry blossoms, in the summer the cuckoo. In autumn the moon, and in winter the snow, clear, cold." Kawabata, "The Nobel Prize in Literature 1968." This is close to the translation by Seidensticker, quoted recently by Steven Heine, who also gives his own translation. Heine, "Dōgen: His Life, Religion, and

Poetry," 35. My translation adheres closer than Seidensticker's to the structure of the original, where the fourth line introduces a verb for the first time and the fifth line—which appears almost lost as a verse of its own in Seidensticker and Kawabata—is set off by its different grammatical structure.

4. 春は花夏ほととぎす秋は月、冬雪さえてすずしかりけり。DZZ II, 412.

5. It is of no consequence to this argument whether the seasons are taken to be a "natural" division of time or a cultural one. Nevertheless, it is worth mentioning that in the case of Japan, the notion of four seasons was a cultural import from the Sinitic sphere that gained traction in court culture (and the urban environment) from the eighth century onward. See Shirane, "Japan and the Culture of the Four Seasons," and his more extensive argument in his monograph of the same title.

6. I have explained this approach in more detail, and with reference to examples from the arts, sciences, and various literary traditions, in Steineck, "Chronographical Analysis."

7. 迷を大悟するは諸佛なり, *Genjō kōan*, DZZ I, 7. この法は、人人の分上にゆたかにそなはれりといへども、いまだ修せざるにはあらはれず、證せざるにはうることなし。 *Bendōwa*, DZZ I, 729.

8. See, for example, Roland Harweg's magisterial survey of chronography in world literatures: Harweg, *Zeit in Mythos und Geschichte*.

9. [しづかに二十年中の消息おもひやるべし、]わするる時なかれ。 DZZ I, 126.

10. See, once more, Harweg, *Zeit in Mythos und Geschichte*.

11. 和尚、この山に住してよりこのかた、多少時也, from the fascicle "Sustained Practice," DZZ I, 129. Cf. Nearman, *The Shōbōgenzō*, 386. Tanahashi, *Treasury*, 341.

12. 一花開五葉. DZZ I, 108.

13. *Kūge* 空華. The term refers to patterns one may perceive in the sky when afflicted by a disease of the eye and is a traditional Buddhist metaphor relating to the illusion that the things perceived in human experience have an enduring substance or essence. In the fascicle in question, Dōgen turns the metaphor around and suggests that insight is found precisely by closely engaging with these "emptiness flowers."

14. Time, to Kant, is a "form of intuition," and as such belongs to a logical dimension separate from that of the categories.

15. In my 2018 essay, I followed Harweg in treating sequence, synchrony, and iteration as parts of chronometry. Upon further reflection, I prefer the grouping suggested here. It also points to the possible, often necessary, co-determination of time via different kinds of categories, such as quantity or relation.

16. Incidentally, that is precisely the point made by Einstein in his explanation of special and general relativity: See Einstein, *Über die spezielle und die allgemeine Relativitätstheorie*, 13–15.

17. 天大雨雪ならずとも、深山高峰の冬夜は、おもひやるに、人物の窓前に立地すべきにあらず。竹節なほ破す、おそれつべき時候なり。DZZ I, 148; Nearman, *The Shōbōgenzō*, 413. Tanahashi, *Treasury*, 363.

18. ひさしく龍潭にとぶらひせば、頭角觸折することもあらまし、領珠を正傳する時節にもあはまし。DZZ I:67; Tanahashi, *Treasury*, 194; Nearman, *The Shōbōgenzō*, 192.

19. たとへば、春の經歴はかならず春を經歴するなり。DZZ I, 192. Cf. Nearman; *The Shōbōgenzō*, 115; Tanahashi, *Treasury*, 108.

20. In the fascicle "Buddha Nature" (*Busshō* 佛性) Dōgen quotes a saying of the 6th ancestor Huineng to the extent that "Impermanence is itself Buddha Nature" and explains that "Supreme, fully perfected enlightenment is Buddha Nature, and hence it is impermanent." Tanahashi, *Treasury*, 243, and Nearman, *The Shōbōgenzō*, 257; and see DZZ I, 21.

21. Based on an electronic search on the digitalized text provided by Shōmon ji: http://www.shomonji.or.jp/soroku/genzou.htm. The automatic count is fifty-seven, but that includes occurrences in other chapter headings and double occurrences in logographic passages and their *kundoku* transcriptions.

22. This is often—a manuscript copy of the *Treasury* included—identified as a statement from the Nirvana Sutra (cf. DZZ I, 16, footnote). However, none of the extant redactions of this sutra contains that expression (Cf. SAT DB database). Cf. Nearman, *The Shōbōgenzō*, 249. Tanahashi, *Treasury*, 238.

23. "They say that, if the time has not arrived, [the Buddha nature] will not appear, even when one inquires about the dharma with a teacher or exerts oneself in negotiating the way. . . . People like that do belong to the extraneous path of the naturalists." 時節いたらざれば、參師問法するにも、辨道功夫するにも、現前せずといふ。... かくのごとくのたぐひ、おそらくは天然外道の流類なり。(DZZ I, 16–17).

24. Elberfeld, *Phänomenologie der Zeit*, 230–39.

25. 先師古佛、正法眼藏あきらかなるによりて、この正法眼藏を、過去・現在・未来の十方に聚会する仏祖に正伝す。DZZ I, 464. Cf. Nearman, *The Shōbōgenzō*, 693; Tanahashi, *Treasury*, 589. Dōgen also uses the abbreviated expression *kagenrai* 過現来 instead of *kako/genzai/mirai* 過去・現在・未来. See for example in the same fascicle, DZZ I, 462.

26. Fasc. 8 of the 12-fascicle composite-vernacular *Treasury*, DZZ I, 682–91; Nearman, *The Shōbōgenzō*, 1028–43; Tanahashi, *Treasury*, 779–819.

27. Kim, *Dōgen Kigen*, 138.

28. Kato and Soothill, *The Threefold Lotus Sutra*, 289.

29. 万物といふは、過現来のみにあらず、威音王以前、乃至未来なり。DZZ I, 462. Cf. Nearman, *The Shōbōgenzō*, 690; Tanahashi, *Treasury*, 586. The first part of the sentence refers to the present eon; the second, via invoking a Buddha from a past eon, to different ones.

30. 正當恁麼時のみなるがゆゑに、有時みな盡時なり、有草有象ともに時なり。DZZ I, 190; 盡時を盡有と究盡するのみ, DZZ I, 192.

31. 諸時また青黄赤白等のいろあるなり。DZZ I, 112. Cf. Nearman, *The Shōbōgenzō*, 559; Tanahashi, *Treasury*, 463.

32. 梁武初見達磨之時、即問、如何是聖諦第一義。From "Sustained Practice, II," DZZ I, 142. Cf. Nearman, *The Shōbōgenzō*, 405; Tanahashi, *Treasury*, 355. This passage is introduced as a quote from a Song period Chinese source, the *Linjian lu* 林間錄, compiled by Huihong 惠洪.

33. のちに出世せりし時、衆にしめしていはく、 from "Paying Obeisance and Obtaining the Mark." DZZ I, 248. Cf. Nearman, *The Shōbōgenzō*, 93; Tanahashi, *Treasury*, 75.

34. 諸法の佛法なる時節・萬法ともにわれにあらざる時節、 DZZ I, 7. Cf. Nearman, *The Shōbōgenzō*, 31; Tanahashi, *Treasury*, 29.

35. Raud, "Existential Moment," 155.

36. From "Buddha Nature," cf. DZZ I, 17; Nearman, *The Shōbōgenzō*, 249; Tanahashi, *Treasury*, 238.

37. From "Buddha Nature," cf. DZZ I, 27. Mazu Daoyi 馬祖道一 (709–788 CE) was a well-known master in the second generation after the sixth patriarch Huineng, so his name would suffice to provide temporal orientation. Cf. Nearman, *The Shōbōgenzō*, 266. Tanahashi, *Treasury*, 250.

38. 聞ヲ昏鐘ヲ、搭シ袈裟ヲ、入テ雲堂ニ、就テ被位ニ座禅ス。DZZ II, 313. Cf. Nearman, *The Shōbōgenzō*, 239. Tanahashi, *Treasury*, 230.

39. DZZ I, 454–57; Nearman, *The Shōbōgenzō*, 156–59; Tanahashi, *Treasury*, 165–68.

40. つらつら釋尊在世をおもひやれば、わづかに二千餘年なり。國寶神器のいまにつたはれるも、これよりもすぎてふるくなれるもおほし。DZZ I, 287. Cf. Nearman, *The Shōbōgenzō*, 122; Tanahashi, *Treasury*, 138.

41. しかありしよりこのかた、すでに二千一百九十四年［當日本寛元三年乙巳歳］なり。DZZ I, 570. Nearman gives 2,094 instead of 2,194 years, *The Shōbōgenzō*, 857. Because of his many inaccuracies pertaining to the translation of numerical chronography, his translations will not be referenced below where chronometrical information is concerned. See also Tanahashi, *Treasury*, 726.

42. 足びきの山鳥の尾のしだり尾の長長し夜も明けてける哉。DZZ II, 413.

43. あし曳の山どりのをのしだりをのながながしよをひとりかもねん。MYS 11.2802

44. Shirane, "Japan and the Culture of the Four Seasons Nature, Literature and the Arts."

45. 南謨佛法僧寶大吉、立春大吉、一家祖師祖宗大吉、佛法弘通大吉大吉、... 寛元五年丁未立春、大吉大吉。DZZ II, 406. "Salutations" here translates the invocatory phrase *namu*, a transliteration of Skt. *oṃ*, which refers to all "three treasures," the Buddha, his teaching, and the community following the teaching.

A plate with the original text, traditionally said to be of Dōgen's own hand, but possibly a copy, can be found in Eiheiji, *Eihei-ji shiryō zensho. Monjohen-1*, 102.

46. Elberfeld, *Phänomenologie der Zeit*, 236–37; Coulmas, *Japanische Zeiten: eine Ethnographie der Vergänglichkeit*, 76–78.

47. See the illustrations and description in Sasaki, "Rōkoku no genri to suii henka no sūchikeisan."

48. DZZ II, 345. See also GG DZZ 15, 188.

49. すなはち梁代の普通八年丁未歳九月二十一日なり。DZZ I, 140. Tanahashi, *Treasury*, 355.

50. (1) From the "Old mirror" fascicle. 仁治二年辛丑九月九日觀音導利興聖寶林寺示衆。DZZ I, 188.

51. 日本國寬元二年甲辰七月十七日、當先師故大宋國慶元府天童寺第三十代堂頭大和尚之諱辰。DZZ II, 515. Qingyuan prefecture corresponds to an area around Ningbo in today's Zhejiang province.

52. Cf. DZZ I, 86, 276.

53. See the above-quoted example from DZZ II, 406 and the formal instruction no. 169 from the *Extensive Record*, DZZ II, 44. Leighton and Okumura, *Extensive Record*, 193.

54. 爾時仁治元年庚子十月十八日子時于時在 _ 觀音導利興聖寶林寺 _ 示衆。DZZ I, 267. Note the two mentions of "time" (時) preceding the specification of the date and the place (in bold). Cf. Nearman, *The Shōbōgenzō*, 155. Tanahashi, *Treasury*, 164.

55. See the next chapter: the section on diurnal rhythms.

56. 嘉禎二年丙申十月十五日, DZZ II, 7. Leighton and Okumura, *Extensive Record*, 75.

57. 寬元四年丙午六月十五日, DZZ II, 46. Leighton and Okumura, *Extensive Record*, 197.

58. 寶治二年甲戌三月十四日, DZZ II, 63. Leighton and Okumura, *Extensive Record*, 246.

59. Compare the list in Leighton and Okumura, *Extensive Record*, 647–52. See also the following chapter: the section on the annual schedule.

60. Cf. DZZ II, 50, 70, 84, 96, 117. These are from 1246 and 1248–1251, respectively.

61. Cf. DZZ II, 97. The date corresponds to Kenchō 2, twelfth month, tenth day, which is January 10, 1251. Leighton and Okumura list it under the year 1250 because they equate the lunisolar with the solar year. Leighton and Okumura, *Extensive Record*, 351.

62. Cf. DZZ II, 90. The date is [Kenchō 2/1250], 6th month, 10th day. Leighton and Okumura, *Extensive Record*, 332.

63. "Great Wisdom Perfection" (*Maka hannya haramitsu* 摩訶般若波羅蜜): the summer retreat; *Manual of Seated Meditation* (*Zazen gi* 坐禪儀): winter.

64. "Explaining the Heart, Explaining the Nature" (*Sesshin sesshō* 説心説性), "The True Attributes of All Dharmas" (*Shohō jissō* 諸法實相), "Buddhist Sutras" (*Bukkyō* 佛經).

65. "The Deportment of the Practicing Buddha" (*Gyōbutsu igi* 行佛威儀): "middle of the 10th month" 十月中旬, DZZ I, 58.

66. "The True Attributes of All Dharmas," cf. DZZ I, 375.

67. "Spring and Autumn" (*Shunjū* 春秋), cf. DZZ I, 330.

68. Barthes, "The Reality Effect."

69. DZZ I, 136–37. The date mentioned is Changqing 長慶 4, the death year of emperor Muzong 穆宗. Xuanzong 宣宗 was Muzong's younger brother, who reinstated Buddhism after the persecutions under his predecessor (and nephew) Wuzong 武宗. Dōgen relates that Wuzong had tried to kill his uncle, but he miraculously came to life again. In another story, it is the master Dayi whose grave opens after his demise, and his body appears to be alive (DZZ I, 151). Note that in this and one more instance (DZZ I, 150), the era name is combined with the position in the sexagenary title, instead of a year number (but month and day are specified with numbers for the resurrection story).

70. Based on a full text search for 年 and 歳 in the 75- and 12-fascicle collections presented on the website of Shōmon ji, http://www.shomonji.or.jp/soroku/genzou.htm.

71. Cf. DZZ I, 298. Tanahashi, *Treasury*, 152.

72. Cf. DZZ I, 26, 431. Tanahashi, *Treasury*, 249.

73. Cf. DZZ I, 570, 14. Tanahashi, *Treasury*, 726, 234.

74. Leighton and Okumura, *Extensive Record*, 246. 寳治二年 戊辰 三月十四日 ノ 上堂 ニ 云 ク、山僧昨年八月初三日、出 デテ レ 山 ヲ赴 キ ニ 相州鎌倉 一、爲 メ ニ 二 檀那俗弟子 ノ 一 説法 ス 。今年今月昨日歸寺 シ 、今朝陞座 ス 。 Cf. DZZ II, 63. The English translation omits the position of the year in the sexagenary cycle, which is "yang earth dragon."

75. このゆゑに、祖師西來よりこのかた、大唐より大宋にいたる數百歳のあひだ、講經の達者、おのれが業を見徹せるもの、おほく教家律等のともがら、佛法にいるとき、從來舊巢の弊衣なる袈裟を抛却して、佛道正傳の袈裟を正受するなり。 DZZ I, 292. Cf. Nearman, *The Shōbōgenzō*, 129; Tanahashi, *Treasury*, 144.

76. Based on a search in the digital edition of Shōmonji, http://www.shomonji.or.jp/soroku/genzou.htm.

77. 雲嚴和尚と道悟と、おなじく藥山に參學して、ともにちかひをたてて、四十年わきを席につけず、一味參究す。法を洞山の悟本大師に傳付す。洞山いはく、われ、欲打成一片、坐禪辨道已二十年。いまその道、あまねく傳付せり。 DZZ I, 126. Cf. Nearman, *The Shōbōgenzō*, 382; Tanahashi, *Treasury*, 337.

78. 佛性かならず成佛と同參するなり。この道理、よくよく參究功夫すべし。三二十年も功夫參學すべし。 DZZ I, 20. Cf. Nearman, *The Shōbōgenzō*, 254; Tanahashi, *Treasury*, 241.

79. See for example, "Buddha Nature," DZZ I, 22, or "The Deportment of the Practicing Buddha," DZZ I, 49.

80. "For some time—for nine years, as it were—he hung his staff at Gaoshan [monastery]." From "Sustained Practice." しばらく嵩山に掛錫すること九年なり。 DZZ I, 142. Cf. Nearman, *The Shōbōgenzō*, 404. Tanahashi, *Treasury*, 356.

Chapter 4

1. For the *Pure Rules for Zen Monasteries,* see the monograph-cum-translation, Yifa, *The Origins of Buddhist Monastic Codes in China: An Annotated Translation and Study of the Chanyuan Qinggui.*

2. T. Griffith Foulk has discussed how Dōgen relied on Zongze's "Pure Rules" in his prescriptions on the handling of temple affairs and officers' duties. Foulk, "'Rules of Purity' in Japanese Zen," esp. 140.

3. DZZ II, 313–19. GG DZZ 15, 31–51 contains a *kakikudashibun* reading plus a translation into modern Japanese; a (not entirely reliable) English translation is included in Leighton and Okumura, *Dōgen's Pure Standards for the Zen Community: A Translation of Eihei Shingi*, 63–81.

4. The name Daibutsuji is given after the title, but not followed by a date. However, Daibutsuji was opened in 1244 and renamed Eihei-ji in 1246, and the *Extensive Record* mentions the influx of newcomers in 1245.

5. Thompson, "Time, Work-Discipline, and Industrial Capitalism."

6. *Shōsō* 聖僧. The statue of an enlightened being (usually either the Arhat Piṇḍola or the Bodhisattva Mañjuśrī) that constitutes the chief venerated icon in the Monks' Hall in Zen and in the refectory in other monasteries.

7. 合掌. A formal gesture of reverence and salute in which the palms of the hands are put together, accompanied by a bow.

8. DZZ II, 314; GG DZZ 15, 32–34. Cf. Leighton and Okumura, *Dōgen's Pure Standards*, 63–64, whose translation mirrors contemporary practice, e.g., in identifying the "holy monk" as Manjushri.

9. DZZ II, 318, 319. Cf. Leighton and Okumura, *Dōgen's Pure Standards*, 71, 73. These glosses could be seen as evidence in support of the received view that aligns the "twelve hours" with the view of the unenlightened. The question remains, however, why Dōgen then later insisted that his monastery maintain a water clock.

10. DZZ II, 345. Cf. Leighton and Okumura, *Dōgen's Pure Standards*, 180. See also GG DZZ 15, 188.

11. GG DZZ 15, 222. This is roughly consistent with Keizan's rules, which state that preparations for the sounding of the bell should start when "one can [still] see the waist of an ant" (*ari no koshi nao miyuru toki* 蟻の腰尚見ゆる時), Kohō, *Jōsai daishi zenshū*, 263–64.

12. DZZ II, 318; GG DZZ 15, 40. The *Daily Essentials for Members of the Congregation* equally refers to this as an "old saying": Wuliang, "Ruzhong Riyong / Nyūshū Nichiyō," 626. See also Foulk, "Daily Life in the Assembly."

13. DZZ II, 319. Leighton and Okumura, *Dōgen's Pure Standards*, 73–74. See below, Table 2, for an overview of the zodiacal hours and their approximate match with modern clock-time.

14. Otherwise, we might expect to read how his intention is conveyed to the monk who sounds the wooden board to mark the end of the session.

15. DZZ II, 316; Leighton and Okumura, *Dōgen's Pure Standards*, 65.

16. DZZ II, 317; Leighton and Okumura, *Dōgen's Pure Standards*, 70–71.

17. Kosaka et al., "Bendō hō," 229, note 6.

18. *Toki o shiri gi o wakatsu beshi.* 知 リ時、別ツベシ宜ヲ。 DZZ II, 345. This is a quote from the *Zen'en shingi*, Zongze, "Chanyuan Qinggui / Zen'en Shingi," 563.

19. *Sono jisetsu o ukagaite, subekaraku goka ni omomuite senmen subeshi. Jisetsu o ukagau towa, taishū no senmen, yaya sono hazama o eru nari.* 伺其時節。須赴後架而洗面。伺時節者。大衆洗面稍得其隙也。 DZZ II, 314. See also Leighton and Okumura, *Dōgen's Pure Standards*, 66.

20. 若欲起坐。徐徐而起。如要下床緩緩而下。不得高足大步急走馳騁。須揖而手於袖裏。莫垂兩袖於下面。不用點頭。祇看脚跟。詳緩而行。不可卒暴。與時低細。如法隨衆。迺辨道之規矩也。 DZZ II, 318; GDG DZZ 15, 48. See also Leighton and Okumura, *Dōgen's Pure Standards*, 72–73.

21. *Toki o shirite yoroshiki o wakatsu beshi* 知時別宜。 DZZ II, 345, see also GG DZZ 15, 188.

22. Morning (*sōshin* 早晨 or *jinjō* 晨朝), noon (*nitchū* 日中), (late) afternoon (*hoji* 晡時 or *nichimotsu* 日没), evening/incipient night (*kōkon* 黄昏 or *shoya* 初夜), midnight (*chūya* 中夜), and late night (*goya* 後夜).

23. On the correlation between the duration of activities and their importance, see Zerubavel, "The Language of Time: Toward a Semiotics of Temporality," 344.

24. *Keizan oshō shingi* 瑩山和尚清規, cf. Kohō, *Jōsai daishi zenshū*, 260–375. The English translation by Ichimura Shōhei (Keizan, and Ichimura, *Zen Master Keizan's Monastic Regulations* = *Keizan zenji (Oshō) Shingi*) is directed at modern practitioners and unfortunately is often imprecise regarding questions of time. On Keizan in general, see Bodiford, *Sōtō Zen in Medieval Japan*, 81–92. On his reception of Dōgen's monastic rules, see esp. ibid., 89.

25. *Nōshū Tōkoku Yōkō ji gyōji jijo* 州洞谷永光寺行事次序. For the stemma and publication history of the document and its changing titles, see Kohō, *Jōsai Daishi zenshū*, 46–47, and Ozaki, " 'Keizan shingi' kaidai," 782–84.

26. Kohō, *Jōsai daishi zenshū*, 265, 702.

27. Yoshinouchi, "Higashiyama gobunkobon 'Nittchū gyōji' ni mieru Heian jidai kyūchū jikoku seido no kōsatsu," 51–56.

28. Kohō, *Jōsai daishi zenshū*, 261, 263; Ishii, "Keizan shingi," 697, 699.

29. Kohō, *Jōsai daishi zenshū*, 263; Ishii, "Keizan shingi," 700.

30. Kohō, *Jōsai daishi zenshū*, 263–65; Ishii, "Keizan shingi," 700–2. The English translation (Ichimura, *Zen Master Keizan's Monastic Regulations*, 23–32) is of no use here. It treats the hours and the night watches as stable, fixed time units, which leads to obvious contradictions (e.g., p. 28 "One Half Past the Period of Tora . . ."; i.e., 4:00 a.m. The drum of the kitchen hall signals the third phase of the fourth night watch (四更三点, 1:48–2:12 a.m.), and it ignores the correlations between them that Keizan explicitly mentions.

31. Bodiford, *Sōtō Zen in Medieval Japan*, 87–92.

32. Zongze, "Chanyuan qinggui," 580–82; Yifa, *Buddhist Monastic Codes*, 198–201.

33. Zongze, "Chanyuan qinggui," 580; Yifa, *Buddhist Monastic Codes*, 198.

34. *Subekaraku kore gokō no kane imada narazaru toki, karugaru toshite mi aku beshi.* 須是五更〻鍾未〻鳴〻、軽々トシテ抬アク身〻。須くこれ五更の鍾未だ鳴らざるとき、軽々として身を抬くべし。 Wuliang, "Ruzhong riyong/Nisshū nichiyō," 625.

35. Wuliang, "Ruzhong riyong/Nisshū nichiyō," 625.

36. *Kōzen gokoku ron.* Cf. T 2543.80: 14; Yifa, *Buddhist Monastic Codes*, 39.

37. Wuliang, "Ruzhong riyong/Nisshū nichiyō," 629–30.

38. Kurebayashi, "Dōgen zenji no kyōgaku to nyūshū nichiyō shingi."

39. Cf. Wuliang, and "Ruzhong riyong/Nisshū nichiyō," 625–26, and GDG DZZ, 348.

40. Ishii, "Kaidai (Sōsetsu)," 750; Ishii, "'Nisshū nichiyō' kaidai," 773.

41. Wuliang, "Ruzhong riyong/Nisshū nichiyō," 628–29.

42. On Lanxi Daolong's biography and teachings, see Döll, *Im Osten des Meeres: chinesische Emigrantenmönche und die frühen Institutionen des japanischen Zen-Buddhismus*, 92–98.

43. *Kenchō kaizan Daikaku zenji bendō shingi* 建長開山大覚禅師弁道清規.

44. A *gāthā* (Jp. *ge* 偈) is an expression in verse. It may concern the teaching, an insight, or resolve; or be used to pay homage.

45. *Seishin o tōsō seyo.* 抖ソウ精神〻; *tōsō* is a translation of skt. *dhuta*, to shake off, to free oneself. The *Ruzhong riyong* uses the same expression to describe early-morning *zazen*. Wuliang, "Ruzhong riyong/Nisshū nichiyō," 625.

46. *Shōgō* 正業, literally "right action." According to Tachi, this remark, like the others in parentheses, is a later addition, which derives from Pure Land terminology. Tachi, "Rankei Dōryū 'Bendō shingi' ni tsuite," 145. I have chosen my translation because the term is used here in contrast to *jogō* 助業, literally "auxiliary action."

47. *Fumonbon* 不門品. This is the abbreviated title of the Lotus Sutra's chapter on the Bodhisattva Avalokiteśvara, or Kannon bosatsu, the *Kanzeon bosatsu fumon bon* 観世音菩薩普門品, also separately known as *Kannon kyō* 観音経. A fairly literal translation of the chapter's title is "The All-Sidedness of the Bodhisattva Regarder of the Cries of the World"; see Kato and Soothill, *The Threefold Lotus Sutra*, 319.

48. I have translated the text after the version given in Tachi's discussion of the document, Tachi, "Rankei Dōryū 'Bendō shingi,'" 143.

49. Döll, *Im Osten des Meeres*, 94.

50. This may be related to difficulties in direct communication; see Tachi's insightful article on the use of Chinese in Kamakura Zen monasteries: Tachi, "Kamakura ki no zenrin ni okeru chūgoku go to nihongo."

51. Wuliang, "Ruzhong riyong/Nisshū nichiyō," 629.

52. *Vinaya* (Jp. *kairitsu* 戒律) was a set of rules regulating behavior of ordained monastics. In East Asian Buddhism, a set of 253 rules for male and 348 rules for female monastics was generally used, but the Tendai School used only a condensed set of ten "Bodhisattva precepts" (Jp. *bosatsu kai* 菩薩戒) from the Brahmajāla Sutra (Jp. *Bonmōkyō* 梵網経). The precise content and relative importance of these regulations was therefore a subject of debate in Japan. See Groner, *Precepts, Ordinations, and Practice in Medieval Japanese Tendai*.

53. The Esoteric Precepts School, a movement that started in the eleventh and gained tractions in the thirteenth century, combined emphasis on monastic rules with practices from the Shingon School of Esoteric Buddhism. See Pinte, "Shingon Risshū."

54. Shirasu, *Myōe shōnin*, 112. An image of the table, which was later covered with lacquer, and a transcript of the text can be found in Shirasu, *Myōe shōnin*, 123. The English translation in Unno, *Shingon Refractions: Myōe and the Mantra of Light*, 153–54, is inaccurate on several counts, including the conversion of *shinkoku* into modern hours, and the description of rituals.

55. Payne, "84. The Fourfold Training in Japanese Esoteric Buddhism," 1025. Interestingly, Dōgen dismisses this technique in one of his formal lectures as a practice of the "lesser vehicle" (*shōjō* 小乗), *Extensive Record*, vol. 5.390, DZZ II, 96; Leighton and Okumura, *Extensive Record*, 348.

56. Also *Shu ryōgon kyō* 首楞厳経; T 945.19: 105–55.

57. The original text of Shunjō's instructions is given in full in Ishida Mitsuyuki, *Shunjō risshi: Kamakura bukkyō seiritsu no kenkyū*, 391–405. For the time regime quoted here, see ibid., 391. Shunjō also has a brief text on seated meditation, see ibid., 407.

58. This fact is highlighted by Eisai following his sketch of the daily schedule in Song period Chan monasteries: *Shikaru ni sunawachi, shiji no zazen o ketai suru koto nashi.* 然則四時坐禪無懈怠。 ("In this manner, they never neglect seated meditation during the four [specified] hours." *Kōzen gokoku ron*, T 2543.80: 14c12–13. On frequency/iteration as a sign of the importance attached to an activity, see Zerubavel, "The Language of Time," 345.

59. See, e.g., the "Reading Sutras" (*Kankin* 看經) lecture of the *Treasury*, DZZ I, 272–76. Further explained below.

60. See the section on the retreat below.

61. Kasulis, *Zen Action/Zen Person*.
62. Suzuki, "Zen: A Reply to Hu Shih," 45.
63. Foulk, "'Rules of Purity' in Japanese Zen," 140. See also his list of Dōgen's writings drawing on the *Chanyuan qinggui*, earlier on that page. Note, however, Ishii's discussion of the changes Dōgen made concerning the distribution of competences and the mode of decision-making. See Ishii, "Eiheiji senjutsu bunken ni miru Dōgen zenji no sōdan un'ei" and below.
64. Zerubavel, "The Language of Time," esp. 347–49. See also Zerubavel, "Timetables and Scheduling: On the Social Organization of Time."
65. DZZ I, 275–76. Cf. Nearman, *The Shōbōgenzō*, 241–42. Tanahashi, *Treasury*, 232–33.
66. See T 2543.80: 15a2–5.
67. DZZ I, 275. Cf. Nearman, *The Shōbōgenzō*, 241. Tanahashi, *Treasury*, 232.
68. DZZ I, 276. Dōgen, *The Shōbōgenzō*, 242. Tanahashi, *Treasury*, 233.
69. Kohō, *Jōsai daishi zenshū*, 265–68, 271.
70. Yifa, *Buddhist Monastic Codes*, 135, 138. Cf. Zongze, "Chanyuan Qinggui," 554. Unfortunately, the passage on informal lectures is missing in this text.
71. Kohō, *Jōsai Daishi zenshū*, 266, 269–72; Ichimura, *Zen Master Keizan's Monastic Regulations*, 38, 55, 57, 63, 66–67.
72. Vol. 2.171, Leighton and Okumura, *Extensive Record*, 195. Cf. DZZ II, 45.
73. Vol. 6.448, Leighton and Okumura, *Extensive Record*, 404. The editors explain in a footnote: "When asked about words that surpass the buddhas and ancestors, Yunmen responded: 'Sesame cake.' [. . .] Dōgen also refers to this story in his mid-autumn Dharma hall discourse 189." Cf. DZZ II, 50, 116.
74. 407 of 531 recorded sermons are without date. Leighton and Okumura (*Extensive Record*, 647–52) give a helpful index of the 124 dated ones. Note, however, that the years given for lectures during the twelfth month of the old calendar, especially those of enlightenment day (eighth day of twelfth month) are misleading: Since enlightenment day occurs on the eighth day of the month *after* winter solstice, it usually falls in the new year of the solar calendar.
75. Vol. 3: seventy-three lectures in fifteen months (seventh month of 1246 to eighth month of 1247, and third to fourth months of 1248). Vol. 4: Eighty-eight lectures in sixteen months (fourth month of 1248 to eighth month of 1249). Vol. 5: apparently less regular, with several clear breaks in chronology and a total number of sixty-eight lectures in sixteen months (eighth month of 1249 to first month of 1251). Vol. 6: Fifty-seven discourses for approximately twelve months (early 1251 to late 1251 or early 1252—the last dated lecture is that on the first day of the tenth month (early November)—followed by eight more, but without a lecture for the winter solstice, which is regularly explicitly mentioned in the other volumes). Vol. 7: sixty-two discourses for twelve months (early 1252 to early 1253).
76. Kohō, *Jōsai Daishi zenshū*, 265–72; Ichimura, *Zen Master Keizan's Monastic Regulations*, 33–75.

77. Ibid.
78. Ōtani, *Dōgen zenji oriori no hōwa*, 37.
79. DZZ I, 88. Cf. Nearman, *The Shōbōgenzō*, 681. Tanahashi, Treasury, 579. This is taken up in Keizan's manual on seated meditation, Kohō, *Jōsai Daishi zenshū*, 248. Cf. also the German translation in Dumoulin, *Dōgen-Zen: Kleine Schriften der Sōtō-Schule*, 66.
80. Ōtani, *Dōgen zenji oriori no hōwa*, 37.
81. English translation slightly modified after Leighton and Okumura, *Extensive Record*, 214–15. Cf. DZZ II, 52, and Ōtani, *Dōgen zenji oriori no hōwa*, 31–32. Leighton and Okumura have detailed the allusions to Zen lore that also refer to the fireplace or its opening. For convenience, I quote their explanation in full (reference style adjusted): "Linji's lump of Red Flesh refers to a famous saying by the great master Linji, 'Here in this lump of red flesh is a True Man with no rank.' See Watson, *The Zen Teachings of Master Lin-Chi*, 13. 'Xuefeng's ancient mirror' refers to a story in which Xuefeng says, 'If the world is ten feet wide, the ancient mirror is ten feet wide. If the world is one foot wide, the ancient mirror is one foot wide.' His disciple Xuansha asked, 'Then how wide is the furnace?' and Xuefeng said, 'As wide as the ancient mirror.' This is recounted in Dōgen's *Shōbōgenzō* essay Kokyō (The Ancient Mirror). [. . .] Danxia Tianran, a disciple of Shitou, is famous for having burned a wooden buddha statue to warm himself. At Shanfu was a huge iron statue of an ox, considered a guardian deity of the Yellow River. Its head and tail were in different provinces, Henan and Hebei, and it was said to have been built by the legendary Emperor Yu of the Xia dynasty (ca. 2200 B.C.E.)." Leighton and Okumura, *Extensive Record*, 214–15, fn. 24, 25.
82. I use the term "economical" here and in the following to indicate actions and expressions geared toward the provisioning and use of goods for human well-being. The formal sermons in question are *Extensive Record*, vols. 1.14 (1240), 1.109 (1242), 3.199 (1246), 4.288 (1248), 5.353 (1249), 5.396 (1250), 6.462 (1251), and 7.528 (1252); cf. also Ōtani, *Dōgen zenji oriori no hōwa*, 32–33.
83. Cf. *Chiji shingi*, DZZ II, 332. Leighton and Okumura, *Dōgen's Pure Standards*, 153.
84. Cf. DZZ II, 128; *kundoku* reading according to Ōtani, *Eihei kōroku*, vol. 2, 91.
85. The name refers to the first day of the horse in the fifth month, but later this event came to be fixed on the fifth day of the fifth month.
86. Ōtani, *Dōgen zenji oriori no hōwa*, 225. The poems are recorded in *Extensive Record*, vol. 10:74, 80–86, cf. DZZ II, 195–97.
87. Kohō, *Jōsai Daishi zenshū*, 309–13, 315, 344, 355, 357; Ichimura, *Zen Master Keizan's Monastic Regulations*, 187–204, 211, 297–98, 337, 345. Keizan starts with the events scheduled for the celebration of the New Year, including again prayers for imperial longevity. On the occasion of describing the rituals

associated with winter solstice, he notices that all four seasonal turning points shall be observed in a similar fashion.

88. *Chiji shingi*, DZZ II, 332; Leighton and Okumura, *Dōgen's Pure Standards*, 153. The custom to hold special meals, tea ceremonies, and, on the *tango*, *tanabata*, and *chōkyū* dates, eggplant-roasting feasts, was already observed in Song period China; see Yifa, *Buddhist Monastic Codes*, 95–96.

89. *In kiwamarite yō shōzu* 陰極而陽生; cf. DZZ II, 33. Leighton and Okumura, *Extensive Record*, 162.

90. *Issen chōshi* 一線長至. *Chōshi* also refers to the summer solstice, the peak of yang forces: Dōgen equates the full growth of yang within its incipient stage, just like he on other occasions equates practice with enlightenment.

91. Kūō[butsu] 空王[仏] and Ion[butsu] 威音[仏]. These are Buddhas of the first eons in the immeasurably remote past.

92. Cf. DZZ II, 34. See also Leighton and Okumura, *Extensive Record*, 163–64. My translation is also informed by Ōtani's paraphrased rendering in modern Japanese. Ōtani, *Dōgen zenji oriori no hōwa*, 45–46.

93. *Rōhatsu* literally simply refers to the date. As Ōtani Tetsuo remarks, enlightenment day was observed by all Buddhist schools, but on different dates. Dōgen insisted that he had established the custom in Japan. Ōtani, *Dōgen zenji oriori no hōwa*, 55–56. Cf. *Extensive Record*, vol. 5.406, DZZ II, 101; Leighton and Okumura, *Extensive Record*, 361–62.

94. The *Extensive Record* contains nine sermons on the occasion of bathing the Buddha: vol. 1.42 (1241), 75 (1242), 98 (1243), vol. 2.155 (1246), vol. 3.236 (1247), 256 (1248), vol. 4.320 (1249), vol. 6.427 (1251), 7.495 (1252)). Eight sermons are recorded for enlightenment day: vol. 1.88 (1242), vol. 2.136 (1246), 213 (1247), 297 (1249), vol. 5.360 (1250), 406 (1251), vol. 7.475 (1252), 506 (1253). The celebration fell on the eighth day of the twelfth month in the lunisolar calendar, and thus regularly in January of the next solar year, a fact ignored by Ōtani, as well as Leighton and Okumura. Parinirvana day is marked by seven formal sermons: vol. 1.121 (1243), vol. 2.146 (1246), vol. 3.225 (1247), vol. 4.311 (1249), vol. 5.367 (1250), vol. 6.418 (1251), vol. 7.486 (1252). Keizan's annual observances obviously also elaborate on these occasions. Since they follow the course of the lunisolar year, they start with Parinirvana day. Kohō, *Jōsai daishi zenshū*, 313–15, 321–23, 357–59; Ichimura, *Zen Master Keizan's Monastic Regulations*: 204–11, 230–37, 346–51.

95. Buddhist monastic tradition demanded two annual retreats, in summer and winter, and Ōtani insists that both were strictly observed in the Sōtō school in Japan (Ōtani, *Dōgen zenji oriori no hōwa*, 195). However, only the summer retreat is singled out by formal sermons in *Extensive Record*, described in the pertinent fascicle "Summer Retreat" of the *Treasury* and detailed in Keizan's rules. Dōgen states in "Summer Retreat" that while winter retreats are required in the *Brahma Net Sutra*, only the procedures for summer retreats have been transmitted, indicating that he did not hold winter retreats (Cf. DZZ I, 571). Dōgen, *The*

Shōbōgenzō, 865. Tanahashi, *Treasury*, 731. Leighton and Okumura, *Extensive Record*, 145; Zongze, "Chanyuan Qinggui." Accordingly, *Eihei kōroku* has seven formal and five informal sermons each for both opening and closing the summer retreat: Opening: vol. 1:44 (1241), 118 (1243), vol. 2.127 (1245), 158 (1246), vol. 3.238 (1247), 257 (1248), vol. 4.322 (1249), and *shōsan* 6, 8, 11, 15, 19; closing vol. 1:102 (1242), 2.130 (1245), 183 (1246), vol. 3.248 (1247), vol. 4.341 (1249), vol. 6.442 (1251), vol. 7.514 (1252); *shōsan* 1, 3, 7, 16, 20. The Treasury Fascicle "Summer Retreat" was delivered roughly eight weeks into the retreat in 1245, on the thirteenth day of the sixth month; cf. DZZ I, 584. This accounts for the years 1241–1243 at Kōshōji and 1245–1249 and 1251–1252 at Eiheiji; however, note the number of informal lectures and the possibility that Dōgen may have repeated himself in formal lectures, which were then not recorded. See also Kohō, *Jōsai daishi zenshū*, 323–53; Ichimura, *Zen Master Keizan's Monastic Regulations*, 239–326.

96. While ritual commemoration for Rujing is first recorded for 1246 (*Extensive Record*, vol. 2.184, with further *jōdō* for this occasion recorded for 1247, 1248, 1249, 1250, and 1252, cf. vol. 3.249, vol. 4.274, 342, vol. 5.384, vol. 7.515), the other two memorials were apparently only established in 1251 (and repeated in 1252, see vol. 6.435 and 441, vol. 7.504 and 512). In the same years, Dōgen also marked the memorial days of his foster father and his mother with dedicated formal discourses. One might argue that he felt or wanted to display a heightened sense of piety toward those who had nurtured him in mundane and spiritual terms in the last years of his life. Note, however, that Dōgen did not have an immediate personal connection with Eisai and that he did not commemorate his first (Tendai) teachers Ryōkan, Kōen, and Kōin in a similar fashion.

97. DZZ II, 128–29; Leighton and Okumura, *Extensive Record*, 436–39. See also the following discourses 492–94, which emphasize good conduct and distance from secular affairs as the hallmarks of renunciant life, and discuss Linji (493) and Dongshan (494) in sequence.

98. Kohō, *Jōsai daishi zenshū*, 352; Ichimura, *Zen Master Keizan's Monastic Regulations*, 326.

99. Kohō, *Jōsai daishi zenshū*, 271–72, 354–55; Ichimura, *Zen Master Keizan's Monastic Regulations*, 62, 66–67.

100. Bodiford, in his discussion of the conflicts arising at Eiheiji in the third generation of abbots, emphasizes that Keizan (who belonged to the fourth generation) had studied with all conflicting parties. Bodiford, *Sōtō Zen in Medieval Japan*, 78. Nonetheless, only Gikai is singled out for commemoration.

101. *Extensive Record*, vol. 3.193 (1246), vol. 4.279 (1248), vol. 5.347 (1249), 389 (1250), vol. 6.451 (1251), and vol. 7.523 (1252).

102. See also *Extensive Record*, vol. 5.390, following the pertinent sermon in 1250, which remarks on the difference between Dōgen's *zazen* and meditative exercises in other schools. DZZ II, 96–97, and Leighton and Okumura, *Extensive Record*, 348–50.

103. DZZ II, 139, and Leighton and Okumura, *Extensive Record*, 465–66.

104. Ishii, "Eiheiji Senjutsu Bunken," 418–19. See also *Extensive Record*, vol. 2, 137–39 (1246), 3.214 (1247), 4.298–300 (1249), 5.401 (undated, but held either 1250 or 1251), *shōsan* 8.5 (undated, but held at Eiheiji), and *hōgo* 8.6 (1240), 8.7 (1241).

105. Cf. Ishii, "Eiheiji senjutsu bunken," 416–20, 427–30. *Chiji shingi* specifies that minor supervising positions and the like were filled by appointment through the chief administrator (*kan'in* 監院); cf. DZZ II, 332; Leighton and Okumura, *Dōgen's Pure Standards*, 153.

106. And note that in Keizan's rules, the New Year rituals included prayers for imperial longevity, with a lengthy written dedication that was apparently sent to court upon completion. Cf. Kohō, *Jōsai daishi zenshū*, 309–13; Ichimura, *Zen Master Keizan's Monastic Regulations*, 187–204.

107. *Kotenbōrin* 古転法輪, *kobusso* 古仏祖. DZZ I, 570. Cf. Nearman, *The Shōbōgenzō*, 858; Tanahashi, *Treasury*, 727.

108. Cf. DZZ I, 571; Nearman, *The Shōbōgenzō*, 865; Tanahashi, *Treasury*, 731.

109. Cf. DZZ I, 583; Nearman, *The Shōbōgenzō*, 869; Tanahashi, *Treasury*, 736. Unfortunately, the practical consequences of including both sexes in the community, irrespective of clerical or lay status, are not discussed in the document, although one passage mentions a "teacher of female renunciants" (*nishi* 尼師) among the officials who exchange formal greetings at the beginning of the retreat (DZZ I, 579). The *dōshi* 道士 (a term that in a Buddhist context usually refers to clerics as opposed to laypersons), mentioned next, might point to a cleric who instructs the lay practitioners, but that conjecture is based on context only.

110. Keizan's rules describe the process and required documents in detail. Most important was the official certificate of ordination, followed by civil documents of descent and certificates of previous summer retreats (*rokunen* 六念). These were copied for temple records and submitted to the abbot, who had to grant permission of residency. Cf. Kohō, *Jōsai daishi zenshū*, 315–16; Ichimura, *Zen Master Keizan's Monastic Regulations*, 212–15.

111. DZZ I, 571–74. Cf. Nearman, *The Shōbōgenzō*, 861; Tanahashi, *Treasury*, 729.

112. On the importance of the *kairō* and the seating order in Buddhist rituals, see also Matsuo, *A History of Japanese Buddhism*, 34–35.

113. DZZ I, 572; Nearman, *The Shōbōgenzō*, 861; Tanahashi, *Treasury*, 729.

114. Yifa, *Buddhist Monastic Codes*, 61–62.

115. For the following, see DZZ I, 573–81; Nearman, *The Shōbōgenzō*, 865–71; Tanahashi, *Treasury*, 731–39.

116. DZZ I, 577; Nearman, *The Shōbōgenzō*, 866; Tanahashi, *Treasury*, 734.

117. DZZ I, 581; Nearman, *The Shōbōgenzō*, 871; Tanahashi, *Treasury*, 739.

118. Cf. DZZ I, 569; Nearman, *The Shōbōgenzō*, 856; Tanahashi, *Treasury*, 725–26.

119. Cf. DZZ I, 581–82; Nearman, *The Shōbōgenzō*, 872–73; Tanahashi, *Treasury*, 740–41.

120. Cf. DZZ I, 582; Nearman, *The Shōbōgenzō*, 873. Tanahashi, *Treasury*, 741.

121. This follows a custom already well established in China; see Yifa, *Buddhist Monastic Codes*, 71–72.

122. English translation, modified after Tanahashi, *Treasury*, 31. The Japanese original is 人のさとりを罣礙せざること、滴露の天月を罣礙せざるがごとし。ふかきことはたかき分量なるべし。時節の長短は、大水小水を撿點し、天月の廣狹を辨取すべし。 DZZ I, 8–9. Tanahashi's and Aitken's otherwise beautiful translation glosses precisely over the differentiations indicated in the last sentences of the second paragraph. Cf. also Nearman, *The Shōbōgenzō*, 33.

123. See, e.g., Yifa, *Buddhist Monastic Codes*, 71–72. Dōgen refers to this practice in his obituary for Myōzen, *Myōzen oshō kaiyō okugaki*, DZZ II, 397.

124. As Zerubavel has observed, "we normally regard temporal precedence as virtually synonymous with priority," but he also cautioned that this mode of ordering may on occasion be reversed. Zerubavel, "The Language of Time," 347.

125. 首座、大衆をひきて入堂し、戒臘によりて巡堂立定す。 DZZ I, 577. Cf. Nearman, *The Shōbōgenzō*, 866. Tanahashi, *Treasury*, 734.

126. Zerubavel, "The Language of Time," 347.

127. Zerubavel, "The Language of Time," 344–45.

128. Zerubavel, however, does not make this connection and believes that the choice between "temporal priority equals higher rank" and "last is most important" is completely arbitrary: "within the essentially artificial realm of the symbolic, one should not expect the relations between most signifiers and signifieds to be anything other than arbitrary" (ibid., 347), although later in the same article he also discusses "the symbolic relation between waiting and power," stating that "it is usually the powerful who have the license to make others wait." Zerubavel, "The Language of Time," 354.

129. *Taitaiko goge jari hō* 對大己五夏闍梨法; short: *Rules for Facing Senior Practitioners.* DZZ II, 308–12.

130. Cf. DZZ II, 309. Leighton and Okumura, *Dōgen's Pure Standards*, 122. An *ajari* 阿闍梨 (derived from Skt. *ācārya* for "preceptor," "mentor") is a senior priest who may instruct and correct junior monks, an *oshō* or in Sanskrit *upadhyāya* is someone's personal teacher. See endnote 1, Kosaka et al., "Taitaiko goge jari hō," GG DZZ 15, 267.

131. Iteration, as a temporal mode of expressing social distinction, is visible again in "Summer Retreat" when formal greetings during the opening of the retreat are described. The number of prostrations or bows in these exchanges is clearly correlated with status. For example, the "dharma relatives" of the abbot bow three times to him, which he returns. His immediate disciples and attendants bow nine times, and novices nine or twelve times, and these courtesies

are simply received with hands clasped in greeting, but not returned. Cf. DZZ I, 577; Nearman, *The Shōbōgenzō*, 866; Tanahashi, *Treasury*, 734. On the matter of bows and prostrations, see also Foulk, "'Just Sitting'? Dogen's Take on Zazen, Sutra Reading, and Other Conventional Buddhist Practice."

132. See Faure, "The Daruma-Shū," 27–35; Ōkubo, "Dōgen zenji no genshi sōdan to Nihon daruma shū to no kankei"; Heine, "Dōgen and the Precepts Revisited," 16–18.

133. On this, see also Dōgen's instruction to the *kan'in*, the most senior temple official, that in monitoring admissions to the monastery, the emphasis should be on maintaining a community of devoted practitioners and not on mere numbers; DZZ II, 333.

134. Cf. DZZ II, 310; Leighton and Okumura, *Dōgen's Pure Standards*, 123.

135. Cf. DZZ II, 310; Leighton and Okumura, *Dōgen's Pure Standards*, 124.

136. Cf. DZZ II, 311; Leighton and Okumura, *Dōgen's Pure Standards*, 124.

137. Obviously, terms such as "subordinate" or "superior" in themselves already embody this metaphorical principle, which is the social application of a more general one expressed by Lakoff and Johnson in their seminal work *Philosophy in the Flesh* as "Control is Up." Lakoff and Johnson list this among the "primary metaphors" anchored in the physical realities of human existence. Lakoff and Johnson, *Philosophy in the Flesh*, 53.

138. Cf. DZZ II, 287. In addition to ordering of names, a thin red line leads from the name of Śākyamuni to that of the first and then to each successive patriarch up to Dōgen, from where it returns toŚākyamuni.

139. Cf. DZZ I, 451–53. At the beginning of this passage, Dōgen uses the rhetorical device of ostensibly addressing a past master (Chenggao chanshi, who claimed to be an heir of Yunmen because he had lived in the vicinity of his stupa) when speaking to Daruma shū members in his assembly: "Even if we concede that you knew and saw great master Yunmen, has great master Yunmen really seen you or not? If he hasn't seen you, you cannot have received succession from him. And because Yunmen hasn't approved of you, you do not say 'Great master Yunmen has seen me.' We thus know that you have not yet met with great master Yunmen. From the seven Buddhas and all Buddhas of the past, present, and future, which Buddha or patriarch has succeeded in the dharma without personally meeting with a master?" Cf. DZZ I, 451; Nearman, *The Shōbōgenzō*, 842–43; Tanahashi, *Treasury*, 576.

140. Allusions to the stories of dharma transmission from Śākyamuni to Kāśyapa, Bodhidharma to Huike, Hongren to Huineng, and Yunyan to Dongshan. For the full lineage leading up to Dōgen, see the above-mentioned document of succession, and *Busso*, DZZ I, 454–57. See also Nearman, *The Shōbōgenzō*, 835; Tanahashi, *Treasury*, 570.

141. DZZ I, 446. Cf. Nearman, *The Shōbōgenzō*, 835; Tanahashi, *Treasury*, 569–70.

142. Yifa, *Buddhist Monastic Codes*, 132–33.

143. Kohō, *Jōsai daishi zenshū*, 270–71.

144. On rigidity and firmness of timing as a sign of importance, see Zerubavel, "The Language of Time," 346–47.

145. The text of the document, together with that of Rujing's answer, is quoted in full at the beginning of *Record from the Baojing Era*, cf. DZZ II, 371. Again, this conforms to Zerubavel's characterization of free access, frequency of contact, and ever-availability as signs of intimacy; cf. Zerubavel, "The Language of Time," 345–46.

146. On this category and its meaning for medieval Japan, see Matsuo, "What Is Kamakura New Buddhism? Official Monks and Reclusive Monks."

147. *Eiheiji jūryo seiki* 永平寺住侶制規 ("Restrictions for resident monks of Eiheiji"), DZZ II, 367.

148. See the colophone and Ōkubo's editorial note, DZZ II, 367.

149. Acting as a ritualist in functions for the deceased was also prohibited. The general intent to prevent involvement with requests (including those concerning spiritual affairs) by outside individuals stands in some contrast to Matsuo's characterization of reclusive monks.

150. *Kisshō-zan Eiheiji shuryō shingi* 吉祥山永平寺衆寮箴規, DZZ II, 363–67. Leighton and Okumura, *Dōgen's Pure Standards*, 109–21.

151. DZZ II, 366; Leighton and Okumura, *Dōgen's Pure Standards*, 114.

152. *Mata shōkyaku, ishi, sōshi nado, oyobi shodō no tomogara to mondō subekarazu*. 又不ㇾ可ㇾ與₋商客・医師・相師等、及諸道輩₋問答ㇾ上。 DZZ II, 363; cf. Leighton and Okumura, *Dōgen's Pure Standards*, 110.

153. *Kashira o atsumete danwa shi, muzan muki ni shite kyoshō subekarazu*. 不ㇾ可ㇾ聚ㇾ頭談話、無慚無愧而戯笑ㇾ。 DZZ II, 364; cf. Leighton and Okumura, *Dōgen's Pure Standards*, 110.

154. *Seken no koto, myōri no koto, kokudo no jiran, kyōshū no sosai o danwa subekarazu* 不ㇾ可ㇾ談₋話世閒事・名利事・國土治亂・共衆麤細ㇾ。 DZZ II, 364; Leighton and Okumura, *Dōgen's Pure Standards*, 111.

155. *Zokuten oyobi tenmon / chiri no sho, oyoso gedō no kyōron, shibu, waka nado no kanjiku o okubekarazu*. 不ㇾ可ㇾ置₋俗典及天文・地理之書、凡外道經論、詩賦等卷軸ㇾ。 DZZ II, 365; Leighton and Okumura, *Dōgen's Pure Standards*, 114.

156. *Eiheiji koin seiki* 永平寺庫院制規, DZZ II, 362.

157. See the chapter on the "Zen Monastic Economy" in Collcutt, *Five Mountains*, 249–89.

158. *Ima yori igo shitagahite teiji subeki koto* 自今已後可₋從ᵗ停止₋事。 DZZ II, 362.

Part II

1. A "two truths" reading of Dōgen is expressly proposed in Yoshimura, "Nāgārjuna (Ryūju) to Dōgen—Nitairon kara no 'Shōbō genzō' dokkai no kokoromi."

Chapter 5

1. Kim, *Dōgen Kigen*, 142.
2. Yanagida, "Zen bukkyō no jikanron"; Rappe, "Time and Nothingness in Aspects of Buddhist Philosophy—From the Beginnings to Dogen's Uji"; Elberfeld, *Phänomenologie der Zeit*.
3. Yanagida, "Zen no jikanron," 79.
4. Ibid., 87. The reference is to *Dabanniepan jing* 大般涅槃經, T 374.
5. Yanagida, "Zen no jikanron," 97–98.
6. Yanagida," Zen no jikanron," 98.
7. *Tonkyō* 頓教.
8. Yanagida, "Zen no jikanron," 100–2.
9. Kim, *Dōgen Kigen*, 138–40; Rappe, "Time and Nothingness," 346–47; Elberfeld, *Phänomenologie der Zeit*, 170–82. On Fazang, see Chen, *Philosopher, Practitioner, Politician: the Many Lives of Fazang (643–712)*.
10. Elberfeld, *Phänomenologie der Zeit*, 203–4. See also Obert, "Zeit als Relationalität und Sprung."
11. *Shi shi zang* 十世章. T 1874.45: 621–22.
12. Elberfeld, *Phänomenologie der Zeit*, 208–12.
13. Ibid., 214–15.
14. "Kann nicht jede Zeit gleichzeitig in gegenwärtige Erscheinung treten": Elberfeld, *Phänomenologie der Zeit*, 214.
15. Rappe, "Time and Nothingness," 347, referring to T 1881.45:609, b8–14: 萬像紛紜參而不雜・雖四像遷移・各住自位・一切即一皆同無性・一即一切因果歷然・力用相收卷舒自在無礙・故名一乘圓教. Rappe gives a translation that is clearly strongly shaped by his own philosophical position, and in his comment he somewhat surprisingly emphasizes an "experience in which everything is in a relationship which is indeterminable."
16. T 1858.45: 151 a8–c29. For an English translation, see Felbur, "Things Do Not Shift."
17. T 1858.45: 151 a12–14. For a more extensive discussion of this argument, see Elberfeld, *Phänomenologie der Zeit*, 186–90.
18. T 1858.45: 151 b3–4.
19. *Extensive Record*, vol. 2,148; see also vol. 7.482, 484, 491. Cf. Leighton and Okumura, *Extensive Record*, 428–29, 430, 436, 437; DZZ II 38, 125, 126, 128–29.
20. Elberfeld, *Phänomenologie der Zeit*, 200.
21. Ibid., 207.
22. Yanagida, "Zen no jikanron," 112–15.
23. Cf. DZZ I, 21.This doctrine formed the title of *Impermanence*, one of the two extant books on time in Dōgen by philosopher Joan Stambaugh.
24. Nearman, *The Shōbōgenzō*, 4. Cf. DZZ I, 731.
25. Nearman, *The Shōbōgenzō*, 5–6. Cf. DZZ I, 731–32.

26. DZZ I, 732. Cf. Nearman, *The Shōbōgenzō*, 6.
27. Cf. DZZ I, 742; Nearman, *The Shōbōgenzō*, 19.
28. Conze, *Buddhist Thought in India: Three Phases of Buddhist Philosophy*, 34–39.
29. Conze, *Buddhist Thought in India*, 122–34; Hakamaya, *Dōgen to bukkyō*, 75–78.
30. He, "Dōgen no shinjōsōmetsuron hihan ni kansuru isshiten"; Kim, *Dōgen Kigen*, 159–62; Heine, *Readings*, 124.
31. Kim, *Dōgen Kigen*, 142. Kim also states that "impermanence was the alpha and omega of religion for Dōgen," ibid., 103. The point has recently been reiterated by Heine, Heine, *Readings*, 119–20.
32. See, for example, Karaki, "Mujō no keijijōgaku," 324–30.
33. Kopf, *Beyond Personal Identity*, 182–83.
34. Heine, *Readings*, 119.
35. Ibid., 120.
36. Stambaugh, *Impermanence*, 30.
37. See, e.g., *Record of Things Heard*. Cf. DZZ II, 433–34 and 445; Masunaga, *A Primer*, 13, 30.
38. My translation, compare DZZ II, 253.
39. Heine, *Did Dōgen Go to China?*, 138–39.
40. See chapter 3, fn. 56 for details of this document.
41. 又只假令ニ觀法ナンドニスベキ事ニ非ラズ、又無事ヲ造テ思フベキ事ニ非ラズ、眞實ニ現前ノ道理也。*Zuimonki*, vol. 3.20, DZZ II, 452; see also Masunaga, *A Primer*, 39.
42. *Kōin o itazura ni sugusaji to omoute* 光陰ヲ徒ニスグサジト思ウテ、*Zuimonki*, vol. 3.23, DZZ II, 453.
43. すでにむまれたる人、いそぎ剃除鬢髪し、著三法衣して、學佛道すべし。[. . .] しかあるを、人間にむまれながら、いたづらに官途世路を貪求し、むなしく國王大臣のつかはしめとして、一生を夢幻にめぐらし、後世は黒闇におもむき、いまだたのむところなきは至愚なり。DZZ I, 615–16. Quoted in Karaki, "Mujō no keijijōgaku," 327–28.
44. For a classic description of the "god's eye view" and its problems, see Putnam, "Two Philosophical Perspectives," 251–56.
45. This point is widely acknowledged in the literature; see, for example: Kim, *Dōgen Kigen*, 146–48; Arifuku, *Dōgen no Sekai*, 225, 236–37; Stambaugh, *Impermanence*, 30–31; Elberfeld, *Phänomenologie der Zeit*, 266–67; Yorizumi, *Dōgen: Jiko, jikan, sekai wa dono yō ni seiritsu suru no ka*, 93; Raud, "Existential Moment," 160. While this conforms with what Putnam in his above-quoted article describes as the "internalist" view, there is some truth in the almost clichéd observation that classical Western philosophy has largely hesitated to think of reality as dependent on the self in more than epistemological terms. There may be good reasons for ultimately holding on to the notion of an independent real-

ity (if only to retain its critical value)—but it is certainly worth considering the position as it is illustrated in the following quote.

46. Kim, *Dōgen Kigen*, 150. Japanese original: 生といふは、たとへば、人のふねにのるときのごとし。このふねは、われ帆をつかひわれかぢをとれり。われさををさすといへども、ふねわれをのせて、ふねのほかにわれなし。われふねにのりて、このふねをもふねならしむ。この正當恁麼時を功夫參學すべし。この正當恁麼時は、舟の世界にあらざることなし。天も水も岸もみな舟の時節となれり、さらに舟にあらざる時節とおなじからず。このゆゑに、生はわが生ぜしむるなり、われをば生のわれならしむるなり。舟にのれるには、身心依正、ともに舟の機關なり。盡大地、盡虛空、ともに舟の機關なり。生なるわれ、われなる生、それかくのごとし。 DZZ I, 203–4. Cf. Nearman, *The Shōbōgenzō*, 526.

47. Nearman, *The Shōbōgenzō*, 16. Japanese original: いはむや常住を談ずる門には萬法みな常住なり、身と心とをわくことなし。寂滅を談ず門には諸法みな寂滅なり。性と相とをわくことなし。

48. Nearman, *The Shōbōgenzō*, 16.

49. Ueda, "Kaisetsu," 93.

50. Kim, *Dōgen Kigen*, 149; Raud, "Existential Moment," 156.

51. Stone, *Original Enlightenment and the Transformation of Medieval Japanese Buddhism*, 381. The passage in question reads 是法住法位世間相常住 ("this dharma abides in its dharma-position, the attributes of the world constantly abide"), T 262.9: 9b10. 法位 also appears with some frequency in the *Prajñāpāramitā* sutras and related commentaries.

52. English translation until "not return to life again after death": Raud, "Existential Moment," 156. The ensuing sentences are my own translation. Japanese original: たき木、はひとなる、さらにかへりてたき木となるべきにあらず。しかあるを、灰はのち、薪はさきと見取すべからず。しるべし、薪は薪の法位に住して、さきありのちあり。前後ありといへども、前後際斷せり。灰は灰の法位にありて、のちありさきあり。かのたき木、はひとなりぬるのち、さらに薪とならざるがごとく、人のしぬるのち、さらに生とならず。しかあるを、生の死になるといはざるは、佛法のさだまれるならひなり、このゆゑに不生といふ。死の生にならざる、法輪のさだまれる佛轉なり、このゆゑに不滅といふ。生も一時のくらゐなり、死も一時のくらゐなり。たとへば、冬と春のごとし。冬の春となるとおもはず、春の夏となるといはぬなり。 DZZ I, 8.

53. Raud, "Existential Moment," 156–57.

54. Ibid., 159. In his ideas about the relation between the moment and duration, Raud's proposition matches with Akiyama's idea mentioned in the preceding chapter. Raud, however, makes no mention of Akiyama's work.

55. See, for example, the pertinent contributions by de la Vallée Poussin, Gupta, and Stcherbatsky in Prasad, *Essays on Time in Buddhism*. See also Rospatt, "The Buddhist Doctrine of Momentariness"; Brown, "Microgenesis and Buddhism: The Concept of Momentariness" for more recent discussions.

56. Akiyama, *Dōgen*, 132–33; Kawamura, " 'Uji' Ni Tsuite," 120; Kim, *Dōgen Kigen*, 148–49; Sugio, "Zengosaidan—setsuna shōmetsu no ronri"; Hoshi, "Dōgen ni okeru jikan," 310–11.

57. Kim, *Dōgen Kigen*, 138.

58. Heine, *Dimensions of Time*, 89; Stambaugh, *Impermanence*, 25; Elberfeld, *Phänomenologie der Zeit*.

59. Raud, "Existential Moment," 153.
A similar statement is made by Stambaugh in *Impermanence*, 48.

60. Raud, "Existential Moment," 160.

61. Ibid., 159.

62. Kim, *Dōgen Kigen*, 148. See also Heine, *Readings*, 133.

Taken from the following passage: しるべし、今生の人身は、四大五蘊、因和合してかりになせり、八苦つねにあり。いはんや刹那刹那に生滅してさらにとどまらず、いはんや一弾指のあひだに六十五の刹那生滅すといへども、みづからくらきによりて、いまだしらざるなり。すべて一日夜があひだに、六十四億九万九千九百八十の刹那ありて五蘊生滅すといへども、しらざるなり。あはれむべし、われ生滅すといへども、みづからしらざること。DZZ I, 607. For other translations, see Nearman, *The Shōbōgenzō*, 911–12; Tanahashi, *Treasury*, 802–3.

63. Notably, Dōgen's calculation deviates from the tradition by roughly 10^{-3}, making the *setsuna* even shorter than the earlier sources: The *Kusharon* 倶舎論, Fasc. 12, calculates 120 *setsuna* = 1 *tasetsuna* 怛刹那 (Skt. *tatkṣaṇa*), 60 *tasetsuna* = 1 *rōbaku* 臘縛 (skt. *lava*, alt. transliteration *rayo* 羅予・羅預), 30 *rōbaku* = 1 *mukoritta* 牟呼栗多 (skt. *muhūrta*, alt. translation *shuyu* 須臾), and 30 *mukoritta* = 1 day and night (T 1558.29: 62b13–19), so 6'480'000 *setsuna* = 24 h = 86400 sec. This means that 75 *setsuna* = 1 sec or 1 *setsuna* = 0.013 sec. The *Maka Sōgiritsu* 摩訶僧祇律, Fasc. 17 calculates 20 *nen* = 1 *shun* 瞬, 20 *shun* = 1 *danji* 弾指 (snap of the fingers), 20 *danji* = 1 *rayo* (*rōbaku*, *lava*), 20 *rayo* = 1 *shuyu* 30 *shuyu* = 1 day and night (T 1425.22: 360a11–16), so 24h = 4'800'000 *setsuna*, leading to 1 *setsuna* = 0.018 sec.

64. Kazue, "Shōbōgenzō no jikanron"; Dumoulin, "Genjōkōan"; Kim, *Dōgen Kigen*, 148–51.

65. Abe, *A Study of Dōgen*, 132.

66. I quote Dumoulin's German in the translation given by Stambaugh, *Impermanence*, 49. For the original, see Dumoulin, "Genjōkōan," 435, fn. 19.

67. Raud, "Existential Moment," 154–57.

68. Kim, *Dōgen Kigen*, 148–49; Sugio, "Zengosaidan—setsuna shōmetsu no ronri"; Hoshi, "Dōgen ni okeru jikan"; Ishii, " 'Zengo saidan' ni tsuite"; Steineck, "Time Is Not Fleeting: Thoughts of a Medieval Zen Buddhist."

69. Kim, *Dōgen Kigen*, 148, 151. Ishii, "Zengo saidan to *Uji* no kyōryaku," forcefully argues in favor of a reading that concedes that dharmas exist for a certain duration of time and undergo changes (coming and going).

70. Yorizumi Mitsuko has pointed to the long history of such a view in the Buddhist tradition. The "Questions of King Milinda" (*Milinda pañha*) already used the example of a lamp burning through the night to explain trans-temporal identity on the basis of impermanence. As Yorizumi sums up: "[The lamp] may not be identical as a fixed substance, but insofar as its flame continues to burn, it is not something separate or different either." つまり、実体として固定されているのでないという意味では同一ではないが、それが焔火として連続性を持つという意味では別異ではないと言うのである。 Yorizumi, *Dōgen: Jiko, jikan, sekai*, 209.

71. Ishii, " 'Zengo saidan' ni tsuite," 47. Ishii's expression is *aru teido no 'ittei shita jōtai' no jizoku* ある程度の「一定した状態」の持続, literally: "the continuance of a 'state' that is, to some degree, 'consistently defined.' "

72. Maraldo, "Negotiating the Divide of Death in Japanese Buddhism: Dōgen's Difference," 17–18.

73. Maraldo himself takes a different approach to these statements, saying that there is "no birth or life, no arising" because "there is nothing to which to contrast birth or life"—probably in the sense that in the situation of life, there is no death, and vice versa (ibid.). I find that difficult to understand, and also an unnecessary imputation, as the denial of an abiding substance suffices to comprehend these statements. Note further that there is another passage in the *Treasury* where Dōgen mentions that at every moment in life, there is also cessation/death within the living body (*Zenki*, DZZ I, 203).

74. *Mu no jikogentei no okoru wa tada kotsuzen toshite okoru nomi, muriyū ni shite higōriteki de aru.* 無の自己限定の起るはただ忽然として起るのみ、無理由にして非合理的である。 ("The self-determination of nothingness occurs spontaneously, it is without reason and irrational.") Akiyama, *Dōgen no kenkyū*, 131.

75. The variety in the possible readings of the Lotus Sutra passage in question is expressed in the following translations: "All dharmas dwell in their Dharma positions; the forms in the world are always present." Hurvitz, *Scripture of the Lotus Blossom of the Fine Dharma*, 41. "All things abide in their fixed order, [hence] the world abides forever"; or "This stable laws and order [are] / Immovable [and] ever abide in the world." Kato and Soothill, *The Threefold Lotus Sutra*, 70. For the history of its interpretation within Japanese, esp. Tendai Buddhism, see Stone, *Original Enlightenment*, 29, and 381–82.

76. See Chapter 3, fn. 56 for details of this document.

77. *Jikō wa oshimu ni yorite todomaruka* 時光ハヲシムニヨリテトドマルカ。 *Zuimonki* vol. 5.5, DZZ II, 470; see also Masunaga, *A Primer*, 64.

78. *Kōin o itazurani sugosu koto naku gakudō seyo*. 時光ヲイタヅラニ過スコトナク學道セヨ. DZZ II, 470.

79. See, e.g., *Zuimonki* 1.7, DZZ II, 422; Masunaga, *A Primer*, 99–100; 103–4.

80. *Zuimonki* 2.19, DZZ II, 437; 3.22, DZZ II, 453; cf. Masunaga, *A Primer*, 40–41.

81. *Zuimonki* 6.25, DZZ II, 492; cf. Masunaga, *A Primer*, 94–95.
82. DZZ II, 362.
83. *Tenzō kyōkun* 典座教訓, DZZ II, 295–303, dated spring Katei 3 (1237). For the reception of this work, see Akitsu, "Dōgen zenji ikō no 'tenzo kyōkun' no denshin to juyō"; Sawashiro, "Sengo kara gendai ni okeru *Tenzo kyōkun* no tenkai: Toku ni shūmon gai de no dōkō ni tsuite." For a recent assimilation into ecological discourse, see Wirth, "When Washing Rice, Know That the Water Is Your Own Life: An Essay on Dōgen in the Age of Fast Food."
84. Cf. DZZ II, 295; Leighton and Okumura, *Dōgen's Pure Standards*, 34–35.
85. Cf. DZZ II, 296–97; Leighton and Okumura, *Dōgen's Pure Standards*, 36.
86. Cf. DZZ II, 298–303; Leighton and Okumura, *Dōgen's Pure Standards*, 39–49. And see Wirth, "When Washing Rice, Know That the Water Is Your Own Life," 243.
87. Nagai, "Tenzo kyōkun senjutsu ito no kōsatsu," 5, 8.

Chapter 6

1. DZZ I, 194.
2. According to Kawamura Kōdō, *Dōgen Zenshi zenshū*, vol. 1, 246. Steven Heine follows Kawamura; see Heine, *Did Dōgen Go to China?*, 242.
3. The colophone of the latter says it was actually delivered as a lecture to the monastery's assembly, while "Transmitting the Robe" is described as simply having been "recorded" (*ki* 記). The most probable interpretation is that Dōgen drafted a manuscript that he used for an informal lecture on the said day and later redacted it repeatedly.
4. *Extensive Record*, vol. 1.14, DZZ II, 10; ET Leighton and Okumura, *Extensive Record*, 86.
5. Winter solstice, according to *Extensive Record*, vol. 1.25, coincided with the new moon/beginning of the eleventh month; there was an intercalary tenth month that year. Cf. DZZ II, 12.
6. In the chronological order of composition, "What Is:Time" is the eleventh text in the 75-fascicle redaction, and the eighth text written after Dōgen started to regularly produce such expositions in the vernacular in 1239. See the table in Heine, *Did Dōgen Go to China?*, 151.
7. On this pattern and its function in Japanese rhetoric, see Senko Kumiya Maynard, *Principles of Japanese Discourse*, 33–39.
8. Adam, *Les Textes: Types et prototypes*.
9. Chapter 1, pp. 17–18.
10. DZZ I, 189. See chapter 1, pp. 1, 17–18. In the following, I will also refer to the section numbering used by Elberfeld (*Phänomenologie der Zeit*, 2004, 385–94; abbreviated here as E), and to the page numbers in the open access

translation by Nearman (Nearman, *The Shōbōgenzō*. abbrevited as N). The first two paragraphs mentioned above correspond to E I and II, and N 108–109.

11. DZZ I, 190; E III–IV; N 109–10.

12. DZZ I, 190; E V; N 110.

13. DZZ I, 190–91; E VI–VIII; N 110–12.

14. The compound consists of the character for "now" 今 (Jp. *ima; kon; kin*) preceded by the conjunctive *shi/ni* 而 ("and; also"); it is often used to indicate either contrast or continuity with a previous state of affairs.

15. Heine, *Dimensions of time*, 128.

16. DZZ I, 191; E IX–X; N 112–13.

17. DZZ I, 191–92; E XI; N 113–14.

17. DZZ I, 192; E XII; N 114.

19. DZZ I, 192; E XIII; N 114.

20. DZZ I, 192; E XIV; N 114–15.

21. Taken from *Zongmen liangdeng huiyao*, chapter 19.

22. Nearman, *The Shōbōgenzō*, 115.

23. DZZ I, 193; E XV–XVI; N 115–16.

24. DZZ I, 193; E XVII; N 116. The source is *Zongmen liangdeng hui yao*, Chapter 12.

25. DZZ I, 193–94; E XVIII; N 117–18. "The time when one looks up and unbolts the barrier gate" is Nearman's translation of *kōjō kanrei* 向上関捩.

26. DZZ I, 194; E XIX–XXI; N 118.

27. The other three are transposition of lexical components; reflexive, self-causative utterances; and use of homophonous expression. See Kim, *Dōgen on Meditation and Thinking: A Reflection on His View of Zen*, 65–77. Kim explicitly cites *uji* as an example of the "explication of semantic attributes," 69–70.

28. Stambaugh, *Impermanence* (1990), 26. To illustrate the consensus, here are a few more examples in addition to those already quoted. Ohe speaks of a "doctrine of the self-identity of time and things." Similarly, Shaner summarizes Dōgen's position as "all beings are times such that each particular thing [. . .] is a time." Heine speaks of "complete and harmoniously interpenetrating self-sameness." Arifuku employs traditional Buddhist expressions such as the copula *soku* 即 and the term "non-dual unity" (*funi ichinyo* 不二一如). Tsunoda, reviewing the Japanese literature up to the year 2000, speaks of "mutual identity" (*sōsoku* 相即). Yorizumi uses the phrase "unity of time and being (*jikan to sonzai to no ittaisei* 時間と存在との一体性). Ohe, "Time, Temporality, and Freedom," 82; Shaner, *The Bodymind Experience in Japanese Buddhism: A Phenomenological Perspective of Kūkai and Dōgen*, 150; Heine, *Dimensions of time*, 31; Arifuku, *Dōgen no sekai*, 225, 232; Tsunoda, "Dōgen no jikanron kenkyū," 188; Yorizumi, *Dōgen: Jiko, jikan, sekai*, 88.

29. Rovelli, "'Forget Time': Essay Written for the FQXi Contest on the Nature of Time"; Callender, "Is Time an Illusion?".

30. Luhmann, "Zeit und Handlung—Eine vergessene Theorie"; Elias, *Time: An Essay*.

31. Nearman, *The Shōbōgenzō*, 111; Tanahashi, *Treasury*, 106. Japanese original: しかあれば、松も時なり、竹も時なり。 Ōkubo, "Uji," 191. Quoted e.g., in Kim, *Dōgen Kigen*, 144; Arifuku, *Dōgen no sekai*, 241.

32. Elberfeld, *Phänomenologie der Zeit*, 229, 244.

33. "das Konstellieren von Daseinsfaktoren ist zugleich das Konstellieren von Weltzusammenhängen." Elberfeld, *Phänomenologie der Zeit*, 244.

34. Kim, *Dōgen Kigen*, 143, 145.

35. Yorizumi, *Dōgen*, 93.

36. Tsujiguchi, *Shōbōgenzō*, 162. For a similar statement in the anglophone literature, see e.g., Kim, *Dōgen Kigen*, 143.

37. "'Zeit' im Sinne Dōgens ist *nicht* meßbar." Elberfeld, *Phänomenologie der Zeit*, 239.

38. Heine, *Readings*, 126.

39. Roberts, *Being-Time: A Practitioner's Guide to Dōgen's Shōbōgenzō Uji*, 87.

40. Kim, *Dōgen on Meditation*, 52.

41. As Kim remarks with regard to a case where Dōgen discusses balancing-scales as a metaphor for insight into emptiness: "Emptiness involves the dynamics of weighing and calibration on the one hand and the principle of fairness and reasonableness on the other [. . .] As a result, discriminative discernment regarding differentiation (duality) in our everyday life is intrinsic, not extrinsic, to equality (nonduality)." Kim, *Dōgen on Meditation*, 46.

42. 十二時の長遠短促、いまだ度量せずといへども、これを十二時といふ。 DZZ I, 189. "One calls them 'twelve hours' without having measured the length or brevity of their duration." Cf. Nearman, *The Shōbōgenzō*, 109. This is the sentence Elberfeld takes as evidence that Dōgen denies the measurability of time. Elberfeld, *Phänomenologie der Zeit*, 239.

43. Entry 而 in *Chinese Etymology* 字源.

44. Elberfeld, *Phänomenologie der Zeit*, 260–61.

45. Yorizumi, *Dōgen*, 99; Kim, *Dōgen Kigen*, 146.

46. そして、「今この一瞬」（而今）とは「空」を体得し、世界を現成させるその「一瞬」である。この瞬間は、「空」という無時間に立脚した時間である。宗教哲学的な用語を使うならば、「永遠の今」ということもできよう。 Yorizumi, *Dōgen*, 99.

47. いはゆる山をのぼり河をわたりし時にわれありき、われに時あるべし。われすでにあり、時さるべからず。 DZZ I, 190. Compare the following alternative translations: "When I waded rivers and ascended mountains, I was there. To [that particular] me belongs a particular time. As I am already here and now, time should not depart from me." Kim, *Dōgen*, 146. Elberfeld interpolates personal memory as a mediating term: "Zu der Zeit (toki) als [*ich nach meiner Erinnerung*] den Berg

bestieg und den Fluß überquerte, war ich ja [*nach meiner Erinnerung*]; so muß es [*diese*] Zeit (ji, toki) [*ineins*] mit mir geben (aru). [. . .] Ich bin (ari) schon, so kann [*diese*] Zeit (ji, toki) nicht verschwinden." Elberfeld, *Phänomenologie der Zeit* (2004), 259, 260. Heine translates *sude ni*, which usually means "already" or "inevitably," as "still," and internalizes time into the I: "At the time the mountain was being climbed and the river was being crossed, I was there [as being-time]. Therefore, the time has to be in me. Inasmuch as I am still here, it cannot be that time passes by." Heine, *Readings*, 128–29.

    48. Italics mine. Cf. the original: 時もし去來の相にあらずは、上山の時は有時の而今なり。DZZ I, 190. Cf. Kim, *Dōgen Kigen*, 146.: "If time does not have the quality of coming and going, the occasion of mountaineering is the absolute now of [my] existence-time." Nearman believes that the statement is problematic for Dōgen, and translates: "If time did not have the characteristic of 'coming and going, being continually in flux,' then the time when this I was 'climbing atop the mountain' would have remained forever, eternally comprised of that particular 'time when.'" Nearman, *The Shōbōgenzō*, 110–11. But there is no evidence that Dōgen weighs this proposition differently from the following, that time has the property of coming and going. His argument precisely tries to bring together both views and explain how they can be reconciled. Note that in both cases, the terms "absolute" and "eternally" have no direct counterpart in the Japanese original.

    49. Holbrook, "Does Time Move?," 198; Raud, "Existential Moment" (2012), 158. See also Stambaugh, *Impermanence* (1990), 46–47.

    50. Kim, *Dōgen Kigen*, 152. The characters for *sōsoku sōnyū* are 相即相入.

    51. Steineck, "Time Is Not Fleeting."

    52. Heine, *Readings*, 137.

    53. Ibid., 138.

    54. 時もし去來の相を保任せば、われに有時の而今ある、これ有時なり。Kim, *Dōgen Kigen*, 146. "If time does come and go, the absolute now of existence-time is [still] mine." My translation is close to that of Elberfeld, *Phänomenologie der Zeit*, 261. "Behält die Zeit (toki) die Weise des Gehens und Kommens, so gibt es [*zusammen*] mit mir das gegenwärtige Jetzt von *uji*; dies ist *uji*."

    55. The pertinent passage reads in full in the original: "Zeit [ist] in einem noch viel tieferen Sinne paradox konstituiert, nämlich als Gleichzeitigkeit des Ungleichzeitigen. [. . .] Deshalb können Vergangenheit und Zukunft als komplementäre Zeithorizonte nur gleichzeitig gegeben sein. Es handelt sich immer um Horizonte der Gegenwart, um eine gegenwärtige Vergangenheit und um eine gegenwärtige Zukunft, wobei Gegenwart nichts anderes ist als die Trennlinie, die Grenze, die die Differenz von Vergangenheit und Zukunft konstituiert. Damit reformulieren wir nur, daß alles, was geschieht, gleichzeitig geschieht, auch wenn am Geschehen Bewegung oder Veränderung und damit Vergangenheits- und Zukunftshorizonte ablesbar sind." Luhmann, "Gleichzeitigkeit und Synchronisation," 96.

56. [丈六八尺も]、すなはちわが有時にて一經す、彼處にあるにたれども而今なり。DZZ I, 191. Cf. Elberfeld, *Phänomenologie der Zeit*, 263–64; Kim, *Dōgen Kigen*, 146.

57. Heine, *Dimensions of time*, 53.

58. Elberfeld, *Phänomenologie der Zeit*, 246–47. And see Kim's description of this rhetorical technique in Kim, *Dōgen on Meditation*, 65–66.

59. Tsujiguchi, *Shōbōgenzō*, 178.

60. Tanahashi, *Treasury*, 106; Raud, "Existential Moment," 165; Elberfeld, *Phänomenologie der Zeit*, 267; Kim, *Dōgen Kigen*, 154; Waddell and Abe, *The Heart of Dōgen's Shōbōgenzō*, 51–52; Heine, *Dimensions of Time*, 157; Abe, *A Study of Dōgen*, 83–85.

61. Nihon kokugo daijiten dainihan henshū iinkai et al., *Nihon kokugo daijiten*. Entry *keireki* 經歷.

62. 有時に經歷の功德あり。いはゆる今日より明日に經歷す、今日より昨日に經歷す、昨日より今日に經歷す。今日より今日に經歷す、明日より明日に經歷す。經歷はそれ時の功德なるがゆゑに。DZZ I, 191.

63. *Gakushikitaru bekarazu* 學しきたるべからず: I have translated the perfective aspect of *gakushikitaru* as "in the usual way" (more literally: "as one has so far come to study it").

64. *Jinkai wa* 盡界は: *jinkai* can be read more simply as "the whole world" or—closer to Buddhist terminology—"all spheres" (meaning the spheres of the sensible forms, of sublimely sensible forms, and that without sensible form), but since the paragraph is an explanation of how "transiting through phases" is the way in which everything depends on "the exertion of my powers," I here read it in a more active sense, as *kai o tsukusu*.

65. 經歷といふは、風雨の東西するがごとく學しきたるべからず。盡界は不動轉なるにあらず、不進退なるにあらず、經歷なり。經歷は、たとへば春のごとし。春に許多般の樣子あり、これを經歷といふ。外物なきに經歷すると參學すべし。たとへば、春の經歷はかならず春を經歷するなり。經歷は春にあらざれども、春の經歷なるがゆゑに、經歷いま春の時に成道せり。審細に參來參去すべし。經歷をいふに、境は外頭にして、能經歷の法は東にむきて百千世界をゆきすぎて、百千劫をふるとおもふは、佛道の參學、これのみを專一にせざるなり。DZZ I, 192.

66. 「時」は時間の経過ではなく「有」（存在）であり「經歷」（在り方）である, Tsunoda, "Dōgen zenji no jikanron," 85.

67. Kim, *Dōgen Kigen*, 148, 151; Tsunoda, "Kenkyū dōkō Dōgen zenji no jikanron kenkyū," 190, 192; Stambaugh, *Impermanence*, 44.

68. Tsujiguchi, *Shōbōgenzō*, 181–82.

69. The various shifts involved are well summed up in Raud, "Existential Moment," 165. However, in line with his reading of Dōgen as a metaphysical momentarist, he takes them to relate to merely a "linguistic model" (ibid.).

70. 時は一向にすぐるとのみ計功して、未到と解會せず。DZZ I, 192.

71. 古今の時、かさなれるにあらず、ならびつもれるにあらざ[る]。 DZZ I, 192.

72. いま世界に排列せるむまひつじをあらしむるも、住法位の恁麼なる昇降上下なり。 DZZ I, 191.

73. われを丈六金身にあらずとのがれんとする、またすなはち有時の片片なり、未證據者の看看なり。 DZZ I, 191.

74. この時、三頭八臂にて盡界を證し、丈六金身にて盡界を證す。それ盡界をもて盡界を界盡するを、究盡するとはいふなり。 DZZ I, 191.

75. 丈六金身をもて丈六金身するを、發心修行菩提涅槃と現成する、すなはち有なり、時なり。盡時を盡有と究盡するのみ。 DZZ I, 191.

76. われを排列しおきて盡界とせり、この盡界の頭頭物物を時時なりと見すべし。物物の相礙せざるは、時時の相礙せざるがごとし。このゆゑに同時發心あり、同心發時あり。および修行成道もかくのごとし。われを排列してわれこれをみるなり。自己の時なる道理、それかくのごとし。 DZZ I, 190. See also Nearman, *The Shōbōgenzō*, 109; Tanahashi, *Treasury*, 105.

77. Ishii, "Zengo saidan to Uji no kyōryaku," 693–95, 698.

78. See above, chapter 3, pp. 59, 70.

79. *Jiji muge* 事々無礙. On the connection to Kegon in this passage, see Elberfeld, *Phänomenologie der Zeit*, 245; Winfield, *Icons and Iconoclasm in Japanese Buddhism*, 46–48; Girard, "Did Huayan's Teachings Influence Dōgen's Thought?," 241–50. Winfield posits that Dōgen's "holochronic" view entails that one "abandons linear thinking" (48). In contrast, Girard emphasizes the link between the holistic and the sequential view, which is closer to the interpretation presented here. To illustrate how Dōgen understands the mutual permeation and non-obstruction of things, Elberfeld helpfully points to the boat-riding passage in the instruction "Comprehensive Occasion" quoted above at pp. 126–27; cf. DZZ I, 203; Nearman, *The Shōbōgenzō*, 526; Tanahashi, *Treasury*, 451.

80. わがいま盡力經歷にあらざれば、一法一物も現成することなし、經歷することなしと參學すべし。 DZZ I, 191.

81. Awaya, "Shōbōgenzō ni okeru jinjippōkai"; "'Shōbōgenzō' ni okeru jin no shisō (Ichi)"; "'Shōbōgenzō' ni okeru jin no shisō (Ni)."

82. Awaya, "'Shōbōgenzō' ni okeru jin no shisō (Ni)," 71.

83. たとひ半究盡の有時も、半有時の究盡なり。 DZZ I, 192.

84. 眉目は山海なるべし、山海は眉目なるゆゑに。その教伊揚は山をみるべし、その教伊瞬は海を宗すべし。[...] 山も時なり、海も時なり。時にあらざれば山海あるべからず、山海の而今に時あらずとすべからず。 DZZ I, 193.

85. For a general critique of reading Dōgen's pertinent writings in line with a phenomenology of experience, instead of a metaphysics, see Schilbrack, "Metaphysics in Dōgen." The main objects of his critique are Kasulis, *Zen Action/Zen Person*; and Shaner, *The Bodymind Experience in Japanese Buddhism*.

Notes to Chapter 7 | 273

Chapter 7

1. *Busso* 佛祖, DZZ I, 454–57.

2. An allusion to the origin story of the "heart to heart" transmission authorizing the various Zen lineages: The Buddha twirls a flower in his fingers in place of a verbal teaching. Cf. Aitken, *The Gateless Gate*, 35; Nishimura, *Mumonkan*, 43.

3. 佛祖の現成は、佛祖を擧拈して奉覲するなり。過現當來のみにあらず、佛向上よりも向上なるべし。まさに佛祖の面目を保任せるを拈じて、禮拜し相見す。佛祖の功徳を現擧せしめて住持しきたり、體證しきたれり。 DZZ I, 454. Cf. Nearman, *The Shōbōgenzō*, 156; Tanahashi, *Treasury*, 165.

4. 古來今の佛事、ことごとくこの圓鑑にむかひてみることをう。 DZZ I, 175, cf. Nearman, *The Shōbōgenzō*, 210; Tanahashi, *Treasury*, 206.

5. 十二時もし鏡にあらずよりは、いかでか照古あらん。十二時もし鏡にあらずは、いかでか照今あらん。いはゆる十二時は十二面なり、十二面は十二鏡なり、古今は十二時の所使なり。 DZZ I, 179, cf. Nearman, *The Shōbōgenzō*, 216; Tanahashi, *Treasury*, 210.

6. *Haku zassui* 百雜碎 cf. DZZ I, 178; Nearman, *The Shōbōgenzō*, 220; Tanahashi, *Treasury*, 209.

7. 明鏡を道得ならしむるに、百雜碎なるべきがゆゑに。雜碎のかかれるところ、明鏡なり。さきに未雜碎なるときあり、のちにさらに不雜碎ならん時節を管見することなかれ。ただ百雜碎なり。 DZZ I, 182. Cf. Nearman, *The Shōbōgenzō*, 220; Tanahashi, *Treasury*, 214.

8. Heine, *Readings*, 125.

9. Heine, *Readings*, 124, 128.

10. いのちは光陰にうつされてしばらくもとどめがたし。紅顔いづくへかさりにし、たづねんとするに蹤跡なし。つらつら觀ずるところに、往事のふたたびあふべからざるをおもし。 DZZ I, 162. Cf. Nearman, *The Shōbōgenzō*, 364; Tanahashi, *Treasury*, 325.

11. 赤心もとどまらず、片片として往來す。たとひまことありといふとも、吾我のほとりにとどこほるものにあらず。 DZZ I, 162. Cf. Nearman, *The Shōbōgenzō*, 364–65; Tanahashi, *Treasury*, 325.

12. いづれの善巧方便ありてか、すぎにし一日をふたたびかへしえたる。 *Gyōji* 行持, DZZ I, 135.

13. 佛祖の大道、かならず無上の行持あり。道環して斷絶せず、發心修行、菩提涅槃、しばらくの間隙あらず、行持道環なり。このゆゑに、みづからの強爲にあらず、他の強爲にあらず、不曾染汚の行持なり。 DZZ I, 122. Cf. Nearman, *The Shōbōgenzō*, 374; Tanahashi, *Treasury*, 332. Note that the expression 道環 is introduced in conjunction with the auxiliary verb *-su*, pointing to an activity and not a fixed structure. Note further that all verbs in the final clause of the quote are active, pointing to a medial understanding of the process: Neither side is an agent working on the passive other, but within and by way of participating in the

process of practice, both sides (Buddha ancestors and practitioners) are sustained in completion of the way.

14. Cf. DZZ I, 122; Nearman, *The Shōbōgenzō*, 374–75; Tanahashi, *Treasury*, 332–33.

15. 一日の行持、これ諸佛の種子なり、諸佛の行持なり。 DZZ I, 123。 Cf. Nearman, *The Shōbōgenzō*, 375; Tanahashi, *Treasury*, 333.

16. 行持のいまは自己の本有元住にあらず、行持のいまは自己に去來出入するにあらず。いまといふ道は、行持よりさきにあるにはあらず、行持現成するをいまといふ。 DZZ I, 123. Cf. Nearman, *The Shōbōgenzō*, 375; Tanahashi, *Treasury*, 333.

17. See chapter 3, p. 164.

18. "Confirmation" / *Juki* 授記, DZZ I, 195–202. Cf. Nearman, *The Shōbōgenzō*, 445–57; Tanahashi, *Treasury*, 387–96.

19. *Bodaisō* 菩提相. DZZ I, 201. Translation after Tanahashi, *Treasury*, 395.

20. 維摩詰所説經, T 475.14: 542b.

21. Tanahashi, *Treasury*, 388. Cf. DZZ I, 195. According to Buddhist and other traditions originating in South Asia, Mount Sumeru is "an enormous mountain . . . at the center of a generally flat, disk-shaped world that is filled with oceans, continents, and smaller mountains . . . [It] is generally understood as the largest single object in the world, and as such it frequently serves as a basis for metaphors of enormity and strength." Huntington, "Buddhist Cosmology," section "Some Common Features of Buddhist Cosmology."

22. DZZ I, 202. Cf. Nearman, *The Shōbōgenzō*, 456; Tanahashi, *Treasury*, 395–96.

23. いはくの成佛は、かならず相繼するなり。 DZZ I, 199. English translation: Tanahashi, *Treasury*, 392.

24. In the course of co-authoring a chapter on time in medieval Japanese religion, December 2020–August 2021.

25. 釋迦牟尼佛、まさしく迦葉佛に嗣法せり、とならひきたるなり。釋迦佛の嗣法してのちに、迦葉佛は入涅槃すと參學するなり。 . . . かくのごとく佛佛相嗣して、いまにおよびきたれるによりて、箇箇佛ともに正嗣なり。つらなるにあらず、あつまれるにあらず。 . . . もしひとへに釋迦佛よりおこれりといはば、わづかに二千餘年なり、ふるきにあらず。 . . . この佛嗣は、しかのごとく學するにあらず。釋迦佛は迦葉佛に嗣法すると學し、迦葉佛は釋迦佛に嗣法せりと學するなり。かくのごとく學するとき、まさに諸佛諸祖の嗣法にてあるなり。 DZZ I, 346. Cf. Nearman, *The Shōbōgenzō*, 171; Tanahashi, *Treasury*, 178–79.

26. Cf. DZZ I, 78; Nearman, *The Shōbōgenzō*, 565; Tanahashi, *Treasury*, 468.

27. The term that forms the title of the instruction usually refers to the practice of Zen novices to travel far and wide to meet and study with enlightened masters. Dōgen in this instruction turns the phrase around to say that it is less about moving around in space than about "penetrating study by fully probing the realm" (*kyūkyō santetsu* 究竟參徹; DZZ I, 489. Cf. Nearman, *The Shōbōgenzō*, 718; Tanahashi, *Treasury*, 609.

28. 釋迦老子は玄沙老漢と同參するゆゑに古佛なり。玄沙老漢は釋迦老子と同參なるゆゑに兒孫なり。...いはゆる釋迦老子と玄沙老漢と、同時同參の時節を遍參功夫するなり。 DZZ I, 491. Cf. Tanahashi, *Treasury*, 612; Nearman, *The Shōbōgenzō*, 522.

29. DZZ I, 525–31, cf. Nearman, *The Shōbōgenzō*, 765–73; Tanahashi, *Treasury*, 646–54.

30. 釋迦牟尼佛言、明星出現時、我與大地有情、同時成道。しかあれば、發心・修行・菩提・涅槃は、同時の發心・修行・菩提・涅槃なるべし。佛道の身心は草木瓦礫なり、風雨水火なり。これをめぐらして佛道ならしむる、すなはち發心なり。 DZZ I, 528. "Thus, aspiration, practice, enlightenment, and nirvana must be simultaneously aspiration, practice, enlightenment, and nirvana [with all sentient beings]. The body and mind of the Buddha way is grass, trees, tiles, and pebbles, as well as wind, rain, water, and fire. To turn them around and make them the Buddha way—this is the aspiration for enlightenment." Tanahashi, *Treasury*, 650.

31. Tanahashi, *Treasury*, 650. 千億發の發心は、さだめて一發心の發なり。千億人の發心は、一發心の發なり。一發心は千億の發心なり、修證轉法もまたかくのごとし。 DZZ I, 528.

32. Yorizumi, *Shōbōgenzō*, 121, 141–43, 147; Heine, *Readings*, 127, 129.

33. 黃金妙相といふは、著衣喫飯なり, DZZ I, 500.

34. Yorizumi, *Dōgen no shisō*, 200, 205.

35. *Milindapañha*. The earliest parts of the text were formulated between 100 BCE and 200 CE, with later accretions. For more background and discussion of sources and origin, see Kubica, "Reading the *Milindapañha*"; Levman, "Revisiting the *Milindapañha*."

36. Yorizumi, *Dōgen no shisō*, 209; cf. Rhys Davids. *The Questions of King Milinda*, 64.

37. "The problem is how to save morality from legalism, conformism, and moralism so as to attain authenticity, freedom, and purity, without retreating from moral involvement." Kim, *Dōgen Kigen*, 213. See also Heine, *Readings*, 224.

38. Yorizumi, *Dōgen no shisō*, 216–17.

39. Ibid., 219.

40. As Akiyama has pointed out, the Edo period Sōtō scholar Tenkei Denson (1648–1735) opened the debate by denying the authenticity of the fascicle on "Deep Certitude about Cause and Effect," which most strongly proposed a linear understanding of karma. Akiyama, *Dōgen no kenkyū*, 174.

41. See chapter 2 and the summaries by Steven Heine, *Shifting Shape, Shaping Text: Philosophy and Folklore in the Fox Kôan*, 109–24; *Did Dōgen Go to China?*, 76–82; *Readings*, 220–25. The first (*Shifting Shape*) is most specific on the topic discussed here.

42. Yorizumi, *Dōgen no shisō*, 231; Kagamishima, *Dōgen zenji to sono shūfū*, 219.

43. Heine, *Readings*, 128. See also ibid., 126–29, which bases itself on Yorizumi, *Shōbōgenzō*, 120–26, 142–53; Yorizumi, *Dōgen no shisō*, 223–39.

44. Kim, *Dōgen Kigen*, 206; Kim, *Dōgen on Meditation*, 1, 75.

45. DZZ I, 544–51; Nearman, *The Shōbōgenzō*, 823–33; Tanahashi, *Treasury*, 705–14, and DZZ I, 676–81; Nearman, *The Shōbōgenzō*, 1019–27; Tanahashi, *Treasury*, 851–57.

46. Rendered, for example, as the second case in the "Gateless Gate" collection, and as case 102 in Dōgen's "300 Cases Treasury," cf. DZZ II, 219–20; Loori and Tanahashi, *The True Dharma Eye*, 136–37.

47. For a review on this question and the creation of Zen monastic rules, see Jia, "The Creation and Codification of Monastic Regulations at Mount Baizhang."

48. For a brief account of Huangbo's position, see Steineck, "Ichlosigkeit als wahres Selbst."

49. Heine, *Shifting Shape, Shaping Text*, 105.

50. Ibid., 106.

51. Yorizumi, *Dōgen no shisō*, 231.

52. Heine, *Shifting Shape, Shaping Text*, 106.

53. This is how Tanahashi, *Treasury*, 707, renders the phrase: いまだかつて落不落の論あらず、昧不昧の道あらず。DZZ I, 545.

54. Heine, *Shifting Shape, Shaping Text*, 120–21. See also DZZ I, 549; Tanahashi, *Treasury*, 707. With regard to Heine's reading of "Great Practice" and "Deep Certitude about Cause and Effect" as ambiguous about the belief in "supernatural beings" (*Shifting Shape, Shaping Text*, 118–19), note that the existence of deities is no more or less in doubt for Dōgen than that of human beings; the question is whether one can rely on them for salvation.

55. Tanahashi, *Treasury*, 711; cf. DZZ I, 549.

56. DZZ I, 545–46. Cf. Nearman, *The Shōbōgenzō*, 825–26. Tanahashi, *Treasury*, 707–8 omits the deictic reference of "cause and effect" to "great practice" in the beginning and is in general less precise.

57. Heine, *Shifting Shape, Shaping Text*, 106.

58. DZZ I, 277–84, dated En'ō 2.8.15 (September 9, 1240). Cf. Nearman, *The Shōbōgenzō*, 79–88; Tanahashi, *Treasury*, 95–103.

59. The passage reads in full: "Cause and effect / fruit of the good here are both actualizations of the *kōan* of 'implementing [the good].' The cause is not before, the effect is not afterwards, instead the cause comes to full completion, the effect comes to full completion. One feels the effect as awaited by the cause, but they are not before and after, because there is the saying that before and after are one." この善の因果、おなじく奉行の現成公案なり。因はさき、果はのちなるにあらざれども、因圓滿し、果圓滿す。因等法等、果等法等なり。因にまたれて果感ずといへども、前後にあらず、前後等の道あるがゆゑに。DZZ I, 281; quoted in Yorizumi, *Dōgen no shisō*, 225.

60. *Shinri sekai* 真理世界.
61. *Kongenteki kiban* 根源的基盤.
62. Yorizumi, *Dōgen no shisō*, 225.
63. 「応報も当為もすべての規範的言説が無化され」, Yorizumi, *Dōgen no shisō*, 231. One can even translate this as "all normative discourse is annihilated."
64. *Eien no shinri no sekai* 永遠の真理の世界, *sōtai teki na mayoi no sekai* 相対的な迷いの世界. Yorizumi, *Dōgen no shisō*, 232.
65. Cf. DZZ I, 691; Nearman, *The Shōbōgenzō*, 1041; Tanahashi, *Treasury*, 791.
66. Note that the same idea of the temporal dilation of retribution is also addressed in a formal instruction from early 1252 (*Extensive Record*, vol. 7.485, DZZ II, 126–27, cf. Leighton and Okumura, *Extensive Record*, 430–32), and that Dōgen repeatedly emphasizes the importance of understanding karma in other formal instructions from the final two years of his life: See vol. 7.504, 510 (on the Fox *kōan*), 517 (again on karma in the three times), DZZ II, 133, 134, 135, 137; cf. Leighton and Okumura, *Extensive Record*, 450, 454–55, 460–61.
67. Cf. *Fushuku hanpō*, DZZ II, 353.
68. *Mappō* 末法.
69. On the origin of the concept, see the classic study by Nattier, *Once Upon a Future Time*, esp. 61–65.
70. For medieval Japan, see, e.g., Ōsumi, "Jizoku to henkaku—shinwa kara rekishi e," 133–34; Mezaki, "Matsudai/mappō to jōdo shinkō;" Eubanks, *Miracles of Book and Body: Buddhist Textual Culture and Medieval Japan*, 100–1.
71. On the question of these calculations, see Fischer, *Studien zur Entwicklungsgeschichte des Mappō-Gedankens und zum Mappō-tōmyō-ki [von Saichō]*, 120–21; Ozawa, *Mappō to masse no shisō*, 65–67.
72. Stone, "Seeking Enlightenment in the Last Age"; Marra, "The Development of 'Mappō' Thought in Japan (I)"; Marra, "The Development of 'Mappō' Thought in Japan (II)."
73. Fischer, *Studien*, 166–69; Orzech, *Politics and Transcendent Wisdom: The Scripture for Humane Kings in the Creation of Chinese Buddhism*, 119–23; Kikutō, "Kamakura kyūbukkyō to mappō shisō."
74. Question 15, DZZ I, 742; cf. Tanahashi, *Treasury*, 17–18; Stone, "Seeking Enlightenment in the Last Age," 38. Ishikawa Rikizan has pointed to a statement in "Things Heard about the Treasury" in which the idea is explicitly characterized as an "expedient means" (*hōben* 方便); Ishikawa, "'Mappō Tōmyōki' to Dōgen Zen," 177, referring to Dōgen et al., *Shōbōgenzō; Shōbōgenzō Zuimonki*, 406–7.
75. DZZ I, 287; cf. Tanahashi, *Treasury*, 139. See also *Kesa kudoku*, DZZ I, 628–30; 637.
76. *Extensive Record*, vol. 5.383, DZZ II, 93–95. The next recorded instruction is from the memorial day of Rujing, which was on the seventeenth day of the seventh lunar month. DZZ I, 95. Note that from the late 1240s onward, the

278 | Notes to Chapter 8

record contains an increased number of explanatory or argumentative formal instructions; possibly, after the completion of the 75-fascicle version, Dōgen used this occasion more than he did previously for a discursive form of teaching.

77. Quotes in English from Leighton and Okumura, *Extensive Record*, 340–41. Cf. DZZ II, 383–84.

78. Cf. DZZ II, 384–85; Leighton and Okumura, 341–44.

Chapter 8

1. This metaphor was famously applied to the history of Japanese thought by Maruyama Masao, see his "Rekishi ishiki no 'kosō.'"

2. DZZ I, 112; see also above, chapter 3, p. 57.

3. Kim, *Dōgen Kigen*, 142; Shaner, *The Bodymind Experience in Japanese Buddhism*, 175–79; Stambaugh, *Impermanence*, 63–66; Goodhew and Loy, "Momo, Dogen, and the Commodification of Time," 236–41; Raud, "Existential Moment." See also the discussion below.

4. See especially Heinemann, *Der Weg des Übens im ostasiatischen Mahāyāna*, 148–59. See also the discussion above in chapter 6,

5. Hoshi, "Dōgen ni okeru jikan," 314–16. For another description and analysis of this graphic representation, which combines a linear with the circular element, see Winfield, *Icons and Iconoclasm in Japanese Buddhism*, 50–52.

6. DZZ I, 224–26.

7. See above, chapter 4.

8. The traditional image of a cycle or wheel of life and death (*shōji rinne* 生死輪廻) is a two-dimensional projection of this movement. Dōgen in "Karma in the Three Times" posits a forward vector of causation-retribution: in this life, in the next life, or in a much later life. If the wheel is accordingly imagined as that of a forward-moving cart (as opposed to that of a watermill), it is evident that a certain point on the wheel touches the ground and the air in different places with every turn.

9. See, e.g., the following statement by Raud: "Western philosophy has traditionally postulated a continuous identity of things for the greater good of (linguistic) clarity and thus has preferred the durational mode of being to the momentary, while most Buddhist philosophers have stubbornly refused to give up immediate existence and are willing to negotiate the stability and precision of their intellectual instruments instead." Raud, "Existential Moment," 154.

10. Raud, "Existential Moment," 156.

11. Heine, *Dimensions of Time*, 127.

12. Roberts, *Being-Time*, 87–89. The reference is to Heine, *Dimensions of Time*, 53.

13. Heine, *Dimensions of Time*, 136.
14. Kopf, *Beyond Personal Identity*, 185.
15. Goodhew and Loy, "Commodification of Time," 100–1.
16. Other forms of goal-directed action (e.g., preserving food and cooking meals for the monastic community) can be integrated into that process, although Dōgen apparently believed that they demand a certain degree of experience and training to avoid becoming preoccupied with them.
17. Yanagida, "Zen no jikanron," 127; Nishio, "Zeami no geijutsuron no tokushitsu to Dōgen no eikyō;" Ōtomo, *Zeami to Zen*. The main reference relating to unceasing practice is to the final chapter of the "Mirror Held to the Flower" (*Kakyō* 花鏡); cf. Ijichi, Omote, and Kuriyama, *Renga ronshū. Nōgaku ronshū. Haironshū*, 339. Ōtomo's argument that Dōgen's texts had a direct influence on Zeami (through the latter's acquaintance with Bonsei, who collated one of the oldest extant copies of the vernacular *Treasury*) deserves closer scrutiny, which I hope to undertake on another occasion.
18. Cf. Eihei shōbō genzō shūsho taisei hankō kai, *Eihei shūsho taisei* 12, 212–13. Yamauchi Shūnyū, to date the most eminent modern commentator on Senne, has surmised that the latter ultimately found these expressions "a nut too hard to crack" (歯が立たないこと), *Shōbō genzō kikigaki shō no kenkyū* 1, 281. However, there is also evidence that he was consciously steering the interpretation of the text in the direction of a "two truths" reading. In a later part of his commentary, he states: "Within the teaching, affairs 事 are treated as different, but the principle 理 is taken to be without differentiation." Eihei shōbō genzō shūsho taisei hankō kai, *Eihei shūsho taisei* 12, 215.
19. Kyōgō simply insists that every instance comprises the totality of time, without any connection to before and after. Consequently, he excludes the notion of "transiting through phases" from the enlightened view of time. In his view, Dōgen only comments on the passage of time because the Buddha's teaching refrains from picking and choosing. Eihei shōbō genzō shūsho taisei hankō kai, *Eihei shūsho taisei* 12, 192.
20. Giun's commentary, recently translated into English by Heine, generally presents four-line verses on 60 fascicles from the composite vernacular *Treasury* corpus. The verse commentary on "What Is:Time" adds two more lines and emphasizes change according to a harmonious natural cycle of events. Cf. Heine, *Flowers Blooming on a Withered Tree*, 118.
21. Satō, *Kamakura bukkyō*, 148–57.
22. Shirane, *Japan and the Culture of the Four Seasons*.
23. Tyler, *The Tale of the Heike*, 3.
24. See the full quote in the introduction, Error: Reference source not found and the pertinent note.
25. Heine, *Flowers Blooming*, 70–75.

26. See his "Essentials on Studying the Way," section 8; DZZ II, 259.

27. Stone, *Original Enlightenment*, 254, 264. See also Steineck, "Time and Eschatology." In addition, Ichikawa Hiroshi has recently shown how an optimistic reading of Japan as a superior realm emerged and coexisted with "Final Dharma Age" thought during the medieval period. Ichikawa, *Nihon chūsei no rekishi ishiki*.

28. Elias, *Time*.

29. Piaget, "Time Perception in Children"; Dux, *Die Zeit in der Geschichte: Ihre Entwicklungslogik vom Mythos zur Weltzeit*, 29–30.

30. Wendorff, *Zeit und Kultur: Geschichte des Zeitbewusstseins in Europa*. See esp. 253–56, 357–76.

31. Dohrn-van Rossum, *Die Geschichte der Stunde: Uhren und moderne Zeitordnungen*; *History of the Hour: Clocks and Modern Temporal Orders*. As Fasolt has observed in his careful review, Dohrn-van Rossum argues against economic and technological variants of determinism and carefully surveys other developments that supported the emerging dominance of abstract global time. Fasolt, "Dohrn-van Rossum, *Geschichte der Stunde*."

32. Maki, *Jikan no hikaku shakaigaku*, 2–12.

33. For a recent example, see Redfield, "Being Time: Zen, Modernity, the Contemporary."

34. Tanaka, *New Times in Modern Japan*.

35. Nagafuji, *Kodai Nihon bungaku to jikan ishiki*; Tanaka, *Das Zeitbewusstsein der Japaner im Altertum*; Coulmas, *Japanische Zeiten*.

36. Maki, *Jikan no hikaku shakaigaku*, 284–302.

37. See, for example, Whitrow, *What Is Time?*, 1–15; Wendorff, *Zeit und Kultur*, 92; Dux, *Die Zeit in der Geschichte*, 331–43; Cohen, *Transformations of Time and Temporality in Medieval and Renaissance Art*, 39–52.

38. Significantly, Dōgen thus demonstrates the capacity for all three operations Piaget defines as sufficient "to develop logical concepts of time": ordering of events, classification of duration, and measurement of time (e.g., relating the age to the sequence of birth dates). Piaget, "Time Perception in Children," 214–15. Note also the contrast to the small range of temporal orientation that Wendorff observes in the European medieval period. Wendorff, *Zeit und Kultur*, 131.

39. Again, as opposed to the European medieval outlook characterized in Wendorff, *Zeit und Kultur*, 128–31.

40. The author is currently preparing with partners from the TIMEJ project an edited volume *Time in Medieval Japan*, forthcoming in DeGruyter's "Worlds of East Asia" series in late 2025. The chapters on court and bakufu, on markets and on historiography provide further information on these topics.

41. Needham, "Time and Knowledge in China and the West," 106–7. The escapement plays a seminal part in Dohrn-van Rossum's Eurocentric discussion of clocks.

42. On Gyōki's charitable projects, see Augustine, "Monks and Charitable Projects." On Eizon and Ninshō, see Quinter, "Creating Bodhisattvas: Eison, Hinin, and the 'Living Mañjuśrī'"; Quinter, "Emulation and Erasure: Eison, Ninshō, and the Gyōki Cult." On Suzuki Shōsan, see Nakamura and Johnston, "Suzuki Shōsan, 1579–1655 and the Spirit of Capitalism in Japanese Buddhism"; Kasai, "Suzuki Shōsan ni okeru 'Keizai rinri' ni tsuite."

Chapter 9

1. Lakoff and Johnson, *Philosophy in the Flesh*, 139.
2. *Kinō to ii, kyō to kurashite, Asukagawa nagarete, hayaku tsukihi narikeri* きのふと言ひ、けふと暮らしてあすか川流れて早く月日なりけり. Kokinshū VI, 341. Harumichi no Tsuraki 春道列樹 (d. 920) was a courtier bureaucrat from the Mononobe clan who was employed as one of twelve document specialists (*monjōshō* 文章生) by the government. I have translated "Asukagawa"—a river in the Nara basin—as "Morrow River" because of the pun on the first two syllables of its name (*asu* = "tomorrow").
3. Heine, *Dimensions of Time*, 53.
4. Hoshi, "Dōgen ni okeru jikan." It is unclear whether the document in question (cf. DZZ II, 287) is truly authentic, but that question need not concern us here.
5. DZZ I, 607.
6. Maki, *Jikan no hikaku shakaigaku*, 158–96, esp. 195. See also Steineck, "Time in Old Japan," 24–29.
7. Lakoff and Johnson, *Philosophy in the Flesh*, 168.
8. Ōmori, *Jikan to Sonzai*, 20, and see above, chapter 1, p. 13; Quine, *From a Logical Point of View*, 2; Hume, *Enquiry*, 2.5; Descartes, *Meditations*, 12–13.
9. The German phenomenologist Hermann Schmitz introduced the term "Halbding (half-thing)" for objects like the wind, which exist in a purely dynamic and discontinuous fashion. Schmitz, *Der unerschöpfliche Gegenstand*, 216–17.
10. I have suggested elsewhere that Dōgen's concept of time might be useful in thinking about the problem of waste. Steineck, "Time, Waste and Enlightment."
11. Barbour, "The Nature of Time," 2.
12. Cf. the report by Craig Callender, "Is Time an Illusion?" or the contribution by Carlo Rovelli, "Forget Time."
13. Wood, "Founder's Lecture: Is Time Out of Joint? Or at a New Threshold? Reflections on the Temporality of Climate Change," 49–50.
14. In the "Natorp Report," not yet available in English, Heidegger writes: "To determine factual life, its mode of objectivity and being without also positing death and life's 'having of death' in a fundamental way that guides the problematic

is a failure that cannot be repaired by way of subsequent supplementation. The pure, constitutively ontological problematic of death's mode of being is completely different from a metaphysics of immortality and the 'hereafter.' The imminence of death that life 'has' [before it] is a constituent of facticity because of its specific way of making visible the presence and pastness (historicity) of life. At the same time, it is the phenomenon from which to explicate the specific 'temporality' of human existence. The meaning of this temporality, and not the formal analysis of a contingent mode of historiography and its assumed temporal directionality, determines the fundamental meaning of the historical." Cf. GA 62, 358–59. See also Heidegger, *Sein und Zeit*, 252–67.

15. Heidegger, *Sein und Zeit*, 257–58.

16. Wolfgang Marx in his groundbreaking work on the logic of categories demonstrated that the fundamental logical functions of determination (of which Kant's table of categories is one attempt at systematization) cannot be separated from each other. In his words, "all categories form a mutually intertwined whole, in which each particular determination in principle affects all others and enters into their content (Alle Kategorien bilden ein ineinander verflochtenes Ganzes, in dem jede einzelne Bestimmung im Prinzip jede andere affiziert und in ihren Gehalt eingeht)" (Marx, *Reflextionstopologie*, 86).

17. Bureau International des Poids et Mesures, *The International System of Units*, 130.

18. See Heidegger's handwritten note in the typoscript of the "Natorp report"; "Zeitlichkeit–Tod, entscheidend Einmaligkeit (temporality—death, singularity decisive)," GA 62, 360. See also Heidegger, *Sein und Zeit*, 258.

19. Heine, *Dimensions of Time*, 1.

20. On this topic, see Moishe Postone's classic study *Time, Labor, and Social Domination: A Reinterpretation of Marx's Critical Theory*.

21. The term "fetish" is here used in a sense inspired by Marx's famous chapter on the "The Fetish of the Commodity and Its Secret" in *Capital*. For a detailed study on the notions of "fetish" and "fetishism" in Marx, see Schulz, "Marx's Distinction between the Fetish Character of the Commodity and Fetishism."

22. Maki, *Jikan no hikaku shakaigaku*, 182–83.

23. Dux, *Die Zeit in der Geschichte*; Dohrn-van Rossum, Gerhard, *History of the Hour*.

24. Postone, *Time, Labor, and Social Domination*.

25. Rosa, *Social Acceleration: A New Theory of Modernity*.

26. Thompson, "Time," 60.

27. Steger, "Japanese Historic 'Timescapes': An Anthropological Approach," 56.

28. DZZ II, 314; see also Leighton and Okumura, *Dōgen's Pure Standards*, 66, and for more details chapter 4, p. 79.

29. Thompson, "Time," 61.

30. O'Malley, "Time, Work and Task Orientation: A Critique of American Historiography"; Ogle, "Time, Temporality and the History of Capitalism."

31. Thompson, "Time," 71.

32. O'Malley, "Time, Work and Task Orientation."

33. Uchiyama Takashi gives a good example for this from the modern workplace in his insightful study of time, *Jikan ni tsuite no jūnishō*, 147–49.

34. Solignac, "Spiritualität," section twentieth century.

35. Hadot, *Exercices spirituels et philosophie antique*. See also Hadot, *Philosophy as a Way of Life*.

36. Hadot (*Exercises spirituels*, 59) refers to Paul Rabbow's identification of spiritual with moral exercises in his monograph *Seelenführung*, 18.

37. Cf. Hadot, *Exercises spirituels*, 15–58.

38. See e.g., Meier et al., *Spirituality and Health: Multidisciplinary Explorations*; Kelemen and Peltonen, "Spirituality: A Way to an Alternative Subjectivity?"

39. Compare, in addition to the above, the survey of notions of spirituality in the health sector by McCarroll et al. ("Assessing Plurality in Spirituality Definitions"), the influential book on *Japanese Spirituality* by Suzuki Daisetz (see also Suzuki, *Nihonteki reisei*), and the recent review of spirituality in present-day Japan by Shimazono Susumu, "Supririchuariti no mirai ni mukete," 8–13.

40. Redfield, "Being Time," and Roberts, *Being-Time*, are examples from North American practitioners.

41. Eliade, *Mythos und Wirklichkeit*, 22–26.

42. On this point, see Roman Pfaller's reflections on "delegated faith" in his *On the Pleasure Principle in Culture: Illusions Without Owners*, 35–72.

43. The fascist movements of the twentieth century, for example, were extremely skillful in staging such experiences and harvesting their emotive power. For an early analysis by an author who inspired this study, see Cassirer, "The Technique of Our Modern Political Myths."

44. "Auguries of Innocence," see Stevenson, *Blake: The Complete Poems*, 615.

Appendix 1

1. I have discussed these dimensions and their implications for the translation and interpretation of Dōgen elsewhere; see Steineck, "When Zen Becomes Philosophy."

2. See chapter 2, section "Religious Writing in Medieval Japan" for an explanation of these styles and their use.

3. Heine, *Dimensions of Time*, 155–62; Nearman, *The Shōbōgenzō*, 106–18; Tanahashi, *Treasury*; Elberfeld, *Phänomenologie der Zeit*, 385–94; Nakamura, *Zen'yaku Shōbō genzō*, 388–98; Takahashi, *Shōbō genzō zenkan gendaiyaku*, 332–42; Tamaki, *Shōbō genzō (jō)*, 232–51.

4. The reference is to Yaoshan Weiyan 藥山惟儼 (Jp. Yakusan Igen; 745–827), and the first two lines are based on his response to a question about the meaning of committing to monastic rules, meditation, and wisdom: "You should right away head for sitting (in meditation) on the high, high mountains or walk the bottom of the deep, deep sea" (直須向高高山頂坐深深海底行, *Jingde chuan deng lu*, T 2076.51: 312b21). The following lines are probably Dōgen's own composition, but they continue to make oblique references to other Zen dialogues, most of which are also in his collection of 300 *kōan* cases. See the notes below.

5. 有時. The earlier manuscripts give the reading *yūji* (DZZ I, 189), but modern sources usually read *uji*. The standard Japanized (*kun*) reading is *aru toki*, "sometimes, at a given time, once." Dōgen, however, later in the text insists on reading the term as an unresolved compound indicating the identity of "what there is" with "time." Therefore, and because Dōgen's reading in effect constitutes a somewhat awkward neologism, I opted for "What Is:Time" as my standard translation. I sometimes omit or replace the "what" where the text specifies the token to be identified with time, but I mostly stay with the third person "is" to indicate that in Dōgen's view, by way of its identity with time, everything there is encompasses a configuration of the whole world. Where "what" is omitted, the term will still be identifiable through the use of the colon between "is" (or, in rare cases, other conjugations of "to be") and "time." See below and chapter 1, pp. 17–18 for a more extensive discussion of my choice of translation, and chapter 6 for an explanation of its implications.

6. "Three heads and eight arms" (Jp. *santō happi* 三頭八臂) can either point to the figure of a "fighting demon" (Jp. *ashura*, see e.g., Tanahashi, 104) or, more probably, to a guardian deity like the Immovable Wisdom King (Jp. *Fudō myōō*, cf. e.g., Takahashi, *Shōbō genzō*, 332). Arifuku (*Dōgen no sekai*, 233), perhaps following a lead in Keizan Jōkin's "Record of the Transmission of Light" (*Denkō roku* 傳光錄; T 2585.82: 358b21), has pointed to the *Lotus Sutra*'s exposition of the 32 forms in which the Bodhisattva Kannon (Skt. Avalokiteśvara; see Kato and Soothill, *The Threefold Lotus Sutra*, 321–23) appears to save suffering beings—making these lines about meeting sentient beings in whatever shape is needed to lead them toward liberation from suffering.

7. "One *jō* six [*shaku*] or eight *shaku*" (Jp. *jō roku hasshaku* 丈六八尺), roughly 4.8 m./16 ft. and 2.4 m./8 ft., respectively. According to traditional iconography, the first is the measures of a standing Buddha/Buddha statue, the second of a seated one.

8. The staff is used by wandering monks, the fly whisk, which signifies abstinence from killing even the lowliest sentient beings, is used by Zen masters during formal instructions as a ritual implement and sign of authority. Cases 1:1, 3:29, 3:56 of Dōgen's "300 Cases Treasury" refer to the whisk, case 1:91 to the staff. See DZZ II, 201, 242, 246; 216 and Loori and Tanahashi, *The True Dharma Eye*, 3, 313, 349; 121.

9. Pillars and lanterns are part of monastic architecture and referred to in cases 1:41, 3:101 (pillar) and 3:96 (lantern) of Dōgen's collection; see DZZ II, 208, 252; 251 and Loori and Tanahashi, *The True Dharma Eye*, 56; 401.

10. Zhang and Li are common Chinese family names, mentioned e.g., in case 1:39 of the "300 Cases Treasury"; see DZZ II, 208 and Loori and Tanahashi, *The True Dharma Eye*, 54. The later-born sons are male children outside of the ancestral line, and here stand for average, inconsequential human beings.

11. The encompassing space of all forms of existence. The sky is mentioned e.g., in case 2:91 of the "300 Cases Treasury;" see DZZ II, 235 and Loori and Tanahashi, *The True Dharma Eye*, 259.

12. "Study and practice" translates *sangaku* 参学, a standard expression for training in a Buddhist and especially Zen Buddhist monastery or congregation.

13. In a later passage, Dōgen will insist that the current body of the practitioner is the golden Buddha body in the second of the four phases of enlightenment: initial aspiration, practice, insight, and nirvana.

14. "Self-identical" here translates *ware*, which can function as a first-person pronoun, but is used in this and other of Dōgen's texts to refer to things insofar as they retain certain essential characteristics over time. In the context of "What is: Time," both meanings are implied because the configuration of the self implies a configuration of the whole world and vice versa—an aspect denoted in "What Is: Time" by the term *hōi* 法位 from the Lotus Sutra. *Ware* may further denote the Indian notion of an eternal, substantial self (*ātman*), a notion generally refuted in Buddhism. Dōgen apparently seeks to replace it here with his vision of a holistic but temporal self. See chapter 6, pp. 153–57 for further discussion of this passage, esp. concerning the connection between "exhausting" (see next note) and "lining up in order."

15. *Jinkai* 盡界. The first character of the compound can be understood as a transitive verb (as in the compound *kyūjin su* 究盡す, which refers to an exhaustive probing or understanding of something) or as an adjective. To account for the ambiguity, I have translated here according to a transitive reading of the compound as *kai o tsukusu* (for a similar reading, see Nearman, *The Shōbōgenzō*, 109), and followed the adjective reading in the sense of "entire world" (Tanahashi, *Treasury*, 105) or "entire [*Dharma-*]realm" (Heine, *Dimensions of Time*, 155) below. See also pp. 155–57 for a discussion of "exhausting."

16. *Sōge sezaru* 相礙せざる is a paraphrase of the Kegon School's notion of "mutual non-obstruction of things" (Jp. *jiji muge* 事事無碍). See again p. 272, n. 79 for further discussion.

17. "Origination of intention" here translates *hosshin* 發心. A more literal translation would be "bringing forth the *bodhi*-mind." This is the first of the four phases of complete liberation, which further include practice, obtaining enlightenment, and nirvana. The full set of four is referenced later in the text. See also *Essentials*, quoted above, p. 125.

18. *Dōji hosshin ari, dōjin hotsuji nari* 同時發心あり、同心發時なり。 I follow DZZ I, 190 here, while the standard edition followed by Shōmonji has *dōjin hotsuji ari,* which would make this a paratactical clause, meaning "There is the same-time arising of the intention, and there is the arising of time from the same intention." See section "Synchrony and Sequence," pp. 161–68.

19. "The way to understand" here translates *dōri* 道理, composed of elements indicating "the way" and a "pattern," respectively.

20. "The self" here translates *jiko* 自己.

21. The "myriad shapes" (*banshō* 萬象) indicate the manifold objects with a sensible form. "Grass" is another metaphor for the same.

22. I.e., between the two ways of looking at things mentioned in the previous sentence.

23. "Field" is *denchi* 田地, a metaphorical expression that ties in with the image of "grass" and indicates the "place" where one "encounters" (*e* 会), that is, apprehends, the "shapes" or objects, and forms an understanding of them.

24. *Ima no toki ni moretaru jin'u jinkai ari ya nashi ya* いまの時にもれたる盡有盡界ありやなしや: Translations vary concerning the interpretation of *moretaru* (perfective form of "leak"), which can mean both "leaking into" (see Nearman, *The Shōbōgenzō*, 110) or "leaking out" (see Tanahashi, *Treasury*, 105). I have opted for the first, because the particle *ni* generally indicates the place to which something is leaking, whereas the place from which it is leaking is indicated by *yori* (see examples in *Zenbun zen'yaku kogo jiten*, https://japanknowledge.com/lib/display/?lid=200380001995800).

25. "I" here translates *ware*, because the word in this context is clearly used as a first-person pronoun.

26. "I" is again used to translate *ware,* because Dōgen here refers to the common view quoted above. However, his use of the word is ambiguous in the sense explained above in fn. 10.

27. "Consummate now" is my translation term for *nikon* 而今, a Sinitic phrase that usually simply means "now," often used to indicate continuation with or contrast to the past. As with *uji,* Dōgen turns it into a technical term that stands for an essential aspect of his view of time. See chapter 6, pp. 148–52 for an extensive discussion.

28. Nearman (*The Shōbōgenzō*, 111), referring to an unidentified "Zen saying," explains: "The bamboo, all up and down its length, has joints (which mark the passage of the seasons); the pine (being ever-green) has no colors to differentiate past from present." The saying in question is probably 「竹有上下節。松無古今青。」 attributed to Daweishan Zuchun 大溈山祖珣 in *Jianzhong jingguo xu denglu* 建中靖國續燈錄, X 78: 1556, 778a2.

29. I have inserted "things" here purely for grammatical reasons to match with the plural in the second part of the sentence.

30. 有時なるによりて吾有時なり。 I read *Uji naru ni yorite waga uji nari* because I take the topic of this sentence to be identical with that of the preceding

sentences. If one assumes that the sentence has a separate topic, one can read *Uji naru ni yorite ware uji nari*, "By way of being what is:time, I am what is:time."

31. "Virtue" here translates *kudoku* 功德, a term that entails both beneficial acts and the benefic karmic effects resulting from them.

32. "Transiting/transition through phases" is my translation of *kyōryaku* 經歷, otherwise translated as "flowing" (Tanahashi, *Treasury*, 106), "shifting" (Raud, "Existential Moment," 165), "event-like passage" (*ereignishaftes Verlaufen*: Elberfeld, *Phänomenologie der Zeit*, 267), "passage" (Kim, *Dōgen Kigen*, 154), "seriatim passage" (Waddell and Abe, *The Heart of Dōgen's Shōbōgenzō*, 51–52), "[totalistic] passage" (Heine, *Dimensions of Time*, 157), and even "passageless passage" (Abe, *A Study of Dōgen*, 83–85). In common usage, *kyōryaku* 經歷—more often read *keireki*—has the dynamic aspect of passing through places or spending time and the aspect of stations in life one has gone through or the sum of one's experiences. Dōgen integrates both these aspects. For a more extensive discussion, see chapter 6, pp. 152–54.

33. Time does not accumulate, neither as a growing uniform block, nor as an augmenting series of discrete portions. See also chapter 6, p. 155 for further discussion.

34. The references are to the Zen masters Qingyuan Xingsi 青原行思 (Jp. Seigen Gyōshi; d. 740), a dharma heir of the famous sixth patriarch Huineng, Huangbo Xiyun 黃檗希運 (Jp. Ōbaku Kiun; d. 850), the teacher of Linji (Jp. Rinzai), Jiangxi 江西—better known as Mazu Daoyi 馬祖道一 (Jp. Baso Dōitsu, 709–88)—and Shitou Xiqian 石頭希遷 (Jp. Sekitō Kisen; 700–90), a dharma heir to Qingyuan. Mazu and Shitou are part of an episode quoted later in the text.

35. *Nyūdei nissui* 入泥入水. "Entering the mud, entering the water" is a metaphor for a Bodhisattva's reentry into the realms of transmigration to save suffering beings (cf. e.g., *Jingdu huowen* 淨土或問, T1972, 47:292c11). "Entering the water" here further connects to the quote from Yaoshan about "walking the bottom of the deep, deep sea."

36. *Dharma* translates *hō* 法. In this context, it indicates the "true reality" of ordinary existence, but the term can also stand for the truth or "law" as exposed in the Buddha's teaching and for the particular constituents of reality. Further down, it is used in this latter sense.

37. *Hōi* 法位. I borrow this translation from Raud, "Existential Moment," 156. Alternative translations include "dharma position" (Kim, *Dōgen Kigen*, 149, Heine, *Dimensions of Time*, 158) or "dharma stage" (Waddell and Abe, *The Heart of Dōgen's Shōbōgenzō*, 52; both Tanahashi, *Treasury*, 107, and Nearman, *The Shōbōgenzō*, 113, skip over the term). See also chapter 5, pp. 127–32.

38. The animals appearing in this and the following sentence are part of the Chinese zodiac and therefore also indicate select stellar hours. The hours of horse and sheep correspond to midday and early afternoon (roughly 11:00 a.m.–3:00 p.m.); those of rat and tiger, mentioned in the following sentence, to midnight and dawn (11:00 p.m.–1:00 a.m. and 3:00–5:00 a.m., respectively).

39. On "exhausting," see above, fn. 15.

40. Briefly said, for Dōgen each dharma implies a configuration that involves the whole world and as such may be said to "exhaust" the whole world. At the same time, it coexists with other dharmas that equally exhaust the whole world. This interplay or "mutual permeation" ensures a shared reality and thereby also forms the basis of clock-time. See chapter 6, sections "Exhausting" and "Conclusion."

41. *Dharma* again translates *hō* 法 and could point to both a "truth" or a "constituent of reality."

42. Dōgen here refutes metaphysical notions of absolute "nothingness" (*mu* 無) or absolute "being" (*yū* 有).

43. 解會は時なりといへども、他にひかるる縁なし。 *Hikaruru* is passive, determining *en*. I read this as indicating that by virtue of being time (in the sense of What Is:Time Dōgen elucidates), understanding is equipped with everything necessary to fully achieve insight.

44. "Leather bag" here translates *hitai* 皮袋, a pejorative expression for the physical body, and thus for a person without insight.

45. *Tennō tenshū* 天王天衆. Major and minor protective deities of Buddhism.

46. This and the following sentences spell out Dōgen's idea that, because one's existence at each and every moment is a configuration of the whole world, the activity maintaining that existence at once sustains everything that exists at that moment. Notably, celestial kings and their retinue belong as much to "normal reality" for Dōgen as the animals of the land and the water.

47. *Gakushikitaru bekarazu* 學しきたるべからず: I have translated the perfective aspect of *gakushikitaru* as "in the usual way" (more literally: "as one has so far come to study it").

48. *Jinkai wa* 盡界は: *jinkai* can be read more simply as "the whole world" or—closer to Buddhist terminology—"all spheres" (meaning the spheres of the sensible forms, of sublimely sensible forms, and that without sensible form), but since the paragraph is an explanation of how "transiting through phases" is the way in which everything depends on "the exertion of my powers," I here read it in a more active sense, as *kai o tsukusu*.

49. *Kyōryaku o iu ni, kyō wa gaizu ni shite, nō kyōryaku no hō wa higashi ni mukite hyakusen sekai o yukisugite, hyakusen gō o furu to omou wa, butsudō no sangaku, kore nomi o sen'ichi ni sezaru nari.* 經歷をいふに、境は外頭にして、能經歷の法は東にむきて百千世界をゆきすぎて、百千劫をふるとおもふは、佛道の參學、これのみを專一にせざるなり。 Translations diverge depending on the identification of the antecedent to *kore* in the last part of the sentence. Tanahashi reads it as referring to *butsudō* and translates: "In your study of flowing [their translation of *kyōryaku*], if you imagine the objective to be outside yourself and that you flow and move through hundreds and thousands of worlds, for hundreds, thousands, and myriad of eaons, you have not devotedly studied the buddha way." Tanahashi, *Treasury*, 108–9. Nearman's and Heine's translations take a similar

direction (Nearman, *The Shōbōgenzō*, 115; Heine, *Dimensions of Time*, 159). I believe, however, that it is more accurate grammatically to relate *kore* to the topic of the sentence, namely the view that separates the agent of transiting from the realm through which it transits. Notably, Dōgen in the previous passages does not completely refute this view, which may be understood as a simple rendering of the Buddhist teaching of transmigration. He asks his disciples to consider in all its details a holistic perspective on transition that involves both the dharma that transits and the realms in which it is situated at each changing moment as connected and interrelated poles of one single reality.

50. 無際大師 (Jp. Musai Daishi), honorific name of Shitou Xiqian 石頭希遷 (Jp. Sekitō Kisen; 700–90).

51. 藥山弘道大師 (Jp. Yakusan Gūdō Daishi). Alternative name of Yaoshan Weiyan, a disciple of Shitou and the author of the initial two lines of the poem at the beginning of "What Is: Time."

52. 江西大寂禪師. Alternative honorific name of Mazu Daoyi 馬祖道一 (Jp. Baso Dōitsu; 709–88).

53. Of those listening directly to the Buddha's teaching, those reaching enlightenment on their own, and those following the Mahāyāna teaching.

54. *Ika naranka kore soshi seirai no i* 如何是祖師西來意. The "ancestor" in question is Bodhidharma, who according to legend brought Zen from India ("the West") to China. The question is used in Zen dialogues to inquire about the meaning of its teaching. *I* 意 primarily refers to intentions or thoughts, but can also refer to the meaning of a phrase, event, or action, which is why I chose a translation that is open to both interpretations.

55. *Kyō* 教 has the literal meaning of "teaching," but is also used as a standard causative form in literary Sinitic. Heine (*Existential . . .*, 159–60) takes it in the literal meaning, but most other translations (modern Japanese, English, and German) stay with the causative, as also indicated by a Japanese reading gloss in the Rurikōji manuscript (cf. DZZ I, 193; and see Tamaki, *Shōbō genzō jō* 246; Nakamura, *Zen'yaku Shōbō genzō*, 395; Takahashi, 339; Nearman, 115; Tanahashi, 109; Elberfeld, 392).

56. Based on chapter 19 of *Zongmeng liangdeng huiyao* 宗門聯燈會要, but Dōgen omits the subject 我 (Ch. *wo*, *ware*) from the sentence, which in the original has the meaning: "At one time, I made him raise his eyebrows and blink his eyes." Cf. X 1556, 79: 163b. *Zengaku daijiten* (entry *yōbi* 揚眉, 1252) states (without giving a reference) that "Raising the eyebrows and blinking the eyes" is an allusion to the episode about Śākyamuni turning a flower in his hands and Kaśyapa smiling that in the Zen tradition forms the beginning of "heart to heart" (*ishin denshin* 以心伝心) transmission.

57. Takahashi's modern Japanese translation links these sentences to Bodhidharma's travel from India across the mountains and the sea (339). Nakamura interpolates an explanatory phrase that points to the oneness of the Buddha with

nature (395). A more obvious connection would be to Yaoshan's lines about standing on the top of the mountain and walking the bottom of the sea quoted at the beginning of the chapter.

58. My translation of the non-standard term *shūsubeshi* 宗すべし (*sōsubeshi* according to one manuscript), taken from the meaning of nominal *shū* 宗 in the Buddhist context, which points to the teaching of the canonical scriptures and the association with Yaoshan's above-mentioned lines. Readings of this expression diverge widely. The Rurikōji manuscript gives the Japanized (*kun*) transcription *atsumuru beshi* (DZZ I, 193), which would translate as "must collect the sea." Perhaps the reason behind this somewhat obscure choice is that 宗 is identified as short for *sō* 綜 ("binding together, collect"), although the logical Japanized transcription would then be *suburu beshi*. Nakamura Sōichi's modern Japanese translation renders the phrase as *manabu*, "learning the sea." (*Zen'yaku Shōbōgenzō*, 395) Tanahashi (*Treasury*, 109) similarly reads "to understand the oceans." Tamaki Kōshirō (*Shōbō genzō [jō]*, 247) has *umi ga miwataseyo* "one is able to survey the sea." (Similarly: Heine, *Existential . . .* , 160; Elberfeld, 392.) Unfortunately, these authors do not explain their choice of translation. Takahashi, *Shōbō genzō zenkan gendaiyaku*, 340) gives a paraphrase: *Daruma ga umi o wataru omomuki ni miru ga yoi*. ("One should see it in Bodhidharma's intent in crossing the sea") that is in line with his explanation mentioned in n. 19, but constitutes a major accretion to the text.

59. A symbol of the attainment of enlightenment. It is said that when Śākyamuni first achieved his decisive insight, the morning star appeared.

60. A symbol of something to be preciously guarded and also of the gist of the Buddhist teaching—see the title of the "Treasury of the True Dharma Eye."

61. This once more alludes to the heart-to-heart transmission of the dharma between Śākyamuni and Kāśyapa.

62. Jp. Sekken (or Shōken) [no] Kisei zenji 葉縣の歸省禪師, tenth–eleventh century. Ye district is an area in northeastern Henan 河南, where Guisheng resided at the Guangjiang subtemple of Baoan monastery founded by his teacher Shoushan Shengnian 首山省念 (Jp. Shuzan Shōnen; 926–93).

63. *I* 意, see n. 51.

64. *Ku* 句, Skt. *pada*. A short sentence or verse.

65. This is an abbreviated version of an episode recounted in the *Zongmen liangdeng hui yao,* chapter 12 (X 1557, 79:105a) and later in the *Wudeng huiyan* (*Gotō egen* 五燈會元, *Assembled Origins of the Five Lamps*) compiled upon imperial command by Dachuan Puji 大川普濟 in 1252. The full account from *Assembled Origins of the Five Lamps* runs as follows: "The master ascended the lecture hall. He first paused for a long time, then spoke thus: 'You traveling Chan monks! Here is something you all need to be aware of: if you want to get closer and not to be led astray by what's going on around you, then you must have the right eye in your study and your understanding. How shall one go about this? [There

are four kinds of situations you need to know:] There is the case of *ju* [saying] arriving but *yi* [intention, meaning] failing to show up. This refers to a situation where imagined things are taken to be real and false distinctions are made on that very ground. There is the case where *yi* is there but *ju* fails to arrive. This refers to a situation where what is being talked about is not unreal, but different people are focusing on different aspects of the thing [so they end up talking past each other]. There is the case where both *ju* and *yi* arrive. When this happens, great illumination is produced, breaking the vast empty space. Finally there is the case where both *ju* and *yi* fail to arrive. We may liken this to the case of a blind man striding haphazardly ahead and falling in a deep pit.'" (English translation quoted after: Zong, *Three Language-related Methods*, 590.

66. Reference to case 2:43 from the "300 Cases Treasury," DZZ II, 227. The English translation of the dialogue in question reads: "Huileng of Changqing studied with Lingyun and asked him, 'What is the essential meaning of the Buddhadharma?' Lingyun said, 'When the donkey matter has not yet left, the horse matter arrives.'" Loori and Tanahashi, *The True Dharma Eye*, 210.

67. Since each what is:time is a configuration of the whole, it does not stand in opposition to or obstruct any other what is: time. Rather, in maintaining certain features as part of this configuration, it restricts itself. See p. 156.

68. Reference to case 1:92 from the "300 Cases Treasury," DZZ II, 216–17; Loori and Tanahashi, *The True Dharma Eye*, 122.

69. "One should perform what is:time": *Uji* is here used as part of the verb phrase *uji subeshi* 有時すべし.

70. These and the lines in small capital below are composed by Dōgen in Literary Sinitic.

71. *Kaitō* 開冬, generally the tenth calendar month, but also its first day (a new moon day).

72. Roughly corresponding to the year 1240. If the date indicates the first day of the tenth month, this would correspond to October 24, 1240.

73. The first year of Kangen, between the fifteenth days of the fourth and seventh month, corresponding to the time between May 12 and August 9, 1243.

Bibliography

Abe, Masao 阿部正雄. *A Study of Dōgen: His Philosophy and Religion*. Edited by Steven Heine. Albany: State University of New York Press, 1992.
———. "Dōgen no jikan-kūkanron 道元の時間・空間論." In *Dōgen shisō no tokuchō* 道元思想 の特徴, edited by Tamaki Kōshirō 玉城康四郎 and Kagamishima Genryū 鏡島元隆, 163–90. Kōza Dōgen 講座道元 4. Tōkyō: Shunjūsha, 1980.
Adam, Jean-Michel. *Les Textes: Types et prototypes. Récit, description, argumentation, explication et dialogue*. Paris: Armand Colin, 2005.
Adolphson, Mikael S. *The Teeth and Claws of the Buddha: Monastic Warriors and Sōhei in Japanese History*. Honolulu: University of Hawai'i Press, 2007.
Adolphson, Mikael, and J. Mark Ramseyer. "The Competitive Enforcement of Property Rights in Medieval Japan: The Role of Temples and Monasteries." *Journal of Economic Behavior & Organization* 71, no. 3 (2009): 660–68.
Aguessy, Honorat, ed. *Time and the Philosophies*. Paris: Unesco, 1977.
Aitken, Robert. *The Gateless Barrier: The Wu-Men Kuan (Mumonkan)*. Berkeley, CA: North Point Press, 2010.
Akitsu Hideaki 秋津秀彰. "Dōgen zenji ikō no 'tenzo kyōkun' no denshin to juyō. Chūsei/Keizan zenji yori Kindai/Senzenki ni kakete 道元禅師以降の『典座教訓』の伝播と受容：中世・瑩山禅師より近代・戦前期にかけて." *Sōtōshū sōgō kenkyū sentā gakujutsu taikai kiyō* 曹洞宗総合研究センター学術大会紀要 21 (2020): 22–31.
Akiyama Hanji 秋山範二. *Dōgen no kenkyū* 道元の研究. Tōkyō: Iwanami shoten, 1935.
Arifuku Kōgaku 有福孝岳. *Dōgen no sekai* 道元の世界. Ōsaka: Ōsaka shoseki, 1985.
Augustine, Jonathan. "Monks and Charitable Projects: The Legacy of Gyoki Bosatsu." *Japanese Religions* 26, no. 1 (2001): 1–22.
Awaya Ryōdō, 粟谷良道. "'Shōbōgenzō' ni okeru jin no shisō 1 『正法眼蔵』における尽の思想 (一)." *Indogaku bukkyōgaku kenkyū* 印度學佛教學研究 37, no. 2 (1989): 748–51.
———. "'Shōbōgenzō' ni okeru jin no shisō 2 「正法眼蔵」における尽の思想-2-." *Shūgaku kenkyū* 宗學研究 31 (1989): 66–71.

———. "Shōbōgenzō ni okeru jinjippōkai 正法眼蔵における尽十方界." *Indogaku bukkyōgaku kenkyū* 印度學佛教學研究 35, no. 1 (1986): 219–22.
Azuma Sen'ichirō 東專一郎. "Shūkyōteki shi to shūkyōteki jikan: Haideggā/Kirukegōru/Dōgen 宗教的死と宗教的時間—ハイデッガー・キルケゴール・道元." *Risō* 443 (1970): 17–28.
Barbour, Julian. "The Nature of Time." Essay. Foundational Questions Institute, December 1, 2008.
Barthes, Roland. "The Reality Effect." In *The Novel: An Anthology of Criticism and Theory, 1900–2000*, edited by Dorothy Hale, 229–34. Chichester: Wiley, 2005.
Bein, Steve. *Purifying Zen: Watsuji Tetsuro's Shamon Dogen*. Honolulu: University of Hawai'i Press, 2011.
Bielefeldt, Carl. *Dōgen's Manuals of Zen Meditation*. Berkeley: University of California Press, 1988.
———. "Recarving the Dragon: History and Dogma in the Study of Dōgen." In *Dōgen Studies*, edited by William LaFleur, 21–54. Honolulu: University of Hawai'i Press, 1985.
Bloom, Alfred. *Shinran's Gospel of Pure Grace*. Tucson: University of Arizona Press, 1965.
Bodiford, William. "Rewriting Dōgen." *Kokusai Zen kenkyū* 国際禅研究 4 (2019): 219–302.
———. *Sōtō Zen in Medieval Japan*. Honolulu: University of Hawai'i Press, 1993.
———. "Zen and the Art of Religious Prejudice: Efforts to Reform a Tradition of Social Discrimination." *Japanese Journal of Religious Studies* 23, no. 1–2 (1996): 1–27.
Bredeson, Garrett Zantow. "On Dōgen and Derrida." *Philosophy East and West* 58, no. 1 (2008): 60–82.
Breugem, Vincent Michaël Nicolaas. *From Prominence to Obscurity: A Study of the Darumashū: Japan's First Zen School: Including Annotated Translations of Jōtōshōgakuron, Kenshōjōbutsugi and Hōmon Taikō*. PhD diss., Leiden University, 2012.
Brown, Jason W. "Microgenesis and Buddhism: The Concept of Momentariness." *Philosophy East and West* 49, no. 3 (1999): 261–77.
Bureau International des Poids et Mesures. *The International System of Units*, 2019. https://www.bipm.org/documents/20126/41483022/SI-Brochure-9.pdf/fcf090b2-04e6-88cc-1149-c3e029ad8232.
Callender, Craig. "Is Time an Illusion?" *Scientific American* 302, no. 6 (2010): 58–65.
Cassirer, Ernst. *An Essay on Man: An Introduction to the Philosophy of Human Culture*. 1944. Reprint. New Haven: Yale University Press, 1992.
———. *Philosophie der symbolischen Formen I: Die Sprache*. Darmstadt: Wissenschaftliche Buchgesellschaft, 1994.
———. "The Technique of Our Modern Political Myths." In *Symbol, Myth, and Culture : Essays and Lectures of Ernst Cassirer, 1935–1945*, edited by Donald Phillip Verene, 242–67. New Haven: Yale University Press, 1979.

Cassirer, Ernst, and Steve G. Lofts. *The Philosophy of Symbolic Forms, Vol. 1: Language*. London: Routledge, 2021.
CBETA, ed. *Xuzangjing* 続蔵經. https://cbetaonline.dila.edu.tw/zh/.
Chen, Jinhua. *Philosopher, Practitioner, Politician: The Many Lives of Fazang (643–712)*. Leiden: Brill, 2007.
Chinese Etymology 字源. //hanziyuan.net.
Cohen, Simona. *Transformations of Time and Temporality in Medieval and Renaissance Art*. Leiden: Brill, 2014.
Collcutt, Martin. *Five Mountains : The Rinzai Zen Monastic Institution in Medieval Japan*. Cambridge, MA: Harvard University Press, 1981.
Conze, Edward. *Buddhist Thought in India: Three Phases of Buddhist Philosophy*. London: Routledge, 2013.
Cornell, Drucilla, and Kenneth Michael Panfilio. *Symbolic Forms for a New Humanity: Cultural and Racial Reconfigurations of Critical Theory*. New York: Fordham University Press, 2010.
Coulmas, Florian. *Japanische Zeiten: eine Ethnographie der Vergänglichkeit*. Reinbek bei Hamburg: Kindler, 2000.
Descartes, René. *Meditations. The Philosophical Writings of Descartes*. Cambridge: University Press, 2008.
Dōgen. *Shōbōgenzō; Shōbōgenzō zuimonki* 正法眼蔵; 正法眼蔵随聞記. Edited by Nishio Minoru 西尾實. Nihon koten bungaku taikei 81. Tōkyō: Iwanami Shoten, 1965.
———. "The Treasury of the Eye of the True Dharma Book 3—Buddha Nature (1)." Translated by Carl Bielefeldt. *Soto Zen Journal: Dharma Eye* 25 (2010): 17–23.
Dohrn-van Rossum, Gerhard. *Die Geschichte der Stunde: Uhren und moderne Zeitordnungen*. München: Deutscher Taschenbuch Verlag, 1995.
———. *History of the Hour: Clocks and Modern Temporal Orders*. Chicago: University of Chicago Press, 1996.
Döll, Steffen. *Im Osten des Meeres: Chinesische Emigrantenmönche und die frühen Institutionen des japanischen Zen-Buddhismus*. Münchner ostasiatische Studien 84. Stuttgart: Franz Steiner Verlag, 2010.
Dumoulin, Heinrich. *A History of Zen Buddhism*. New York: McGraw-Hill, 1965.
———. "Das Buch Genjōkōan. Aus dem Shōbōgenzō des Zen-Meisters Dōgen." *Monumenta Nipponica* 15, no. 3–4 (1960, 1959): 425–40.
———. *Dōgen-Zen: Kleine Schriften der Sōtō-Schule*. Zürich, München: Theseus-Verlag, 1990.
Dux, Günter. *Die Zeit in der Geschichte: Ihre Entwicklungslogik vom Mythos zur Weltzeit*. Frankfurt am Main: Suhrkamp, 1992.
Eihei shōbō genzō shūsho taisei hankō kai 永平正法眼藏蒐書大成刊行會. *Eihei shōbō genzō shūsho taisei 12* 永平正法眼藏蒐書大成. Vol. 12. Tōkyō: Daishukan shoten, 1974.
Eiheiji 永平寺. *Eiheiji shiryō zensho. Monjohen-1*. 永平寺史料全書. 文書編第 1 巻 文書編第 1 巻. Daihonzan Eiheiji, 2012.

Einstein, Albert. *Über die spezielle und die allgemeine Relativitätstheorie*. 24th ed. Berlin, Heidelberg: Springer Berlin Heidelberg, 1969.

Elberfeld, Rolf. *Phänomenologie der Zeit im Buddhismus : Methoden interkulturellen Philosophierens*. Philosophie Interkulturell 1. Stuttgart-Bad Cannstatt: Frommann-Holzboog, 2004.

Eliade, Mircea. *Mythos und Wirklichkeit*. Frankfurt am Main: Insel Verlag, 1988.

Elias, Norbert. *Time: An Essay*. Cambridge: Cambridge University Press, 1992.

Eubanks, Charlotte. *Miracles of Book and Body: Buddhist Textual Culture and Medieval Japan*. Berkeley: University of California Press, 2011.

Farris, William Wayne. *Japan to 1600: A Social and Economic History*. Honolulu: University of Hawai'i Press, 2009.

Fasolt, Constantin. "Dohrn-van Rossum, Geschichte der Stunde." *Medieval Review*, December 1, 1993. https://scholarworks.iu.edu/journals/index.php/tmr/article/view/14162/20280.

Faure, Bernard. "The Daruma-Shū, Dōgen and Sōtō Zen." *Monumenta Nipponica* 42, no. 1 (1987): 25–55.

Favuzzi, Pellegrino, Tobias Endres, and Timo Klattenhoff. "Cassirer, Globalized—Über Sinn und Zweck eines Neulesens." In *Philosophie der Kultur- und Wissensformen: Ernst Cassirer neu lesen*, 9–22. Frankfurt: Peter Lang, 2016.

Felbur, Rafal, trans. "Things Do Not Shift." In *Three Short Treatises by Vasubandhu, Sengzhao, and Zongmi*, 65–70. BDK English Tripiṭaka Series. Moraga, CA: BDK America, 2017.

Fischer, Peter. *Studien zur Entwicklungsgeschichte des Mappō-Gedankens und zum Mappō-tōmyō-ki [von Saichō]*. Mitteilungen der Gesellschaft für Natur- und Völkerkunde Ostasiens, 65. Hamburg: Gesellschaft für Natur- und Völkerkunde, 1976.

Foshay, Toby Avard. "Denegation, Nonduality, and Language in Derrida and Dōgen." *Philosophy East and West* 44, no. 3 (1994): 543–58.

Foulk, T. Griffith. "Daily Life in the Assembly." In *Buddhism in Practice. Abridged Edition*, edited by D. S. Lopez, 339–56. Princeton, NJ: Princeton University Press, 2007.

———. "'Just Sitting'? Dogen's Take on Zazen, Sutra Reading, and Other Conventional Buddhist Practice." In *Dōgen: Textual and Historical Studies*, edited by Steven Heine, 76–105. New York: Oxford University Press, 2012.

———. "'Rules of Purity' in Japanese Zen." In *Zen Classics: Formative Texts in the History of Zen Buddhism*, edited by Steven Heine and Dale S. Wright, 137–70. New York: Oxford University Press, 2006.

Fraleigh, Matthew. *Plucking Chrysanthemums: Narushima Ryūhoku and Sinitic Literary Traditions in Modern Japan*. Vol. 390. Harvard East Asian Monographs. Cambridge, MA: Harvard University Asia Center, 2016.

Freudenthal, Gideon. "Der fehlende Kern von Cassirers Philosophie: Homo faber in abstracto." In *Ethik oder Ästhetik?: Zur Aktualität der neukantianischen*

Kulturphilosophie, edited by Peter-Ulrich Merz-Benz and Ursula Renz, 261–86. Würzburg: Königshausen und Neumann, 2004.

Furuta Shōkin 古田紹欽. *Nihon Zenshū shi no nagare* 日本禅宗史の流れ. Kyōto: Jinbun Shoin, 1983.

Garrett, Philip. "Getting Away from 'Religion' in Medieval Japan." *Religions* 13, no. 4 (April 2022): 288.

Giles, James. "To Practise One Thing: Kierkegaard through the Eyes of Dogen." In *Kierkegaard and Japanese Thought*, edited by James Giles, 87–105. Basingstoke: Palgrave Macmillan, 2008.

Girard, Frédéric. *Les dialogues de Dōgen en Chine*. Genève: Droz, 2016.

———. "Did Huayan's Teachings Influence Dōgen's Thought?: Dōgen's Treatment of Huayan Concepts of Mind-Only and One-and-Allness (Part 1: The Intellectual Relationship Between Dōgen and Huayan)." *Oriental Studies* 東洋学研究 27 (2020): 237–50.

Goodhew, Linda, and David Loy. "Momo, Dogen, and the Commodification of Time." *KronoScope* 2, no. 1 (2002): 97–107.

Groner, Paul. *Precepts, Ordinations, and Practice in Medieval Japanese Tendai*. University of Hawai'i Press, 2022.

———. *Ryōgen and Mount Hiei : Japanese Tendai in the Tenth Century*. Studies in East Asian Buddhism 15. Honolulu: University of Hawai'i Press, 2002.

———. *Saichō: The Establishment of the Japanese Tendai School*. Berkeley: University of California Press, 1984.

Haas, Hans. *"Amida Buddha unsere Zuflucht": Urkunden zum Verständnis des japanischen Sukhāvatī-Buddhismus*. Göttingen: Vandenhoeck & Ruprecht; J.C. Hinrichs'sche Buchhandlung, 1910.

Hadot, Pierre. *Exercices spirituels et philosophie antique*. Etudes augustiniennes [Série Antiquité 88]. Paris: Etudes augustiniennes, 1981.

———. *Philosophy as a Way of Life: Spiritual Exercises from Socrates to Foucault*. Oxford: Blackwell, 1995.

Hakamaya Noriaki 袴谷憲昭. *Dōgen to bukkyō* 道元と仏教. Tōkyō: Daizō Shuppan, 1992.

———. *Dōgen to bukkyō: Jūnikanbon "Shōbōgenzō" no Dōgen* 道元と仏教: 十二巻本『正法眼蔵』の道元. Tōkyō: Daizō shuppan, 1992.

———. *Honkaku shisō hihan* 本覚思想批判. Tōkyō: Daizō shuppan 大蔵出版, 1989.

Hakeda, Yoshito S. *Kūkai: Major Works. Translated, with an Account of His Life and a Study of His Thought*. New York: Columbia University Press, 1972.

Harweg, Roland. *Zeit in Mythos und Geschichte: Weltweite Untersuchungen zu mythographischer und historiographischer Chronographie vom Altertum bis zur Gegenwart. Chronographie im Orient vom Altertum bis zur Gegenwart*. Vol. 3. Münster: LIT Verlag, 2009.

Hashimoto Hideki 橋本英樹. "'Zuimonki' no seiritsu o kangaeru (Josetsu)「随聞記」の成立を考える(序説)." *Komazawa daigaku bukkyō gakubu ronshū* 駒沢大学仏教学部論集 27 (October 1996): 203–13.

He Yangsheng 何燕生. "Dōgen no shinjōsōmetsuron hihan ni kansuru isshiten 道元の心常相滅論 批判に関する一視点." *Shūkyō kenkyū* 宗教研究 69, no. 3 (1995): 125–47.

Heidegger, Martin. *Gesamtausgabe*. 90 vols. Frankfurt am Main: Klostermann, 1975.

———. *Sein und Zeit*. 17th ed. Tübingen: Niemeyer, 1993.

Heine, Steven. "Critical Buddhism (Hihan Bukkyō) and the Debate Concerning the 75-Fascicle and 12-Fascicle Shōbōgenzō Texts." *Japanese Journal of Religious Studies* 21, no. 1 (1994): 37–72.

———. *Did Dōgen Go to China? What Dōgen Wrote and When He Wrote It*. New York: Oxford University Press, 2006.

———. "Dōgen and the Precepts Revisited." In *Buddhist Studies from India to America: Essays in Honor of Charles S. Prebish*, edited by Damien Keown, 9–27. London: Routledge, 2006.

———. "Dōgen: His Life, Religion, and Poetry." *Education About ASIA* 20, no. 2 (2015).

———. *Existential and Ontological Dimensions of Time in Heidegger and Dōgen*. Albany: State University of New York Press, 1985.

———. *Flowers Blooming on a Withered Tree: Giun's Verse Comments on Dōgen's Treasury of the True Dharma Eye*. New York: Oxford University Press, 2020.

———. *Readings of Dōgen's Treasury of the True Dharma Eye*. New York: Columbia University Press, 2020.

———. *Shifting Shape, Shaping Text: Philosophy and Folklore in the Fox Kôan*. Honolulu: University of Hawai'i Press, 1999.

———. "The Dōgen Canon. Dōgen's Pre-Shōbōgenzō Writings and the Question of Change in His Later Works." *Japanese Journal of Religious Studies* 24, no. 1–2 (1997): 39–85.

Heinemann, Robert Klaus. *Der Weg des Übens im Ostasiatischen Mahāyāna: Grundformen seiner Zeitrelation zum Übungsziel in der Entwicklung bis Dōgen*. Wiesbaden: Harrassowitz, 1979.

Hodgkin, Katharine, and Susannah Radstone. *Contested Pasts: The Politics of Memory*. London: Routledge, 2003.

Holbrook, Dwight. "Does Time Move? Dogen and the Art of Understanding the Moment." *Analecta Husserliana* 74 (2002): 193–200.

Hoshi Shundō 星俊道. "Dōgen zenji ni okeru shūkyōteki jikan no tokushitsu 道元禅師における 宗教的時間の特質." *Komazawa daigaku bukkyō gakubu ronshū* 駒沢大学仏教学部論集 23 (October 1992): 309–18.

Hubbard, Jamie, and Paul L. Swanson, eds. *Pruning the Bodhi Tree: The Storm over Critical Buddhism*. Nanzan Library of Asian Religion and Culture. Honolulu: University of Hawai'i Press, 1997.

Huntington, Eric. "Buddhist Cosmology." In *Oxford Research Encyclopedia of Religion*, 2022. https://doi.org/10.1093/acrefore/9780199340378.013.1050.

Nishimura Eshin 西村惠信, ed. *Mumonkan* 無門関 [=Chin. *Wu Men Guan*]. Tōkyō: Iwanami Shoten, 1994.

Hume, David. *An Enquiry concerning Human Understanding*. In "Hume Texts Online." https://davidhume.org/texts/e/2.

Hurvitz, Leon. *Scripture of the Lotus Blossom of the Fine Dharma*. New York: Columbia University Press, 1976.

Husserl, Edmund. *Cartesian Meditations: An Introduction to Phenomenology*. Translated by Dorion Cairns. The Hague: M. Nijhoff, 1960.

Ichikawa Hirofumi 市川浩史. *Nihon chūsei no rekishi ishiki: Sangoku mappō Nihon* 日本中世の歴史意識：三国・末法・日本. Kyōto: Hōzōkan, 2005.

Ichimura, Shōhei. *Zen Master Keizan's Monastic Regulations = Keizan zenji (Oshō) Shingi*. Tsurumi: Daihonzan Sōjiji, 1994.

Ijichi Tetsuo 伊地知鐵男, Omote Akira 表章, and Kuriyama Riichi 栗山理一. *Renga ronshū. Nōgaku ronshū. Haironshū*. 連歌論集; 能楽論集; 俳論集. Tōkyō: Shōgakkan, 1973.

Imaeda Aishin 今枝愛真. *Dōgen: Zazen hitosuji no shamon* 道元：坐禪ひとすじの沙門. *Nihon hōsō shuppan kyōkai*, 1976.

Ishida Mitsuyuki 石田充之. *Shunjō risshi: Kamakura bukkyō seiritsu no kenkyū* 俊芿律師：鎌倉仏教成立の研究. Kyōto: Hōzōkan, 1972.

Ishii Kiyozumi [Seijun] 石井清純. "'Zengo saidan' ni tsuite「前後際断」について." *Shūgaku Kenkyū* 宗學研究 40 (1998): 43-48.

———. "Zengo saidan to Uji no kyōryaku 前後際断と有時の経歴." *Indogaku bukkyōgaku kenkyū* 印度學佛教學研究 63, no. 2 (2015): 692-99.

———. "Eiheiji senjutsu bunken ni miru Dōgen zenji no sōdan un'ei 永平寺撰述文献に見る道元禅師の僧団運営." In *Dōgen zenji kenkyū ronshū: Dōgen zenji 750kai dai onki kinen shuppan* 道元禪師研究論集：道元禪師七百五十回大遠忌記念出版, edited by Daihonzan Eiheiji daionkikyoku bunka jigyō senmon bukai shuppan iinkai 大本山 永平寺大遠忌局文化事業專門部会出版委員会, 409-40. Tōkyō: Daishūkan shoten, 2002.

Ishii Shūdō 石井修道. "Kaidai (Sōsetsu) 解題（総説）." In *Zenshū shingi shū* 禅宗清規集, edited by Ishii Shūdō, 739-56. Kyōto: Rinsen shoten, 2014.

———, ed. "Keizan shingi 瑩山清規." In *Zenshū shingi shū* 禅宗清規集, edited by Ishii Shūdō, 645-717. Kyōto: Rinsen Shoten, 2014.

———. "'Nisshū nichiyō' kaidai 『入衆日用』解題." In *Zenshū shingi shū* 禅宗清規集, edited by Ishii Shūdō, 772-79. Kyōto: Rinsen Shoten, 2014.

Ishikawa Rikizan 石川力山. "'Mappō tōmyōki' to Dōgen Zen 『末法燈明記』と道元禅." *Indo gaku bukkyō gaku kenkyū* 45, no. 1 (1996): 174-80.

Izutsu Toshihiko 井筒俊彦. "Tōyō tetsugaku no tame ni—4—sōzō fudan—Tōyō-teki jikan ishiki no genkei—ge—Dōgen no 'Uji' ni tsuite 東洋哲学のために-4-創造不断―東洋的時間意識の元型-下-道元の「有時」について." *Shisō* 思想 742 (1986): 49-70.

Jaeschke, Walter. "Die List der Vernunft." *Hegel-Studien* 43 (2008): 87–102.
Jakobson, Roman. "Closing Statement: Linguistics and Poetics." In *Style in Language*, edited by Thomas A. Sebeok, 350–77. Cambridge, MA: MIT Press, 1960.
Jia, Jinhua. "The Creation and Codification of Monastic Regulations at Mount Baizhang." *Journal of Chinese Religions* 33, no. 1 (2005): 39–59.
Kagamishima Genryū 鏡島元隆, ed. *Dōgen zenji goroku* 道元禅師語錄. Tōkyō: Kōdansha, 1990.
———. *Dōgen zenji to sono shūfū* 道元禅師とその宗風. Tōkyō: Shunjūsha, 1994.
———, general ed. *Genbun taishō gendaigo yaku Dōgen zenji zenshū* 原文対照現代語訳道元禅師全集. 17 vols. Tōkyō: Shunjūsha, 1999–2013.
Kamo no Chōmei 鴨長明. *Shintei hōjōki* 新訂方丈記. Edited by Ichiko Teiji 市古貞次. Tōkyō: Iwanami, 1989.
Kamo Chōmei, and Arthur Lindsay Sadler. *The Ten Foot Square Hut; And, Tales of the Heike*. Tuttle Classics. North Clarendon: Tuttle Publishing, 2006.
Karaki Junzō 唐木順三. "Mujō no keijijōgaku 無常の形而上学." In *Dōgen shisō kenkyū kakuron* 道元思想研究各論, edited by Tsunoda Tairyū 角田泰隆, 322–74. Dōgen Shisō Taikei/Shisōhen 道元思想大系 思想篇 6. Kyōto: Dōhōsha, 1995.
Kasai Akira 笠井哲. "Suzuki shōsan ni okeru 'Keizai rinri' ni tsuite 鈴木正三における「経済倫理」について [On the Economic Ethics of Suzuki Shosan]." *Indogaku bukkyōgaku kenkyū* 印度學佛教學研究 42, no. 5 (2006): 791–97.
Kasulis, Thomas P. *Zen Action/Zen Person*. Honolulu: University of Hawai'i Press, 1981.
Kato, Bunno, and William Edward Soothill. *The Threefold Lotus Sutra*. New York: Weatherhill, 1975.
Kaufmann, Paulus, and Raji C. Steineck. "Another Discourse on the Method: Understanding Philosophy through Rhetorical Analysis." *European Journal of Japanese Philosophy* 3 (2018): 59–86.
Kawabata, Yasunari. "The Nobel Prize in Literature 1968." https://www.nobelprize.org/prizes/literature/1968/kawabata/lecture.
Kawamura Kōdō 河村孝道, ed. *Dōgen Zenshi zenshū* 道元禅師全集. 河村孝道. Tōkyō: Shunjūsha, 1988.
———. *Shōbōgenzō no seiritsushiteki kenkyū* 正法眼蔵の成立史的研究. Tōkyō: Shunjūsha 春秋社, 1987.
———. "Shōbōgenzō 'Uji' ni tsuite—Busshō no mondai to no kanren ni oite 正法眼蔵「有時」について仏—性の問題との関連に於いて." *Shūgaku kenkyū* 宗學研究 3 (1961): 117–25.
Kelemen, Mihaela, and Tuomo Peltonen. "Spirituality: A Way to an Alternative Subjectivity?" *Organization Management Journal* 2, no. 1 (May 1, 2005): 52–63.
Kikutō Myōdō 菊藤明道. "Kamakura kyūbukkyō to mappō shisō 鎌倉旧仏教と末法思想." *Indogaku bukkyōgaku kenkyū* 23, no. 1 (1974): 235–38.

Kim, Hee Jin. *Dōgen Kigen, Mystical Realist* [2nd printing]. Monographs of the Association for Asian Studies. Tucson: University of Arizona Press, 1980.
———. *Dōgen on Meditation and Thinking a Reflection on His View of Zen.* Albany: State University of New York Press, 2007.
Kohō Chisan 孤峰智璨, ed. *Jōsai daishi zenshū* 常濟大師全集. 2nd ed. Kanagawa: Daihonzan Sōjiji, 1967.
Kopf, Gereon. *Beyond Personal Identity. Dōgen, Nishida, and a Phenomenology of No-Self.* Richmond: Curzon Press, 2001.
Kornicki, Peter. *The Book in Japan: A Cultural History from the Beginnings to the Nineteenth Century.* Leiden: Brill, 1998.
Kosaka Kiyū 小坂機融, Hareyama Shun'ei 晴山俊英, Iwanaga Shōsei 岩永正晴, Tsunoda Tairyū 角田泰隆, and Itō Shūken 伊藤秀憲, eds. "Bendō hō 弁道法." In GG DZZ 15:31-51.
———, ed. "Taitaiko goge jari hō 大己五夏闍梨法." In GG DZZ 15:95-105, 267-80, 362-66.
Kubica, Olga. "Reading the *Milindapañha*: Indian Historical Sources and the Greeks in Bactria." In *The Graeco-Bactrian and Indo-Greek World*, 430-45. London: Routledge, 2020.
Kurebayashi Kōdō 樺林皓堂. "Dōgen zenji no kyōgaku to nyūshū nichiyō shingi 道元禪師の教學と入衆日用清規." *Komazawa daigaku jissen shūjō kenkyūkai nenpō* 駒沢大学実践宗 乗研究会年報 8 (1940): 17-27.
Kuroda, Toshio. "The Development of the Kenmitsu System as Japan's Medieval Orthodoxy." *Japanese Journal of Religious Studies* 23, no. 3-4 (1996): 233-69.
Lakoff, George, and Mark Johnson. *Philosophy in the Flesh: The Embodied Mind and Its Challenge to Western Thought.* New York: Basic Books, 1999.
Leighton, Taigen Daniel, and Shōhaku Okumura, eds. *Dōgen's Extensive Record: A Translation of the Eihei Koroku.* Boston: Wisdom Publications, 2004.
———. *Dōgen's Pure Standards for the Zen Community: A Translation of Eihei Shingi.* Albany, NY: State University of New York Press, 1996.
Levman, Bryan G. "Revisiting Milindapañha." *Journal Asiatique* 309, no. 1 (2021): 107-30.
Loori, John Daido, and Kazuaki Tanahashi, trans. *The True Dharma Eye: Zen Master Dogen's Three Hundred Kōans.* Boston: Shambhala, 2005.
Luhmann, Niklas. "Gleichzeitigkeit und Synchronisation." In *Soziologische Aufklärung 5*, 92-125. VS Verlag für Sozialwissenschaften, 2005.
———. "Zeit und Handlung—Eine vergessene Theorie." In *Soziologische Aufklärung 3*, 101-25. VS Verlag für Sozialwissenschaften, 1981.
Maki Yūsuke 真木悠介. *Jikan no hikaku shakaigaku* 時間の比較社会学. Tōkyō: Iwanami shoten, 2003.
Maraldo, John. "Negotiating the Divide of Death in Japanese Buddhism: Dōgen's Difference." In *Dōgen and Sōtō Zen*, edited by Steven Heine, 109-37. Oxford: Oxford University Press, 2015.

Marra, Michele. "The Development of 'Mappō' Thought in Japan (I)." *Japanese Journal of Religious Studies* 15, no. 1 (1988): 25–54.

———. "The Development of 'Mappō' Thought in Japan (II)." *Japanese Journal of Religious Studies* 15, no. 4 (1988): 287–305.

Maruyama Masao 丸山真男. "Rekishi ishiki no 'kosō' 歴史意識の「古層」." In *Maruyama Masao shū* 丸山真男集, 10:3–64. Tōkyō: Iwanami, 1996.

Marx, Wolfgang. *Reflexionstopologie*. Tübingen: Mohr, 1984.

Masunaga, Reihō. *A Primer of Sōtō Zen*. Honolulu: University of Hawai'i Press, 1971.

———. *The Soto Approach to Zen*. Tōkyō: Layman Buddhist Society Press, 1958.

Masunaga Reihō. "Dōgen zenji no tachiba to sono jikanron 道元禪師の立場とその時間論." *Indogaku bukkyōgaku kenkyū* 1, no. 2 (1953): 269–78.

Matsumoto Shirō 松本史朗. *Engi to kū: Nyoraizō shisō hihan* 縁起と空: 如来蔵思想批判. Tōkyō: Daizō shuppan, 1989.

Matsunami Naohiro 松波直弘. *Kamakura bukkyō zenshū shisōshi no kenkyū: "Nihon zenshū" no keisei* 鎌倉期禅宗思想史の研究:「日本禅宗」の形成. Tōkyō: Perikan sha, 2011.

Matsuo, Kenji. *A History of Japanese Buddhism*. Folkestone: Global Oriental, 2007.

———. "What Is Kamakura New Buddhism? Official Monks and Reclusive Monks." *Japanese Journal of Religious Studies* 24, no. 1–2 (1997): 179–89.

McCarroll, Pam, Thomas St. James O'Connor, and Elisabeth Meakes. "Assessing Plurality in Spirituality Definitions." In *Spirituality and Health: Multidisciplinary Explorations*, edited by Augustine Meier et al., 43–59. Waterloo, Ontario: Wilfrid Laurier University Press, 2005.

Maynard, Senko Kumiya. *Principles of Japanese Discourse: A Handbook = Nihongo*. Cambridge: Cambridge University Press, 1998.

Meier, Augustine, Thomas St. James O'Connor, and Peter L. VanKatwyk. *Spirituality and Health: Multidisciplinary Explorations*. Waterloo, Ontario: Wilfrid Laurier University Press, 2005.

Mezaki Tokue 目崎徳衛. "Matsudai/Mappō to jōdo shinkō 末代・末法と浄土信仰." In *Jikan* 時間, edited by Sagara Tōru 相良亨 et al., 37–78. Nihon shisō 日本思想 4. Tōkyō: Daigaku Shuppankai, 1984.

Mills, Ian. "Aeterno Modo: The Expression of an Integral Consciousness in the Work of Kierkegaard and Dogen." In *Kierkegaard and Japanese Thought*, edited by James Giles, 106–23. Basingstoke: Palgrave Macmillan, 2008.

Moriya Shigeru 守屋茂. "Dōgen zenji to hokuetsu ishaku no shinsō—Zenji no ketsudan to Hakusan Tendai no eikyō 道元禅師と北越移錫の真相-禅師の決断と白山天台の影響." *Shūgaku kenkyū* 宗學研究 30 (1988): 19–24.

Müller, Klaus. *Wirtschafts- und Technikgeschichte Japans*. Handbuch der Orientalistik. Fünfte Abteilung: Japan 3. Leiden: Brill, 1988.

Murphy, Tim. "Religionswissenschaft as Colonialist Discourse: The Case of Rudolf Otto." *Temenos—Nordic Journal of Comparative Religion* 43, no. 1 (2007).

Nagafuji Yasushi 永藤靖. *Kodai Nihon bungaku to jikan ishiki* 古代日本文学と時間意識. Tōkyō: Miraisha, 1979.

Nagai Kenryū 永井賢隆. "*Tenzo kyōkun* senjutsu ito no kōsatsu 『典座教訓』撰述意図の考察." *Zengaku Kenkyū* 98 (2020): 1–15.

Nahm, Kiho. "Hegels Begriff der List." *Tijdschrift voor Filosofie* 78, no. 2 (2016): 329–64.

Nakamura Hajime 中村元, and Kino Kazuyoshi 紀野一義, eds. *Hannyashingyō/Kongōhannyakyō* 般若心經・金剛般若經. Tōkyō: Iwanami Shoten, 1960.

Nakamura, Hajime, and William Johnston. "Suzuki Shōsan, 1579–1655 and the Spirit of Capitalism in Japanese Buddhism." *Monumenta Nipponica* 22, no. 1, no. 2 (1967): 1–14.

Nakamura Sōichi 中村宗一. *Zen'yaku Shōbō genzō* 全訳正法眼蔵. Vol. 1. Tōkyō: Seishin Shobō, 1971.

Nakaseko Shōdō 中世古祥道. *Dōgen zenji den kenkyū* 道元禅師伝研究. Tōkyō: Kokushokankōkai, 1979.

———. *Shin Dōgen zenji den kenkyū* 新道元禅師伝研究. Tōkyō: Kokusho kankōkai, 2002.

———. *Dōgen zenji den kenkyū : 2*. 道元禅師伝研究. Tōkyō: Kokusho kankōkai, 1997.

Nattier, Jan. *Once upon a Future Time: Studies in a Buddhist Prophecy of Decline*. Berkeley: Asian Humanities Press, 1991.

Nearman, Hubert. *The Shōbōgenzō, or, The Treasure House of the Eye of the True Teachings*. Translated by Hubert Nearman. Mount Shasta: Shasta Abbey, 1996. https://www.urbandharma.org/udharma12/shobo.html.

Needham, Joseph. "Time and Knowledge in China and the West." In *The Voices of Time: A Cooperative Survey of Man's Views of Time as Expressed by the Sciences and by the Humanities*, edited by J. T. Fraser, 92–137. New York: G. Braziller, 1966.

Nieda, Rokusaburo. "'Nothing' in Zen." *Numen* 9, no. 1 (January 1, 1962): 37–44.

Nihon kokugo daijiten dainihan henshū iinkai 日本国語大辞典第二版編集委員会, Shōgakukan Kokugo Jiten Henshūbu 小学館国語辞典編集部. *Nihon kokugo daijiten* 日本国語大辞典. Shōgakukan, 2003.

Nishio Minoru 西尾実. "Zeami no geijutsuron no tokushitsu to Dōgen no eikyō 世阿弥の芸術論の特質と道元の影響." In *Dōgen zenji to sōtōshū* 道元禅師と曹洞宗, edited by Kawamura Kōdō 河村孝道, Ishikawa Rikizan 石川力山, 335–52. Yoshikawa kōbunkan, 1985.

Obert, Mathias. "Zeit als Relationalität und Sprung bei Fazang." In *Zeit: Anfang und Ende*, edited by Walter Schweidler, 111–23. Sankt Augustin: Academia Verlag, 2004.

Ogle, Vanessa. "Time, Temporality and the History of Capitalism." *Past & Present* 243, no. 1 (2019): 312–27.

Ohe, Seizo. "Time, Temporality, and Freedom." In *Time and the Philosophies*, edited by Honorat Aguessy, 81–89. Paris: Unesco, 1977.

Ōkubo Dōshū, 大久保道舟. *Dōgen zenji den no kenkyū (Kaitei Zōho)* 道元禪師傳の研究 (改訂増補). Tōkyō: Chikuma Shobō, 1966.

———. "Dōgen zenji no genshi sōdan to Nihon daruma shū to no kankei 道元禅師の原始僧団と日本達磨宗との関係." In *Dōgen no shōgai 3: Kōshōji kaisō, Hokuetsu ishaku* 道元の生涯 3: 興聖寺開創・北越移錫, edited by Takahashi Shūei 高橋秀栄, 201–17. Dōgen shisō taikei 道元思想大系 3. Kyōto: Dōhōsha, 1995.

———, ed. *Dōgen zenji zenshū* 道元禅師全集. Tōkyō: Chikuma Shobō, 1969.

Olson, Carl. "The Leap of Thinking: A Comparison of Heidegger and the Zen Master Dōgen." *Philosophy Today* 25, no. 1 (1981): 55–62.

O'Malley, Michael. "Time, Work and Task Orientation: A Critique of American Historiography." *Time & Society* 1, no. 3 (1992): 341–58.

Ōmori Shōzō 大森荘蔵. *Jikan to sonzai* 時間と存在. Tōkyō: Seidosha, 1994.

Orzech, Charles D. *Politics and Transcendent Wisdom: The Scripture for Humane Kings in the Creation of Chinese Buddhism*. University Park: Pennsylvania State University Press, 1998.

Ōsumi Kazuo 大隅和雄. "Jizoku to henkaku—shinwa kara rekishi e 持続と変革〜神話から歴史へ." In *Jikan* 時間, edited by Sagara Tōru 相良亨 et al., 133–65. Nihon shisō 日本思想 4. Tōkyō: Tōkyō daigaku shuppankai, 1984.

Ōtani Tetsuo 大谷哲夫. *Dōgen zenji oriori no hōwa: Eihei kōroku ni manabu* 道元禅師おりおりの法話: 永平広録に学ぶ. Tōkyō: Sōtō shū shūmuchō, 1999.

———, eds. *Eihei kōroku: Kunchū* 永平廣錄: 訓註. 2 vols. Tōkyō: Daizō Shuppan, 1996.

———. *Eihei no kaze: Dōgen no shōgai* 永平の風: 道元の生涯. Tōkyō: Bungeisha, 2001.

Ōtomo Taishi 大友泰司. *Zeami to zen* 世阿弥と禅. Tōkyō: Kanrin shobō, 2007.

Ōtsuka Tadahide 大塚忠秀. "Dōgen to Meruro Ponti ni okeru jikan 道元とメルロポンティにおける時間 'Time' in Merleau-Ponty and Dogen." *Hikaku shisō kenkyū* 比較思想研究 2 (1975): 1–13.

Otto, Rudolf. "Über Zazen als Extrem des numinosen Irrationalen." In *Aufsätze, das Numinose betreffend*. Stuttgart: Perthes, 1923.

Ozaki Shōzen 尾崎正善 (崎」replaces「山奇」). "'Keizan shingi' kaidai 『瑩山清規』解題." In *Zenshū shingi shū* 禅宗清規集, edited by Ishii Shūdō, 780–92. Kyōto: Rinsen Shoten, 2014.

Ozawa Tomio 小沢富夫. *Mappō to masse no shisō* 末法と末世の思想. Tōkyō: Yūzankaku shuppan, 1974.

Ozeki, Ruth L. *The Book of Form and Emptiness*. New York: Viking, 2021.

Payne, Richard K. "84. The Fourfold Training in Japanese Esoteric Buddhism." In *Esoteric Buddhism and the Tantras in East Asia*, edited by Charles D. Orzech, Henrik H. Sørensen, and Richard K. Payne, 1024–28. Leiden: Brill, 2011.

Pinte, Klaus. "Shingon Risshū: Esoteric Buddhism and Vinaya Orthodoxy in Japan." In *Esoteric Buddhism and the Tantras in East Asia*, edited by Charles D. Orzech, Henrik H. Sørensen, and Richard K. Payne, 845–53. Leiden: Brill, 2011.

Pfaller, Robert. *On the Pleasure Principle in Culture: Illusions Without Owners*. London: Verso Books, 2014.

Piaget, Jean. "Time Perception in Children." In *The Voices of Time: A Cooperative Survey of Man's Views of Time as Expressed by the Sciences and by the Humanities*, edited by J. T. Fraser, 202–16. New York: G. Braziller, 1966.

Postone, Moishe. *Time, Labor, and Social Domination: A Reinterpretation of Marx's Critical Theory*. Cambridge: Cambridge University Press, 2006.

Prasad, Hari S. *Essays on Time in Buddhism*. Vol. no. 78. Bibliotheca Indo-Buddhica. Delhi: Sri Satguru, 1991.

Putnam, Hilary. "Two Philosophical Perspectives." In *The Nature of Truth: Classic and Contemporary Perspectives*, edited by Michael Patrick Lynch, 251–58. Cambridge, MA: MIT Press, 2001.

Quine, Willard van Orman. *From a Logical Point of View: Logico-Philosophical Essay*. 2nd ed. New York: Harper and Row, 1963.

Quinter, David. "Creating Bodhisattvas: Eison, Hinin, and the 'Living Mañjuśrī.'" *Monumenta Nipponica* 62, no. 4 (2007): 437–58.

———. "Emulation and Erasure: Eison, Ninshō, and the Gyōki Cult." *The Eastern Buddhist* 39, no. 1 (2008): 29–60.

Rabbow, Paul. *Seelenführung: Methodik der Exerzitien in der Antike*. München: Kösel, 1954.

Rappe, Guido. "Time and Nothingness in Aspects of Buddhist Philosophy—From the Beginnings to Dogen's Uji." In *Interkulturelle Philosophie und Phänomenologie in Japan: Beiträge zum Gespräch über Grenzen hinweg*, edited by Tadashi Ogawa, Michael Lazarin, and Guido Rappe, 325–65. München: Iudicium, 1998.

Raud, Rein. "The Existential Moment: Rereading Dōgen's Theory of Time." *Philosophy East and West* 62, no. 2 (2012): 153–73.

Redfield, James Adam. "Being Time: Zen, Modernity, the Contemporary." *Diogenes* 58, no. 4 (2011): 123–46.

Ricoeur, Paul. "The History of Religions and the Phenomenology of Time Consciousness." In *The History of Religions: Retrospect and Prospect*, edited by Joseph M. Kitagawa, 13–30. New York: Macmillan, 1985.

Roberts, Shinshu. *Being-Time: A Practitioner's Guide to Dōgen's Shōbōgenzō Uji*, 2018.

Rosa, Hartmut. *Social Acceleration: A New Theory of Modernity*. Translated by Jonathan Trejo-Mathys. New York: Columbia University Press, 2016.

Rospatt, Alexander von. "The Buddhist Doctrine of Momentariness: A Survey of the Origins and Early Phase of This Doctrine up to Vasubandhu." Stuttgart: Steiner, 1995.

Rovelli, Carlo. "'Forget Time': Essay Written for the FQXi Contest on the Nature of Time." August 24, 2008. 8. http://fqxi.org/data/essay-contest-files/Rovelli_Time.pdf? phpMyAdmin=0c371ccdae9b5ff3071bae814fb4f9e9.

Sango, Asuka. "Buddhist Debate in Medieval Japan." *Religion Compass* 9, no. 7 (2015): 216–25.

Sasaki Katsuhiro 佐々木勝浩 "Rōkoku no genri to suii henka no sūchikeisan" 漏刻の原理と水位変化の数値計算." *Kokuritsu kagaku hakubutsukan kenkyū hōkoku E rui (rikōgaku)* 国立科学博物館研究報告 E 類 (理工学) 26 (2003): 21–31.

Satō Hiroo 佐藤弘夫. *Kamakura bukkyō* 鎌倉仏教. Tōkyō: Chikuma shobō, 2014.

Sawashiro Kunio 澤城邦生. "Sengo kara gendai ni okeru *Tenzo kyōkun* no tenkai: Toku ni shūmon gai de no dōkō ni tsuite 戦後から現代における『典座教訓』の展開: 特に宗門外での動向について." *Sōtōshū sōgō kenkyū sentā gakujutsu taikai kiyō* 曹洞宗総合研究センター学術大会紀要 21 (2020): 32–37.

Schilbrack, Kevin. "Metaphysics in Dōgen." *Philosophy East and West* 50, no. 1 (2000): 34–55.

Schmitz, Hermann. *Der unerschöpfliche Gegenstand*. Bonn: Bouvier, 1995.

Schulz, Guido. "Marx's Distinction between the Fetish Character of the Commodity and Fetishism." *Studies in Social & Political Thought* 20 (2012): 25–45.

Shaner, David Edward, ed. *The Bodymind Experience in Japanese Buddhism: A Phenomenological Perspective of Kūkai and Dōgen*. SUNY Series in Buddhist Studies. Albany: State University of New York Press, 1985.

Shimazono Susumu 島薗進. "Supirichuariti no mirai ni mukete: Genkai ishiki no supirichuaritie to iu shiten kara スピリチュアリティの未来に向けて: 限界意識のスピリチュアリティという視点から." *Gendai shisō* 現代思想 51, no. 12 (October 2023): 8–19.

Shinohara Hisao 篠原寿雄. *Gakudō yōjin shū: Dōgen gakushū to shugyō no kokoroe* 学道用心集: 道元学習と修行のこころえ. Tōkyō: Daitō Shuppansha, 1990.

Shirane, Haruo. "Canon Formation in Japan: Genre, Gender, Popular Culture, and Nationalism." *Reading East Asian Writing: The Limits of Literary Theory* 12 (2003): 22.

———. *Japan and the Culture of the Four Seasons: Nature, Literature, and the Arts*. New York: Columbia University Press, 2012.

———. "Japan and the Culture of the Four Seasons Nature, Literature and the Arts." In *Rethinking Nature in Japan from Tradition to Modernity*, 9–25, 2017.

Shirasu Masako 白洲正子. *Myōe shōnin* 明恵上人. Tōkyō: Kōdansha, 2002.

Solignac, Aimé. "Spiritualität." In *Historisches Wörterbuch der Philosophie online*. Basel: Schwabe, 2017. https://doi.org/10.24894/HWPh.4013.

Stambaugh, Joan. *Impermanence Is Buddha-Nature: Dōgen's Understanding of Temporality*. Honolulu: University of Hawai'i Press, 1990.

Steger, Brigitte. "Japanese Historic 'Timescapes': An Anthropological Approach." *KronoScope* 17, no. 1 (2017): 37–60.

Steineck, Christian. "Time Is Not Fleeting: Thoughts of a Medieval Zen Buddhist." *KronoScope* 7, no. 1 (2007): 33–47.

Steineck, Raji C. "A Zen Philosopher?—Notes on the Philosophical Reading of Dōgen's *Shōbōgenzō*." In *Concepts of Philosophy in Asia and the Islamic World, Vol. 1: China and Japan*, edited by Raji C. Steineck, Elena L. Lange, Ralph Weber, and Robert H. Gassmann, 577–606. Leiden: Brill, 2018.

———. "Chronographical Analysis: An Essay in Methodology." *KronoScope* 18, no. 2 (2018): 171–98.

———. "From *Uji* to Being-Time (and Back): Translating Dōgen into Philosophy." In *Dōgen's Texts*, edited by Ralf Müller and George Wrisley. Berlin: Springer, 2023.

———. "Ichlosigkeit als wahres Selbst. Reflexionen zu einer religiösen Subjektivitätskonstruktion." In *Die Relationalität des Subjektes im Kontext der Religionshermeneutik*, edited by Gerhard Oberhammer and Marcus Schmücker, 213–30. Beiträge zur Kultur- und Geistesgeschichte 70. Wien: ÖAW Verlag der Österreichischen Akademie der Wissenschaften, 2011.

———. "Kritik der Kultur. Überlegungen zu Cassirers Konzept der symbolischen Form." *Zeitschrift für Kulturphilosophie* 14, no. 1 (2020): 137–52.

———. *Kritik der symbolischen Formen I: Symbolische Form und Funktion*. Stuttgart: Frommann-Holzboog, 2014.

———. "'Religion' and the Concept of the Buddha Way: Semantics of the Religious in Dōgen." *Asiatische Studien—Études Asiatiques* 72, no. 1 (2018): 177–206.

———. "Time and Eschatology." In *Brill's Encyclopedia of Buddhism*. Vol. 3, forthcoming.

———. "Time in Old Japan: In Search of a Paradigm." *KronoScope* 17, no. 1 (March 28, 2017): 16–36.

———. "Time, Waste and Enlightenment, or: On Leaving No Trace." In *Time and Trace: Multidisciplinary Investigations of Temporality*, edited by Sabine Gross and Steve Ostovich. Brill, 2016.

———. "When Zen Becomes Philosophy: The Case of Dōgen's Uji." *Journal of Chan Buddhism* 3 (2023): 107–28.

Stevenson, W. H., ed. *Blake: The Complete Poems*. 3rd ed. Harlow: Pearson Education Ltd., 2007.

Steiniger, Brian. "Manuscript Culture and Chinese Learning in Medieval Kamakura." *Harvard Journal of Asiatic Studies* 78, no. 2 (2018): 339–69.

Stone, Jackie. "Seeking Enlightenment in the Last Age: 'Mappō' Thought in Kamakura Buddhism: Part I." *The Eastern Buddhist* 18, no. 1 (1985): 28–56.

———. "Seeking Enlightenment in the Last Age: Mappō Thought in Kamakura Buddhism: Part II." *The Eastern Buddhist* 18, no. 2 (1985): 35–64.

Stone, Jacqueline. *Original Enlightenment and the Transformation of Medieval Japanese Buddhism*. Studies in East Asian Buddhism 12. Honolulu: University of Hawai'i Press, 1999.

———. *Original Enlightenment and the Transformation of Medieval Japanese Buddhism*. Studies in East Asian Buddhism. Honolulu: University of Hawai'i Press, 1999.

Sueki Fumihiko 末木文美士. "Shisō/Shisō shi/Shisō shigaku: Futatsu no Nihon shisōshi kōza to Nihon shisōshi no toikata 思想/思想史/思想史学：二つの日本思想史講座と日本思想史 の問い方." *Nihon shisōshi gaku* 日本思想史学 48 (2016): 13–21.

Sugio Genyū 杉尾玄有. "Zengosaidan—setsuna shōmetsu no ronri 前後際断・刹那生滅の論理." *Sōtōshū sōgō kenkyū* 20 (1978): 29–34.

———. "Haideggā saikin no kyōgai to Dōgen Zen ハイデッガー最近の境涯と道元禅." *Indogaku bukkyōgaku kenkyū* 印度學佛教學研究 19, no. 2 (1971): 709–12.

Suzuki, Daisetz Teitaro 鈴木大拙. *Japanese Spirituality*. Tokyo: Japan Society for the Promotion of Science, 1972.

———. *Nihonteki reisei* 日本的霊性. Tōkyō: Daito Shuppansha, 1946.

———. "Zen: A Reply to Hu Shih." *Philosophy East and West* 3, no. 1 (1953): 25–46.

Tachi Ryūshi 舘隆志. "Kamakura ki no zenrin ni okeru chūgoku go to nihongo 鎌倉期の禅林における中国語と日本語." *Komazawa daigaku bukkyōgaku ronshū* 駒沢大学仏教学部論集 45 (2014): 259–86.

———. "Rankei dōryū 'Bendō shingi' ni tsuite 蘭渓道隆『弁道清規』について." *Indogaku bukkyōgaku kenkyū* 印度學佛教學研究 59, no. 1 (2010): 141–45.

Tajima Hakudō 田島柏堂. "Sōtōshū ni okeru tenseki kaihan no rekishi 曹洞宗における典籍開版の歴史." In *Dōgen zenji to Sōtōshū* 道元禅師と曹洞宗, edited by Kawamura Kōdō 河村孝道 and Ishikawa Rikizan 石川力山, 292–319. Yoshikawa kōbunkan, 1985.

Takahashi Kenjin 高橋賢陳. "Dōgen ni okeru sonzaijikan no ronri 道元に於ける存在時間の論理." *Onomichi tanki daigaku kiyō* 尾道短期大学研究紀要, 2 (1953): 47–70.

———. *Shōbō genzō zenkan gendaiyaku. Jō* 正法眼蔵全巻現代訳・上. Tōkyō: Risōsha, 1971.

Takakusu Junjirō 高楠順次郎, Watanabe Kaigyoku 渡邊海旭 et al., eds. *Taishō shinshū daizōkyō:* 大正新修大蔵経. Tōkyō: Taishō issaikyō kankōkai, 1931.

Takayanagi Hideo 高柳央雄. "Jitsuzon tetsugaku to Dōgen 2: Jikanron o megutte 実存哲学と道元禅-2-時間論をめぐって." *Shizuokajoshidaigaku kenkyū kiyō* 静岡女子大学研究紀要 15 (1981): 235–45.

Tamaki Kōshirō 玉城康四郎. *Shōbō genzō-jō* 正法眼蔵 上. Tōkyō: Daizō shuppan, 1993.

Tanabe Hajime 田邊元. *Shōbōgenzō no tetsugaku shikan* 正法眼蔵の哲学私観. Tōkyō: Iwanami shoten, 1939.

Tanahashi, Kazuaki. *Enlightenment Unfolds: The Essential Teachings of Zen Master Dogen*. Boston: Shambhala, 1999.

———, ed. *Moon in a Dewdrop*. San Francisco: North Point Press, 1985.

———. *Treasury of the True Dharma Eye: Zen Master Dogen's Shobo Genzo*. Boston: Shambhala, 2010.

Tanaka, Gen. *Das Zeitbewusstsein der Japaner im Altertum: Struktur und Entwicklung*. Edited by Thomas Leims. Wiesbaden: Otto Harrassowitz, 1993.

Tanaka, Stefan. *New Times in Modern Japan*. Princeton, NJ: Princeton University Press, 2004.

Tellenbach, Hubertus, and Bin Kimura. "Some Meanings of the Concept 'Nature' in European Vernacular Languages and Their Correspondences in Japanese." *International Philosophical Quarterly* 19, no. 2 (1979): 177–85.

Thompson, E. P. "Time, Work-Discipline, and Industrial Capitalism." *Past & Present* 38 (1967): 56–97.

Totman, Conrad, ed. *A History of Japan*. Malden, MA: Blackwell, 2000.

Tsujiguchi Yūichirō 辻口雄一郎. *Shōbōgenzō no shisōteki kenkyū* 正法眼蔵の思想的研究. Tōkyō: Hokuju shuppan, 2012.

Tsunoda Tairyū 角田泰隆. *Dōgen zenji kenkyū niokeru shomondai: kindai no shūgaku ronsō o chūshin toshite* 道元禅師研究における諸問題: 近代の宗学論争を中心として. Tōkyō: Shunjūsha, 2017.

———. "Dōgen zenji no daigitai to sono kaiketsu 道元禅師の大疑滞とその解決." In *Dōgen zenji kenkyū ronshū: Dōgen zenji 750kai dai onki kinen shuppan* 道元禪師研究論集: 道元禪師七百五十回大遠忌記念出版, edited by Daihonzan Eiheiji daionkikyoku bunka jigyō senmon bukai shuppan iinkai 大本山永平寺大遠忌局文化事業専門部会出版委員会, 216–35. Tōkyō: Daishūkan shoten, 2002.

———. "Dōgen zenji no jikanron—Shōbōgenzō 'Uji' o chūshin ni shite 道元禅師の時間論—『正法眼蔵』「有時」を中心にして" *Komazawa daigaku bukkyō gakubu ronshū* 駒沢大学仏教学部論集 7 (October 2001): 77–92.

———. "Dōgen zenji no jikanron kenkyū 道元禅師の時間論研究." *Komazawa tanki daigaku bukkyō ronshū* 駒澤短期大學佛教論集 8 (2002): 187–204.

Tyler, Royall, trans. *The Tale of the Heike*. London: Penguin, 2012.

Uchiyama Takashi 内山節. *Jikan ni tsuite no jūnishō* 時間についての十二章. Vol. 9. Uchiyama Takashi chosakushū. Tōkyō: Nōsan Gyoson Bunka Kyōkai, 2015.

Ueda Shizuteru 上田閑照. "Kaisetsu 解説." In *Dōgen* 道元, edited by Ueda Shizuteru 上田閑照 and Yanagida Seizan 柳田聖山, 93–255. Daijō butten 大乗仏典 23. Tōkyō: Chūō Kōronsha, 1995.

Unno, Mark. *Shingon Refractions: Myōe and the Mantra of Light*. Boston, MA: Wisdom Publications, 2004.

Wakatsuki Shōgo 若月正吾. "Shōwa zenki ni okeru shūgaku kenkyū no 'shūhen' (1): Akiyama Hanji cho 'Dōgen no kenkyū' ni tsuite 昭和前期における宗学研究の「周辺」（1）-秋山範二著「道元の研究」について- [Outlook on the Studies of Soto Doctrine in the Former Term of Showa (I) : On the Study of Dogen by Hanji Akiyama]." *Komazawa daigaku bukkyō gakubu ronshū* 駒澤大学仏教学部論集 8 (October 1977): 29–41.

Watson, Burton. *The Zen Teachings of Master Lin-Chi: A Translation of the Linji Lu*. Boston: Shambhala Publications, 1993.

Watsuji Tetsurō 和辻哲郎. "Shamon Dōgen 沙門道元." In *Nihon seishinshi kenkyū* 日本精神史研究, 237–356. Tōkyō: Iwanami shoten, 1992.

Wendorff, Rudolf. *Zeit und Kultur: Geschichte des Zeitbewusstseins in Europa*. 2. Aufl. Wiesbaden: Westdeutscher Verl, 1981.

Whitrow, G. J. *What Is Time?* Oxford: Oxford University Press, 2003.

Winfield, Pamela. *Icons and Iconoclasm in Japanese Buddhism: Kukai and Dogen on the Art of Enlightenment*. Oxford: Oxford University Press, 2013.

Wirth, Jason M. "When Washing Rice, Know That the Water Is Your Own Life: An Essay on Dōgen in the Age of Fast Food." In *Ontologies of Nature: Continental Perspectives and Environmental Reorientations*, edited by Gerard Kuperus and Marjolein Oele, 235–44. Contributions to Phenomenology. Cham: Springer International Publishing, 2017.

Wood, David. "Founder's Lecture: Is Time Out of Joint? Or at a New Threshold? Reflections on the Temporality of Climate Change." *Time in Variance*, September 20, 2021, 43–65.

Wuliang Zongshou 無量宗寿. "Ruzhong riyong [nyūshū nichiyō] 入衆日用." In *Zenshū shingi shū* 禅宗清規集, edited by Ishii Shūdō 石井修道, 625–41. Kyōto: Rinsen shoten, 2014.

Yamauchi Shun'yū 山内舜雄. *Shōbō genzō kikigaki shō no kenkyū* 『正法眼蔵聞書抄』の研究, 7 vols. Daizō Shuppan, 1988.

Yanagida Seizan 柳田聖山. "Zen bukkyō no jikanron 禅仏教の時間論." In *Jikan* 時間, edited by Sagara Tōru 相良亨 et al., 79–131. Nihon shisō 日本思想 4. Tōkyō: Daigaku Shuppankai, 1984.

Yifa. *The Origins of Buddhist Monastic Codes in China: An Annotated Translation and Study of the Chanyuan Qinggui*. Classics in East Asian Buddhism. Honolulu: University of Hawai'i Press, 2002.

Yorizumi Mitsuko 頼住光子. *Dōgen: Jiko, jikan, sekai wa dono yōni seiritsu suru no ka* 道元: 自己・時間・世界はどのように成立するのか. Tōkyō: Nihon Hōsō Shuppan Kyōkai, 2009.

———. *Dōgen no shisō: Daijō bukkyō no shinzui o yomitoku* 道元の思想: 大乗仏教の真髄を読み解く. Tōkyō: NHK, 2011.

———. *Shōbōgenzō nyūmon*. Vol. H-114-1. Kadokawa sofia bunko. Tōkyō: Kadokawa, 2014.

Yoshimura Hitoshi 吉村均. "Nāgārjuna (Ryūju) to Dōgen—Nitairon kara no 'Shōbō genzō' dokkai no kokoromi ナーガールジュナ(龍樹)と道元二—諦論からの『正法眼蔵』読解の試み." *Hikaku shisō kenkyū* 比較思想研究 34 (2007): 54–63.

Yoshinouchi Kei 芳之内圭. "Higashiyama gobunkobon 'Nittchū gyōji' ni mieru Heian jidai kyūchū jikoku seido no kōsatsu: 'Naiju sōji no koto,' konoeji yakō no koto" no kentō o chūshin ni 東山御文庫本『日中行事』にみえる平安時代宮中時刻制度の考察:「内豎奏時事」・「近衛陣夜行事」の検討を中心に." *Shigaku zasshi* 史学雑誌 17, no. 8 (2008): 1414–34.

Waddell, Norman and Abe, Masao, trans. *The Heart of Dōgen's Shōbōgenzō*. Albany: State University of New York Press, 2002.

Zengaku daijiten hensanjo 禪學大辭典編纂所. *Zengaku daijiten* 禪學大辭典. Tōkyō: Taishûkan Shoten, 1985.

Zerubavel, Eviatar. "The Language of Time: Toward a Semiotics of Temporality." *Sociological Quarterly* 28, no. 3 (1987): 343–56.

———. "Timetables and Scheduling: On the Social Organization of Time." *Sociological Inquiry* 46, no. 2 (1976): 87–94.

Zongze 宗賾 [Changlu Zongze 長蘆宗賾]. "Chanyuan qinggui [Zen'en shingi] 禅苑清規." In *Zenshū shingi shū* 禅宗清規集, edited by Ishii Shūdō 石井修道, 543–621. Rinsen Shoten, 2014.

———. "Chanyuan qinggui 禪苑清規." In *Manji zokuzō kyō* 卍續藏經 No. 1245, 63:522ff. Tōkyō: Shin bunhō shuppan, 1994.

Index of Names

Akiyama Hanji 秋山範二, 2, 14–15, 133, 189–90
Arifuku Kōgaku 有福孝岳, 13

Baizhang Huaihai 百丈懷海, 170–72
Blake, William, 15
Bodhidharma, 6, 38, 57, 63, 144
Bodiford, William, 28–29, 239n7, 257n100
Bonsei 梵清, 279n17

Cassirer, Ernst, 19–20

Dahui Zonggao 大慧宗杲, 39, 87
Dainichibō Nōnin 大日房能忍, 34, 105, 107
Dōgen 道元: family background, relations, 35–36, 241n34; and Bodhidharma, 38; and Huineng, 39; and Kegon doctrine, 156; and medieval society; and modern philosophy, 13–15; as philosopher, 9–10; political and economic support of, 37–39, 41–42, 242n49
Dumoulin, Heinrich, 130
Dux, Günter, 71, 196–97

Einstein, Albert, 245n16
Eisai 榮西, 31, 37, 87, 92, 98, 253n58, 257n96

Ejō 懷奘, 38, 40, 98, 109, 126, 156, 159, 161, 243n59
Elberfeld, Rolf, 18, 56, 121–22, 139, 141, 146–47, 272n80
Enni Ben'en 圓爾辯圓, 41

Fazang 法藏, 121–22
Fujiwara Michiie. *See* Kujō Michiie
Fujiwara Moroie. *See* Kujō Moroie
Fujiwara Motofusa 藤原基房, 35–36
Fujiwara Motomichi. *See* Konoe Motomichi

Giun 義雲, 192, 195, 279n20

Hadot, Pierre, 214
Hakamaya Noriaki 袴谷憲昭, 29
Hatano Yoshishige, 41, 43, 243n53
Heidegger, Martin, 2, 17, 125, 207, 209, 281–82n14
Hōjō Tokiyori 北条時賴, 43, 49, 87
Heine, Steven, 2, 25, 28–29, 36, 40, 44–45, 125, 129, 142, 147, 150–51, 163, 170–71, 173, 189, 195, 204, 243n59, 268n29
Hōnen 法然, 31–36 passim
Huangbo Xiyun 黃檗希運, 66, 171
Husserl, Edmund, 14

Ishi 伊子, 35

313

Index of Names

Ishii Kiyozumi (=Ishii Seijun) 石井清純, 99, 132, 155–56, 158–59

Jakobson, Roman, 21, 238n29

Kakinomoto no Hitomaro 柿本人麻呂, 60
Kamo no Chōmei 鴨長明, 30–31
Kant, Immanuel, 5–6, 14, 19–20, 50–54, 146, 210, 245n14
Kawamura Kōdō 河村孝道, 28–29
Keizan Jōkin 瑩山紹瑾, 6, 60, 74, 82–93, 96–98, 108–109, 113–14, 255n87, 258n106
Kim, Hee-Jin, 56, 119, 124, 126–27, 129–31, 145, 147–49, 263n31, 269n42
Konoe Motomichi 近衛基通, 39, 41
Kujō Michiie 九条道家, 41
Kujō Moroie 九条師家, 39, 41
Kuroda Toshio 黒田俊雄, 34
Kyōgō 經豪, 192, 279n19

Lakoff, George, 21, 205, 260n137
Lanxi Daolong. See Rankei Dōryū
Linji 臨済, 38–39, 41, 57, 66, 98–99, 143–44, 173, 226, 255n81, 257n97

Maki Yūsuke 真木悠介, 21, 197, 205, 207
Marx, Karl, 212, 282n21
Marx, Wolfgang, 282n16
Matsumoto Shirō 松本史朗, 29
Matsunami Taiun 松波諦雲, xi
Matsuo Kenji 松尾剛次, 30, 261n146, 261n149
Minamoto Michichika 源通親, 35–36
Minamoto Michitomo 源通具, 35–36
Minamoto Yoshinaka 源義仲, 35–36
Minamoto Yoritomo 源頼朝, 35–36
Myōe 明恵, 32, 89–90, 114, 253n54

Nāgārjuna, 125
Nakaseko Shōdō 中世古祥道, 28–29, 35–36, 41, 43, 242n49, 243n53
Nichiren 日蓮, 31, 32, 34, 177, 196
Nishida Kitarō 西田幾多郎, 14, 189, 235n4, 237n14
Nishio Minoru 西尾実, 279n17

Ōe Seizō 大江精三 (=Ohe, Seizo), 11–16
Ōmori Shōzō 大森荘蔵, 13–14, 205
Otto, Rudolf, 22–23
Ozeki, Ruth, 218

Piaget, Jean, 196
Postone, Moishe, 282n20

Rankei Dōryū (Lanxi Daolong) 蘭渓道隆, 87–88, 91, 109
Rappe, Guido, 119, 121, 262n15
Raud, Rein, 16, 25, 58, 127–31, 149, 154, 158, 188, 206, 264n54, 278n9
Ricoeur, Paul, 238n28
Roberts, Shinshū, 147–48, 189
Rosa, Hartmut, 211
Rovelli, Carlo, 268n30
Rujing 如浄, 37–38, 41–42, 45, 63, 67, 98, 107, 109, 113, 165–67, 257n96, 277n76
Ryōken 良顕, 36

Satō Hiroo 佐藤弘夫, 30, 34, 192
Sengzhao 僧肇, 122
Senne 詮慧, 109, 192, 279n18
Shinran 親鸞, 31, 34, 177, 196
Shitou Xiqian 石頭希遷, 143, 224, 226, 255n81, 287n34, 289n50
Shōkaku 性覚, 39
Shōkū 證空, 36
Shunjō 俊芿, 89, 90, 114

Stambaugh, Joan, 2, 15–16, 125, 146, 154
Sueki Fumihiko 末木文美士, 37
Suzuki, Daisetz Teitaro, 91
Suzuki Shōsan 鈴木正三, 199

Tanabe Hajime 田邊元, 16, 23
Thompson, E. P., 75–76, 212–13
Tsujiguchi Yōichirō 辻口雄一郎, 147, 152, 154
Tsunoda Tairyū 角田泰隆, 28, 29, 154

Watsuji Tetsurō 和辻哲郎, 2, 23

Yanagida Seizan 柳田聖山, 119–20, 122
Yaoshan Weiyan, 13, 17, 69, 139–45 passim, 157, 225, 226, 236n4, 284n4, 289n51
Yorizumi Mitsuko, 25, 147, 149, 165–70 passim, 173–74
Yōsai. *See* Eisai

Zeami, 279n17
Zerubavel, Eliatar, 91–92, 104–105, 259n128, 261n144, 261n145
Zhiyi, 120

Index of Terms

absolute now, 14–15, 28, 149, 167, 237, 271n58. *See also* consummate now
alienation, 190–91, 210, 214
anātman. See self
ātman. See self; *ware*

Being and Time, 3, 207. *See also* Heidegger, Martin
birth and death: cycle of, 120, 124, 125, 138
Buddha Dharma (*buppō*), 58, 113, 124, 160, 236n11
Buddha Way (*butsudō*), 7, 20, 165, 167, 225, 236n11, 238n24, 275n30, 288n49
buppō 仏法. *See* Buddha Dharma
butsudō 仏道. *See* Buddha Way

calendar: time, 50, 61, 192–93; ritual, 5, 97, 210–11
chronoaesthetics, 51, 53, 61, 87, 126, 181–82, 186, 187, 200–201
chronography. *See* chronometry, chronothesis, chronotypology
chronology, 3, 6, 58, 65–66, 147, 183
chronometry, 21, 52, 79, 147, 174, 182–86, 192–93, 198, 239; absolute, 52–53; formal, 52; nominal, 52, 65; numerical, 52, 61–69, 76–78, 87, 183; material, 52, 60, 70; relational, 52–53
chronopolitics, 22, 95, 73–116, 160, 193
chronothesis, 52, 54–56, 146
chronotypology, 53–54, 167, 175, 182, 185–86
clock-time, 15, 77, 83, 139, 147, 159, 189–90
consummate now (*nikon/shikin*), 7, 142, 148–52, 160, 164, 184–85, 187, 204, 223, 286n27
Critical Buddhism, 28–29, 43–44, 169–70

datsuraku shinjin 脱落身心. *See* dropping off/dropped off body and mind
dharma-configuration or dharma-position (*hōi*), 127–33, 142–43, 146, 153–54, 224
dropping off/dropped off body and mind (*datsuraku shinjin*), 74, 99
dualism: between rational thinking and spiritual experience, 3, 216; between "lived" and "measured" time, 3, 207–208; non-dualism, 25, 126, 149, 175, 187, 195
duration, 3–4, 7, 15, 67–69, 105, 114, 127, 130–33, 147, 164, 182

economy, 74, 95, 110–11, 134, 199–200, 255n82
emptiness, 4, 25, 148–49, 162–63, 169–70, 194–95, 269n42
epistemology, 14–16, 22, 215
epoché, 14
eternity, 129, 163; eternalism, 124, 155. *See also* absolute now
existentialism: existentialist interpretations of Dōgen, 2–3, 125, 147

Final Dharma Age (*mappō*), 30, 124, 176–78, 196–97
form, 4, 127, 194–95, 205, 218, 222–23, 271n65, 286n21, 288n48; symbolic, 19–20, 23, 200
freedom: free will, 167–68, 176, 186–88

historical materialism, 20
hōi 法位. *See* dharma-configuration or dharma-position
holism, 16, 142, 151, 155–58, 167, 184, 214, 215, 217, 224
hour(s), 77, 80–82, 142, 198, 208, 213, 222, 224; zodiacal, 12, 62, 84–85, 89, 162, 192–93; system of, 62–64, 83–86, 147

immortality, 124, 127, 182, 281n14
impermanence, 7, 15, 55, 123–26, 138, 163, 175, 182, 194, 246n20
iteration, 53, 105, 259n131

karma, 8, 150, 168–78, 186–88, 216–19, 276n59, 277n66
kyōryaku 經歷. *See* transiting through phases

language, 145, 188–89; communication, 21, 122; metaphorical, 8, 21, 120, 204–205, 260n137

mappō 末法. *See* Final Dharma Age
meditation, 13–14, 94, 99, 123–25. See also *zazen*
memorial days, 6, 97–99, 113, 193
moment (*setsuna*), 14–15, 129–30, 164, 188, 265n63
momentarism, 129, 149–50, 154, 182
monastery: monastic life, 3, 73–75, 186–87; monastic hierarchy, 6–7, 22, 101, 105
month, 62, 91–94, 193–94
mountain time, 157–58
muga 無我. *See* self
mysticism, 15–16; mystical unity, 37, 114, 124, 150

nature: love of, 42, 49; knowledge/study of, 111, 199–200, 201, 207
night, 59–60, 62, 76–78
night-watches, 62, 77–78
nikon 而今. *See* consummate now
non-duality, 25, 117–18, 125, 148–49, 162–63, 170, 187, 192, 194–95
now of eternity, 237n14. *See also* absolute now

omnipresence, 1, 124, 145–46. *See also* Buddha Dharma
ontology, 2, 4, 15, 25, 138, 157, 181–82, 188–89
operational competence, 109, 112, 134, 196, 200, 280n38

past, present, and future, 121, 142, 150–51, 160, 165, 168–69, 187; limits of, 56; relative weight, 111–14, 125, 188–90
patronage, 38–39, 41–42, 66, 92
periodization, 120, 169–70
persistence. *See* duration
phenomenology, 14–15, 158, 272n86
planning for the future, 78, 80, 112, 134
printing, 31–32

Index of Terms | 319

reading, 32–33
relativity theory, 198–99

schedule, 65, 212–13; scheduling, 75–82, 108, 109–10, 193
seasons, 49–50, 61, 94–97, 143, 193–94, 206–207, 245n5
self, 7, 12, 124–26, 128–29, 155–58, 164, 188, 285n14; eternal (*ātman*), 124, 151, 155, 285n14; no-self (*anātman/muga*), 124
sequence, 6, 14, 52–53, 58–59, 61, 70, 78–79, 104–106, 125, 147, 154, 161–68, 189
setsuna 刹那. *See* moment
shikin 而今. *See* consummate now
shinjin datsuraku 身心脱落. *See* dropping off/dropped off body and mind
sleep time, 82, 86–87
soteriology, 13, 23–24, 151, 159–60, 184–86; salvation, 16–18, 23, 34, 138, 194–95. *See also under* time
substance, 53, 55, 124, 127, 130–32, 135, 154, 194
suffering, 123, 138, 152, 157, 186–87, 194. *See also* birth and death
synchrony, 3, 53, 146, 150, 214–16; synchronization, 5, 79–80, 92–94, 123, 139, 152, 157, 160, 161–68, 178, 185, 193, 212–13

task-orientation, 73, 75–76, 83, 211–14
temporal: location, 6, 17, 22, 59, 62–63, 65, 168; distinction, 7–8, 16, 146, 149, 154, 165, 167–68
time: abstract global, 183, 196–98, 200, 210–11; as container, 14, 57, 147–48; as hyperonym/general notion, 56–57, 69, 182; as number, 8, 70; as salvific, 2, 18, 138, 176, 186; cyclical, 71, 95–96, 120, 164, 185, 193–94, 278n8, 279n20; "empty", 66–67, 184, 197; intrinsic to things, 139, 144, 145–46, 182, 206; "language of " (Zerubavel), 104; linearity of, 14, 71, 107, 149–50, 165–66, 168–70, 174, 185; metaphors of, 8, 205; morphology of, 21–22, 71, 113, 164–66, 184–88, 203–205; six periods of day, 193, 251n22; "of action" (Dux), 71, 75; (not) flying past, 138, 149, 154, 204–205; -oriented organisation, 73, 75–76; regimes, 8, 73–74, 88–91, 109, 197, 211, 213; travel, 97; unidirectional flow of, 142, 143, 147, 160
time and history, 8, 196–201. *See also* Final Dharma Age
transiency, 123–25, 127, 175
transiting through phases (*kyōryaku*), 142, 152–54, 164, 225

uji 有時 (term): translation/meaning of, 1–2, 7, 11–13, 17–18, 55, 139, 144–48. *See also* what is:time
unity (of practitioners and Buddhas), 123, 135, 139, 143, 146, 154, 165–68
urgency (sense of), 7, 51, 126, 134, 201

ware われ・我: as first-person pronoun, 151, 155; as self-identical, 151, 155, 172–73, 221, 285n14, 286n25, 286n26. *See also* self
week, 93
what is:time, 2, 18, 57, 110, 118, 139, 143–48, 149–52 passim, 157, 158–60, 165, 178, 198, 217–18. *See also uji*

zazen 坐禅, 37–39, 80–82, 86, 88, 114, 223, 226–27, 257n102. *See also* meditation

www.ingramcontent.com/pod-product-compliance
Ingram Content Group UK Ltd.
Pitfield, Milton Keynes, MK11 3LW, UK
UKHW041937210426
5322IPUK00016B/230